SOCIAL SECURITY LE
SUPPLEMENT 2024/25

General Editor
Nick Wikeley, M.A. (Cantab)

Commentary by
Ian Hooker, LL.B.
Formerly Lecturer in Law, University of Nottingham
Formerly Chairman, Social Security Appeal Tribunals

John Mesher, B.A., B.C.L. (Oxon), LL.M. (Yale)
Retired Judge of the Upper Tribunal
Emeritus Professor of Law, University of Sheffield

Edward Mitchell, LL.B.
Judge of the Upper Tribunal

Will Rolt, LL.B.
Judge of the First-tier Tribunal

Tom Royston, M.A. (Cantab)
Barrister

Christopher Ward, M.A. (Cantab)
Judge of the Upper Tribunal

Nick Wikeley, M.A. (Cantab)
Judge of the Upper Tribunal,
Emeritus Professor of Law, University of Southampton

Consultant Editor
Child Poverty Action Group

Sweet & Maxwell

Thomson Reuters™

Published in 2025 by Thomson Reuters,
trading as Sweet & Maxwell.
Registered in England & Wales. Company No. 1679046.
Registered office and address for service: 5 Canada Square, Canary Wharf, London, E14 5AQ.

For further information on our products and services, visit
http://www.sweetandmaxwell.co.uk.

Typeset by Cheshire Typesetting Ltd, Cuddington, Cheshire
Printed in Great Britain by Hobbs the Printers Ltd, Totton, Hampshire, SO40 3WX

A CIP catalogue record for this book is available from the British Library.

ISBN (print): 978-0-41412-522-3
ISBN (e-book): 978-0-41412-524-7
ISBN (print and e-book): 978-0-41412-523-0

PREFACE

This is the Supplement to the 2024/25 edition of *Social Security Legislation*, which was published in September 2024 in four volumes. Part I of this Supplement contains new legislation, presented in the same format as in the main volumes. Parts II, III, IV and V contain the standard updating material—a separate Part for each volume of the main work—which amends the legislative text and key aspects of the commentary, drawing attention to important recent case law, so as to be up to date as at December 9, 2024 (although we have squeezed in some more recent case law developments thanks to the generous understanding of our publishers Sweet & Maxwell). Part VI comprises the cumulative updating material for Volume V, *Income Support and the Legacy Benefits*, which was last published in the 2021/22 edition (and so Part VI lists the cumulative updates by reference to the pagination of the 2021/22 edition of Volume V). Finally, Part VII gives some notice of changes forthcoming between December 2024 and the date to which the main work (2025/26 edition) will be up to date (mid-April 2025), along with the April 2025 benefit rates.

The updating changes in this Supplement include a multitude of amendments to both the primary and secondary legislation governing social security provision (including the new infected blood compensation scheme). There is further analysis of the developing case law on universal credit, now the main means-tested benefit, together with detailed discussion of new Upper Tribunal case law on the various personal independence payment (PIP) descriptors. There have in addition been a myriad of amendments to devolved social security provision in Scotland.

As always, we welcome comments from those who use this Supplement. Please address these to the General Editor, Nick Wikeley, c/o School of Law, The University of Southampton, Highfield, Southampton SO17 1BJ (njw@soton.ac.uk).

Ian Hooker
John Mesher
Edward Mitchell
Tom Royston

Will Rolt
Christopher Ward
Nick Wikeley

February 4, 2025

CONTENTS

USING THE UPDATING MATERIAL IN THIS SUPPLEMENT

For the most part any relevant new legislation since the main volumes of *Social Security Legislation 2024/25* were published is contained in Part I, while amendments to existing legislative provisions are contained in Parts II–VI respectively, together with commentary on new case law. The amendments and updating material contained in Parts II–V of this Supplement are keyed to the page numbers of the relevant main volume of *Social Security Legislation 2024/25*. Part VI differs in that the cumulative updates are by reference to page numbers in the 2021/22 Volume V, covering Income Support and the Legacy Benefits. As such Part VI supersedes the last cumulative Volume V Supplement to be found at the back of the 2024/25 Volume II.

Where there have been a significant number of changes to a provision, the whole section, subsection, paragraph or regulation, as amended will tend to be reproduced. Other changes may be noted by an instruction to insert or substitute new material or to delete part of the existing text. The date the change takes effect is also noted. Where explanation is needed of the change, or there is updating relating to existing annotations but no change to the legislation, you will also find commentary in this Supplement. The updating material explains new statutory material, takes on board Upper Tribunal or court decisions, or gives prominence to points which now seem to warrant more detailed attention.

This Supplement amends the text of the main volumes of *Social Security Legislation 2024/25* to be up-to-date as at December 9, 2024.

Nick Wikeley
General Editor

PAGES OF MAIN VOLUMES AFFECTED BY MATERIAL IN THIS SUPPLEMENT

Main volume page affected	Relevant paragraph in supplement
p.808	3.034
p.811	3.035
p.817	3.036
p.833	3.037
p.838	3.038
p.857	3.039
p.870	3.040
p.870	3.041
p.887	3.042
pp.887–888	3.043
p.888	3.044
p.919	3.045
p.929	3.046
p.957	3.047
p.969	3.048
p.986	3.049
p.1005	3.050

VOLUME III

pp.20–23	4.001
pp.97–98	4.002
pp.157–158	4.003
p.257	4.004
p.328	4.005
p.391	4.006
p.420	4.007
p.432	4.008
pp.458–459	4.010
pp.489–490	4.011
p.502	4.012
pp.569–570	4.013
pp.571–572	4.014
pp.572–574	4.015
pp.595–596	4.016
p.684	4.017
p.1061	4.018
p.1062	4.019
p.1067	4.020
p.1068	4.021
p.1084	4.022
p.1086	4.023
p.1190	4.024
p.1221	4.025
p.1222	4.026
p.1245	4.027
p.1270	4.028
p.1274	4.029
p.1285	4.030

Main volume page affected	Relevant paragraph in supplement
p.1292	4.031
p.1301	4.032
p.1317	4.033
p.1318	4.035
p.1324	4.036
pp.1334 and 1357	4.037
p.1404	4.038
p.1500	4.039
p.1524	4.040
p.1529	4.041
pp.1531–1535	4.042
pp.1566–1567	4.043
pp.1567–1568	4.044
p.1575	4.045
p.1575	4.046
p.1599	4.047
pp.1600–1601	4.048
p.1602	4.049
pp.1606–1607	4.050
p.1608	4.051
p.1627	4.052
p.1628	4.053
p.1631	4.054
p.1632	4.055
p.1638	4.056
p.1644	4.057
p.1686–1691	4.058

VOLUME IV

p.322	5.001
p.551	5.002
p.561	5.003
p.578	5.004
p.578	5.005
p.579	5.006
p.588	5.007
p.588	5.008
p.589	5.009
p.591	5.010
p.591	5.011
p.677	5.012
p.678	5.013
p.761	5.014
p.1145	5.015
p.1147	5.016
p.1289	5.017
p.1290	5.018
p.1294	5.019
p.1296	5.020

Main volume page affected	Relevant paragraph in supplement
VOLUME V	
p.15	6.001
p.18	6.002
pp.19–20	6.003
p.33	6.004
p.72	6.005
p.81	6.006
p.124	6.007
p.133	6.008
p.226	6.009
p.229	6.010
p.275	6.011
p.314	6.012
pp.329–331	6.013
p.355	6.014
pp.382–385	6.015
p.385	6.016
pp.393–396	6.017
p.403	6.018
p.412	6.019
p.421	6.020
pp.431–433	6.021
pp.433–436	6.022
p.438	6.023
p.439	6.024
pp.440–441	6.025
p.443	6.026
p.446	6.027
p.449	6.028
p.451	6.029
p.467	6.031
p.482	6.032
pp.485–486	6.033
pp.520–523	6.034
p.526	6.035
p.527	6.036
p.539	6.037
p.542	6.038
p.550	6.039
pp.571–572	6.040
p.605	6.041
p.606	6.042
p.631	6.043
p.642	6.044
p.644	6.045
p.646	6.046
p.648	6.047
p.651	6.048

Main volume page affected	Relevant paragraph in supplement
p.1540	6.151
p.1542	6.152
p.1544	6.153
p.1546	6.154
p.1549	6.155
p.1554	6.156
p.1556	6.157
p.1556	6.158
pp.1558–1559	6.159
p.1559	6.160
p.1563	6.161
pp.1565–1566	6.162
p.1579	6.163
p.1579	6.164
p.1613	6.165
p.1613	6.166
p.1615	6.167
pp.1663–1664	6.168
pp.1670–1672	6.169
pp.1670–1672	6.170
p.1674	6.171
p.1681	6.172
pp.1681–1683	6.173
p.1732	6.174
p.1733	6.175
p.1734	6.176
p.1734	6.177
p.1735	6.178
pp.1735–1736	6.179
p.1737	6.180
p.1738	6.181
p.1738	6.182
p.1741	6.183
p.1742	6.184
p.1745	6.185
p.1793	6.186
p.1798	6.187
pp.1826–1829	6.188
p.1831	6.189
pp.1889–1891	6.190
p.1890	6.191
pp.1891–1892	6.192
pp.1892–1893	6.193
p.1893	6.194

TABLE OF ABBREVIATIONS USED IN THIS SERIES

1975 Act	Social Security Act 1975
1977 Act	Marriage (Scotland) Act 1977
1979 Act	Pneumoconiosis (Workers' Compensation) Act 1979
1986 Act	Social Security Act 1986
1996 Act	Employment Rights Act 1996
1998 Act	Social Security Act 1998
2002 Act	Tax Credits Act 2002
2004 Act	Gender Recognition Act 2004
2006 Act	Armed Forces Act 2006
2008 Act	Child Maintenance and Other Payments Act 2008
2013 Act	Marriage (Same Sex Couples) Act 2013
2014 Act	Marriage and Civil Partnership (Scotland) Act 2014
2018 Act	Social Security (Scotland) Act 2018
A1P1	Art.1 of Protocol 1 to the European Convention on Human Rights
AA	Attendance Allowance
AA 1992	Attendance Allowance Act 1992
AAC	Administrative Appeals Chamber
AACR	Administrative Appeals Chamber Reports
A.C.	Law Reports, Appeal Cases
A.C.D.	Administrative Court Digest
Admin	Administrative Court
Admin L.R.	Administrative Law Reports
Administration Act	Social Security Administration Act 1992
Administration Regulations	Statutory Paternity Pay and Statutory Adoption Pay (Administration) Regulations 2002
AIP	assessed income period
All E.R.	All England Reports
All E.R. (E.C.)	All England Reports (European Cases)
AMA	Adjudicating Medical Authorities
AO	Adjudication Officer
AOG	*Adjudication Officers Guide*
art.	article
Art.	Article
ASD	Autistic Spectrum Disorder
ASPP	Additional Statutory Paternity Pay
A.T.C.	Annotated Tax Cases

Attendance Allowance Regulations	Social Security (Attendance Allowance) Regulations 1991
AWT	All Work Test
BA	Benefits Agency
Benefits Act	Social Security Contributions and Benefits Act 1992
B.H.R.C.	Butterworths Human Rights Cases
B.L.G.R.	Butterworths Local Government Reports
Blue Books	*The Law Relating to Social Security*, Vols 1–11
B.P.I.R.	Bankruptcy and Personal Insolvency Reports
B.T.C.	British Tax Cases
BTEC	Business and Technology Education Council
B.V.C.	British Value Added Tax Reporter
B.W.C.C.	Butterworths Workmen's Compensation Cases
c.	chapter
C	Commissioner's decision
C&BA 1992	Social Security Contributions and Benefits Act 1992
CAA 2001	Capital Allowances Act 2001
CAB	Citizens Advice Bureau
CAO	Chief Adjudication Officer
CB	Child Benefit
CBA 1975	Child Benefit Act 1975
CBJSA	Contribution-Based Jobseeker's Allowance
C.C.L. Rep.	Community Care Law Reports
CCM	HMRC *New Tax Credits Claimant Compliance Manual*
C.E.C.	European Community Cases
CERA	cortical evoked response audiogram
CESA	Contribution-based Employment and Support Allowance
CFS	chronic fatigue syndrome
Ch.	Chancery Division Law Reports; Chapter
Charter	Charter of Fundamental Rights of the European Union
Citizenship Directive	Directive 2004/38/EC of the European Parliament and of the Council of April 29, 2004
CJEC	Court of Justice of the European Communities
CJEU	Court of Justice of the European Union
Claims and Payments Regulations	Social Security (Claims and Payments) Regulations 1987
Claims and Payments Regulations 1979	Social Security (Claims and Payments) Regulations 1979
Claims and Payments Regulations 2013	Universal Credit, Personal Independence Payment, Jobseeker's Allowance and Employment and Support Allowance (Claims and Payments) Regulations 2013
CM	Case Manager
CMA	Chief Medical Adviser

CMEC	Child Maintenance and Enforcement Commission
C.M.L.R.	Common Market Law Reports
C.O.D.	Crown Office Digest
COLL	*Collective Investment Schemes Sourcebook*
Community, The	European Community
Computation of Earnings Regulations	Social Security Benefit (Computation of Earnings) Regulations 1978
Computation of Earnings Regulations 1996	Social Security Benefit (Computation of Earnings) Regulations 1996
Consequential Provisions Act	Social Security (Consequential Provisions) Act 1992
Contributions and Benefits Act	Social Security Contributions and Benefits Act 1992
Contributions Regulations	Social Security (Contributions) Regulations 2001
COPD	chronic obstructive pulmonary disease
CP	Carer Premium; Chamber President
CPAG	Child Poverty Action Group
CPR	Civil Procedure Rules
Cr. App. R.	Criminal Appeal Reports
CRCA 2005	Commissioners for Revenue and Customs Act 2005
Credits Regulations 1974	Social Security (Credits) Regulations 1974
Credits Regulations 1975	Social Security (Credits) Regulations 1975
Crim. L.R.	Criminal Law Review
CRU	Compensation Recovery Unit
CSA 1995	Children (Scotland) Act 1995
CSIH	Inner House of the Court of Session (Scotland)
CSM	Child Support Maintenance
CS(NI)O 1995	Child Support (Northern Ireland) Order 1995
CSOH	Outer House of the Court of Session (Scotland)
CSPSSA 2000	Child Support, Pensions and Social Security Act 2000
CTA	Common Travel Area
CTA 2009	Corporation Tax Act 2009
CTA 2010	Corporation Tax Act 2010
CTB	Council Tax Benefit
CTC	Child Tax Credit
CTC Regulations	Child Tax Credit Regulations 2002
CTF	child trust fund
CTS	Carpal Tunnel Syndrome
DAC	Directive 2011/16/ EU (Directive on administrative co-operation in the field of taxation)
DAT	Disability Appeal Tribunal
dB	decibels
DCA	Department for Constitutional Affairs
DCP	Disabled Child Premium

Decisions and Appeals Regulations 1999	Social Security Contributions (Decisions and Appeals) Regulations 1999
Dependency Regulations	Social Security Benefit (Dependency) Regulations 1977
DfEE	Department for Education and Employment
DHSS	Department of Health and Social Security
Disability Living Allowance Regulations	Social Security (Disability Living Allowance) Regulations
DIY	do it yourself
DLA	Disability Living Allowance
DLA Regs 1991	Social Security (Disability Living Allowance) Regulations 1991
DLAAB	Disability Living Allowance Advisory Board
DLADWAA 1991	Disability Living Allowance and Disability Working Allowance Act 1991
DM	Decision Maker
DMA	Decision-making and Appeals
DMG	*Decision Makers' Guide*
DMP	Delegated Medical Practitioner
DP	Disability Premium
DPT	diffuse pleural thickening
DPTC	Disabled Person's Tax Credit
DRO	Debt Relief Order
DSD	Department for Social Development (Northern Ireland)
DSM IV; DSM-5	Diagnostic and Statistical Manual of Mental Disorders of the American Psychiatric Association
DSS	Department of Social Security
DTI	Department of Trade and Industry
DWA	Disability Working Allowance
DWP	Department for Work and Pensions
DWPMS	Department for Work and Pensions Medical Service
EAA	Extrinsic Allergic Alveolitis
EAT	Employment Appeal Tribunal
EC	European Community
ECHR	European Convention on Human Rights
ECJ	European Court of Justice
E.C.R.	European Court Reports
ECSC	European Coal and Steel Community
ECSMA	European Convention on Social and Medical Assistance
EEA	European Economic Area
EEA EFTA Separation Agreement	Agreement on arrangements between Iceland, the Principality of Liechtenstein, the Kingdom of Norway and the United Kingdom of Great Britain and Northern Ireland following the withdrawal of the United Kingdom from the European Union, the EEA Agreement and other agreements applicable between the United Kingdom and the EEA EFTA

	States by virtue of the United Kingdom's membership of the European Union
EEA Regulations 2016	Immigration (European Economic Area) Regulations 2016
EEC	European Economic Community
EESSI	Electronic Exchange of Social Security Information
E.G.	Estates Gazette
E.G.L.R.	Estates Gazette Law Reports
EHC plan	education, health and care plan
EHIC	European Health Insurance Card
EHRC	European Human Rights Commission
E.H.R.R.	European Human Rights Reports
EL	employers' liability
E.L.R	Education Law Reports
EMA	Education Maintenance Allowance
EMP	Examining Medical Practitioner
Employment and Support Allowance Regulations	Employment and Support Allowance Regulations 2008
EPS	extended period of sickness
Eq. L.R.	Equality Law Reports
ERA	evoked response audiometry
ERA scheme	Employment, Retention and Advancement scheme
ES	Employment Service
ESA	Employment and Support Allowance
ESA Regs 2013	Employment and Support Allowance Regulations 2013
ESA Regulations	Employment and Support Allowance Regulations 2008
ESA WCAt	Employment and Support Allowance Work Capability Assessment
ESC	employer supported childcare
ESE Scheme	Employment, Skills and Enterprise Scheme
ESE Regulations	Jobseeker's Allowance (Employment, Skills and Enterprise Scheme) Regulations 2011
ESES Regulations	Jobseeker's Allowance (Employment, Skills and Enterprise Scheme) Regulations 2011
ETA 1973	Employment and Training Act 1973
ETA(NI) 1950	Employment and Training Act (Northern Ireland) 1950
ETS	European Treaty Series
EU	European Union
Eu.L.R.	European Law Reports
EWCA Civ	Civil Division of the Court of Appeal (England and Wales)
EWHC Admin	Administrative Court, part of the High Court (England and Wales)
FA 1993	Finance Act 1993
FA 1996	Finance Act 1996

FA 2004	Finance Act 2004
Fam. Law	Family Law
FAS	Financial Assistance Scheme
F.C.R.	Family Court Reporter
FEV	forced expiratory volume
FIS	Family Income Supplement
FISMA 2000	Financial Services and Markets Act 2000
F.L.R.	Family Law Reports
FME	further medical evidence
F(No.2)A 2005	Finance (No.2) Act 2005
FOTRA	Free of Tax to Residents Abroad
FRAA	flat rate accrual amount
FRS Act 2004	Fire and Rescue Services Act 2004
FSCS	Financial Services Compensation Scheme
FTT	First-tier Tribunal
General Benefit Regulations 1982	Social Security (General Benefit) Regulations 1982
General Regulations	Statutory Shared Parental Pay (General) Regulations 2014
GMCA	Greater Manchester Combined Authority
GMFRA	Greater Manchester Fire and Rescue Authority
GMP	Guaranteed Minimum Pension
GMWDA	Greater Manchester Waste Disposal Authority
GNVQ	General National Vocational Qualification
GP	General Practitioner
GRA	Gender Recognition Act 2004
GRB	Graduated Retirement Benefit
GRP	Graduated Retirement Pension
HB	Housing Benefit
HB (WSP) R (NI) 2017	Housing Benefit (Welfare Social Payment) Regulations (Northern Ireland) 2017
HBRB	Housing Benefit Review Board
HCA	Homes and Communities Agency
HCD	House of Commons Debates
HCP	healthcare professional
HCV	Hepatitis C virus
Health Service Act	National Health Service Act 2006
Health Service (Wales) Act	National Health Service (Wales) Act 2006
HIV	Human Immunodeficiency Virus
HL	House of Lords
H.L.R.	Housing Law Reports
HMIT	Her Majesty's Inspector of Taxes
HMRC	Her Majesty's Revenue and Customs
HMSO	Her Majesty's Stationery Office
Hospital In-Patients Regulations 1975	Social Security (Hospital In-Patients) Regulations 1975
Housing Benefit Regulations	Housing Benefit Regulations 2006
HP	Health Professional

HPP	Higher Pensioner Premium
HRA 1998	Human Rights Act 1998
H.R.L.R.	Human Rights Law Reports
HRP	Home Responsibilities Protection
HSE	Health and Safety Executive
IAC	Immigration and Asylum Chamber
IAP	Intensive Activity Period
IB	Incapacity Benefit
IB PCA	Incapacity Benefit Personal Capability Assessment
IB Regs	Social Security (Incapacity Benefit) Regulations 1994
IB Regulations	Social Security (Incapacity Benefit) Regulations 1994
IB/IS/SDA	Incapacity Benefits Regime
IBJSA	Income-Based Jobseeker's Allowance
IBS	Irritable Bowel Syndrome
ICA	Invalid Care Allowance
I.C.R.	Industrial Cases Reports
ICTA 1988	Income and Corporation Taxes Act 1988
IFW Regulations	Incapacity for Work (General) Regulations 1995
IH	Inner House of the Court of Session
I.I.	Industrial Injuries
IIAC	Industrial Injuries Advisory Council
IIDB	Industrial Injuries Disablement Benefit
ILO	International Labour Organization
Imm. A.R.	Immigration Appeal Reports
Incapacity for Work Regulations	Social Security (Incapacity for Work) (General) Regulations 1995
Income Support General Regulations	Income Support (General) Regulations 1987
IND	Immigration and Nationality Directorate of the Home Office
I.N.L.R.	Immigration and Nationality Law Reports
I.O.	Insurance Officer
IPPR	Institute of Public Policy Research
IRESA	Income-Related Employment and Support Allowance
I.R.L.R.	Industrial Relations Law Reports
IS	Income Support
IS Regs	Income Support Regulations
IS Regulations	Income Support (General) Regulations 1987
ISA	Individual Savings Account
ISBN	International Standard Book Number
ITA 2007	Income Tax Act 2007
ITEPA 2003	Income Tax, Earnings and Pensions Act 2003
I.T.L. Rep.	International Tax Law Reports
I.T.R.	Industrial Tribunals Reports
ITS	Independent Tribunal Service

ITTOIA 2005	Income Tax (Trading and Other Income) Act 2005
IVB	Invalidity Benefit
IW (General) Regs	Social Security (Incapacity for Work) (General) Regulations 1995
IW (Transitional) Regs	Incapacity for Work (Transitional) Regulations
Jobseeker's Allowance Regulations	Jobseeker's Allowance Regulations 1996
Jobseeker's Regulations 1996	Jobseeker's Allowance Regulations 1996
JSA	Jobseeker's Allowance
JSA 1995	Jobseekers Act 1995
JSA (NI) Regulations	Jobseeker's Allowance (Northern Ireland) Regulations 1996
JSA (Transitional) Regulations	Jobseeker's Allowance (Transitional) Regulations 1996
JSA Regs 1996	Jobseeker's Allowance Regulations 1996
JSA Regs 2013	Jobseeker's Allowance Regulations 2013
JS(NI)O 1995	Jobseekers (Northern Ireland) Order 1995
J.S.S.L.	Journal of Social Security Law
J.S.W.L.	Journal of Social Welfare Law
K.B.	Law Reports, King's Bench
L.& T.R.	Landlord and Tenant Reports
LCW	limited capability for work
LCWA	Limited Capability for Work Assessment
LCWRA	limited capability for work-related activity
LDEDC Act 2009	Local Democracy, Economic Development and Construction Act 2009
LEA	local education authority
LEL	Lower Earnings Limit
LET	low earnings threshold
LGA 2003	Local Government Act 2003
L.G. Rev.	Local Government Review
L.G.L.R.	Local Government Reports
L.J.R.	Law Journal Reports
LRP	liable relative payment
L.S.G.	Law Society Gazette
Luxembourg Court	Court of Justice of the European Union (also referred to as CJEC and ECJ)
MA	Maternity Allowance
MAF	Medical Assessment Framework
Maternity Allowance Regulations	Social Security (Maternity Allowance) Regulations 1987
MDC	Mayoral development corporation
ME	myalgic encephalomyelitis
Medical Evidence Regulations	Social Security (Medical Evidence) Regulations 1976
MEN	Mandatory Employment Notification
Mesher and Wood	*Income Support, the Social Fund and Family Credit: the Legislation* (1996)
M.H.L.R.	Mental Health Law Reports
MHP	mental health problems

MIF	minimum income floor
MIG	minimum income guarantee
Migration Regulations	Employment and Support Allowance (Transitional Provisions, Housing Benefit and Council Tax Benefit (Existing Awards) (No.2) Regulations 2010
MP	Member of Parliament
MRSA	methicillin-resistant Staphylococcus aureus
MS	Medical Services
MWA Regulations	Jobseeker's Allowance (Mandatory Work Activity Scheme) Regulations 2011
MWAS Regulations	Jobseeker's Allowance (Mandatory Work Activity Scheme) Regulations 2011
NCB	National Coal Board
NDPD	Notes on the Diagnosis of Prescribed Diseases
NHS	National Health Service
NI	National Insurance
N.I.	Northern Ireland Law Reports
NICA	Northern Ireland Court of Appeal
NICom	Northern Ireland Commissioner
NICs	National Insurance Contributions
NINO	National Insurance Number
NIRS 2	National Insurance Recording System
N.L.J.	New Law Journal
NMC	Nursing and Midwifery Council
Northern Ireland Contributions and Benefits Act	Social Security Contributions and Benefits (Northern Ireland) Act 1992
N.P.C.	New Property Cases
NRCGT	non-resident capital gains tax
NTC Manual	Clerical procedures manual on tax credits
NUM	National Union of Mineworkers
NUS	National Union of Students
OCD	obsessive compulsive disorder
Ogus, Barendt and Wikeley	A. Ogus, E. Barendt and N. Wikeley, *The Law of Social Security* (1995)
Old Cases Act	Industrial Injuries and Diseases (Old Cases) Act 1975
OPB	One Parent Benefit
O.P.L.R.	Occupational Pensions Law Reports
OPSSAT	Office of the President of Social Security Appeal Tribunals
Overlapping Benefits Regulations	Social Security (Overlapping Benefits) Regulations 1975
P	retirement pension case
P. & C.R.	Property and Compensation Reports
para.	paragraph
Pay Regulations	Statutory Paternity Pay and Statutory Adoption Pay (General) Regulations 2002; Statutory Shared Parental Pay (General) Regulations 2014

PAYE	Pay As You Earn
PC	Privy Council
PCA	Personal Capability Assessment
PCC	Police and Crime Commissioner
PD	Practice Direction; prescribed disease
Pens. L.R.	Pensions Law Reports
Pensions Act	Pension Schemes Act 1993
PEP	Personal Equity Plan
Persons Abroad Regulations	Social Security Benefit (Persons Abroad) Regulations 1975
Persons Residing Together Regulations	Social Security Benefit (Persons Residing Together) Regulations 1977
PIE	Period of Interruption of Employment
PILON	pay in lieu of notice
Pilot Scheme Regulations	Universal Credit (Work-Related Requirements) In Work Pilot Scheme and Amendment Regulations 2015
PIP	Personal Independence Payment
P.I.Q.R.	Personal Injuries and Quantum Reports
Polygamous Marriages Regulations	Social Security and Family Allowances (Polygamous Marriages) Regulations 1975
PPF	Pension Protection Fund
Prescribed Diseases Regulations	Social Security (Industrial Injuries) (Prescribed Diseases) Regulations 1985
PSCS	Pension Service Computer System
Pt	Part
PTA	pure tone audiometry
P.T.S.R.	Public and Third Sector Law Reports
PTWR 2000	Part-time Workers (Prevention of Less Favourable Treatment) Regulations 2000
PVS	private and voluntary sectors
Q.B.	Queen's Bench Law Reports
QBD	Queen's Bench Division
QCS Board	Quality Contract Scheme Board
QEF	qualifying earnings factor
QYP	qualifying young person
r.	rule
R	Reported Decision
R.C.	Rules of the Court of Session
REA	Reduced Earnings Allowance
Reciprocal Agreement with Ireland	Convention on Social Security between the Government of the United Kingdom and Northern Ireland and the Government of Ireland
reg.	regulation
REULRRA	Retained EU Law (Revocation and Reform) Act 2023
RIPA	Regulation of Investigatory Powers Act 2000
RMO	Responsible Medical Officer
rr.	rules

RR	reference rate
RSI	repetitive strain injury
RTI	Real Time Information
R.V.R.	Rating & Valuation Reporter
s.	section
S	Scottish Decision
SAP	Statutory Adoption Pay
SAPOE Regulations	Jobseeker's Allowance (Schemes for Assisting Persons to Obtain Employment) Regulations 2013
SAWS	Seasonal Agricultural Work Scheme
SAYE	Save As You Earn
SB	Supplementary Benefit
SBAT	Supplementary Benefit Appeal Tribunal
SBC	Supplementary Benefits Commission
S.C.	Session Cases
S.C. (H.L.)	Session Cases (House of Lords)
S.C. (P.C.)	Session Cases (Privy Council)
S.C.C.R.	Scottish Criminal Case Reports
S.C.L.R.	Scottish Civil Law Reports
Sch.	Schedule
SDA	Severe Disablement Allowance
SDP	Severe Disability Premium
SEC	Social Entitlement Chamber
SEN	special educational needs
SERPS	State Earnings Related Pension Scheme
ShPP	statutory shared parental pay
ShPP Regulations	Statutory Shared Parental Pay (General) Regulations 2014
SI	Statutory Instrument
SIP	Share Incentive Plan
S.J.	Solicitors Journal
S.J.L.B.	Solicitors Journal Law Brief
SLAN	statement like an award notice
S.L.T.	Scots Law Times
SMP	Statutory Maternity Pay
SMP (General) Regulations 1986	Statutory Maternity Pay (General) Regulations 1986
Social Security Directive	Council Directive 79/7/EEC of 19 December 1978 on the progressive implementation of the principle of equal treatment for men and women in matters of social security
SPC	State Pension Credit
SPC Regulations	State Pension Credit Regulations 2002
SPCA 2002	State Pension Credit Act 2002
SPL Regulations	Shared Parental Leave Regulations 2014
SPP	Statutory Paternity Pay
ss.	sections
SS (No.2) A 1980	Social Security (No.2) Act 1980

SSA 1975	Social Security Act 1975
SSA 1977	Social Security Act 1977
SSA 1978	Social Security Act 1978
SSA 1979	Social Security Act 1979
SSA 1981	Social Security Act 1981
SSA 1986	Social Security Act 1986
SSA 1988	Social Security Act 1988
SSA 1989	Social Security Act 1989
SSA 1990	Social Security Act 1990
SSA 1998	Social Security Act 1998
SSAA 1992	Social Security Administration Act 1992
SSAC	Social Security Advisory Committee
SSAT	Social Security Appeal Tribunal
SSCBA 1992	Social Security Contributions and Benefits Act 1992
SSCB(NI)A 1992	Social Security Contributions and Benefits (Northern Ireland) Act 1992
SSCPA 1992	Social Security (Consequential Provisions) Act 1992
SSD	Secretary of State for Defence
SSHBA 1982	Social Security and Housing Benefits Act 1982
SSHD	Secretary of State for the Home Department
SSI	Scottish Statutory Instrument
SS(MP)A 1977	Social Security (Miscellaneous Provisions) Act 1977
SSP	Statutory Sick Pay
SSP (General) Regulations	Statutory Sick Pay (General) Regulations 1982
SSPA 1975	Social Security Pensions Act 1975
SSPP	statutory shared parental pay
SS(S)A 2018	Social Security (Scotland) Act 2018
SSWP	Secretary of State for Work and Pensions
State Pension Credit Regulations	State Pension Credit Regulations 2002
S.T.C.	Simon's Tax Cases
S.T.C. (S.C.D.)	Simon's Tax Cases: Special Commissioners' Decisions
S.T.I.	Simon's Tax Intelligence
STIB	Short-Term Incapacity Benefit
subpara.	subparagraph
subs.	subsection
Swiss Citizens' Rights Agreement	Agreement between the United Kingdom of Great Britain and Northern Ireland and the Swiss Confederation on citizens' rights following the withdrawal of the United Kingdom from the European Union and the Free Movement of Persons Agreement
T	Tribunal of Commissioners' Decision
T.C.	Tax Cases
TCA 1999	Tax Credits Act 1999
TCA 2002	Tax Credits Act 2002
TCC	Technology and Construction Court

TCEA 2007	Tribunals, Courts and Enforcement Act 2007
TCGA 1992	Taxation of Chargeable Gains Act 2002
TCTM	*Tax Credits Technical Manual*
TEC	Treaty Establishing the European Community
TENS	transcutaneous electrical nerve stimulation
TEU	Treaty on European Union
TFC	tax-free childcare
TFEU	Treaty on the Functioning of the European Union
TIOPA 2010	Taxation (International and Other Provisions) Act 2010
TMA 1970	Taxes Management Act 1970
T.R.	Taxation Reports
Transfer of Functions Act	Social Security Contributions (Transfer of Functions etc.) Act 1999
Tribunal Procedure Rules	Tribunal Procedure (First-tier Tribunal) (Social Entitlement Chamber) Rules 2008
UB	Unemployment Benefit
UC	Universal Credit
UC Regs 2013	Universal Credit Regulations 2013
UC Transitional Regulations	Universal Credit (Transitional Provisions) Regulations 2014
UCB	Unacceptable Customer Behaviour
UCITS	Undertakings for Collective Investments in Transferable Securities
UKAIT	UK Asylum and Immigration Tribunal
UKBA	UK Border Agency of the Home Office
UKCC	United Kingdom Central Council for Nursing, Midwifery and Health Visiting
UKFTT	United Kingdom First-tier Tribunal Tax Chamber
UKHL	United Kingdom House of Lords
U.K.H.R.R.	United Kingdom Human Rights Reports
UKSC	United Kingdom Supreme Court
UKUT	United Kingdom Upper Tribunal
UN	United Nations
Universal Credit Regulations	Universal Credit Regulations 2013
URL	uniform resource locator
USI Regs	Social Security (Unemployment, Sickness and Invalidity Benefit) Regulations 1983
USI Regulations	Social Security (Unemployment, Sickness and Invalidity Benefit) Regulations 1983
UT	Upper Tribunal
VAT	Value Added Tax
VCM	vinyl chloride monomer
Vol.	Volume
VWF	Vibration White Finger
W	Welsh Decision
WCA	Work Capability Assessment
WCAt	limited capability for work assessment

WFHRAt	Work-Focused Health-Related Assessment
WFI	work-focused interview
WFTC	Working Families Tax Credit
Wikeley, Annotations	N. Wikeley, "Annotations to Jobseekers Act 1995 (c.18)" in *Current Law Statutes Annotated* (1995)
Wikeley, Ogus and Barendt	Wikeley, Ogus and Barendt, *The Law of Social Security* (2002)
Withdrawal Agreement	Agreement on the Withdrawal of the United Kingdom of Great Britain and Northern Ireland from the European Union and the European Atomic Energy Community 2019
W.L.R.	Weekly Law Reports
WLUK	Westlaw UK
Workmen's Compensation Acts	Workmen's Compensation Acts 1925 to 1945
WP	Widow's Pension
WPS	War Pensions Scheme
WRA 2007	Welfare Reform Act 2007
WRA 2009	Welfare Reform Act 2009
WRA 2012	Welfare Reform Act 2012
W-RA Regulations	Employment and Support Allowance (Work-Related Activity) Regulations 2011
WRAAt	Work-Related Activity Assessment
WRPA 1999	Welfare Reform and Pensions Act 1999
WRP(NI)O 1999	Welfare Reform and Pensions (Northern Ireland) Order 1999
WRWA 2016	Welfare Reform and Work Act 2016
WSP (LCP) R (NI) 2016	Welfare Supplementary Payment (Loss of Carer Payments) Regulations (Northern Ireland) 2016
WSP (LDRP) R (NI) 2016	Welfare Supplementary Payment (Loss of Disability-Related Premiums) Regulations (Northern Ireland) 2016
WSPR (NI) 2016	Welfare Supplementary Payment Regulations (Northern Ireland) 2016
WTC	Working Tax Credit
WTC Regulations	Working Tax Credit (Entitlement and Maximum Rate) Regulations 2002

TABLE OF CASES

TABLE OF COMMISSIONERS' DECISIONS

TABLE OF EUROPEAN LEGISLATION

TABLE OF STATUTES

TABLE OF STATUTORY INSTRUMENTS

PART I

NEW LEGISLATION

NEW STATUTES

Neonatal Care (Leave and Pay) Act 2023

(2023 c.20)

Neonatal care leave and pay

1. In the Schedule— 1.001

(a) Part 1 creates a statutory entitlement to neonatal care leave,

(b) Part 2 creates a statutory entitlement to neonatal care pay, and

(c) Part 3 contains related amendments.

Power to make consequential provision

2. *[not yet in force]* 1.002

Extent, commencement and short title

3.—(1) An amendment or repeal made by the Schedule has the same extent as the provision to which it relates. 1.003

(2) Otherwise, this Act extends to England and Wales, Scotland and Northern Ireland.

(3) Section 1, section 2 and the Schedule come into force on such day as the Secretary of State may by regulations made by statutory instrument appoint; and different days may be appointed for different purposes.

(4) This section comes into force on the day on which this Act is passed.

(5) This Act may be cited as the Neonatal Care (Leave and Pay) Act 2023.

SCHEDULE – *[not yet in force]*

GENERAL NOTE

This Act will amend or insert a number of provisions into the Employment Rights Act 1996 and the Social Security Contributions and Benefits Act 1992. These provide powers to make regulations to create an entitlement to Neonatal Care Leave and Pay for eligible employees with parental or other relevant personal relationship with a child who is receiving, or has received, neonatal care. In particular, the Act's powers allow provision to be made for Neonatal Care Leave—a right for employed parents to be absent from work for a prescribed period (to be set at a minimum of one week and a maximum of 12 weeks) in respect of a child who is receiving, or has received, neonatal care (with associated employment protections). All employees who meet the eligibility conditions will be entitled to this leave, regardless of how long they have worked for their employer. The leave must be taken before the end of a period of at least 68 weeks beginning with the date of the child's birth. In addition, the Act's powers allow provision to be made for Neonatal Care Pay—a right for those eligible parents who meet minimum requirements relating to continuity of employment (at least 26 weeks with their current employer) and earnings to be paid during that leave at a prescribed rate. In line with other entitlements to paid statutory leave, the Act enables provision to be made for employers to reclaim payments from the Government. It is anticipated that the new provisions will be in force as from April 2025. 1.004

Victims and Prisoners Act 2024

(2024 c.21)

An Act to make provision about victims of criminal conduct and others affected by criminal conduct; about the appointment and functions of advocates for victims of major incidents; for an infected blood compensation scheme; about the release of prisoners; about the membership and functions of the Parole Board; to prohibit certain prisoners from forming a marriage or civil partnership; and for connected purposes.

ARRANGEMENT OF SECTIONS REPRODUCED

PART 3

INFECTED BLOOD COMPENSATION

[ss. 1–47 omitted]

GENERAL NOTE

1.005 See the General Note to the Infected Blood Compensation Scheme Regulations 2024 (SI 2024/872).

PART 3

INFECTED BLOOD COMPENSATION

Infected Blood Compensation Authority

1.006 **48.**—(1) A body corporate called the Infected Blood Compensation Authority is established.

(2) In this Part that body is referred to as "the IBCA".

(3) Schedule 1 contains further provision about the IBCA.

Infected blood compensation scheme

49.—(1) The Secretary of State or the Minister for the Cabinet Office must by regulations within three months of the passing of this Act establish a scheme (the "infected blood compensation scheme") for making payments to eligible persons. 1.007

(2) "Eligible persons" means such persons within subsection (3) as the regulations provide are to be eligible persons.

(3) The persons within this subsection are persons who—

(a) have been infected as a result of being treated with blood, blood products or tissue,

(b) have been infected as a result of another person being treated with blood, blood products or tissue, or

(c) have been affected by another person being infected as described in paragraph (a) or (b).

(4) The regulations may define an eligible person by reference to matters including (but not limited to)—

(a) the kind of infection;

(b) the duration or effect of an infection;

(c) when the treatment occurred;

(d) where the treatment was given;

(e) who gave the treatment;

(f) whether a person was treated with blood, blood products or tissue;

(g) in the case of a person within subsection (3)(b), how the person was infected and their connection with the person who was treated;

(h) in the case of a person within subsection (3)(c), how the person has been affected and their connection with the person who has been infected.

(5) The regulations must provide for payments under the scheme to be made by, and the scheme to be otherwise administered by, the IBCA.

Payments

50.—(1) The amount of a payment under the infected blood compensation scheme is to be determined in accordance with regulations under section 49. 1.008

(2) The regulations may make provision for the amount payable to eligible persons—

(a) to be a specified amount;

(b) to be an amount within a specified range;

(c) not to exceed a specified amount.

(3) The regulations may make provision—

(a) for payments to be made as a lump sum or periodically;

(b) for payments to be held on trust;

(c) for interest to be payable on payments;

(d) for the amount of any periodic payment to be increased to take account of changes in the value of money.

(4) The regulations may make provision for payments to be made subject to conditions.

(5) The regulations may make provision for payments under the scheme to be repaid to the IBCA (in whole or in part) in specified circumstances.

(6) In this section "specified" means specified in the regulations.

Applications and procedure

1.009 **51.**—Regulations under section 49 may deal with the procedure for the making and deciding of applications for payments under the infected blood compensation scheme and, in particular, may—

(a) impose time limits for making an application or taking other steps;
(b) make provision about evidence.

Reviews and appeals

1.010 **52.**—(1) Regulations under section 49—

(a) may make provision for the IBCA to review decisions taken under the infected blood compensation scheme;
(b) must confer a right of appeal to the First-tier Tribunal against a decision taken under the scheme.

(2) If the regulations make provision under subsection (1)(a), they may provide for the right of appeal to be exercisable only if the IBCA has reviewed the decision.

Information: infected blood compensation scheme

1.011 **53.**—(1) The IBCA may provide information to another person, and a person may provide information to the IBCA, for the purposes of any matter connected with the administration of the infected blood compensation scheme.

(2) The IBCA may by notice in writing require a person to provide information to the IBCA for the purposes of any matter connected with the administration of the infected blood compensation scheme.

(3) If a person fails to comply with a notice under subsection (2), the IBCA may apply to the appropriate court for an order requiring the person to comply with the notice.

(4) The information referred to in this section may comprise or include personal data.

(5) This section does not limit the circumstances in which information may be disclosed apart from this section.

(6) Except as provided by subsection (7), a disclosure of information authorised by or required under this section does not breach—

(a) any obligation of confidence owed by the person making the disclosure, or
(b) any other restriction on the disclosure of information (however imposed).

(7) This section does not authorise or require the processing of information if the processing would contravene the data protection legislation (but in determining whether it would do so, take into account the powers conferred and duties imposed by this section).

(8) In this section—

"the appropriate court" means—

(a) in England and Wales and Northern Ireland, the High Court;
(b) in Scotland, the Court of Session;

"personal data", "processing" and "the data protection legislation" have the meanings given by section 3 of the Data Protection Act 2018.

Duty to co-operate with the IBCA

54.—(1) Each relevant person must co-operate with the IBCA on any matter connected with the making of payments to persons in connection with those persons, or other persons, being treated with infected blood, infected blood products or infected tissue. **1.012**

(2) The relevant persons are—

(a) the Secretary of State;

(b) the Minister for the Cabinet Office;

(c) a Special Health Authority established under section 28 of the National Health Service Act 2006;

(d) the Welsh Ministers;

(e) a National Health Service trust established under section 18 of the National Health Service (Wales) Act 2006;

(f) a Special Health Authority established under section 22 of the National Health Service (Wales) Act 2006;

(g) the Scottish Ministers;

(h) a person who has at any time been appointed by the Scottish Ministers under subsection (4)(d) of section 28 of the Smoking, Health and Social Care (Scotland) Act 2005 (asp 13) to manage a scheme made under that section;

(i) the Department of Health in Northern Ireland;

(j) the Regional Business Services Organisation established by section 14 of the Health and Social Care (Reform) Act (Northern Ireland) 2009 (c. 1 (N.I.));

(k) any other persons specified as relevant persons in regulations made by the Secretary of State or the Minister for the Cabinet Office for the purposes of this section.

(3) Regulations under subsection (2)(k)—

(a) may not specify a Welsh body as a relevant person unless the Welsh Ministers consent;

(b) may not specify a Scottish body as a relevant person unless the Scottish Ministers consent;

(c) may not specify a Northern Ireland body as a relevant person unless the Department of Health in Northern Ireland consents.

(4) In subsection (3)—

"Welsh body" means—

(a) a devolved Welsh authority as defined in section 157A of the Government of Wales Act 2006;

(b) a person providing services to a person within paragraph (a);

"Scottish body" means—

(a) a person who is a part of the Scottish Administration;

(b) a Scottish public authority with mixed functions or no reserved functions (within the meaning of the Scotland Act 1998);

(c) a person providing services to a person within paragraph (a) or (b);

"Northern Ireland body" means—

(a) a Northern Ireland department;

(b) a public authority whose functions are exercisable only or mainly in or as regards Northern Ireland and relate only or mainly to transferred matters (within the meaning of the Northern Ireland Act 1998);

(c) a person providing services to a person within paragraph (a) or (b).

Provision of support and assistance

1.013 **55.**—(1) The Secretary of State or the Minister for the Cabinet Office may make such arrangements as they consider appropriate for the provision of support and assistance to applicants (or potential applicants) for compensation under the infected blood compensation scheme.

(2) The arrangements may be for the provision of support and assistance by the IBCA or any other person.

Payments to personal representatives of qualifying infected persons

1.014 **56.**—(1) The Secretary of State or the Minister for the Cabinet Office must make arrangements for the personal representatives of a qualifying infected person (in their capacity as such) to receive a payment of £100,000.

(2) A "qualifying infected person" is a deceased person—

(a) who was registered as an infected person under an infected blood support scheme, or with a relevant organisation, before 17 April 2024, or

(b) whose death was registered as the death of an infected person under an infected blood support scheme, or with a relevant organisation, before 17 April 2024,

and to or in respect of whom no payment has been made under the Infected Blood Interim Compensation Payment Scheme.

(3) An "infected blood support scheme" means—

(a) the England Infected Blood Support Scheme established under section 2 of, and paragraph 7C of Schedule 1 to, the National Health Service Act 2006,

(b) the Wales Infected Blood Support Scheme established under sections 1 to 3 of the National Health Service (Wales) Act 2006,

(c) the Scottish Infected Blood Support Scheme established partly under section 28 of the Smoking, Health and Social Care (Scotland) Act 2005 (asp 13), and

(d) the Infected Blood Payment Scheme for Northern Ireland established under section 3 of the Health and Social Care (Reform) Act (Northern Ireland) 2009 (c. 1 (N.I.)).

(4) A "relevant organisation" means—

(a) the Caxton Foundation (charity number 1142529),

(b) the Eileen Trust (charity number 1028027),

(c) the Macfarlane Trust (charity number 298863),

(d) the Macfarlane (Special Payments) Trust established on 29 January 1990,

(e) the Macfarlane (Special Payments) (No. 2) Trust established on 3 May 1991,

(f) MFET Limited (company number 07121661), and

(g) the Skipton Fund Limited (company number 5084964).

(5) A payment is made in respect of a deceased person under the Infected Blood Interim Compensation Payment Scheme if a payment under that scheme is made to the person's personal representatives (in their capacity as such) or the person's bereaved partner.

(6) The Infected Blood Interim Compensation Payment Scheme means the scheme of that name administered by the persons who administer the

infected blood support schemes (whether or not in conjunction with other persons).

(7) The arrangements under subsection (1)—

(a) must include provision about the procedure for making payments to the personal representatives of qualifying infected persons;

(b) may include arrangements for one or more other persons (which may in particular include relevant persons) to administer the making of payments, in accordance with that procedure, on behalf of the Secretary of State or the Minister for the Cabinet Office.

(8) The arrangements under subsection (1) may be made, in whole or in part, by exercising powers conferred on the Secretary of State or the Minister for the Cabinet Office apart from this section.

(9) In this section—

"personal representatives", in relation to a deceased person, means the persons responsible for administering the deceased person's estate;

"relevant person" has the same meaning as in section 54.

(10) The Secretary of State or the Minister for the Cabinet Office may by regulations repeal or amend subsections (1) to (9).

Information: payments to personal representatives

57.—(1) A person may provide information to— **1.015**

(a) the Secretary of State or the Minister for the Cabinet Office, or

(b) a person administering the making of payments under section 56 by virtue of section 56(7)(b),

for the purposes of any matter connected with the making of payments to personal representatives under that section.

(2) The information referred to in subsection (1) may comprise or include personal data.

(3) Subsection (1) does not limit the circumstances in which information may be disclosed apart from that subsection.

(4) Except as provided by subsection (5), a disclosure of information authorised by this section does not breach—

(a) any obligation of confidence owed by the person making the disclosure, or

(b) any other restriction on the disclosure of information (however imposed).

(5) Subsection (1) does not authorise the processing of information if the processing would contravene the data protection legislation (but in determining whether it would do so, take into account the power conferred by that subsection).

(6) In this section "personal data", "processing" and "the data protection legislation" have the meanings given by section 3 of the Data Protection Act 2018.

[ss.58–82 omitted]

[Schs 1 and 2 omitted]

NEW REGULATIONS

The Welfare Reform Act 2012 (Commencement No. 31 and Savings and Transitional Provisions) (Amendment) Order 2024

(SI 2024/604)

Made *7th May 2024*

The Secretary of State makes this Order in exercise of the powers conferred by section 150(3) and (4)(c) of the Welfare Reform Act 2012.

Citation, extent and effect

1.016 **1.**—(1) This Order may be cited as the Welfare Reform Act 2012 (Commencement No. 31 and Savings and Transitional Provisions) (Amendment) Order 2024.

(2) This Order extends to England and Wales and Scotland.

(3) The amendment in article 2 has effect from 8th June 2024.

Preservation of saving for mixed-age couples migrated to universal credit

1.017 **2.**—(1) The Welfare Reform Act 2012 (Commencement No. 31 and Savings and Transitional Provisions and Commencement No. 21 and 23 and Transitional and Transitory Provisions (Amendment)) Order 2019 is amended as follows.

(2) In article 4 (savings) after paragraph (2) insert—

"(3) Nothing in regulation 6A (restriction on claims for housing benefit, income support or a tax credit) of the Transitional Regulations prevents a claim for housing benefit by a member of a mixed-age couple referred to in paragraph (1) where—

(a) they have been issued with a migration notice;

(b) they make the claim for housing benefit within three months beginning with—

(i) in the case of a person who became entitled to universal credit by claiming before the final deadline, the day after their award of universal credit terminates; or

(ii) in the case of a person who did not claim universal credit, or claimed before the final deadline but was not entitled, the day after their award of housing benefit terminates; and

(c) they meet the conditions for entitlement to housing benefit on that day.

(4) Where a person mentioned in sub-paragraph (b)(i) of paragraph (3) claims—

(a) housing benefit; or

(b) state pension credit (whether or not they also claim housing benefit),

within three months beginning with the day mentioned in that sub-paragraph, any days on which they were entitled to universal credit are to be disregarded for the purposes of paragraph (2).

(5) In this article "Transitional Regulations" means the Universal Credit (Transitional Provisions) Regulations 2014 and "final deadline" and "migration notice" have the same meaning as in those Regulations.".

The Social Security (State Pension Age Claimants: Closure of Tax Credits) (Amendment) Regulations 2024

(SI 2024/611)

Made	*7th May 2024*
Laid before Parliament	*9th May 2024*
Coming into force	*8th June 2024*

The Secretary of State makes these Regulations in exercise of the powers conferred by sections 122(1), 123(1)(d), 135(1), 137(1), 175(1), (3) to (5) of, and paragraphs 2(2), 3B(5)(b)(iii) and 7B(5)(b)(iii) of Schedule 5 to, the Social Security Contributions and Benefits Act 1992, section 5(1)(a) and (k) and 189(1) and (3) to (6) of the Social Security Administration Act 1992, sections 2(3)(b), 15(6)(a) and 19(1) of the State Pension Credit Act 2002, sections 32, 42(1) to (3) and 96(1) and (4)(c) of, and paragraph 4(1) and (3) of Schedule 1 to, and paragraphs 1(1), 4(1)(a) and (b) and (2)(c) and (d) of Schedule 6 to, the Welfare Reform Act 2012.

In accordance with section 173(1)(b) of the Social Security Administration Act 1992, the Social Security Advisory Committee has agreed that the proposals in respect of these Regulations should not be referred to it.

In accordance with section 176(1)(a) of that Act, in so far as these Regulations relate to housing benefit, the Secretary of State has consulted with organisations appearing to him to be representative of the authorities concerned in respect of the proposals for these Regulations.

Citation, commencement and extent

1.—(1) These Regulations may be cited as the Social Security (State Pension Age Claimants: Closure of Tax Credits) (Amendment) Regulations 2024 and come into force on 8th June 2024. **1.018**

(2) This regulation and regulation 3 extend to England and Wales, Scotland and Northern Ireland.

(3) Regulation 2 and regulations 4 to 7 extend to England and Wales and Scotland.

Closure of tax credits – migration of pension age claimants to universal credit

2.—(1) The Universal Credit (Transitional Provisions) Regulations 2014 are amended as follows. **1.019**

(2) In regulation 2 (interpretation) in the appropriate place insert—

""tax credit closure notice" means a notice issued under article 3A (tax credit closure notice) of the Welfare Reform Act 2012 (Commencement No. 32 and Savings and Transitional Provisions) Order 2019;".

(3) In regulation 44 (migration notice)—

(a) after paragraph (3) insert—

"(3A) But where a migration notice is issued after cancellation of a previous migration notice or after cancellation of a tax credit closure notice the deadline day may be within such shorter period as the Secretary of State considers appropriate."; and

(b) after paragraph (5) insert—

"(5A) In a case referred to in paragraph (5)(a) the Secretary of State may, instead of cancelling the migration notice, treat that notice as if it were a tax credit closure notice issued to that person and may treat the deadline day in the migration notice as if it were the deadline day in a tax credit closure notice.".

(4) In regulation 56 (circumstances in which transitional protection ceases)—

(a) in paragraph (1) after "paragraph (2)" insert ", (3A)";

(b) in paragraph (2) after "assessment period", where it is first mentioned, insert "other than an assessment period in relation to an award of universal credit mentioned in regulation 60A(1) (waiver of upper age limit for claimants migrated from tax credits)"; and

(c) after paragraph (3) insert—

"(3A) This paragraph applies to an assessment period in relation to an award of universal credit mentioned in regulation 60A(1) (waiver of upper age limit for claimants migrated from tax credits) which—

(a) is not one of the first 12 assessment periods; and

(b) is the assessment period after the third consecutive assessment period in which the claimant's earned income, (or, if the claimant is a member of a couple the couple's combined earned income) is less than the amount that a person would be paid at the hourly rate set out in regulation 4 of the National Minimum Wage Regulations for 16 hours a week converted to a monthly amount by multiplying by 52 and dividing by 12.".

(5) After regulation 60 (protection for full-time students until course completed) insert—

"Waiver of upper age limit for claimants migrated from tax credits

60A.—(1) Where a qualifying claim is made by—

(a) a single claimant who, at the time the migration notice is issued—

(i) has reached the qualifying age for state pension credit;

(ii) is entitled to an award of working tax credit; and

(iii) is not entitled to an award of state pension credit; or

(b) joint claimants both of whom satisfy the criteria in sub-paragraph (a)(i) to (iii) at the time the migration notice is issued,

then, subject to paragraphs (2) and (3), the condition in section 4(1)(b) of the Act (claimant has not reached the qualifying age for state pension credit) is not to apply for the purposes of determining entitlement to universal credit in respect of the qualifying claim or any award made in respect of that claim.

(2) The reference in paragraph (1) to a person who is entitled to an award of working tax credit includes a person who meets the entitlement conditions for both that credit and child tax credit.

(3) Paragraph (1) ceases to apply in respect of an award of universal credit mentioned in paragraph (1) in an assessment period in which—

(a) a transitional element or transitional capital disregard would cease to apply by virtue of regulation 56 (circumstances in which transitional protection ceases) or regulation 57 (application of transitional protection to a subsequent award); or

(b) a person who is entitled to an award of universal credit by virtue of paragraph (1) makes a claim for state pension credit.

Deferral of retirement pension income

60B.—(1) Where, at the time a migration notice is issued, the notified person—

(a) has reached the qualifying age for state pension credit;

(b) is entitled to an award of a tax credit; and

(c) has not made an application for retirement pension income to which they might expect to be entitled,

regulation 74 (notional unearned income) of the Universal Credit Regulations is not, subject to paragraph (2), to apply in relation to that person for the purpose of calculating the amount of an award of universal credit (including the indicative UC amount) until the assessment period following the first 12 assessment periods of an award made in respect of a claim by that person.

(2) This regulation ceases to apply in an assessment period in which a transitional element or transitional capital disregard would cease to apply by virtue of regulation 56 (circumstances in which transitional protection ceases) or regulation 57 (application of transitional protection to a subsequent award).

(3) In this regulation "retirement pension income" has the same meaning as in regulation 67 of the Universal Credit Regulations.

Exemption from the benefit cap

60C. Where a qualifying claim is made by a single claimant who has, or joint claimants both of whom have, reached the qualifying age for state pension credit, regulation 79 (circumstances where the benefit cap applies) of the Universal Credit Regulations is not to apply for the purpose of calculating the amount of an award of universal credit (including the indicative UC amount).".

Closure of tax credits — claimants not moving to universal credit

3.—(1) The Welfare Reform Act 2012 (Commencement No. 32 and Savings and Transitional Provisions) Order 2019 is amended as follows. **1.020**

(2) In article 1 (citation and interpretation) insert at the appropriate place—

""migration notice" means a notice under regulation 44 (migration notice) of the Universal Credit (Transitional Provisions) Regulations 2014 or a notice under regulation 45 (migration notice) of the Universal Credit (Transitional Provisions) Regulations (Northern Ireland) 2016;";

""notified person" means a person to whom a notice has been issued under article 3A (tax credit closure notice);";

““state pension credit” means state pension credit under the State Pension Credit Act 2002 or the State Pension Credit Act (Northern Ireland) 2002;”.

(3) In article 3 (savings) in paragraph (1) at the beginning insert “Subject to articles 3A (tax credit closure notice) and 3B (saving to cease following issue of tax credit closure notice),”.

(4) After article 3 insert—

“Tax credit closure notice

3A.—(1) The Secretary of State (or, in Northern Ireland, the Department) may, at any time, issue a notice (“a tax credit closure notice”) to—

(a) a person who is entitled to an award of child tax credit, but not an award of working tax credit, and is—

(i) a single person who has reached the qualifying age;

(ii) a member of a couple both members of which have reached that age; or

(iii) a member of a protected mixed-age couple; or

(b) a person who is entitled to both an award of a tax credit and an award of state pension credit,

informing the person that their tax credit award is to end by a specified day (“the deadline day”).

(2) The tax credit closure notice may contain such other information as the Secretary of State or the Department considers appropriate.

(3) The deadline day must not, subject to paragraph (4), be within the period of three months beginning with the day on which the tax credit closure notice is issued.

(4) The deadline day may be within such shorter period as the Secretary of State or the Department considers appropriate where—

(a) the person is entitled to an award of state pension credit when the tax credit closure notice is issued; or

(b) the tax credit closure notice is issued after cancellation of a previous tax credit closure notice or after cancellation of a migration notice issued to that person.

(5) If the tax credit award is to joint claimants the Secretary of State or the Department must issue a tax credit closure notice to each claimant.

(6) The Secretary of State or the Department may determine that the deadline day should be changed to a later day either—

(a) on the Secretary of State’s or the Department’s own initiative; or

(b) if the notified person requests such a change before the deadline day,

if there is a good reason to do so.

(7) Where the Secretary of State or the Department changes the deadline day in accordance with paragraph (6) they must inform the notified person or persons of the new deadline day.

(8) The Secretary of State or the Department may cancel a tax credit closure notice issued to any person—

(a) if it has been issued in error;

(b) in any other circumstances where the Secretary State or the Department considers it necessary to do so in the interests of the person, or any class of person, or to safeguard the efficient administration of state pension credit.

(9) In a case referred to in paragraph (8)(a) the Secretary of State or the Department may, instead of cancelling the tax credit closure notice, treat that notice as if it were a migration notice issued to that person and as if the deadline day in the tax credit closure notice were the deadline day in a migration notice.

(10) In this article—

"the Department" means the Department for Communities in Northern Ireland;

"protected mixed-age couple" means a mixed-age couple to whom article 4 (savings) of the Welfare Reform Act 2012 (Commencement No. 31 and Savings and Transitional Provisions and Commencement No. 21 and 23 and Transitional and Transitory Provisions (Amendment)) Order 2019 or article 4 (savings) of the Welfare Reform (Northern Ireland) Order 2015 (Commencement No. 13 and Savings and Transitional Provisions and Commencement No. 8 and Transitional and Transitory Provisions (Amendment)) Order 2019 applies,

and the reference in paragraph (1) to a person who is entitled to a tax credit includes a person who is treated as being so entitled by virtue of regulation 11(1) (ongoing awards of tax credits) of the Universal Credit (Transitional Provisions) Regulations 2014 or regulation 9(1) (ongoing awards of tax credits) of the Universal Credit (Transitional Provisions) Regulations (Northern Ireland) 2016.

Saving to cease following issue of tax credit closure notice

3B.—(1) Paragraph (1) of article 3 (savings) shall cease to apply to a notified person in relation to any of the cases mentioned in that article on—

(a) where the person makes a claim for state pension credit on or before the deadline day, the day on which the claim is made (or if, in the case of joint tax credit claimants there is more than one such claim, the day on which the first claim is made); or

(b) in any other case, the deadline day.

(2) Where article 3 ceases to apply in relation to an award of a tax credit in accordance with this article during a tax year, the amount of the tax credit to which the person is entitled for that tax year is to be calculated in accordance with the Tax Credits Act 2002 and regulations made under that Act as modified by Schedule 1 (modification of tax credits legislation (finalisation of tax credits)) to the Universal Credit (Transitional Provisions) Regulations 2014 or Schedule 1 (modification of tax credits legislation (finalisation of tax credits)) to the Universal Credit (Transitional Provisions) Regulations (Northern Ireland) 2016 in the same way as if—

(a) the claim for state pension credit had been a claim for universal credit; or

(b) the deadline day in the tax credit closure notice had been the deadline day in a migration notice.".

Closure of tax credits – transitional protection in state pension credit

4.—(1) The State Pension Credit Regulations 2002 are amended as follows. 1.021

(2) In regulation 1 (citation, commencement and interpretation) in the appropriate place insert—

"“tax credit closure notice” means a notice issued under article 3A (tax credit closure notice) of the Welfare Reform Act 2012 (Commencement No. 32 and Savings and Transitional Provisions) Order 2019;".

(3) In regulation 6 (amount of the guarantee credit) after paragraph (6)(c) omit "or" and after paragraph (6)(d) insert—

"or

(e) in accordance with Schedule IIB (transitional protection on closure of tax credits).".

(4) In regulation 18 (notional income)—

(a) in paragraph (1A) for "and (1CB)" substitute ", (1CB) and (5A)";

(b) in paragraphs (1D) and (2) at the beginning insert "Subject to paragraph (5A),"; and

(c) after paragraph (5) insert—

"(5A) Where a person—

(a) makes a claim for state pension credit on or after the issue of a tax credit closure notice and before the expiry of one month beginning with the deadline day specified in that notice; and

(b) has not, at the time the notice is issued, made an application for retirement pension income to which they might expect to be entitled,

paragraphs (1), (1D) and (2) are not to apply for a period beginning with the first day on which the person is entitled to an award of state pension credit as a consequence of that claim and ending after 52 weeks or, if sooner, on the day the person ceases to be entitled to state pension credit.".

(5) After Schedule IIA (additional amount applicable for claimants responsible for a child or qualifying young person) insert—

"SCHEDULE IIB — regulation 6(6)

TRANSITIONAL PROTECTION ON CLOSURE OF TAX CREDITS

Interpretation

1. In this Schedule—

"HMRC" means His Majesty's Revenue and Customs;

"indicative SPC amount" has the meaning given in paragraph 5;

"migration day" in relation to a claimant means the day before the day specified in paragraph (1) of article 3B (saving to cease following issue of tax credit closure notice) of the No. 32 Order;

"the No. 32 Order" means the Welfare Reform Act 2012 (Commencement No. 32 and Savings and Transitional Provisions) Order 2019;

"tax credit", "child tax credit" and "working tax credit" have the same meaning as in the Tax Credits Act 2002.

Claimants eligible for protection

2.—(1) This Schedule applies where the claimant has been issued with a tax credit closure notice and—

(a) the claimant was entitled to an award of child tax credit on the migration day; and

(b) either—

(i) the claimant was entitled to an award of state pension credit when the tax credit closure notice was issued; or

(ii) the claimant made a claim for state pension credit on or after the issue of the tax credit closure notice and before the expiry of one month beginning with the deadline day specified in that notice.

(2) This Schedule does not apply where—

(a) the claimant was a member of a couple for the purposes of the child tax credit award when the tax credit closure notice was issued but is a single person or a member of a different couple for the purposes of state pension credit on the migration day; or

(b) the claimant was a single person for the purposes of the child tax credit award when the tax credit closure notice was issued but is a member of a couple for the purposes of state pension credit on the migration day.

Transitional additional amount

3. An additional amount of the appropriate minimum guarantee ("the transitional additional amount") applies in accordance with regulation 6(6)(e) if the weekly amount determined in accordance with paragraph 4 (representative weekly amount of child tax credit), combined with the weekly amount of state pension credit (if any) to which the claimant was entitled on the migration day, is greater than the weekly amount determined in accordance with paragraph 5 (indicative SPC amount).

Representative weekly amount of child tax credit

4.—(1) To calculate the representative weekly amount of an award of child tax credit—

(a) take the figure for the daily rate of the award on the migration day provided by HMRC and calculated on the basis of the information as to the claimant's circumstances held by HMRC on that day; and

(b) convert to a weekly figure by multiplying by 7.

(2) For the purposes of sub-paragraph (1)(a) "the daily rate" is—

(a) in a case where section 13(1) of the Tax Credit Act 2002 (relevant income does not exceed the income threshold or the claimant is entitled to a prescribed social security benefit) applies, the maximum rate of each element to which the claimant is entitled on the migration day divided by 365; and

(b) in any other case, the rate that would be produced by applying regulations 6 to 9 of the Tax Credits (Income Thresholds and Determination of Rates) Regulations 2002 as if the migration day were a relevant period of one day.

Indicative SPC amount

5.—(1) The indicative SPC amount is the weekly amount to which a claimant would be entitled if an award of state pension credit were calculated in accordance with the Act and these Regulations by reference to the claimant's circumstances on the migration day—

(a) disregarding any amount of working tax credit to which the person may be entitled on that day;

(b) including an additional amount in accordance with Schedule IIA (additional amount applicable for claimants responsible for a child or qualifying young person); and

(c) applying the assumptions in sub-paragraph (2).

(2) The assumptions are—

(a) the claimant is responsible for any child or qualifying young person in respect of whom the individual element of child tax credit is payable;

(b) the amount of the claimant's earned income is the annual amount of any employment income or trading income, as defined by regulation 4 or 6 respectively of the Tax Credits (Definition and Calculation of Income) Regulations 2002, by reference to which the representative weekly rate of that tax credit is calculated for the purposes of paragraph 4(1) converted to a net weekly amount by—

(i) dividing by 52; and

(ii) deducting such amount for income tax and national insurance contributions as the Secretary of State considers appropriate.

(3) If the claimant would not satisfy the condition in section 2(1) (guarantee credit) of the Act because the claimant has income which exceeds the appropriate minimum guarantee, the claimant is to be treated for the purposes of calculating the indicative SPC amount as if they were entitled to a guarantee credit of a nil amount.

Initial calculation of the transitional additional amount

6. The initial amount of the transitional additional amount is—

(a) if the amount of the guarantee credit in the indicative SPC amount is greater than nil, the amount by which the representative weekly amount of child tax credit combined with the weekly amount of state pension credit (if any) to which the claimant was entitled on the migration day, exceeds the weekly amount of the indicative SPC amount;

(b) if the amount of the guarantee credit in the indicative SPC amount is nil—

(i) the sum of the representative weekly amount of child tax credit and the amount, if any, by which the income deducted in the calculation of the indicative SPC amount exceeds the amount of the appropriate minimum guarantee; minus

(ii) the amount of the maximum saving credit, but only if the indicative SPC amount includes a savings credit or would do but for the claimant's income being such that the condition in section 3(2)(b) of the Act is not met.

Reduction of the transitional additional amount

7.—(1) Whenever there is a relevant increase after the first day on which the transitional additional amount applies, the transitional additional amount is to be reduced by an amount equal to that increase.

(2) A relevant increase is an increase in the standard minimum guarantee or in any additional amount prescribed under section 2(3) of the Act, including where that additional amount is applied for the first time or reapplied following a change of circumstances.

Circumstances in which the transitional additional amount ceases

8.—(1) A transitional additional amount is no longer applicable if—

(a) the transitional additional amount is reduced to nil in accordance with paragraph 7;

(b) the claimant was a member of a couple and ceases to be a member of that couple or becomes a member of a different couple;

(c) the claimant was single and becomes a member of a couple; or

(d) the claimant is no longer responsible for any child or qualifying young person for whom they were responsible at the time the tax credit closure notice was issued.

(2) Where the claimant ceases to be entitled to state pension credit, the transitional additional amount is not, subject to sub-paragraph (3), to apply to a subsequent award to the claimant or, if the claimant is a member of a couple, their partner.

(3) Where an award ("the subsequent award") is made to a person who moves from Northern Ireland when they are entitled to an award of state pension credit that includes a transitional additional amount then, provided their circumstances are otherwise unchanged, the subsequent award is to include a transitional additional amount calculated as if the subsequent award were a continuation of the award made in Northern Ireland.

Effect of revision, appeal etc. of an award of a tax credit

9.—(1) Nothing in paragraph 4 or 5 requiring a calculation in relation to the transitional additional amount to be made on the basis of information held by HMRC on the migration day prevents the Secretary of State from revising or superseding a decision in relation to a claim for, or an award of, state pension credit where—

(a) in the opinion of the Secretary of State, the information held on that day was inaccurate or incomplete in some material respect because of—

(i) a misrepresentation by a claimant;

(ii) a failure to report information that a claimant was required to report where that failure was advantageous to the claimant; or

(iii) an official error; or

(b) a decision has been made on or after the migration day on—

(i) an application made before the migration day to revise a decision in relation to an award of a tax credit (including the report of a change of circumstances); or

(ii) an appeal in relation to such an application.

(2) In this paragraph "official error" means an error that—

(a) was made by an officer of, or an employee of a body acting on behalf of, the Department for Work and Pensions or HMRC; and

(b) was not caused, or materially contributed to, by any person outside that body or outside the Department or HMRC,

but excludes any error of law which is shown to have been such by a subsequent decision of the Upper Tribunal or of a court as defined in section 27(7) of the Social Security Act 1998.".

Supplementary provision relating to persons moving to state pension credit: time for claiming and part-week payments

1.022 **5.**—(1) Where a person who is not entitled to an award of state pension credit is issued with a tax credit closure notice then, notwithstanding anything in regulation 19(2) (time for claiming benefit) of the Social Security (Claims and Payments) Regulations 1987, the prescribed times for making a claim for state pension credit are as follows—

(a) if the person is claiming in respect of a period that begins before the deadline day specified in that notice, the first day of that period;

(b) if the person is claiming in respect of a period that begins on the deadline day, within three months beginning with the deadline day.

(2) Where, by virtue of paragraph (1), state pension credit is awarded from a day which is not the first day of a benefit week then, notwithstanding anything in regulation 16A of those Regulations, entitlement shall begin on the first day of the award and the amount payable in respect of that part-week shall be determined by—

(a) dividing by 7 the weekly amount which would be payable in respect of the full week; and then

(b) multiplying the resulting figure by the number of days in the part-week.

(3) But paragraph (2) does not apply if the claimant's entitlement to state pension credit is unlikely to continue throughout the first full benefit week that follows the part-week.

(4) In this regulation—

"benefit week" means—

(a) where state pension credit is paid in advance, the period of 7 days beginning on the day on which, in the claimant's case, that benefit would (if not for paragraph (2)) be payable;

(b) where state pension credit is paid in arrears, the period of 7 days ending on the day on which, in the claimant's case, that benefit would (if not for paragraph (2)) be payable; and

"tax credit closure notice" means a notice issued under article 3A (tax credit closure notice) of the Welfare Reform Act 2012 (Commencement No. 32 and Savings and Transitional Provisions) Order 2019.

Abolition of the two child limit for pension age housing benefit

6. Regulation 22 of the Housing Benefit (Persons who have attained the qualifying age for state pension credit) Regulations 2006 (applicable amounts) is amended as follows— **1.023**

(a) in paragraph (1)(b)—

(i) omit "up to two individuals who are either"; and

(ii) omit "and";

(b) omit paragraphs (5A) to (5D).

Amendments regarding the deferral of State Pension

7.—(1) In regulation 4 of the Social Security (Widow's Benefit and Retirement Pensions) Regulations 1979 (days to be treated as days of increment) at the end of paragraph (1)(b) for "and" substitute— **1.024**

"or

(vi) universal credit; and".

(2) In regulation 3 of the Social Security (Deferral of Retirement Pensions) Regulations 2005 (amount of retirement pension not included in the calculation of the lump sum) at the end of paragraph (1)(a) insert—

"(vi) universal credit under Part 1 of the Welfare Reform Act 2012;".

The Social Fund Winter Fuel Payment Regulations 2024

(SI 2024/869)

Made under ss.138(2) and 175(1) and (3) to (5) of the Social Security Contributions and Benefits Act 1992, ss.5(1)(a) and (i) and 189(1) and (4) to (6) of the Social Security Administration Act 1992, ss.16(1) and 79(1) and (4) of, and para.3 of Sch.5 to, the Social Security Act 1998 and s.71(1)(a), (2)(a), (3) and (5) of the Scotland Act 2016.

Not referred in advance to the Social Security Advisory Committee, in accordance with section 173(1)(a) of the Social Security Administration Act 1992, on the ground that it appeared to the Secretary of State that by reason of the urgency of this matter it was inexpedient to do so.

General Note

1.025 The principal continuity between this scheme, and the previous scheme existing under the Social Fund Winter Fuel Payment Regulations 2000 (SI 2000/729), is that both schemes provided a cash payment, in winter, to people of pensionable age. The principal difference between the two schemes is that in the new scheme, a recipient must now be entitled to a qualifying means-tested benefit: reg.2(2)(b). It is no longer a universal scheme. One other notable difference is that after the 2024/25 winter, the scheme will no longer apply to anyone resident abroad: reg.7(2). Presumably the legislator took the view that there is no legal obligation under the Withdrawal Agreement to permit exportation of payments made under the 2024 scheme.

On 20 September 2024 the chair of the Social Security Advisory Committee wrote to the Secretary of State criticising the use of the urgency provisions to avoid referring the draft regulations to the Committee, setting out the Committee's view that the urgency exception should only be used in exceptional circumstances and stating:

> "This Committee has a strong track record of supporting successive Secretaries of State respond at pace to emerging crises and risks. We have often arranged additional meetings to enable scrutiny to take place at short notice, in an attempt to avoid the need for invoking the urgency procedure."

The Committee chair also stated:

> "We were disappointed that an assessment of impact was not presented to the Committee alongside the regulations on 11 September 2024. It has subsequently been confirmed that a full assessment of impact does not exist."

Judicial review proceedings have been commenced in both England and Scotland to challenge the lawfulness of the means testing aspect of the 2024 Regulations. The Scotland claim, *Fanning v Secretary of State for Work and Pensions*, has permission and, at the time of writing, is expected to be heard in early 2025. The England claim is being brought by the trade union Unite and is, at the time of writing, at a pre-permission stage.

Citation, commencement, extent and interpretation

1.026 **1.**—(1) These Regulations may be cited as the Social Fund Winter Fuel Payment Regulations 2024 and come into force on 16th September 2024.

(2) Subject to paragraph (3), these Regulations extend to England and Wales only.

(3) Regulations 1 and 7(1), and Schedule 2 (revocations), also extend to Scotland.

(4) In these Regulations—

"child tax credit" and "working tax credit" have the same meanings as in the Tax Credits Act 2002;

"couple" means—

(a) two people who are married to, or civil partners of, each other and are members of the same household; or

(b) two people who are not married to, or civil partners of, each other but are living together as if they were a married couple or civil partners;

"polygamous marriage" means any marriage which took place under the laws of a country which permits polygamy where—

(a) any member of the marriage is for the time being married to more than one person; and

(b) all the members of the marriage are members of the same household;

"qualifying week" means in respect of any year the week beginning on the third Monday in the September of that year.

Entitlement to a Winter Fuel Payment

2.—(1) Subject to regulation 4, the Secretary of State must pay a winter fuel payment out of the social fund to a person where— **1.027**

(a) that person has reached pensionable age in or before the qualifying week; and

(b) in respect of any day falling within the qualifying week, paragraph (2) or (3) applies to the person.

(2) This paragraph applies if the person is—

(a) ordinarily resident in England and Wales; and

(b) entitled to—

(i) a relevant benefit; or

(ii) an award of child tax credit or working tax credit of not less than £26 in respect of the tax year 2024–25.

(3) This paragraph applies if the person is—

(a) habitually resident in any of the countries listed in Schedule 1;

(b) covered by—

(i) Title III of Part 2 of the withdrawal agreement, as set out at Article 30 of that agreement;

(ii) Title III of Part 2 of the EEA EFTA separation agreement, as set out at Article 29 of that agreement;

(iii) Part Three of the Swiss citizens' rights agreement, as set out at Article 25 of that agreement; or

(iv) the Convention on Social Security between the Government of the United Kingdom of Great Britain and Northern Ireland and the Government of Ireland signed at Dublin on 1st February 2019, as set out in Article 2 of that Convention; and

(c) able to demonstrate—

(i) entitlement to a benefit payable in the country in which the person is habitually resident that is equivalent to a relevant benefit; and

(ii) a genuine and sufficient link to the United Kingdom.

(4) In this regulation—

"pensionable age" has the meaning given by the rules in paragraph 1 of Schedule 4 to the Pensions Act 1995 (c. 26);

"relevant benefit" means—

(a) income support under Part 7 of the Social Security Contributions and Benefits Act 1992;

(b) an income-based jobseeker's allowance under the Jobseekers Act 1995;

(c) state pension credit under the State Pension Credit Act 2002;

(d) an income-related employment and support allowance under Part 1 of the Welfare Reform Act 2007;

(e) universal credit under Part 1 of the Welfare Reform Act 2012;

"withdrawal agreement", "EEA EFTA separation agreement" and "Swiss citizens' rights agreement" have the same meanings as in section 39(1) of the European Union (Withdrawal Agreement) Act 2020.

(5) The reference in paragraph (2)(b) and (3)(c)(i) to a person being entitled to a relevant benefit or tax credit includes where the person is a member of a couple or polygamous marriage and the other member of the couple or another member of that marriage is entitled to the benefit or tax credit.

DEFINITIONS

"child tax credit" and "working tax credit"—see reg.1(4).
"couple"—see reg.1(4).
"polygamous marriage"—see reg.1(4).
"qualifying week"—see reg.1(4).

GENERAL NOTE

1.028 Until the winter of 2015/16, winter fuel payments were payable under the Social Fund Winter Fuel Payment Regulations 2000 (SI 2000/729) to people who were habitually resident in any EEA state (or Switzerland) rather than only to those who were habitually in a scheduled country. The effect of the amendment made by SI 2014/3270 with effect from September 21, 2015, which is carried through into the new scheme for 2024/25, was that those who are habitually resident in Cyprus, France, Greece, Malta, Portugal and Spain no longer qualify, but other EEA states and Switzerland do.

According to the explanatory memorandum to SI 2014/3270 the average winter temperature (November to March) in the warmest part of the United Kingdom is 5.6°C. The policy is to exclude from entitlement those who are habitually resident in EEA states where the average winter temperature is warmer. The memorandum goes on to state:

> "7.7 DWP is aware there will be people who live in cold regions of "warm" countries who will not be eligible for a Winter Fuel Payment. However, we would have to implement the scheme on a regional basis throughout the EEA in order to make a Winter Fuel Payment for even some of these people. DWP considered this very carefully but concluded that it would introduce disproportionate complexity and administrative costs. Therefore, the scheme has to be administered on a countrywide basis using the average winter temperature for each EEA country to determine where Winter Fuel Payments will be payable."

Under the new scheme, the provision for payments to persons habitually resident in the European Economic Area and Switzerland will expire altogether on April 1, 2025: see reg.7(2).

Amount of a Winter Fuel Payment

3. The amount of a winter fuel payment is as follows— **1.029**

(a) if the person has reached the age of 80 in or before the qualifying week, £300;

(b) if the person has not reached the age of 80 in or before the qualifying week but they are a member of a couple or a polygamous marriage and the other member of the couple or another member of that marriage has reached that age in or before that week, £300; or

(c) in any other case, £200.

DEFINITIONS

"couple"—see reg.1(4).
"polygamous marriage"—see reg.1(4).
"qualifying week"—see reg.1(4).

Persons not entitled to a Winter Fuel Payment

4.—(1) Regulation 2 does not apply in respect of a person who— **1.030**

(a) throughout the qualifying week, is—

(i) one member of a couple where the Secretary of State has paid a winter fuel payment in respect of the qualifying week to the other member of that couple;

(ii) a member of a polygamous marriage where the Secretary of State has paid a winter fuel payment in respect of the qualifying week to another member of that marriage;

(iii) receiving free in-patient treatment and has been receiving free in-patient treatment for a period of at least 52 weeks ending immediately before the qualifying week;

(iv) detained in custody under a sentence imposed by a court; or

(v) in residential care and has been in residential care for a period of at least 12 weeks ending immediately before the qualifying week;

(b) having been ordinarily resident in England and Wales on a day falling within the qualifying week, becomes ordinarily resident in Scotland or Northern Ireland by the last day of that week; or

(c) subject to paragraph (2), has not made a claim for a winter fuel payment on or before 31st March following the qualifying week in respect of the winter following that week.

(2) Paragraph (1)(c) does not apply where—

(a) a payment has been made by virtue of regulation 5(1) in respect of the winter following the qualifying week; or

(b) regulation 5(2) applies.

(3) In this regulation—

"care home" in England, has the meaning assigned to it by section 3 of the Care Standards Act 2000, and in Wales, means a care home service within the meaning of Part 1 of the Regulation and Inspection of Social Care (Wales) Act 2016 which is provided wholly or mainly to persons aged 18 or over;

"free in-patient treatment" is to be construed in accordance with regulation 2(4) and (5) of the Social Security (Hospital In-Patients) Regulations 2005;

"independent hospital" means—

(a) in England, a hospital as defined by section 275(1) of the National Health Service Act 2006 that is not a health service hospital as defined by that section;

(b) in Wales, has the meaning assigned to it by section 2 of the Care Standards Act 2000;

(c) in relation to Scotland, means an independent health care service as defined in section 10F(1)(a) and (b) and (2) of the National Health Service (Scotland) Act 1978;

"residential care" means, disregarding any period of temporary absence, a person residing in—

(a) a care home;

(b) an independent hospital; or

(c) accommodation provided under section 3(1) of the Polish Resettlement Act 1947.

DEFINITIONS

"couple"—see reg.1(4).
"polygamous marriage"—see reg.1(4).
"qualifying week"—see reg.1(4).

GENERAL NOTE

1.031 Regulation 4 excludes certain people from entitlement to a winter fuel payment even if they fall within reg.2(1)(a) and (b). There are in substance five categories:

(a) partners of people who have been paid a winter fuel payment (reg.4(1)(a)(i) and (ii)). This is to prevent double payment;

(b) people who, throughout the qualifying week, have been receiving free in-patient treatment (see the notes to reg.21(3) of the Income Support Regulations) for more than 52 weeks (reg.4(1)(a)(iii));

(c) people serving a custodial sentence throughout the qualifying week (reg.4(1)(a)(iv)). Note that the reference to "a sentence imposed by a court" excludes those in prison on remand;

(d) people in residential care who have been in residential care for a period of at least 12 weeks ending immediately before the qualifying week (reg.4(1)(a)(iv)); and

(e) anyone who does not automatically receive a winter fuel payment under reg.5 and who fails to claim it by March 31 in the following year (reg.4(1)(c)). This is subject to the Reg. 4(2)(b) exception for people who become retrospectively entitled to a qualifying benefit. In *CIS 2337/2004*, Commissioner Jacobs held that the time limit (in the equivalent provision of the 2000 regulations) did not infringe claimants' rights under art.1 of the First Protocol to the European Convention on Human Rights even when a payment has been made without a claim in respect of previous years. The time limit did not deprive claimants of any rights but merely defined the scope of those rights. A claim for a winter fuel payment may be made using one of the forms at http:// www.gov.uk. Typing the words "winter fuel payment claim" into the search box on the home page gives a link to the forms (one for those living in Great Britain and the other for those living in one of the countries listed in Schedule 1 to the 2024 regulations). Proof of age will usually be required. Claiming in other ways may be acceptable, as long as it is done in writing, but—unless to do so would risk missing the absolute time limit for claiming—it is better to use the appropriate form, if possible.

Making a Winter Fuel Payment without a claim

5.—(1) The Secretary of State may, on or before the 31st March following the qualifying week, pay a winter fuel payment in respect of the winter following the qualifying week to a person who (disregarding regulation 4(1)(c)) appears to the Secretary of State to be entitled to a payment under regulation 2. 1.032

(2) Where a person becomes entitled to state pension credit, universal credit, child tax credit or working tax credit in respect of any day falling within the qualifying week by virtue of a decision made after that week by the Secretary of State, the Commissioners for His Majesty's Revenue and Customs, the First-tier Tribunal or the Upper Tribunal, the Secretary of State may pay a winter fuel payment to that person in respect of the winter following the qualifying week if (disregarding regulation 4(1)(c)) it appears to the Secretary of State that person is entitled to a payment under regulation 2.

(3) Subject to paragraph (4), for the purposes of paragraphs (1) and (2), official records held by the Secretary of State as to a person's circumstances are sufficient evidence for the purpose of deciding a person's entitlement to a winter fuel payment and its amount.

(4) Paragraph (3) does not apply so as to exclude the revision of a decision under section 9 of the Social Security Act 1998 (revision of decisions) or the supersession of a decision under section 10 of that Act (decisions superseding earlier decisions) or the consideration of fresh evidence in connection with the revision or supersession of a decision.

Definitions

"child tax credit" and "working tax credit"—see reg.1(4).
"qualifying week"—see reg.1(4).

General Note

Regulation 5 empowers (but does not oblige) the Secretary of State to make winter fuel payments on the basis of Benefits Agency records and without an express claim being made. At the outset, the information in those records is deemed to be sufficient evidence of entitlement or non-entitlement (see reg.5(3)) but reg.5(4) permits the initial decision to be revised or superseded in the normal way if further information comes to light. Those who consider themselves to be entitled to a winter fuel payment but do not receive one automatically may make a claim for it, provided they do so by March 31 in the year following the qualifying week (see reg.4(1)(c)). In cases where the Secretary of State does not make an automatic payment, there is no right of appeal against that omission. This is because omitting to make a payment does not give rise to a "decision" against which there is a right of appeal (see *CIS/751/2005* and *CIS/840/2005*, the latter decision doubting the decision of the Deputy Commissioner in *CIS/4088/2004*). In *CIS/840/2005*, the Commissioner explained the point as follows: 1.033

"9. . . . I do not consider that, where the Secretary of State does not decide to make a payment . . . he is obliged to issue a decision not to make a payment. Indeed, it seems to me that he is not entitled, before 31 March of the relevant year, to issue a decision not to make a payment to a person who may be entitled to one, because that person may still make a claim within the time allowed by regulation 3(1)(b) and might establish his entitlement on the claim. He can make a decision under regulation 4 to make a payment but otherwise it seems to me that he must leave matters open and await a possible claim."

And, of course, after March 31 the Secretary of State's power to make the payment ends in any event by virtue of reg.4(1)(c).

Consequential amendments to the Social Security (Claims and Payments) Regulations 1987

1.034 **6.**—[omitted]

Revocations and expiry

1.035 **7.**—(1) [omitted]

(2) The following provisions cease to have effect on 1st April 2025—

(a) in regulation 2—

(i) in paragraph (1)(b), the words "or (3)";

(ii) paragraph (3);

(iii) in paragraph (4), the definition of "withdrawal agreement", "EEA EFTA separation agreement" and "Swiss citizens' rights agreement"; and

(iv) in paragraph (5), the words "and (3)(c)(i)"; and

(b) Schedule 1.

SCHEDULE 1 [Regulation 2(3)(a)]

Countries

1.036 Republic of Austria
Kingdom of Belgium
Republic of Bulgaria
Republic of Croatia
Czech Republic
Kingdom of Denmark
Republic of Estonia
Republic of Finland
Federal Republic of Germany
Hungary
Iceland
Republic of Ireland
Italian Republic
Republic of Latvia
the Principality of Liechtenstein
Republic of Lithuania
Grand Duchy of Luxembourg
Kingdom of the Netherlands
Kingdom of Norway
Republic of Poland
Romania
Slovak Republic
Republic of Slovenia
Kingdom of Sweden
Swiss Confederation

SCHEDULE 2 [Regulation 7(1)]

Regulations [1 and Orders] revoked

1.037 [Omitted]

AMENDMENT

1. Social Fund Winter Fuel Payment (Amendment) Regulations 2024 (SI 2024/898), regs. 1(1), 2(3)(a) (September 16, 2024).

The Infected Blood Compensation Scheme Regulations 2024

(SI 2024/872)

Made	*22 August 2024*
Laid before Parliament	*at 10.00 am on 23 August 2024*
Coming into force	*at 11.00 pm on 23 August 2024*

PART 1

GENERAL

PART 2

ESTABLISHMENT AND ADMINISTRATION OF THE INFECTED BLOOD COMPENSATION SCHEME

PART 3

MEANING OF "ELIGIBLE INFECTED PERSON"

PART 4

COMPENSATION PAYMENTS – CORE ROUTE

CHAPTER 1

PRELIMINARY

CHAPTER 2

DETERMINING THE AMOUNT OF A COMPENSATION PAYMENT

PART 5

COMPENSATION PAYMENTS – IBSS ROUTE

PART 6

APPLICATIONS FOR COMPENSATION PAYMENT FROM THE SCHEME

PART 7

REVIEWS AND APPEALS

PART 8

RECOVERY OF OVERPAYMENTS

SCHEDULE

INFECTION SEVERITY LEVELS FOR HEPATITIS B AND HEPATITIS C

GENERAL NOTE

Thousands of NHS patients in the UK between the 1970s and early 1990s contracted HIV or hepatitis viruses (or both) after receiving contaminated blood, blood products and tissue as part of medical treatments and procedures, such as blood transfusions. The Infected Blood Inquiry, chaired by Sir Brian Langstaff, examined the circumstances that led to individuals being given contaminated blood and blood products. It also scrutinised the response of the government, health services and professionals. Its final report was published on May 20, 2024 and estimated that more than 3,000 deaths amongst some 30,000 patients were attributable to infected blood, blood products and tissue. The inquiry's primary recommendation was that the government should immediately establish a compensation scheme for those "infected and affected", with affected people being "those who have suffered the impacts of infected blood through their relationship with a living or deceased infected person" (see *Infected Blood Compensation Scheme Proposal summary* May 21, 2024). **1.038**

The Victims and Prisoners Act 2024, which received Royal Assent on May 24, 2024, set up the Infected Blood Compensation Authority (IBCA) and required the government to establish a compensation scheme "within three months of the passing" of the Act (s.49(1)). This meant that the regulations establishing the compensation scheme had to be in place by August 24, 2024. This instrument duly came into force one hour before midnight on August 23, 2024. These regulations enable compensation payments to be made via the 'core route', namely to infected persons, both living and deceased. The government has said that a second set of regulations would follow to "ensure that the IBCA can begin compensation payments to affected persons in 2025".

The scheme established under this instrument goes far further than previous arrangements. In 1989 a scheme was set up which provided limited financial support for people who had been infected with HIV from contaminated blood products. This was followed by a scheme established in 2004 to support those infected with hepatitis C. In 2017 the existing schemes were replaced by the Infected Blood Support Scheme (or IBSS, actually four separate schemes with one for each country in the UK). Interim compensation payments of £100,000 and subsequently £210,000 have been payable under the IBSS. Under the new scheme, compensation will be assessed according to a tariff-based approach using set criteria and rates. Accordingly, the amount of compensation due to an infected person will be the total of that awarded across the five different compensation categories: the injury impact, social impact, autonomy, financial loss, and care awards. Some of these awards will be a fixed payment and some will vary (for example, based on loss of earnings). For the injury impact, social impact and autonomy awards, the compensation assessment will take into account the severity of infection and whether someone had multiple infections.

PART 1

GENERAL

Citation, commencement and extent

1.039 **1.**—(1) These Regulations may be cited as the Infected Blood Compensation Scheme Regulations 2024.

(2) These Regulations come into force at 11.00 p.m. on 23rd August 2024.

(3) These Regulations extend to England and Wales, Scotland and Northern Ireland.

Interpretation

1.040 **2.**—(1) In these Regulations—

"the Act" means the Victims and Prisoners Act 2024;

"applicant" means a person who makes an application under regulation 30;

"application" means, except in regulations 5 and 33(2) and (3), an application under regulation 30;

"care" includes—

(a) domestic support or household maintenance;
(b) personal care;
(c) nursing care;
(d) end of life care;

"co-infection" means infection with two or more of Hepatitis B, Hepatitis C or HIV;

"compensation payment" means a payment paid, or to be paid, under the Scheme—

(a) in relation to an eligible infected person who is not an IBSS-registered person, under the core route;
(b) in relation to an IBSS-registered person, under the IBSS route;

the "consumer price index" means the general index of consumer prices (for all items) published by the Statistics Board, a body corporate established by section 1 of the Statistics and Registration Service Act 2007;

"core route" means the process for determining and making a compensation payment in accordance with Part 4;

"eligible infected person" has the meaning given by regulation 7;

"first year of infection", in relation to an eligible infected person ("P"), means—

(a) where P has a single infection—

(i) the year in which P contracted the infection, or

(ii) the earliest year in which P could have contracted the infection, if it is not possible to establish the year in which the infection was contracted;

(b) where P has a co-infection—

(i) the earliest year in which P contracted one or more infections, or

(ii) the earliest year in which P could have contracted one or more infections, if it is not possible to establish the year in which the first infection was contracted;

"healthy life expectancy", in relation to an eligible infected person, means the number of years that person could expect to live if they had no serious health conditions, calculated for that person as at the date of the application and by reference to the typical life expectancies in the actuarial tables for use in personal injury and fatal accident cases published by the Government Actuary's Department in 2020 and updated in 2022;

"HIV" means human immunodeficiency virus;

"IBSS route" means the process for determining and making a compensation payment in accordance with Part 5;

"IBSS-registered person" means an eligible infected person who, on the date of the application, was registered under an infected blood support scheme, and—

(a) who was so registered on or before 31st March 2025, or

(b) who applied, or on whose behalf someone else applied, to be so registered on or before 31st March 2025, and became so registered after that date;

"infected blood support scheme" has the meaning given by section 56(3) of the Act;

"loss of services" includes costs incurred in the provision of—

(a) childcare or other care, and

(b) domestic support;

"infection", in relation to an eligible infected person, means an infection of the person of such description and which was contracted in such a manner as to cause them to be an eligible infected person, and "infected" is to be construed accordingly;

a "periodic payment" has the meaning given in regulation 13(1);

a "periodic payment election" has the meaning given in regulation 8(4);

"personal representatives" has the meaning given in section 56(9) of the Act, and a reference to personal representatives is a reference to them acting in their capacity as such;

"relevant person" means the person to whom a compensation payment is to be paid in accordance with regulation 9;

"relevant date", in relation to an eligible infected person, means—

(a) where the person was deceased on the date of the application, the date of the person's death;

(b) otherwise, the date of the application;

"the Scheme" means the infected blood compensation scheme established by regulation 3(1);

"single infection" means infection with only one of Hepatitis B, Hepatitis C or HIV;

"support scheme payment"—

(a) means a regular payment made, or to be made, to a person ("P") under an infected blood support scheme,

(b) includes a regular payment made, or to be made, to P for the purpose of helping P meet expenses for heating which have been or are likely to be incurred in cold weather, but

(c) does not include a payment which is only payable subject to P fulfilling conditions or meeting criteria beyond those required to be eligible for registration under the infected blood support scheme.

(2) In these Regulations, in relation to the severity of—

(a) a Hepatitis C infection, "level 1" means an infection described in the first row of the table in the Schedule;

(b) a Hepatitis B infection, a Hepatitis C infection, or a co-infection of Hepatitis B and Hepatitis C—

(i) "level 2" means an infection described in the second row of the table in the Schedule;

(ii) "level 3" means an infection described in the third row of the table in the Schedule;

(iii) "level 4" means an infection described in the fourth row of the table in the Schedule;

(c) a Hepatitis B infection, "level 5" means an infection described in the fifth row of the table in the Schedule.

(3) For the purpose of determining the amount of the compensation award in relation to an eligible infected person ("P") in accordance with regulation 11(2) or 23(2)—

(a) except in regulation 21(6) to (8)—

(i) a reference to a year is a reference to the 12-month period from January to December;

(ii) where P was infected for only part of a year, they are to be treated as if they were infected for the whole of that year;

(iii) where P dies partway through a year, they are to be treated as if they had died at the end of that year;

(b) where P has an infection of Hepatitis B or Hepatitis C (or both)—

(i) where the severity level of the infection varied over the course of a year, the severity level for the whole year is the highest severity level of the infection in that year;

(ii) where, on the date of the application, P is not deceased and has not attained the age of their healthy life expectancy, the severity level of the infection for the period between the date of the application and the year in which P is expected to attain the age of their healthy life expectancy is be treated as the severity level on the date of the application;

(c) where P attains a specified age partway through a year, they are to be treated as if they had attained that age at the beginning of that year.

PART 2

ESTABLISHMENT AND ADMINISTRATION OF THE INFECTED BLOOD COMPENSATION SCHEME

Establishment of the Scheme

3.—(1) The infected blood compensation scheme for the making of payments in relation to eligible infected persons is established in accordance with these Regulations. **1.041**

(2) Payments under the Scheme must be made, and the Scheme must otherwise be administered, by the IBCA.

Eligibility criteria for appointment as a member of the IBCA

4.—(1) A person who meets the criteria specified in paragraph (3) is eligible for appointment as the Chair or any other non-executive member of the IBCA. **1.042**

(2) At least one of the non-executive members of the IBCA must have experience of risk and audit.

(3) The criteria are that the person—

(a) has not within the preceding five years had passed on them in the United Kingdom, the Channel Islands or the Isle of Man a sentence of imprisonment (whether suspended or not) for a period of three months or more without the option of a fine,

(b) is not the subject of—

(i) a bankruptcy restrictions order or an interim bankruptcy restrictions order under Schedule 4A to the Insolvency Act 1986 ("the 1986 Act") or Schedule 2A to the Insolvency (Northern Ireland) Order 1989 ("the 1989 Order"), or

(ii) a debt relief restrictions order or an interim debt relief restrictions order under Schedule 4ZB to the 1986 Act or Schedule 2ZB to the 1989 Order,

(c) has not within the preceding five years been dismissed, otherwise than by reason of redundancy, from any paid employment with a body listed in the Schedule to the Public Bodies (Admission to Meetings) Act 1960,

(d) has not had their tenure of office as the Chair, a member, or a director of a body listed in the Schedule to the Public Bodies (Admission to Meetings) Act 1960 terminated on the grounds—

(i) that it was not in the interests of that body that they should continue to hold the office,

(ii) of non-attendance at meetings,

(iii) of non-disclosure of a pecuniary interest, or

(iv) of misbehaviour, misconduct or failure to carry out their duties,

(e) is not subject to a disqualification order under the Company Directors Disqualification Act 1986, the Company Directors (Northern Ireland) Disqualification Order 2002 or to an order made under section 429(2) of the 1986 Act,

(f) has not been removed from the office of charity trustee or trustee for a charity by a relevant order on the grounds of—

(i) any misconduct or mismanagement in the administration of the charity for which they were responsible or to which they were privy,

(ii) that they knew of the misconduct or mismanagement and failed to take reasonable steps to oppose it, or

(iii) that their conduct contributed to or facilitated the misconduct or mismanagement,

(g) has not been removed by the Court of Session under section 34(5)(e) of the Charities and Trustee Investment (Scotland) Act 2005 from being concerned in the management or control of a charity or other body, or

(h) is not, in the opinion of the appropriate person, a person who has a conflict of interest which would affect their ability to carry out the functions of the Chair or a non-executive member of the IBCA if they were to be appointed as such.

(4) If the Chair or a non-executive member of the IBCA, during their term of appointment as such, no longer meets the criteria specified in paragraph (3), their appointment must be terminated.

(5) In this regulation—

"appropriate person" has the same meaning as in paragraph 5(5) of Schedule 1 to the Act;

"relevant order" means an order made by—

(a) the Charity Commission under section 79(4) of the Charities Act 2011,

(b) the Charity Commission for Northern Ireland under section 33(2)(b)(i) of the Charities Act (Northern Ireland) 2008, or

(c) the High Court.

Cessation of disqualification from eligibility for appointment to the IBCA

1.043 **5.**—(1) Subject to paragraph (2), where a person is disqualified under regulation 4(3)(c) or (f), they may, after the expiry of two years beginning with the date on which they were dismissed or, as the case may be, removed, apply in writing to the Minister for the Cabinet Office or the Secretary of State to remove the disqualification, and the Minister for the Cabinet Office or the Secretary of State may direct that the disqualification must cease.

(2) Where the Minister for the Cabinet Office or the Secretary of State refuses an application to remove a disqualification, no further application may be made by that person until the expiry of the period of two years beginning with the date of the application and this paragraph applies to any subsequent application.

(3) Where a person is disqualified under regulation 4(3)(d), the disqualification ceases on the expiry of the period of two years beginning on the date of the termination of their tenure of office but the Minister for the Cabinet Office or the Secretary of State may, on an application being made to the Minister for the Cabinet Office or the Secretary of State by that person, reduce the period of disqualification.

Duties of the IBCA in relation to sums repaid to it

1.044 **6.**—(1) The IBCA must retain any payments it recovers under regulation 43.

(2) The IBCA must use any such payments for—
(a) administering the Scheme, or
(b) making compensation payments under the Scheme.

PART 3

MEANING OF "ELIGIBLE INFECTED PERSON"

Meaning of "eligible infected person"

7.—(1) For the purposes of these Regulations, a person is an eligible infected person where paragraph (2), (6), (7) or (8) applies to that person, whether or not that person is deceased. 1.045

(2) Subject to paragraph (5), this paragraph applies to a person who—
(a) has received, in the course of NHS treatment or armed forces treatment overseas, infected blood treatment,
(b) was subsequently diagnosed with an infection specified in paragraph (3), and
(c) began, or continued, receiving the infected blood treatment during the period specified in paragraph (4).

(3) The infections are—
(a) HIV;
(b) Hepatitis C;
(c) Hepatitis B, where—
(i) the infection caused the person's death within a period of 12 months beginning with the date that the infected blood treatment began, or
(ii) the infection did not cause the person's death but continued for a period of at least six months beginning with the date that the infected blood treatment began.

(4) The period specified for the purposes of paragraph (2)(c) is—
(a) for a person diagnosed with HIV, 1st January 1982 to 1st November 1985;
(b) for a person diagnosed with Hepatitis C, 1st January 1952 to 1st September 1991;
(c) for a person diagnosed with Hepatitis B, 1st January 1952 to 1st December 1972.

(5) Paragraph (2) does not apply to a person whom the IBCA is satisfied did not become infected with an infection specified in paragraph (3) as a result of the infected blood treatment.

(6) This paragraph applies to a person—
(a) who has received, in the course of NHS treatment or armed forces treatment overseas, infected blood treatment,
(b) who was subsequently diagnosed with an infection specified in paragraph (3),
(c) who began, or continued, receiving the infected blood treatment after the period specified in paragraph (4), and
(d) who satisfies the IBCA that the infected blood treatment caused the person to become infected with that infection.

(7) Subject to paragraph (9), this paragraph applies to a person who has been diagnosed with an infection specified in paragraph (3) and who satisfies the IBCA that they became so infected as a result of its transmission to them from a person to whom paragraph (2) or (6) applies by means of—

(a) sexual contact, where the person to whom the infection was transmitted and the person to whom paragraph (2) or (6) applies were in a long-term relationship at the time of the contact,

(b) direct vertical transmission from mother to child,

(c) accidental needle stick injury, or

(d) another method of transmission resulting from living in close proximity to a person to whom paragraph (2) or (6) applies.

(8) Subject to paragraph (9), this paragraph applies to a person who has been diagnosed with an infection specified in paragraph (3) and who satisfies the IBCA that they became so infected as a result of its transmission to them by a person to whom paragraph (7) applies by means of—

(a) sexual contact, where the person to whom paragraph (7) applies and the person to whom the infection was transmitted were in a long-term relationship at the time of the contact,

(b) direct vertical transmission from mother to child,

(c) accidental needle stick injury, or

(d) another method of transmission resulting from living in close proximity to a person to whom paragraph (7) applies.

(9) Paragraphs (7) and (8) do not apply in relation to transmission caused by the sharing of needles for the purpose of intravenous drug use.

(10) In this regulation—

"armed forces" means the naval, military and air forces of the Crown, excluding the forces of a Commonwealth country other than the United Kingdom;

"armed forces treatment overseas" means treatment received outside the United Kingdom by a person who was, at the time of their treatment—

(a) acting in their capacity as a serving member of the armed forces;

(b) acting in their capacity as a person employed by or in the service of the Government of the United Kingdom whose sole or main role was to work—

  (i) in support of the armed forces, or

  (ii) for or in support of the administration of the Sovereign Base Areas of Akrotiri and Dhekelia in the Island of Cyprus;

(c) acting in their capacity as an employee of an organisation—

  (i) which provided support to the armed forces outside the United Kingdom, and

  (ii) for the employees of which the Government of the United Kingdom arranged or provided treatment;

(d) a family member of a person acting in a capacity described in paragraphs (a) to (c) and who resided with that person;

"diagnosed" means diagnosed by a registered medical practitioner;

"infected blood treatment" means treatment with blood, blood products or tissue known to be capable of transmitting an infection specified in paragraph (3);

"long-term relationship" means a relationship between two people where—

(a) the people are married to each other or civil partners of each other, or

(b) the people—
  (i) could have married or formed a civil partnership if the rules that apply to marrying or forming a civil partnership on the date of the application applied at the time of the infection, and
  (ii) lived with each other as if they were married or civil partners;

"NHS treatment" means treatment arranged or provided as part of the health service—

(a) continued under section 1(1) of the National Health Service Act 2006;
(b) continued under section 1(1) of the National Health Service (Wales) Act 2006;
(c) continued under section 1(1) of the National Health Service (Scotland) Act 1978;
(d) under section 1 of the Health Services Act (Northern Ireland) 1948, section 1 of the Health Services Act (Northern Ireland) 1971, Article 4 of the Health and Personal Social Services (Northern Ireland) Order 1972 or section 2(1) of the Health and Social Care (Reform) Act (Northern Ireland) 2009.

GENERAL NOTE

Regulation 7 defines the concept of an "eligible infected person" by reference to four separate categories. The first two categories deal with the situation where the person received infected blood and so experienced direct infection (reg.7(2) and (6)). The third and fourth categories apply where the person shows that they became infected as a result of transmission of the infection to them, i.e. indirect infection (reg.7(7) and (8)). **1.046**

The first category, as set out in reg.7(2), applies to a person who has received in the course of NHS treatment (or armed forces treatment overseas) infected blood treatment and who was subsequently diagnosed with HIV, Hepatitis C or Hepatitis B and, in the case of Hepatitis B, –

- the infection caused that person's death within a period of 12 months beginning with the date that the infected blood treatment began, or
- continued for at least 6 months beginning with the date the infected blood treatment began.

Thus, in line with the Inquiry's recommendation, those who are solely infected with Hepatitis B will only be eligible where the case is chronic or the person died as a result of the infection within the acute period. By para.(4), the treatment for the purposes of reg.7(2) must have begun or have continued during the following periods:

- For HIV, 1st January 1982 to 1st November 1985;
- For Hepatitis C, 1st January 1952 to 1st September 1991;
- For Hepatitis B, 1st January 1952 to 1st December 1972.

Consequently, where a person was treated with blood, blood products or tissue within the specified dates, they will be eligible for compensation on the basis that treatment during those dates is more likely to have resulted in transmission of HIV, Hepatitis C or Hepatitis B. Paragraph (5) additionally deals with causation by providing that para.(2) does not apply where the IBCA is satisfied that the person did not become infected with any of the conditions listed above as a result of the infected blood treatment.

The second category of direct infection is set out in reg.7(6). This applies to a person who received the same type of treatment as in para.(2), who was subsequently diagnosed with HIV, Hepatitis C or Hepatitis B, and who began or continued receiving infected blood treatment after the specified periods set out in para (4). It is this which differentiates this category from the first category. In addition, by reg.7(6)(d), the person must satisfy the IBCA that the infected blood treatment caused the person to be infected with that infection.

The third category under reg.7(7), namely the first of the two indirect categories, applies where a person diagnosed with any of the conditions listed above shows that they became infected by a person who satisfies paras (2) or (6) (i.e. who was directly infected themselves) as a result of –

- sexual contact in a long-term relationship,
- direct transmission from mother to child,
- accidental needle stick injury, or
- another method of transmission resulting from living in close proximity to the person originally infected.

"Long-term-relationship" is (partially at least) defined in reg.7(10) and includes people who are married or civil partners of each other, or living together as if they were married or civil partners.

The fourth and final category, under regulation 7(8), applies where the person diagnosed with the infection shows that they became infected by a person who satisfies the criteria set out in reg.7(7) as a result of the four criteria that apply in relation to reg.7(7).

Note that, by reg.7(9), any person following the routes under regs.7(7) and 7(8) is not entitled to compensation where the transmission is caused by the sharing of needles for the purposes of intravenous drug use.

PART 4

COMPENSATION PAYMENTS – CORE ROUTE

CHAPTER 1

PRELIMINARY

Compensation payments

1.047 **8.**—(1) A compensation payment is to be paid under the Scheme in relation to an eligible infected person ("P") who is not an IBSS-registered person in accordance with this Part.

(2) The compensation payment must be paid to the relevant person.

(3) The IBCA must—

(a) determine the amount of the compensation payment to be paid in relation to P in accordance with regulation 11,

(b) notify the relevant person of an offer in accordance with regulation 10,

(c) if the offer is accepted in accordance with regulation 10, as soon as reasonably practicable—

(i) pay the compensation payment as a lump sum, or

(ii) where the relevant person makes a periodic payment election, commence periodic payments in accordance with regulation 13.

(5) The IBCA may extend the time limit specified in paragraph (3) upon a request of the relevant person.

(6) If the relevant person does not accept the offer in accordance with this regulation, the offer expires (and, accordingly, no compensation payment is payable in relation to P pursuant to that offer).

GENERAL NOTE

Before a compensation payment becomes payable, the IBCA must provide an eligible infected person with a document setting out the offer of payment to them (para.(1)). Within three months, the eligible infected person must either notify the IBCA of acceptance of this offer, or they may apply to have the IBCA decision reviewed (para.(3)). If the offer is not accepted within the specified period, and any review or appeal is not exercised or concluded, the offer expires and no compensation is paid under it (para.(6)). This does not prevent a new application being made. If the compensation offer is reviewed or appealed, there will be a further three month period after the review or appeal decision to accept the offer. 1.052

CHAPTER 2

DETERMINING THE AMOUNT OF A COMPENSATION PAYMENT

Amount of a compensation payment

11.—(1) The amount of the compensation payment in relation to an eligible infected person ("P") is T – (D + I + S), where— 1.053

(a) "T" is the amount of the compensation award determined in relation to P in accordance with paragraph (2);

(b) "D" is the sum of any relevant damages payments within the meaning of regulation 12 made in relation to P;

(c) "I" is the sum of any amounts awarded in relation to P by way of—

(i) a payment under—

(aa) section 56(1) of the Act;

(bb) the Infected Blood Interim Compensation Payment Scheme as defined in section 56(6) of the Act;

(cc) the Infected Blood Further Interim Compensation Payment Scheme, being the scheme of that name administered by the persons who administer the infected blood support schemes (whether or not in conjunction with other persons);

(ii) compensation, paid pursuant to a scheme established by or under statute, in respect of the same or similar losses as those described in the categories of award listed in paragraph (2);

(d) "S" is the sum of any support scheme payments made to P in relation to any period after 31st March 2025.

(2) The amount of the compensation award in relation to P is the sum of—

(a) the injury impact award determined in relation to P in accordance with regulation 14,

(b) the social impact award determined in relation to P in accordance with regulation 15,

(c) the autonomy award determined in relation to P in accordance with regulation 16,
(d) the basic financial loss award determined in relation to P in accordance with regulation 17,
(e) the additional financial loss award determined in relation to P in accordance with regulation 18 together with whichever of regulation 19 or 20 applies in relation to P, and
(f) the care award determined in relation to P in accordance with regulation 21.

(3) Where a provision referred to in paragraph (2) relating to a category of award does not establish an amount for an eligible infected person in P's circumstances, the amount of that award for the purposes of this regulation is £0.

(4) For the purpose of determining the amount of the compensation award in relation to P, the IBCA must determine—
(a) P's healthy life expectancy, and
(b) where P has an infection of Hepatitis B or Hepatitis C (or both), the level of severity of that infection in each year during the period beginning with (and including) P's first year of infection and ending with (and including)—
 (i) the year in which P would attain the age of their healthy life expectancy, or
 (ii) if P died before attaining that age, the year in which P died.

(5) In this Chapter, "compensation award" means the award described in paragraph (2).

General Note

1.054 Compensation potentially consists of six elements (para.(2)): an injury impact award, a social impact award, an autonomy award, a basic financial loss award, an additional financial loss award, and a care award. These components align with the awards recommended by the Inquiry. The amount of compensation due to an eligible infected person is the total of the different categories of compensation awarded to them, less certain deductions. The relevant deductions include: the amount of payments which the person has already received under the Act or existing compensation schemes; any litigation damages paid in relation to infected blood; and support scheme payments which relate to a period after March 31, 2025.

The Injury Impact Award (reg.14) compensates for past and future physical and mental injury and emotional distress and injury to feelings caused by, or that will in the future be felt as a result of, the infection and treatments for infected blood.

The Social Impact Award (reg.15) compensates for past and future social consequences of the infection, including stigma and social isolation.

The Autonomy Award (reg.16) compensates for the distress and suffering caused by the impact of the infection on and the interference with that person's family and private life and autonomy. This includes instances of loss of marriage or partnership prospects, the loss of opportunity to have children and the impact on that person of personal attacks on their home.

Where the eligible infected person has Hepatitis B or Hepatitis C, compensation for each of the three elements above (regs 14–16) is determined by a tariff framework based on the eligible infected person's severity level of the infection, to be decided by the IBCA by reference to the clinical markers set out in the Schedule to these Regulations.

There are two parts to the Financial Loss award—the basic financial loss award (reg.17) and the additional financial loss award (regs 18, 19 and 20). An eligible infected person with acute Hepatitis B (level 5) or acute Hepatitis C (level 1) will receive the basic financial loss award. All other Hepatitis B or C severity levels and eligible infected persons with HIV will be able to claim both the basic and additional financial loss awards. The flat-rate basic financial loss award provides compensation for notional expenses incurred as a consequence of an infection, such as travelling to and from medical appointments or additional insurance costs. The additional financial loss award compensates for past and future financial loss, including loss of services such as childcare, care or domestic support. The total awards are calculated on the basis of amounts payable in relation to each year of a person's infection, as set out in the regulations. The underlying basis of the award is the UK median salary as of early 2024 plus 5 per cent, and net of tax.

The sums awarded are different depending on whether the eligible infected person has Hepatitis B or C, and the severity of that infection, or whether they have HIV. For those with Hepatitis B or C, the rate for years following the introduction of effective treatment is lower in recognition that effective treatment is likely to have resulted in improved ability to work. This reduction does not apply to those who were 55 or older at the time effective treatment was introduced, given their proximity to retirement age and associated difficulty with return to the workplace. Where the eligible infected person is deceased, this award will only pay for financial loss during the period where the person was alive.

The Care Award (reg.21) compensates for losses resulting from care required as a result of the infection in the past and future. Where an eligible infected person is deceased, this is calculated on the basis of the amounts set out in the regulations. The total amount of the Care Award is based on an estimated number of years that the person required care, with a maximum depending on their infection and severity, and allocates to each year an expected level of care, and associated cost, based on the eligible infected person's expected care profile. The most complex - and therefore the most expensive - years of care are calculated first. Effectively, compensation is calculated by "working back" from a person's year of death to ensure that expensive end-of-life care is always compensated for. Where an eligible infected person is living, a flat rate is paid on the assumption that the maximum number of years will be reached during the person's lifetime - as such the regulations can simply refer to a flat rate for the people who are living and infected. Awards for the deceased eligible infected are discounted by 25%, to reflect that much past care will have been provided gratuitously and so will not have been subject to tax or national insurance.

Court and other payments: avoidance of double recovery

12.—(1) A "relevant damages payment" means any payment which it appears to the IBCA— **1.055**

(a) has been, or is to be, made in respect of an eligible infected person ("P")—

(i) pursuant to an award of a court or tribunal anywhere in the world, or

(ii) in settlement or compromise of a court action commenced anywhere in the world,

(b) relates to a head of loss which corresponds, or broadly corresponds, to any category of award listed in regulation 11(2), and

(c) was determined without taking into account the amount of any compensation payment made, or to be made, in relation to P under the Scheme.

(2) A payment received from an organisation listed in section 56(4) of the Act is not a relevant damages payment.

(3) The IBCA may require a relevant person to give—

(a) details of any steps taken, or planned to be taken, to obtain a relevant damages payment in respect of the same or similar losses as those described in the categories of award listed in regulation 11(2);

(b) a written undertaking that if a relevant damages payment is received the relevant person will notify the IBCA.

Amount of periodic payments

1.056 **13.**—(1) Where a compensation payment is to be paid in accordance with a periodic payment election—

(a) an amount of that compensation payment is payable in respect of each month of the term of payment (a "periodic payment"),

(b) after each periodic payment, the remaining amount of the compensation payment is to be reduced by the amount of the periodic payment, and

(c) at the beginning of each payment period other than the first period (and before a periodic payment is paid in respect of the first month of such payment period), the remaining amount of the compensation payment is to be increased by the same percentage as the percentage increase (if any) in the consumer price index over the 12-month period up to the month of September before the beginning of the payment period.

(2) The amount of the periodic payment in respect of each month of a payment period is CR ÷ (MT – MP), where—

(a) "CR" is the remaining amount of the compensation payment at the beginning of the payment period (and before a periodic payment is paid in respect of the first month of the payment period);

(b) "MT" is the total number of months in the term of payment;

(c) "MP" is the number of months in respect of which a periodic payment had been paid immediately before the beginning of the payment period.

(3) For the purposes of this regulation, the payment periods are—

(a) the first period, being—

(i) where the first periodic payment is payable in respect of March, that March only;

(ii) otherwise, the period which—

(aa) begins with the month in respect of which the first periodic payment is payable, and

(bb) ends with the following March,

(b) each subsequent period of 12 months beginning with April and ending with March, until such period which is immediately before the final period, and

(c) the final period, being the period which—

(i) begins with the April in which (counting that month) there are fewer than 13 months remaining of the term of payment, and

(ii) ends with the month in respect of which the final periodic payment is payable.

(4) In this regulation—

the "remaining amount of the compensation payment" means the amount of the compensation payment that remains for the time being after each reduction under paragraph (1)(b) (if any) and each increase under paragraph (1)(c) (if any);

"term of payment" means the fixed term over which a compensation payment is payable in accordance with a periodic payment election.

Injury impact award

14.—(1) The compensation award in relation to an eligible infected person ("P") must include an amount by way of injury impact award for the purpose of compensating for— 1.057

(a) past and future physical and mental injury;

(b) emotional distress and injury to feelings caused by, or that will in the future be felt as a result of, the infection and treatments for it.

(2) The amount of the injury impact award is, where on the relevant date P has a single infection of—

(a) Hepatitis C of severity level 1, £10,000;

(b) Hepatitis B or Hepatitis C, and the severity of the infection is—

(i) level 2, £60,000;

(ii) level 3, £120,000;

(iii) level 4, £180,000;

(c) Hepatitis B of severity level 5, £180,000;

(d) HIV, £180,000.

(3) The amount of the injury impact award is, where on the relevant date P has a co-infection of—

(a) Hepatitis B and Hepatitis C (but not HIV), and the severity of the infection is—

(i) level 2, £75,000;

(ii) level 3, £150,000;

(iii) level 4, £225,000;

(b) HIV and—

(i) Hepatitis C of severity level 1, £182,500;

(ii) Hepatitis B or Hepatitis C (or both), and the severity of the infection is—

(aa) level 2, £195,000;

(bb) level 3, £240,000;

(cc) level 4, £270,000;

(iii) Hepatitis B of severity level 5, £270,000.

Social impact award

15.—(1) The compensation award in relation to an eligible infected person ("P") must include an amount by way of social impact award for the purpose of compensating for the past and future social consequences of the infection including stigma and social isolation. 1.058

(2) The amount of the social impact award is, where on the relevant date P has a single infection of—

(a) Hepatitis C of severity level 1, £5,000;

(b) Hepatitis B or Hepatitis C of severity level 2 to 4 or HIV, £50,000;

(c) Hepatitis B of severity level 5, £50,000.

(3) Where P has a co-infection, the amount of the social impact award is £70,000.

Autonomy award

16.—(1) The compensation award in relation to an eligible infected person ("P") must include an amount by way of autonomy award for the purpose of compensating for the distress and suffering caused by the impact of the infection on, and the interference with, that person's family and private life and autonomy, including— 1.059

(a) the loss of marriage or partnership prospects;
(b) the loss of the opportunity to have children;
(c) the impact on that person of attacks on that person's home as a consequence of the infection.

(2) The amount of the autonomy award is, where on the relevant date P has a single infection of—

(a) Hepatitis C of severity level 1, £10,000;
(b) Hepatitis B or Hepatitis C, and the severity of the infection is—
  (i) level 2 or level 3, £40,000;
  (ii) level 4, £50,000;
(c) Hepatitis B of severity level 5, £50,000;
(d) HIV, £60,000.

(3) Where P has a co-infection, the amount of the autonomy award is £70,000.

Basic financial loss award: eligible infected persons

1.060 **17.**—(1) The compensation award in relation to an eligible infected person ("P") must include an amount by way of basic financial loss award for the purpose of compensating for notional expenses incurred by P as a consequence of the infection, including expenses incurred as a result of—

(a) travelling to and from medical appointments;
(b) additional insurance costs.

(2) The amount of the basic financial loss award is—

(a) where on the relevant date P had an infection of Hepatitis B of severity level 5, £17,500;
(b) in any other case, £12,500.

Additional financial loss award

1.061 **18.**—(1) The compensation award in relation to an eligible infected person ("P") must, except where P had a single infection of Hepatitis B of severity level 5 or of Hepatitis C of severity level 1, include an amount by way of additional financial loss award for the purpose of compensating for—

(a) past financial loss including loss of services suffered by P during the period—
  (i) beginning with—
    (aa) P's first year of infection, or
    (bb) where P was under 16 in their first year of infection, the year in which P attains 16 years of age, and
  (ii) ending with the date of the application;
(b) where P is not deceased on the date of the application, future financial loss including loss of services which is likely to be suffered by P during the period beginning with the day after the date of P's application and ending with the date when P would attain the age of their healthy life expectancy.

(2) The amount of the additional financial loss award is to be determined in accordance with—

(a) where P has Hepatitis B or Hepatitis C (or both, but not HIV), regulation 19;
(b) where P has HIV (whether or not they also have Hepatitis B or Hepatitis C), regulation 20.

Additional financial loss award: eligible infected persons with Hepatitis B or Hepatitis C

19.—(1) The amount of the additional financial loss award for an eligible infected person ("P") with Hepatitis B or Hepatitis C (or both) is the sum of the annual amounts determined in relation to each year of P's infection as follows. **1.062**

(2) For the purposes of paragraph (1), "each year of P's infection" means each year during the period—

(a) beginning with (and including)—

(i) P's first year of infection, or

(ii) if P was under 16 in their first year of infection, the year in which P attains the age of 16, and

(b) ending with (and including)—

(i) the year P attained, or is expected to attain, the age of their healthy life expectancy, or

(ii) if P dies before the date of the application, the year that P died.

(3) Subject to paragraph (4), where P was born—

(a) in or before the relevant year, and the severity of P's infection in a year is—

(i) level 2, the annual amount for that year is £11,863;

(ii) level 3, the annual amount for that year is £23,726;

(iii) level 4, the annual amount for that year is £29,657;

(b) after the relevant year, and the severity of P's infection in a year is—

(i) level 2, the annual amount for that year is—

(aa) if the year is the year of effective treatment or any previous year, £11,863;

(bb) if the year is after the year of effective treatment, £5,931;

(ii) level 3, the annual amount for that year is—

(aa) if the year is the year of effective treatment or any previous year, £23,726;

(bb) if the year is after the year of effective treatment, £17,794;

(iii) level 4, the annual amount for that year is £29,657.

(4) The annual amount for any year in which P is, or would be, 66 or older is 50% of the annual amount that would (but for this paragraph) be determined in accordance with paragraph (3).

(5) In paragraph (3)—

(a) "the relevant year" is, where P is infected with—

(i) Hepatitis B and is not co-infected with Hepatitis C, 1953;

(ii) Hepatitis C (whether or not P is co-infected with Hepatitis B), 1961;

(b) "the severity of P's infection", in relation to a year, is—

(i) the level of severity of P's infection which has been established in relation to that year to the IBCA's satisfaction;

(ii) where insufficient evidence has been provided to establish the level of severity of P's infection in relation to that year, to be determined in accordance with paragraph (6);

(c) "the year of effective treatment" is, where P is infected with—

(i) Hepatitis B and is not co-infected with Hepatitis C, 2008;

(ii) Hepatitis C (whether or not P is co-infected with Hepatitis B), 2016.

(6) Where, on the relevant date, the severity of P's infection is—
(a) level 2, the severity of P's infection is deemed to be level 2 for every year of P's infection;
(b) level 3, the severity of P's infection is deemed to be—
(i) level 3 for the year in which the relevant date falls and for the 5 years previous to that year, and
(ii) level 2 for every other year of P's infection previous to the year in which the relevant date falls;
(c) level 4, the severity of P's infection is deemed to be—
(i) level 4 for the year in which the relevant date falls and for the 3 years previous to that year,
(ii) level 3 for the year 4 years before the year in which the relevant date falls and for the 5 years previous to that year, and
(iii) level 2 for every other year of P's infection previous to the year in which the relevant date falls.

Additional financial loss award: eligible infected persons with HIV

1.063 **20.**—(1) The amount of the additional financial loss award for an eligible infected person ("P") with HIV (whether or not they also have Hepatitis B or Hepatitis C) is the sum of the annual amounts determined in relation to each year of P's infection (within the meaning of regulation 19(2)) as follows.

(2) Subject to paragraph (3), where P is infected with—
(a) a single infection of HIV or a co-infection of HIV and Hepatitis B of severity level 5—
(i) the annual amount for each year between (and including each of) P's first year of infection and for the year before the year in which P was diagnosed as infected with HIV is £14,829;
(ii) the annual amount for the year in which P was diagnosed as infected with HIV and for each subsequent year is £29,657;
(b) HIV and is co-infected with Hepatitis B (other than a Hepatitis B infection of severity level 5) or Hepatitis C (or both)—
(i) the annual amount for each year between (and including each of) P's first year of infection and for the year before the year in which P was diagnosed as infected with HIV is, where, on the relevant date, the severity of P's—
(aa) Hepatitis C infection is level 1, £18,536;
(bb) Hepatitis B or Hepatitis C infection is level 2, £18,536;
(cc) Hepatitis B or Hepatitis C infection is level 3 or level 4, £22,243;
(ii) the annual amount for the year in which P was diagnosed as infected with HIV and for each subsequent year is £29,657.

(3) The annual amount for any year in which P is, or would be, 66 or older is 50% of the annual amount that would (but for this paragraph) be determined in accordance with paragraph (2).

Care award

1.064 **21.**—(1) The compensation award in relation to an eligible infected person ("P") must include an amount by way of care award for the purpose of compensating for—

(a) loss incurred in respect of the cost of care necessitated by the eligible infected person's infection, and
(b) the cost of the future care needs for that person.

(2) Where P had a Hepatitis B infection of level 5, the amount of the care award in relation to P is £41,188.40.

(3) Where P is not deceased, the amount of the care award in relation to P is—

(a) where on the relevant date P has a Hepatitis C infection of severity level 1, £500;
(b) where on the relevant date P has Hepatitis B or Hepatitis C (or both, but not HIV) and the severity of P's infection is—
(i) level 2, £54,600;
(ii) level 3, £195,148.32;
(iii) level 4, £446,751.74;
(c) where on the relevant date P has HIV (whether or not they also have Hepatitis B or Hepatitis C), £679,756.62.

(4) Where P is deceased and P's period of infection was equal to or longer than the relevant period, the amount of the care award in relation to P is—

(a) where P had a single infection of Hepatitis C of severity level 1, £375;
(b) where P had Hepatitis B or Hepatitis C (or both, but not HIV) and the severity of P's infection at the time of their death was—
(i) level 2, £40,950;
(ii) level 3, £146,361.24;
(iii) level 4, £335,063.81;
(c) where P had HIV (whether or not they also had Hepatitis B or Hepatitis C), £509,817.47.

(5) Where P is deceased and P's period of infection was less than the relevant period, the amount of the care award in relation to P is the sum of the amounts determined as set out in paragraph (6) or (7).

(6) Where P had Hepatitis B or Hepatitis C (or both, but not HIV) and the severity of P's infection at the time of their death was—

(a) level 2, the amount for each year of P's infection is £4,095;
(b) level 3, the amount for—
(i) each of the first 6 years of P's infection is £17,568.54;
(ii) each subsequent year of P's infection is £4,095;
(c) level 4, the amount for—
(i) the first 6 months of P's infection is £41,188.49;
(ii) the subsequent year of P's infection is £47,056.80;
(iii) the subsequent 6 months of P's infection is £23,528.40;
(iv) each of the subsequent 2 years of P's infection is £38,464.44;
(v) each of the subsequent 6 years of P's infection is £17,568.54;
(vi) each subsequent year of P's infection is £4,095.

(7) Where P had HIV (whether or not they also had Hepatitis B or Hepatitis C), the amount for—

(a) the first 6 months of P's infection is £41,188.49;
(b) the subsequent year of P's infection is £47,056.80;
(c) the subsequent 6 months of P's infection is £23,528.40;
(d) each of the subsequent 7 years of P's infection is £38,464.44;
(e) each of the subsequent 5 years of P's infection is £17,568.54;
(f) each subsequent year of P's infection is £4,095.

(8) For the purposes of paragraphs (6) and (7), where P died partway through a period for which an amount is specified, they are to be treated as having died at the end of that period (and, accordingly, the care award comprises the full amount in relation to that period).

(9) In this regulation—

"P's period of infection" means the period beginning with (and including) P's first year of infection and ending with (and including) the year in which P died;

"the relevant period" means, where P had—

(a) Hepatitis B or Hepatitis C (or both), and the severity of P's infection at the time of their death was—

(i) level 2, 10 years;

(ii) level 3, 16 years;

(iii) level 4, 20 years;

(b) HIV, 24 years.

PART 5

COMPENSATION PAYMENTS – IBSS ROUTE

Compensation payments under the IBSS route

1.065 **22.**—(1) A compensation payment is to be paid under the Scheme in relation to an IBSS-registered person ("P") who is not deceased in accordance with this Part.

(2) Regulations 8(2) and (4) to (6), 9 and 10, 11(1) to (4), and 12 to 16 apply—

(a) in relation to a compensation payment under the IBSS route as they apply in relation to a compensation payment under the core route, and

(b) in relation to an IBSS-registered person as they apply in relation to an eligible infected person who is not an IBSS-registered person.

(3) The IBCA must—

(a) determine the amounts of each compensation payment in relation to P in accordance with—

(i) regulation 11(1) to (3) ("the core route amount"), and

(ii) regulation 23 ("the IBSS route amount"),

(b) make an offer to the relevant person in accordance with regulation 10, and, in addition to the matters set out in regulation 10(2), the offer must also include—

(i) the IBSS route amount, and

(ii) information about the election that may be made in accordance with paragraph (4) (including that electing for the core route amount means that the amount of the compensation payment set out in the offer may not reflect the final amount of the payment, as it will be reduced by the amount of any support scheme payments received in relation to the period after 31st March 2025), and

(c) if the offer is accepted in accordance with regulation 10 (and subject to paragraph (5)), as soon as reasonably practicable—

(i) pay the compensation payment as a lump sum, or
(ii) where the relevant person makes a periodic payment election, commence periodic payments in accordance with regulation 13.

(4) The relevant person may, when accepting an offer made pursuant to paragraph (3)(b), elect to receive a compensation payment of the core route amount or the IBSS route amount and if no such election is made the compensation payment will be of the IBSS route amount.

(5) But if the relevant person elects to receive a compensation payment of the core route amount, the compensation payment is not payable until the IBCA is satisfied that P is no longer registered under an infected blood support scheme.

(6) Where the IBCA is satisfied that P is no longer registered under an infected blood support scheme—
(a) P is no longer to be treated as an IBSS-registered person,
(b) P is to be treated as if Part 4 applies, and had always applied, in relation to them (and, accordingly, that any steps taken in relation to P under the provisions of Part 4 as applied by this Part had been taken under Part 4), and
(c) this Part no longer applies in relation to P.

General Note

1.066 Part 5 of the regulations makes provision for assessment and payments to be made from the new scheme to eligible infected persons who are also registered under an existing IBSS - this is referred to as the 'IBSS route'. This is equivalent to the core route set out in Part 4, but treats annual entitlements under IBSS as comparable to compensation for future financial loss and future care. The IBSS route is available to those living eligible infected persons registered (or who have applied and are subsequently registered) on an IBSS on or before March 31, 2025.

Amount of compensation payment under the IBSS route

1.067 **23.**—(1) The amount of a compensation payment in relation to an IBSS-registered person ("P") is T – (D + I), where—
(a) "T" is the amount of the compensation award determined in relation to P in accordance with paragraph (2);
(b) "D" is the sum of all relevant damages payments within the meaning of regulation 12 made in relation to P;
(c) "I" is the sum of any amounts awarded in relation to P by way of—
(i) a payment under—
(aa) section 56(1) of the Act;
(bb) the Infected Blood Interim Compensation Payment Scheme as defined in section 56(6) of the Act;
(cc) the Infected Blood Further Interim Compensation Payment Scheme, being the scheme of that name administered by the persons who administer the infected blood support schemes (whether or not in conjunction with other persons);
(ii) compensation, paid pursuant to a scheme established by or under statute, in respect of the same or similar losses as those described in the categories of award listed in paragraph (2).

(2) The amount of the compensation award in relation to P is the sum of—

(a) the injury impact award determined in relation to P in accordance with regulation 14,
(b) the social impact award determined in relation to P in accordance with regulation 15,
(c) the autonomy award determined in relation to P in accordance with regulation 16,
(d) the past financial loss award determined in accordance with regulation 25,
(e) the past care award determined in accordance regulation 26, and
(f) the support scheme top-up award payment determined in accordance with regulation 27.

(3) Where a provision referred to in paragraph (2) relating to an award does not establish an amount for an IBSS-registered person in P's circumstances, the amount of that award for the purposes of this regulation is £0.

Interpretation of regulations 25 to 27

1.068 **24.** In a formula set out in regulations 25 to 27—
"CP" is the care award determined in relation to an IBSS-registered person in accordance with regulation 21;
"FL" is the sum of—
(a) the basic financial loss award determined in relation to an IBSS-registered person in accordance with regulation 17, and
(b) the additional financial loss award determined in accordance with regulation 18 together with whichever of regulation 19 or 20 applies in relation to the IBSS-registered person;
"HLE", in relation to an IBSS-registered person, means the year in which that person would attain the age of their healthy life expectancy;
"YI", in relation to an IBSS-registered person, means that person's first year of infection.

Past financial loss award

1.069 **25.** The amount of the past financial loss award in relation to an IBSS-registered person is (((2024 – YI) ÷ (HLE – YI)) × FL) + ((FL ÷ (HLE – YI)) × 0.25).

Past care award

1.070 **26.** The amount of the past care award in relation to an IBSS-registered person is ((((2024 – YI) ÷ (HLE – YI)) × CP) + ((CP ÷ (HLE – YI)) × 0.25)) × 0.75.

Support scheme top-up award

1.071 **27.**—(1) The amount of the support scheme top-up award in relation to an IBSS-registered person ("P") is (FFL + FCP) – ((S × (HLE – 2025)) + (S × 0.75)), where—
(a) "FFL" is the future financial loss award in relation to P, being (((HLE – 2025) ÷ (HLE – YI)) × FL) + ((FL ÷ (HLE – YI)) × 0.75);
(b) "FCP" is the future care award in relation to P, being (((HLE – 2025) ÷ (HLE – YI)) × CP) + ((CP ÷ (HLE – YI)) × 0.75);
(c) "S" is the amount of the relevant support scheme payment.

(2) In paragraph (1)(c), "relevant support scheme payment" means the sum of the annual rates of any support scheme payments payable in relation to P immediately before 1st April 2025.

(3) Where the amount of the support scheme top-up award is less than £0, that amount is to be treated as £0.

Future financial loss and future care awards where an IBSS-registered person dies

28.—(1) Where the IBCA is notified that an IBSS-registered person has died, the IBCA must determine which is the greater of— **1.072**

(a) the sum of—

(i) the future financial loss award determined in relation to P in accordance with regulation 27(1)(a) as increased in accordance with paragraph (3) of this regulation, and

(ii) the future care award determined in relation to P in accordance with regulation 27(1)(b) as increased in accordance with paragraph (3) of this regulation, and

(b) the sum of all support scheme payments paid in relation to P in relation to the period beginning with 1st April 2025 and ending with the date of P's death.

(2) Where the amount described in paragraph (1)(a) is greater than the amount described in paragraph (1)(b), the IBCA must pay an amount equal to the difference between those amounts to P's personal representatives as a lump sum.

(3) For the purposes of paragraph (1), the future financial loss award and the future care award are to be treated as if they had been, at the beginning of each April during the period—

(a) beginning with the month in which the compensation payment became payable in relation to P (but if the compensation payment became payable in April, that April is be disregarded), and

(b) ending with the date of P's death,

increased by the same percentage as the percentage increase (if any) in the consumer price index over the 12-month period up to the month of September before that April.

PART 6

APPLICATIONS FOR COMPENSATION PAYMENT FROM THE SCHEME

Giving of notices and documents

29.—(1) This regulation applies where a provision in these Regulations requires or authorises a person to— **1.073**

(a) notify another person ("A") of something, or

(b) give a document to A (whether the provision uses the word "give" or some other term).

(2) The notification or document must be given to A—

(a) by sending it by post in a pre-paid envelope—

(i) addressed to A at A's last known place of residence, or

(ii) if A has given an address for service, addressed to A at that address, or

(b) if A has given an address for service using electronic communications, by sending it to A at that address using an electronic communication method which complies with the conditions in paragraph (3).

(3) The conditions are that the notification or document is—

(a) capable of being accessed by A,

(b) legible in all material respects, and

(c) capable of being used for subsequent reference.

(4) A notification or document given in accordance with these Regulations, is—

(a) if given electronically, to be treated for the purposes of these Regulations as having been given, unless the contrary is proved, on the day on which the electronic communication was sent;

(b) if given to the IBCA other than electronically, to be treated as having been given on the day it is received by the IBCA;

(c) if given by the IBCA other than electronically, to be treated as having been given on the day that it was sent.

Applications

1.074 **30.**—(1) An application for a compensation payment under the Scheme must be made to the IBCA.

(2) An application must be made by the person who is seeking to establish that they are an eligible infected person, unless such is sought to be established in relation to a person ("B") who—

(a) is under 18, in which case the application must be made by a person with parental responsibility (within the meaning of regulation 9(2)) for B;

(b) lacks capacity (within the meaning of regulation 9(3)) to make some or all decisions about applying for a compensation payment, in which case the application must be made by a person who, in relation to B, is a person described in one of paragraphs (i) to (v) of regulation 9(1)(b);

(c) is deceased, in which case the application must be made by B's personal representatives.

(3) An application must be—

(a) in writing,

(b) in a form approved by the IBCA,

(c) subject to paragraph (4), accompanied by the evidence specified in regulation 37,

(d) signed by the applicant, and

(e) received by the IBCA by the end of the period specified in regulation 32.

(4) An application need not be accompanied by the evidence specified in regulation 37 where—

(a) the IBCA is satisfied of the matter which the evidence would prove on the basis of evidence it has otherwise obtained, and

(b) the IBCA has notified the applicant that the application need not contain the evidence.

Date of application

1.075 **31.** An application is deemed to have been made on the date on which it is received by the IBCA.

Time limit for making an application

32. An application must be made by— 1.076

(a) the end of 31st March 2031, or

(b) if later, the end of the period of six years beginning with the day on which the person to whom the application relates was diagnosed with an infection specified in regulation 7(3).

Applications for those registered under an infected blood support scheme

33.—(1) Before deciding an application, the IBCA must determine whether the person ("B") in respect of whom the application is made is registered under an infected blood support scheme ("IBSS-registered"), and— 1.077

(a) if B is not IBSS-registered, whether B is in the process of applying to be IBSS-registered;

(b) if B is IBSS-registered, whether B is in the process of applying to have their treatment under the infected blood support scheme varied because of a change in the severity of their infection.

(2) If B is in the process of either of the applications described in paragraph (1)(a) or (b) (an "IBSS application"), then the IBCA must defer consideration of any matter in the application under this Part until the IBSS application has been finally determined.

(3) An IBSS application is finally determined if—

(a) it is decided or withdrawn, and

(b) all routes of review or appeal of a decision on the application have been exhausted (including where any periods for requesting a review or bringing an appeal have expired).

(4) The IBCA may by written notice require the applicant to provide any information relevant to establishing a matter which the IBCA must determine in accordance with this regulation.

Amendment or withdrawal of application by the applicant

34.—(1) An applicant may amend an application by notice given to the IBCA at any time before notice of the decision on the application has been given to the applicant by the IBCA. 1.078

(2) An applicant may, by giving notice to the IBCA, withdraw their application at any time before the IBCA has made a decision on it.

(3) Any notice of withdrawal given in accordance with paragraph (2) has effect when it is received by the IBCA.

(4) Where an applicant has withdrawn an application under paragraph (2)—

(a) that application may not be reinstated, but

(b) the applicant may make a further application in accordance with the provisions of these Regulations.

Duty of applicants

35.—(1) As soon as reasonably practicable, an applicant must inform the IBCA of— 1.079

(a) any matter that comes to the applicant's attention which may be relevant to the question of whether a person is eligible for a payment, or the amount of such a payment, under the Scheme, and

(b) any change in—
 (i) the applicant's address for correspondence, or
 (ii) the bank details of any person who is to receive a payment under the Scheme.

(2) An applicant must, so far as reasonably practicable and within any period specified by the IBCA, provide any other assistance to the IBCA which the IBCA requests in connection with the consideration of the application.

Death before an application has been finally determined

1.080 **36.**—(1) Paragraph (2) applies where—

(a) an application ("the original application") is made by or on behalf of a person ("B") who is not deceased when the application is made, and
(b) B dies—
 (i) before the IBCA has decided in accordance with regulation 39(1)(a) whether B is an eligible infected person,
 (ii) where the IBCA has made an offer in accordance with regulation 10, before the offer is accepted, or
 (iii) where the IBCA has decided in accordance with regulation 39(1)(a) that B is not an eligible infected person, before the right to request a review of that decision under regulation 40 has been exhausted.

(2) Where this paragraph applies—

(a) the original application is to be treated as if it had been withdrawn,
(b) any offer made in accordance with regulation 10 is revoked, and
(c) no review may be commenced under regulation 40 in respect of the original application, and any review so commenced is to be treated as if it had not been commenced.

Evidence

1.081 **37.**—(1) An application must be accompanied by evidence as to—

(a) the diagnosis of the infection caused as a result of the person receiving treatment with blood, blood products or tissue known to be capable of transmitting an infection specified in regulation 7(3),
(b) the date on which that diagnosis was given,
(c) which of paragraph (2), (6), (7) or (8) of regulation 7 applies as to the cause or origin of the infection, and
(d) where the person is infected with Hepatitis B or Hepatitis C (or both), the severity of the infection.

(2) Where the application relates to an IBSS-registered person, the application need not contain the evidence described in paragraph (1)(a) or (c).

(3) Where the application relates to a deceased person (so that the application is made by the person's personal representatives), the application must also be accompanied by a document that is by law sufficient evidence of—

(a) the grant of probate of the person's will,
(b) the grant of letters of administration of the person's estate, or
(c) confirmation as the person's executor.

(4) Nothing in this regulation prevents the IBCA from requesting, or from seeking the production of, evidence to enable the application to be

determined in such cases or in such circumstances as the IBCA considers appropriate.

Burden of proof and standard of proof

38.—(1) The burden of proving any issue is on the applicant. 1.082

(2) The standard of proof applicable in any decision which is required to be made under these Regulations is the balance of probabilities.

Decisions

39.—(1) The IBCA must decide, in relation to each application— 1.083

(a) whether the person to whom the application relates is an eligible infected person, and

(b) any other question arising out of the application.

(2) The IBCA must notify the applicant of any decision under this regulation.

(3) A notice referred to in paragraph (2) must—

(a) give reasons for the decision,

(b) inform the applicant of the right—

(i) to request a review of the decision under regulation 40;

(ii) to appeal to the First-tier Tribunal following any such review, and

(c) specify the period within which the rights in sub-paragraph (b) must be exercised.

Part 7

Reviews and Appeals

Review initiated by the applicant

40.—(1) The IBCA must, on the request of an applicant, review a decision ("the original decision")— 1.084

(a) in accordance with regulation 39(1)(a) that the person to whom an application relates is not an eligible infected person;

(b) where an offer made in accordance with regulation 10 has not been accepted, about—

(i) the person to whom the compensation payment is to be paid in accordance with regulation 9;

(ii) the amount of the compensation payment determined in accordance with regulation 11 or 23.

(2) The request referred to in paragraph (1) must—

(a) be in writing,

(b) be signed by the applicant,

(c) specify the grounds on which the request for a review is made, and

(d) be given to the IBCA within a period of 3 months beginning with the day on which the original decision is given to the applicant.

(3) The applicant may submit further evidence in connection with the request to review the original decision which the IBCA must consider when conducting the review.

(4) Evidence may only be submitted under paragraph (3)—

(a) within the period of 6 months beginning with the day on which the request referred to in paragraph (1) is given to the IBCA, or

(b) where the IBCA determines that it is reasonable to extend that period, within the period of 12 months beginning with the day that request is given to the IBCA.

(5) The IBCA must take reasonable steps to ensure that the review is carried out by a member of the IBCA's staff who had no involvement in the making of the original decision.

(6) The decisions that may be made on a review are—

(a) to confirm the original decision, or

(b) to revoke the original decision and make a new decision on the application in accordance with these Regulations.

(7) The IBCA must notify the applicant of the decision on the review.

(8) The notice under paragraph (7) must—

(a) state—

(i) that the original decision has been confirmed or revoked and remade, and

(ii) the terms of any new decision which has been made on the application,

(b) give reasons for the decision made on the review,

(c) state that the applicant may appeal to the First-tier Tribunal against the decision made on review, and

(d) state the period within which such an appeal is to be made and provide information as to how to make such an appeal.

(9) Nothing in this regulation requires the IBCA to review a decision made under this regulation or under regulation 41.

Review initiated by the IBCA

1.085 **41.**—(1) The IBCA may, at any time after a decision is made under regulation 39 ("the original decision"), decide on its own initiative to conduct a review of that decision or any matter it has determined in relation to the decision under these Regulations.

(2) Where the IBCA decides to conduct a review of the original decision under paragraph (1), it must notify the applicant of the review and the reasons for it unless the IBCA considers that such notification would jeopardise the proper administration of the Scheme.

(3) The grounds on which the IBCA may conduct a review under this regulation include that—

(a) whether fraudulently or otherwise, any person has misrepresented or failed to disclose a material fact and the original decision was made in consequence of the misrepresentation or failure,

(b) the decision to make any compensation payment was based on a mistake as to a material fact, or

(c) there was an error or omission which affected the substance of the original decision whether to make a compensation payment under or the amount of any compensation payment made.

(4) The applicant may submit written representations to the IBCA about the IBCA's decision to conduct a review and about any information on which the decision to conduct a review was based.

(5) Any representation which is made under paragraph (4) must be sent so that it is received by the IBCA not later than 28 days after the date of the IBCA's notice of the review under paragraph (2).

(6) The IBCA may extend the time limit in paragraph (5) by a further period where the IBCA considers that there was good reason for the failure to submit written representations before the end of that initial period and for any delay since then in submitting written representations.

(7) The decisions that may be made on a review under paragraph (1) are—

(a) to confirm the original decision, or

(b) to revoke the original decision and make a new decision on the application in accordance with these Regulations.

(8) Where the IBCA conducts a review under paragraph (1), it must notify the applicant of the decision on the review.

(9) The notice under paragraph (8) must—

(a) state—

(i) that the original decision has been confirmed or revoked and remade, and

(ii) the terms of any new decision which has been made on the application,

(b) give reasons for the decision made on the review,

(c) state that the applicant may appeal to the First-tier Tribunal against the decision made on review, and

(d) state the period within which such an appeal is to be made and provide information as to how to make such an appeal.

Appeals

42. An applicant may appeal to the First-tier Tribunal from a decision that has been made on a review under regulation 40(1) or 41(1). **1.086**

PART 8

RECOVERY OF OVERPAYMENTS

Recovery of overpayments

43.—(1) This regulation applies where a payment has been made to a person under the Scheme which the IBCA has determined, pursuant to a review under regulation 41, exceeds the amount that was payable to that person under the Scheme (and the "excess amount" is the difference between the amount the person was paid and the amount that was payable). **1.087**

(2) The IBCA may, by a notice given to the relevant person, require the relevant person to repay the excess amount.

(3) The notice must state—

(a) the excess amount, and

(b) the period within which the excess amount must be repaid.

(4) The excess amount is recoverable as a civil debt.

SCHEDULE Regulation 2(2)

INFECTION SEVERITY LEVELS FOR HEPATITIS B AND HEPATITIS C

Infection severity level	*Description of infection severity level*
Level 1: Hepatitis C only	Acute infection, being a transient, self-cleared infection
Level 2: Hepatitis B and/or Hepatitis C	Chronic infection characterised by: (a) Hepatitis B – infection with confirmed Hepatitis B surface antigen (HBsAg) positivity for longer than 6 months with detectable Hepatitis B virus DNA on a polymerase chain reaction test, if not on antiviral therapy (b) Hepatitis C – infection with replicating Hepatitis C virus RNA
Level 3: Hepatitis B and/or Hepatitis C	(1) Cirrhosis, characterised by serious scarring (fibrosis) of the liver caused by long-term liver damage caused by infection (2) Treatment of B–cell non-Hodgkin's lymphoma caused by infection – single round treatment (first line therapy) (3) Type 2 or 3 cryoglobulinemia caused by infection accompanied by membranoproliferative glomerulonephritis
Level 4: Hepatitis B and/or Hepatitis C	(1) Decompensated cirrhosis caused by infection, characterised by: (a) the presence of hepatic encephalopathy (confusion due to liver damage), (b) ascites (accumulation of fluid in the abdomen), (c) variceal haemorrhage (bleeding from dilated veins in the gullet or stomach), or (d) a Child-Pugh score greater than 7 (2) Treatment of B-cell non-Hodgkin's lymphoma caused by infection – multiple round treatment (second line therapy) (3) Long-term liver damage caused by infection necessitating liver transplantation (4) Presence of liver cancer caused by infection
Level 5: Hepatitis B only	Infection resulting in acute liver failure within 12 months of infection

(a) frequent attention throughout the day in connection with their bodily functions, or
(b) continual supervision throughout the day in order to avoid substantial danger to themselves or others.

(3) An individual meets the night-time condition if they are so severely disabled physically or mentally that, at night,—

(a) they require from another person prolonged or repeated attention in connection with their bodily functions, or
(b) in order to avoid substantial danger to themselves or others they require another person to be awake for a prolonged period or at frequent intervals for the purpose of watching over them.

(4) For the purposes of paragraphs (2) and (3), the individual shall not be taken to satisfy paragraph (2)(a) or paragraph (3)(a) unless the attention the severely disabled person requires from another person is required to be given in the physical presence of the severely disabled person.

(5) In this regulation—

"attention" means the provision of personal care, prompting or motivation in relation to bodily functions or assistance with communication needs,

"require" means reasonably require and cognate expressions are to be construed accordingly, and

"supervision" means the continual presence of another person for the purpose of reducing the real risk of harm to the individual and to others.

(6) An individual is not entitled to Pension Age Disability Payment at the lower rate or higher rate unless throughout the period of 26 weeks immediately preceding the date on which the award would begin ("the required period"), the individual has satisfied or is likely to satisfy—

(a) the daytime condition,
(b) the night-time condition, or
(c) both.

(7) Paragraph (6) does not apply where regulation 18 (entitlement under special rules for terminal illness) applies.

(8) In this regulation and in regulation 7—

"bodily functions" means the normal actions of any organ of the body, including the brain, or of a number of organs acting together, and

"day" is to be construed in relation to the ordinary domestic routine of the household in which the individual lives.

Eligibility criteria: rates of Pension Age Disability Payment

6.—(1) An individual may be awarded Pension Age Disability Payment at either the lower rate or the higher rate. **1.095**

(2) An individual is entitled to Pension Age Disability Payment at the lower rate if they meet either the daytime condition or the night-time condition.

(3) An individual is entitled to Pension Age Disability Payment at the higher rate if they meet both the daytime condition and the night-time condition.

Entitlement to Pension Age Disability Payment when undergoing renal dialysis

1.096 **7.**—(1) Except as provided in paragraph (3), an individual suffering from renal failure who is undergoing the treatment specified in paragraph (2) is treated as meeting the condition—

(a) in paragraph (2) of regulation 5 where they undergo renal dialysis by day,

(b) in paragraph (3) of regulation 5 where they undergo renal dialysis by night, or

(c) in either paragraph (2) or paragraph (3) of regulation 5, but not both, if they undergo renal dialysis by day and by night.

(2) The treatment referred to in paragraph (1) is the undergoing of renal dialysis—

(a) two or more times a week, and

(b) which either—

(i) is of a type which normally requires the attendance of or supervision by another person during the period of dialysis, or

(ii) which, because of the particular circumstances of their case, in fact requires another person, during the period of dialysis, to attend in connection with the bodily functions of the individual undergoing renal dialysis or to supervise that individual in order that they avoid substantial danger to themselves.

(3) Paragraph (1) does not apply to an individual undergoing the treatment specified in paragraph (2) where the treatment—

(a) is provided under the National Health Service (Scotland) Act 1978, the National Health Service Act 2006, the National Health Service (Wales) Act 2006 or the Health and Personal Social Services (Northern Ireland) Order 1972,

(b) is in a hospital or similar institution,

(c) is out-patient treatment, and

(d) takes place with the assistance or supervision of any member of staff of the hospital or similar institution.

(4) In this regulation a "hospital or similar institution" means—

(a) a health service hospital (within the meaning of section 108(1) of the National Health Service (Scotland) Act 1978) in Scotland,

(b) a health service hospital (within the meaning of section 275(1) of the National Health Service Act 2006) in England,

(c) a hospital in Wales vested in—

(i) an NHS trust,

(ii) a Local Health Board, or

(iii) the Welsh Ministers,

(d) a hospital (within the meaning of the Health and Personal Social Services (Northern Ireland) Order 1972 or the Health and Personal Social Services (Northern Ireland) Order 1991) in Northern Ireland.

(5) For the purposes of determining whether an individual is to treated as meeting one of the conditions specified in paragraph (1), any period of time where paragraph (3) applies to the individual can be included for the purposes of calculating the period of 26 weeks required by regulation 5(6).

PART 4

PENSION AGE DISABILITY PAYMENT AFTER AN INTERVAL

Pension Age Disability Payment after an interval

8.—(1) Where an individual makes an application for Pension Age Disability Payment and that individual had a previous award of Attendance Allowance or Pension Age Disability Payment which ended not more than two years before the date on which that application is made, regulation 5(6) (required period) does not apply to that individual. **1.097**

(2) Paragraph (1) applies only where the determination of the application mentioned in paragraph (1) results in an award of Pension Age Disability Payment at the same rate as, or a lower rate than, the previous award.

PART 5

RESIDENCE AND PRESENCE CONDITIONS

Residence and presence conditions

9.—(1) An individual satisfies the residence and presence conditions where on any day that individual— **1.098**

(a) is ordinarily resident in Scotland,
(b) is habitually resident in the common travel area,
(c) is not a person subject to immigration control within the meaning of section 115(9) of the Immigration and Asylum Act 1999,
(d) is present in the common travel area, and
(e) has been present in the common travel area for a period of, or for periods amounting in the aggregate to, not less than 26 weeks out of the 52 weeks immediately preceding that day.

(2) In this Part, "common travel area" has the meaning given in section 1(3) of the Immigration Act 1971.

(3) The residence condition set out in paragraph (1)(a) does not apply where on any day the individual—

(a) is habitually resident in Ireland,
(b) has a genuine and sufficient link to Scotland, and
(c) is an individual—
 (i) to whom the Convention on Social Security between the Government of the United Kingdom of Great Britain and Northern Ireland and the Government of Ireland signed at Dublin on 1 February 2019, as modified from time to time in accordance with any provision of it, applies, and
 (ii) in respect of whom the United Kingdom is, as a result, competent for payment of long term care benefits.

(4) The reference in paragraph (3)(b) to an individual's link to Scotland being sufficient is to it being sufficiently close that if the individual were not entitled to Pension Age Disability Payment, paragraph (3) would

be incompatible with the Convention on Social Security between the Government of the United Kingdom of Great Britain and Northern Ireland and the Government of Ireland signed at Dublin on 1 February 2019.

(5) Paragraph (1)(c) does not apply to an individual who is a person subject to immigration control within the meaning of section 115(9) of the Immigration and Asylum Act 1999 where the person—

(a) is lawfully working in United Kingdom and is a national of a state with which the United Kingdom has concluded an agreement which replaces in whole or in part an agreement under Article 217 of the Treaty on the Functioning of the European Union which has ceased to apply to, and in, the United Kingdom, providing, in the field of social security, for the equal treatment of workers who are nationals of the signatory state and their families,

(b) is a member of the family of, and living with, a person specified in sub-paragraph (a), or

(c) has been given leave to enter, or remain in, the United Kingdom by the Secretary of State upon an undertaking by another person or persons pursuant to the immigration rules, to be responsible for their maintenance and accommodation.

(6) The past presence condition in paragraph (1)(e) does not apply where an individual has a terminal illness within the meaning of regulation 18.

(7) The residence and presence conditions set out in paragraphs (1)(b) and (1)(e) do not apply where an individual is a person who—

(a) has leave to enter or remain in the United Kingdom granted under the immigration rules by virtue of—

(i) the Afghan Relocations and Assistance Policy, or

(ii) the previous scheme for locally-employed staff in Afghanistan (sometimes referred to as the ex-gratia scheme),

(b) has been granted discretionary leave outside the immigration rules as a dependant of a person referred to in sub-paragraph (a),

(c) has leave granted under the Afghan Citizens Resettlement Scheme,

(d) has leave to enter or remain in the United Kingdom granted under or outside the immigration rules, has a right of abode in the United Kingdom within the meaning given in section 2 of the Immigration Act 1971 or does not require leave to enter or remain in the United Kingdom in accordance with section 3ZA of that Act, where the individual—

(i) was residing in Ukraine immediately before 1 January 2022, and

(ii) left Ukraine in connection with the Russian invasion which took place on 24 February 2022, or

(e) has leave to enter or remain in the United Kingdom granted under or outside the immigration rules, has a right of abode in the United Kingdom within the meaning given in section 2 of the Immigration Act 1971 or does not require leave to enter or remain in the United Kingdom in accordance with section 3ZA of that Act, where the individual—

(i) was residing in Sudan before 15 April 2023, and

(ii) left Sudan in connection with the violence which rapidly escalated on 15 April 2023 in Khartoum and across Sudan,

(f) has leave to enter or remain in the United Kingdom granted under or outside the immigration rules, has a right of abode in the United

Kingdom within the meaning given in section 2 of the Immigration Act 1971 or does not require leave to enter or remain in the United Kingdom in accordance with section 3ZA of that Act, where the individual—

(i) was residing in Israel, the West Bank, the Gaza Strip, East Jerusalem, the Golan Heights or Lebanon immediately before 7 October 2023, and

(ii) left Israel, the West Bank, the Gaza Strip, East Jerusalem, the Golan Heights or Lebanon in connection with the Hamas terrorist attack in Israel on 7 October 2023 or the violence which rapidly escalated in the region following the attack.

(8) For the purposes of paragraph (7), "the Afghan Citizens Resettlement Scheme" means the scheme announced by the United Kingdom Government on 18 August 2021.

Temporary absence from the common travel area

10.—(1) Where an individual is temporarily absent from the common travel area, the individual is to be treated as present in the common travel area for— **1.099**

(a) the first 13 weeks of that absence for any reason, or

(b) the first 26 weeks of that absence where—

(i) after the first 13 weeks, the absence is in connection with arrangements made for the medical treatment of the individual for a disease or bodily or mental disablement which commenced before leaving the common travel area, and

(ii) the arrangements relate to medical treatment—

(aa) outside the common travel area,

(bb) during the period when the individual is temporarily absent from the common travel area, and

(cc) by, or under the supervision of, a person appropriately qualified to carry out that treatment.

(2) For the purposes of paragraph (1)—

(a) an individual is "temporarily absent" if, at the beginning of the period of absence, that absence is unlikely to exceed 52 weeks, and

(b) "medical treatment" means medical, surgical, psychological or rehabilitative treatment (including any course or diet regimen).

Serving members of His Majesty's forces, civil servants and their family members

11.—(1) A relevant individual is treated as meeting the residence and presence conditions set out in regulation 9(1)(a), (b) and (d) where on any day that individual is outside the common travel area— **1.100**

(a) by reason of their capacity mentioned in paragraph (3)(a) provided that the individual satisfied the residence and presence conditions set out in regulation 9(1)(a), (b) and (d) immediately prior to the start of their employment mentioned in paragraph (3)(a), or

(b) by reason of being a person mentioned in paragraph (3)(b) living with an individual to whom paragraph (3)(a) applies.

(2) The past presence condition set out in regulation 9(1)(e) does not apply to a relevant individual.

(3) A "relevant individual" in paragraphs (1) and (2) means an individual who is—

(a) outside of the common travel area in their capacity as a—

(i) serving member of His Majesty's forces, or

(ii) civil servant, or

(b) living with a person mentioned in sub-paragraph (a) and—

(i) is the child, step-child or child in care of that person,

(ii) is the parent, step-parent or parent-in-law of that person, or

(iii) is married to or in a civil partnership with that person, or is living together with that person as if they were married or in a civil partnership.

(4) In this regulation—

"child in care" means—

(a) under the law of Scotland, a child in respect of whom a relevant individual listed in paragraph (3)(a)—

(i) is a foster carer within the meaning of regulation 2 of the Looked After Children (Scotland) Regulations 2009,

(ii) is a kinship carer within the meaning of regulation 2 of the Looked After Children (Scotland) Regulations 2009,

(iii) has a kinship care order within the meaning of section 72 of the Children and Young People (Scotland) Act 2014, or

(b) under the law of England and Wales and Northern Ireland, a child in respect of whom a person listed in paragraph (3)(a) has a relationship equivalent to those listed under the law of Scotland,

"civil servant" has the meaning given by section 1(4) of the Constitutional Reform and Governance Act 2010, and

"serving member of His Majesty's forces" means a member of a regular force or a reserve force ("M") as defined, in each case, by section 374 (definitions applying for purposes of the whole Act) of the Armed Forces Act 2006, unless—

(c) M is under the age of 16,

(d) M is committing an offence under section 8 of the Armed Forces Act 2006 (desertion),

(e) the force concerned is one of His Majesty's naval forces which M locally entered at an overseas base without—

(i) previously being an insured person under the National Insurance Act 1965, or

(ii) paying or having previously paid one or more of the following classes of contributions under the Social Security Act 1975 or the Social Security Contributions and Benefits Act 1992—

(aa) primary Class 1,

(bb) Class 2, or

(cc) Class 3, or

(f) the force concerned is one of His Majesty's military forces or His Majesty's air forces which M entered, or was recruited for, outside the United Kingdom and—

(i) where that force is one of His Majesty's military forces, the depot for M's unit is outside the United Kingdom, or

(ii) where that force is one of His Majesty's air forces, M is liable under the terms of M's engagement to serve only in a specified area outside the United Kingdom.

Aircraft workers, mariners and continental shelf operations

12.—(1) An individual is to be treated as meeting the presence conditions set out in regulation 9(1)(d) and (e) for any period where that individual is— **1.101**

(a) outside the common travel area in their capacity as an aircraft worker or a mariner, or

(b) in employment prescribed for the purposes of section 120 (employment at sea (continental shelf operations)) of the Social Security Contributions and Benefits Act 1992(15) in connection with continental shelf operations.

(2) In this regulation—

"aircraft worker" means a person who is, or has been, employed under a contract of service either as a pilot, commander, navigator or other member of the crew of any aircraft, or in any other capacity on board any aircraft where—

(a) the employment in that other capacity is for the purposes of the aircraft or its crew or of any passengers or cargo or mail carried on that aircraft, and

(b) the contract is entered into in the United Kingdom with a view to its performance (in whole or in part) while the aircraft is in flight,

but does not include a person so far as that employment is as a serving member of His Majesty's forces, and

"mariner" means a person who is, or has been, in employment under a contract of service either as a master or member of the crew of any ship or vessel, or in any other capacity on board any ship or vessel where—

(a) the employment in that other capacity is for the purposes of that ship or vessel or its crew or any passengers or cargo or mail carried by the ship or vessel, and

(b) the contract is entered into in the United Kingdom with a view to its performance (in whole or in part) while the ship or vessel is on voyage,

but does not include a person in so far as that employment is as a serving member of His Majesty's forces.

Persons residing in the United Kingdom to whom a relevant EU regulation applies

13. The past presence condition set out in regulation 9(1)(e) does not apply where on any day the individual is— **1.102**

(a) ordinarily resident in Scotland,

(b) habitually resident in the United Kingdom,

(c) an individual—

(i) to whom the rules set out in a relevant EU regulation apply by virtue of—

(aa) Title III of Part 2 of the EU withdrawal agreement,

(bb) Part 3 or Article 23(4) of the Swiss citizens' rights agreement (as defined in section 39(1) of the European Union (Withdrawal Agreement) Act 2020 ("the 2020 Act")(16),

(cc) Title III of the EEA EFTA separation agreement (as defined in section 39(1) of the 2020 Act), or

(dd) the agreement constituted by the exchange of letters set out in the schedule of the Family Allowances, National

Insurance and Industrial Injuries (Gibraltar) Order 1974(17), and
(ii) in respect of whom the United Kingdom is, as a result, competent for payment of sickness benefits in cash.

Persons residing outside the United Kingdom to whom a relevant EU regulation applies

1.103 **14.**—(1) The residence and presence conditions set out in regulation 9(1) do not apply in relation to Pension Age Disability Payment where on any day the individual satisfies the conditions in paragraph (2).

(2) The conditions referred to in paragraph (1) are that the individual must—

(a) be an individual—
 (i) to whom the rules set out in a relevant EU regulation apply by virtue of—
  (aa) Title III of Part 2 of the EU withdrawal agreement,
  (bb) Part 3 or Article 23(4) of the Swiss citizens' rights agreement (as defined in section 39(1) of the European Union (Withdrawal Agreement) Act 2020 ("the 2020 Act")),
  (cc) Title III of the EEA EFTA separation agreement (as defined in section 39(1) of the 2020 Act), or
  (dd) the agreement constituted by the exchange of letters set out in the schedule of the Family Allowances, National Insurance and Industrial Injuries (Gibraltar) Order 1974, and
 (ii) in respect of whom the United Kingdom is, as a result, competent for payment of sickness benefits in cash,
(b) be habitually resident in—
 (i) Switzerland,
 (ii) an EEA state, or
 (iii) Gibraltar, and
(c) have a genuine and sufficient link to Scotland.

(3) The reference in paragraph (2)(c) to an individual's link to Scotland being sufficient is to it being sufficiently close that if the individual were not entitled to Pension Age Disability Payment, paragraph (2) would be incompatible with the applicable agreement mentioned in sub-paragraph (a)(i) of that paragraph.

(4) In this regulation, "EEA State" means—
(a) any member state of the European Union, or
(b) any other state that is party to the agreement on the European Economic Area signed at Oporto on 2 May 1992, together with the Protocol adjusting that Agreement signed at Brussels on 17 March 1993, as modified or supplemented from time to time.

Refugees

1.104 **15.** The residence and presence conditions set out in regulation 9(1)(b) and (e) do not apply where an individual has—
(a) been granted refugee status or humanitarian protection under the immigration rules, or
(b) leave to enter or remain in the United Kingdom as the dependant of a person granted refugee status or humanitarian protection under the immigration rules.

Persons to whom a relevant EU regulation applies and entitlement to Pension Age Disability Payment

16. An individual to whom a relevant EU regulation applies is not entitled to Pension Age Disability Payment for a period unless during that period the United Kingdom is competent for payment of sickness benefits in cash to the person for the purposes of the relevant EU regulation in question. **1.105**

PART 6

ENTITLEMENT UNDER RULES RELATING TO AGE

Age Criteria

17.—(1) Pension Age Disability Payment may be paid in respect of an individual who has reached pensionable age (within the meaning given by the rules in paragraph 1 of schedule 4 of the Pensions Act 1995). **1.106**

(2) Where an individual was born on 29 February, their birthday is to be taken to fall on 28 February in a year which is not a leap year.

PART 7

ENTITLEMENT UNDER SPECIAL RULES FOR TERMINAL ILLNESS

Entitlement under special rules for terminal illness

18.—(1) An individual who has a terminal illness is to be treated as satisfying the conditions for the higher rate of Pension Age Disability Payment. **1.107**

(2) Paragraph (1) applies regardless of the period of time for which the individual has had the terminal illness.

(3) Subject to paragraphs (4) and (5), the individual's entitlement to the rate referred to in paragraph (1) begins on the date on which—

(a) the individual's application for Pension Age Disability Payment was made, where the application included information about the individual's terminal illness,

(b) the Scottish Ministers became aware of the individual's terminal illness (whether as a result of the individual notifying a change in circumstances or otherwise), where the individual was previously awarded, and has an ongoing entitlement to, Pension Age Disability Payment, on the basis of a determination that the individual was entitled to Pension Age Disability Payment in relation to a condition other than terminal illness, or

(c) the clinical judgement was made in accordance with paragraphs (6) and (7) ("the judgement"),

whichever is the earlier.

(4) Where the judgement mentioned in paragraph (3)(c) is dated not more than 26 weeks earlier than whichever date in paragraph (3)(a) or (b)

applies ("the applicable date"), the Scottish Ministers have the power, when making their determination, to specify that an individual's entitlement begins—

(a) up to a maximum of 26 weeks prior to the applicable date, and

(b) on or after the day these Regulations come into force.

(5) Where the judgement mentioned in paragraph (3)(c)—

(a) is dated more than 26 weeks earlier than whichever date in paragraph (3)(a) or (b) applies ("the applicable date"), and

(b) an appropriate healthcare professional confirms that the judgement is still accurate by making a judgement in accordance with paragraphs (6) and (7),

an individual's entitlement can only begin—

(c) up to a maximum of 26 weeks prior to the applicable date, and

(d) on or after the day these Regulations come into force.

(6) For the purposes of these Regulations an individual is to be regarded as having a terminal illness for the purpose of determining entitlement to Pension Age Disability Payment if it is the clinical judgement of an appropriate healthcare professional that the individual has a progressive disease that can reasonably be expected to cause the individual's death.

(7) Subject to paragraph (8), an appropriate healthcare professional exercising the judgement described in paragraph (6) must have regard to the guidance prepared and made publicly available by the Chief Medical Officer of the Scottish Administration in accordance with paragraph 1(3) of schedule 5 of the 2018 Act.

(8) Where regulation 14 (persons residing outside the United Kingdom to whom a relevant EU regulation applies) applies to the individual, an appropriate healthcare professional mentioned in paragraph (9)(b) need not have regard to the guidance mentioned in paragraph (7) where it would not be reasonable in the circumstances to insist on the judgement being formed with regard to that guidance.

(9) In this regulation, "an appropriate healthcare professional" means—

(a) a registered medical practitioner or a registered nurse who is—

(i) involved in the diagnosis or care of the individual, and

(ii) acting in their professional capacity, or

(b) where regulation 14 applies to the individual, a person who—

(i) has equivalent qualifications to a registered medical practitioner or a registered nurse in an EEA state, Gibraltar or Switzerland,

(ii) is a member of the professional body equivalent to the General Medical Council or Nursing and Midwifery Council in that EEA state, Gibraltar or Switzerland, and

(iii) meets the requirements of sub-paragraph (a)(i) and (ii).

(10) Where an individual has previously received Pension Age Disability Payment at the lower rate or a benefit listed in paragraph (11)(a) for a period and a determination is subsequently made that the individual is entitled to Pension Age Disability Payment at the higher rate for that period by virtue of this regulation, that individual will be entitled to the difference between the value of entitlement to Pension Age Disability Payment under the subsequent determination and the value of Pension Age Disability Payment or the benefit listed in paragraph (11)(a) to which that individual was previously entitled for that period.

(11) For the purposes of paragraph (10)—

(a) the benefits are—

(i) armed forces independence payment,

(ii) Attendance Allowance,

(iii) Disability Living Allowance,

(iv) Personal Independence Payment, or

(v) Adult Disability Payment, and

(b) regulation 4 (entitlement to other benefits) is treated as omitted.

Part 8

Effect of time spent in care homes, hospital and legal detention

Effect of admission to a care home on ongoing entitlement to Pension Age Disability Payment

19.—(1) This regulation applies where an individual who has an ongoing entitlement to Pension Age Disability Payment becomes a resident of a care home. 1.108

(2) Subject to paragraph (4) and regulation 21 on the day after the day on which the individual has been resident in a care home for 28 days, and for so long as the individual continues to reside in such a home, the value of Pension Age Disability Payment that is to be given to the individual is to be £0 instead of the values set out in regulation 26 (amount and form of Pension Age Disability Payment).

(3) The 28 days referred to in paragraph (2) may comprise two or more separate periods, provided that there is no more than 28 days between each period.

(4) Paragraph (2) does not apply to a resident in a care home, where the full costs of any qualifying services are met—

(a) entirely out of the resources of the individual for whom the qualifying services are provided,

(b) partly out of the resources of the individual for whom the qualifying services are provided and partly out of the resources of another person (other than a local authority) or assistance from a charity, or

(c) entirely out of the resources of another person (other than a local authority) or assistance from a charity.

Effect of admission to hospital on ongoing entitlement to Pension Age Disability Payment

20.—(1) This regulation applies where an individual who has an ongoing entitlement to Pension Age Disability Payment— 1.109

(a) is undergoing medical or other treatment as an in-patient at a hospital or similar institution, and

(b) any of the costs of the treatment, accommodation and any related services provided for them are borne out of public funds.

(2) Subject to regulation 21, on the day after the day on which the individual has been an in-patient in a hospital or similar institution for 28 days,

and for so long as the individual continues to be an in-patient in such an institution, the value of Pension Age Disability Payment that is to be given to the individual is £0 instead of the values set out in regulation 26 (amount and form of Pension Age Disability Payment).

(3) The 28 days referred to in paragraph (2) may comprise two or more separate periods, provided that there is no more than 28 days between each period.

(4) For the purposes of paragraph (1), the costs of treatment, accommodation or any related services are borne out of public funds if the individual is undergoing medical or other treatment as an in-patient in—

(a) a hospital or similar institution under—
  (i) the National Health Service Act 2006,
  (ii) the National Health Service (Wales) Act 2006, or
  (iii) the National Health Service (Scotland) Act 1978, or
  (iv) the Health and Personal Social Services (Northern Ireland) Order 1972 or the Health and Personal Social Services (Northern Ireland) Order 1991, or

(b) a hospital or similar institution maintained or administered by the Defence Council.

Exception: Hospices

1.110 **21.**—(1) Regulations 19(2) and 20(2) do not apply where the individual is residing in a hospice and has a terminal illness.

(2) In this regulation, "hospice" means a hospital or other institution whose primary function is to provide palliative care for persons resident there who are suffering from a progressive disease in its final stages, other than—

(a) a health service hospital (within the meaning of section 108(1) of the National Health Service (Scotland) Act 1978) in Scotland,

(b) a health service hospital (within the meaning of section 275(1) of the National Health Service Act 2006) in England,

(c) a hospital in Wales vested in—
  (i) an NHS trust,
  (ii) a Local Health Board, or
  (iii) the Welsh Ministers,

  for the purpose of functions under the National Health Service (Wales) Act 2006,

(d) a hospital or similar institution within the meaning of Article 2(2) of the Health and Personal Social Services (Northern Ireland) Order 1972 or the Health and Personal Social Services (Northern Ireland) Order 1991, or

(e) a hospital maintained or administered by the Defence Council, or

(f) an institution similar to a hospital mentioned in any of the preceding sub-paragraphs.

(3) In this regulation—

"NHS trust" means a body established under section 18 of the National Health Service (Wales) Act 2006, and

"Local Health Board" means a body established under section 11 of that Act.

Effect of legal detention on ongoing entitlement to Pension Age Disability Payment

22.—(1) This regulation applies where an individual who has an ongoing entitlement to Pension Age Disability Payment begins a period of legal detention. 1.111

(2) For the purposes of this regulation, an individual is to be treated as though they are not in legal detention on any day on which they are an in-patient in a hospital or in a hospice.

(3) On the day after the day on which the individual has been in legal detention for 28 days, and for so long as the individual continues to be in legal detention, instead of the values set out in regulation 26 (amount and form of Pension Age Disability Payment) the value of Pension Age Disability Payment that is to be given to the individual is to be £0.

(4) The 28 days referred to in paragraph (3) may comprise two or more separate periods, provided there is no more than one year between each period.

(5) Paragraph (3) of this regulation does not apply to an individual where—

(a) the individual is undergoing legal detention outside the United Kingdom, and

(b) in similar circumstances in Scotland, the individual would have been excepted from the application of that paragraph by virtue of the operation of any provision of this regulation.

Calculation of periods of time spent in a care home, hospital or legal detention

23.—(1) Subject to paragraphs (3) to (6), a period during which an individual is— 1.112

(a) resident in a care home for the purpose of regulation 19,

(b) an in-patient in hospital or similar institution for the purpose of regulation 20,

(c) in legal detention for the purpose of regulation 22, or

(d) resident in a care home, an in-patient in a hospital or similar institution, or in legal detention for the purposes of regulation 24,

is to be determined in accordance with this regulation.

(2) Such a period is to be taken to—

(a) begin on the day after the day on which the individual enters the place, and

(b) end on the day before the day on which the individual leaves the place.

(3) Where an individual takes a period of leave from a place mentioned in paragraph (1), the days on which the individual begins and returns from leave are not to be counted as days of residence in that place.

(4) Days constituting a period of leave are not to be counted as days of residence in a place.

(5) Where an individual enters a place ("the second place") under paragraph (1) as a result of transfer from another place ("the first place") under that paragraph—

(a) the day of transfer is to be counted as a day of residence in the second place,

(b) for the purposes of calculating when the individual has been in the second place for 28 days for the purposes of regulations 19(2), 20(2) and 22(3)—

(i) the days that they were resident in the first place are to be treated as days of residence in the second place,

(ii) if they were resident in the first place for more than 28 days, the individual is to be treated as though they have been resident in the second place for 28 days on the day before the day of transfer, and

(c) the period of residence in the first place is deemed to end on the day on which the period of residence in the second place ends.

(6) For the purposes of this regulation, "days of residence" means days—

(a) resident in a care home in terms of regulation 19 or 24,

(b) as an in-patient in hospital or similar institution in terms of regulation 20 or 24, and

(c) in legal detention in terms of regulation 22 or 24.

Entitlement beginning while in alternative accommodation

1.113 **24.**—(1) This regulation applies where an individual is resident in a care home, an in-patient in a hospital or similar institution, or in legal detention on the day on which their entitlement to Pension Age Disability Payment begins.

(2) On and after that day, and for so long as the individual continues to reside in a place mentioned in paragraph (1), instead of the values set out in regulation 26 (amount and form of Pension Age Disability Payment), in respect of Pension Age Disability Payment, the individual is to be given the value of £0 where the individual is—

(a) resident in a care home,

(b) undergoing medical or other treatment as an in-patient in a hospital or similar institution where any of the costs of the treatment, accommodation and any related services provided for them are borne out of public funds within the meaning of regulation 20(4), or

(c) in legal detention.

(3) Paragraphs (1) and (2) do not apply where the individual is a resident in a care home, and the full costs of any qualifying services are met—

(a) entirely out of the resources of the individual for whom the qualifying services are provided,

(b) partly out of the resources of the individual for whom the qualifying services are provided and partly out of the resources of another person (other than a local authority) or assistance from a charity, or

(c) entirely out of the resources of another person (other than a local authority) or assistance from a charity.

Part 9

Making of applications and payments and duration of eligibility

Making payments

25.—(1) Where Pension Age Disability Payment is payable in respect of an individual, the Scottish Ministers may, where they consider it appropriate, make the payment to another person to be used for the benefit of the individual. 1.114

(2) Where the Scottish Ministers consider, for any reason, that it is no longer appropriate for a particular person who falls within paragraph (1) to continue to receive the payment, they may cease making payment to that person.

Amount and form of Pension Age Disability Payment

26.—(1) The weekly rate of payment of Pension Age Disability Payment is, where the individual is entitled to— 1.115

(a) the lower rate, £72.65, or

(b) the higher rate, £108.55.

(2) Where an individual is entitled to payment of Pension Age Disability Payment for a period shorter than one week, payment is to be made at one-seventh of the relevant weekly rate, for each day of entitlement.

(3) For any week where an individual is entitled to—

(a) Pension Age Disability Payment, and

(b) payment of an amount in respect of constant attendance under section 104 of the Social Security Contributions and Benefits Act 1992, section 104 of the Social Security Contributions and Benefits (Northern Ireland) Act 1992, or article 8 of the Naval, Military and Air Forces etc. (Disablement and Death) Service Pensions Order 2006,

the amount of Pension Age Disability Payment that is to be given to the individual is to be reduced by the amount paid under that section or article, as the case may be.

(4) For the purpose of calculating the amount of the Pension Age Disability Payment that is to be given to the individual, in accordance with paragraph (3), where the amount in respect of constant attendance is equal to or greater than the amount of Pension Age Disability Payment, the value of the Pension Age Disability Payment that is to be given to the individual is to be £0.

(5) Pension Age Disability Payment is only to be given in the form of money, except as provided for by regulation 36 (form of payment – giving Pension Age Disability Payment by way of deduction).

When an application is to be treated as made and beginning of entitlement to assistance

27.—(1) An application for Pension Age Disability Payment is to be treated as made— 1.116

(a) on the day it is received by the Scottish Ministers, or

(b) if applicable, on the day identified by the Scottish Ministers in accordance with paragraph (2).

(2) If, before making a determination on the basis of an application, the Scottish Ministers consider that the individual in respect of whom the application is made—

(a) would not satisfy a requirement in—

(i) regulation 5 (eligibility criteria: daytime and night-time condition and required period),

(ii) regulation 7 (entitlement to Pension Age Disability Payment when undergoing renal dialysis),

(iii) regulations 9 to 16 (residence and presence conditions), or

(iv) regulation 17 (age criteria),

if the application were treated as made on the day it was received, and

(b) would likely be entitled to receive Pension Age Disability Payment if those requirements were satisfied within a 26 week period beginning on the day it was received,

the Scottish Ministers may choose the date within that 26 week period on which the application is to be treated as made.

(3) Where, on the basis of an application, a determination is made that an individual is entitled to Pension Age Disability Payment, the date on which entitlement begins is to be identified in accordance with paragraphs (4) to (6).

(4) Where an application is made within 8 weeks of the day on which the full name and date of birth of an individual ("the required data") is submitted by, or on behalf of, the individual to the Scottish Ministers for the purpose of an application for Pension Age Disability Payment, entitlement begins on whichever is the later of the day—

(a) on which the required data was submitted, or

(b) identified in accordance with paragraph (2).

(5) Subject to paragraph (6), where an application is made after the 8 week period described in paragraph (4), entitlement begins on the day on which the application is treated as made in accordance with paragraph (1).

(6) Where the Scottish Ministers are satisfied that there is good reason why an application was made after the 8 week period described in paragraph (4), they may treat the application as having been made within that period.

(7) For the purposes of section 38(3) (application for assistance) of the 2018 Act, the period covered by an application for Pension Age Disability Payment—

(a) under paragraph (1)(a)—

(i) begins on the day on which the application is treated as having been made, and

(ii) ends on the day on which the determination of entitlement is made, and

(b) under paragraph (1)(b)—

(i) is deemed to begin on the day before the determination of entitlement is made provided that the requirements are satisfied, and

(ii) ends on the day on which the determination of entitlement is made.

Time of payment

1.117 **28.** Where an award of Pension Age Disability Payment is made, the Scottish Ministers are to make—

(a) the first payment of assistance on a date specified in the notice of determination, and
(b) any subsequent payment—
 (i) 4 weekly in arrears, or
 (ii) where regulation 18 (entitlement under special rules for terminal illness) applies, weekly in advance.

Continuing eligibility

29.—(1) Subject to paragraphs (3) and (4), a determination that an individual is entitled to Pension Age Disability Payment in respect of a period is to be made on the basis that the individual has an ongoing entitlement to Pension Age Disability Payment after the end of that period, except where paragraph (2) applies. **1.118**

(2) This paragraph applies where, after the end of the period mentioned in paragraph (1), the individual no longer satisfies the eligibility rules.

(3) A determination of ongoing entitlement is made on the basis that—
(a) the individual will continue to be entitled to Pension Age Disability Payment for a fixed or indefinite period as specified in the notice of determination, and
(b) the decision that the individual is entitled to Pension Age Disability Payment for each subsequent 4-week period is to be taken in accordance with these Regulations, on the strength of the assumptions set out in paragraph (4).

(4) The assumptions are that—
(a) the individual continues to satisfy the eligibility criteria which were satisfied to be entitled to Pension Age Disability Payment under the determination mentioned in paragraph (1),
(b) the information on which the determination mentioned in paragraph (1) was made still applies and is relevant in the individual's case, and
(c) there is no change in circumstances of the individual which would require to be notified under section 56 (duty to notify change of circumstances) of the 2018 Act.

Circumstances in which assistance may be suspended

30.—(1) The Scottish Ministers may decide that an individual who has an ongoing entitlement to Pension Age Disability Payment in respect of a period by virtue of regulation 29 (continuing eligibility) is not to become entitled to be given some or all of Pension Age Disability Payment at the time at which the individual otherwise would in accordance with that regulation, as read with regulation 28 (time of payment) (referred to in these Regulations as a decision to suspend the individual's Pension Age Disability Payment). **1.119**

(2) Where such a decision is made in respect of an individual, payments of Pension Age Disability Payment to that individual are to be suspended until such a time as the Scottish Ministers decide that the individual is once again to become entitled to be given Pension Age Disability Payment.

(3) The Scottish Ministers may decide to suspend an individual's Pension Age Disability Payment only in the circumstances where—
(a) section 54(1A) of the 2018 Act applies, or
(b) the Scottish Ministers have made arrangements (whether under section 85B of the 2018 Act (or otherwise) for a person to receive

the Pension Age Disability Payment on the individual's behalf, and the Scottish Ministers consider that it is necessary to suspend the Pension Age Disability Payment—

(i) in order to protect the individual from the risk of financial abuse, or

(ii) because the person with whom the Scottish Ministers have made arrangements is unable to continue to receive the Pension Age Disability Payment.

(4) In this regulation, "financial abuse" includes—

(a) having money or other property stolen,

(b) being defrauded,

(c) being put under pressure in relation to money or other property,

(d) having money or other property misused.

Having regard to financial circumstances

1.120 **31.** The Scottish Ministers must have regard to an individual's financial circumstances prior to making a decision to suspend payment to the individual of some or all of Pension Age Disability Payment.

Information to be given following suspension

1.121 **32.**—(1) Having made a decision to suspend an individual's Pension Age Disability Payment, the Scottish Ministers must inform the individual of—

(a) their decision to suspend the individual's Pension Age Disability Payment,

(b) the reasons for their decision,

(c) any steps which might be taken by the individual in order for the Scottish Ministers to consider ending the suspension, and

(d) the individual's right under regulation 33 to require the Scottish Ministers to review their decision to suspend the individual's Pension Age Disability Payment.

(2) The Scottish Ministers must fulfil their duty under paragraph (1) in a way that leaves the individual with a record of the information which the individual can show to, or otherwise share with, others.

Right to review suspension

1.122 **33.**—(1) An individual may require the Scottish Ministers to review their decision to suspend that individual's Pension Age Disability Payment.

(2) The Scottish Ministers must—

(a) complete a review mentioned in paragraph (1) within 31 days beginning with the day when they received notice from the individual requiring them to review their decision,

(b) inform the individual of the outcome of the review including reasons for their decision.

(3) The Scottish Ministers must fulfil their duty under paragraph (2)(b) in a way that leaves the individual with a record of the information which the individual can show to, or otherwise share with, others.

Ending a suspension

1.123 **34.** The Scottish Ministers are to make a decision to end a suspension where—

(a) the individual provides the information requested under section 54(1) of the 2018 Act and the Scottish Ministers consider that they do not require to make a determination without application,

(b) regulation 30(3)(a) applies and the Scottish Ministers make a determination without application under regulation 39 (consideration of entitlement after specified period), 40 (determination following change of circumstances etc.), 41 (determination following official error – underpayments), 42 (determination following error – overpayments) or 43 (determination to effect a deduction decision),

(c) the Scottish Ministers make a determination under section 54(2) of the 2018 Act,

(d) the circumstances mentioned in regulation 30(3)(b) no longer apply, or

(e) the Scottish Ministers consider it appropriate in the circumstances, including having regard to the financial circumstances of the individual.

Effect of suspension ending

35. When— **1.124**

(a) the suspension of an individual's Pension Age Disability Payment ends, and

(b) under the latest determination of the individual's entitlement to Pension Age Disability Payment relating to the period of the suspension the individual would have become entitled to be given Pension Age Disability Payment during that period,

the individual is immediately to be given the Pension Age Disability Payment that the individual would have become entitled to be given under the determination during the period of suspension.

Form of payment – giving Pension Age Disability Payment by way of deduction

36.—(1) Where an individual has a liability to the Scottish Ministers under section 63 of the 2018 Act (liability for assistance given in error), the individual's payment of Pension Age Disability Payment may be given (in whole or in part) by way of deduction, at a reasonable level, from that liability either— **1.125**

(a) with the agreement of the individual, or

(b) without the individual's agreement, where the individual has unreasonably refused to agree to the assistance being given in that form.

(2) For the purpose of paragraph (1), "reasonable level" means a level that is reasonable having regard to the financial circumstances of the individual.

When an increase in level of entitlement takes effect

37.—(1) Where, as a result of a determination without an application, the rate of Pension Age Disability Payment payable in respect of an individual is increased, the change takes effect— **1.126**

(a) in the case of an increase pursuant to a determination made under regulation 40(c) or 40(d) (determination following change of circumstances etc.) on the day after the day on which Attendance Allowance ceased to be paid in respect of the individual,

(b) in the case of an award of entitlement or increase pursuant to a determination made in accordance with regulation 40(a) that affects their eligibility under regulation 5 (eligibility criteria: daytime and night-time condition and required period), on the date when—
  (i) if as a result of the individual reporting the change—
    (aa) if the individual reports the change within one month of the change occurring, the individual first satisfies the requirements for the higher rate of Pension Age Disability Payment,
    (bb) if the individual reports the change within more than one month but not more than 13 months of the change occurring, the individual first satisfies the requirements for a higher rate of Pension Age Disability Payment, but only if the Scottish Ministers consider that the individual had good reason for not notifying the change within one month, or
    (cc) in any other case, the individual reports the change,
  (ii) if as a result of the Scottish Ministers becoming aware that a determination of an individual's entitlement was made in ignorance of a material fact, on the date when the Scottish Ministers make the determination,

(c) in the case of an earlier determination which was based on official error within the meaning of regulation 41 (determination following official error – underpayments) or on error within the meaning of regulation 42 (determination following error – overpayments), on the date when the earlier determination took effect,

(d) in the case of a determination made in accordance with regulation 40(a), where the period that an individual has been—
  (i) resident in a care home for the purpose of regulation 19,
  (ii) an in-patient in hospital or similar institution for the purpose of regulation 20,
  (iii) in legal detention for the purpose of regulation 22, or
  (iv) resident in a care home, an in-patient in a hospital or similar institution, or in legal detention for the purposes of regulation 24,

  has come to an end, on the day on which the individual leaves the place, or

(e) in any other case, on the date when the Scottish Ministers make the determination.

(2) Where the Scottish Ministers consider that in all the circumstances it would be unjust not to do so, they may, when making their determination, set an earlier date for the purposes of paragraph (1) (b), (c), (d) or (e).

(3) This regulation does not apply to an individual to whom regulation 18 (entitlement under special rules for terminal illness) applies.

(4) Where an individual has previously received Pension Age Disability Payment for a period and a determination without application has subsequently been made that the same individual is entitled to Pension Age Disability Payment at a higher rate for that period, that individual will be entitled to the difference between the value of entitlement to Pension Age Disability Payment under the subsequent determination and the value of Pension Age Disability Payment to which that individual was previously entitled for that period.

When a decrease in level or cessation of entitlement takes effect

38.—(1) Where, as a result of determination without an application, the rate of Pension Age Disability Payment payable in respect of an individual is decreased or their entitlement is ceased, the change takes effect— 1.127

(a) in the case of a decrease pursuant to a determination made under regulation 40(c) or 40(d) (determination following change of circumstances etc.) on the day after the day on which Attendance Allowance ceased to be paid in respect of the individual,

(b) in the case of a determination without application under regulation 39 or 40(a), on the date—

(i) where the individual was required to notify a change under section 56 of the 2018 Act, if the individual—

(aa) knowingly fails to notify a change, or

(bb) fails to notify the change as soon as reasonably practicable after it occurred,

the individual should have notified the Scottish Ministers of the change, or

(ii) in any other case, the Scottish Ministers make the determination,

(c) in the case of a determination under regulation 40(b), on the date of the individual's death,

(d) in the case of an earlier determination which was based on official error within the meaning of regulation 41 (determination following official error – underpayments) or on error within the meaning of regulation 42 (determination following error – overpayments), on the date when the earlier determination took effect,

(e) in any other case, on the date when the Scottish Ministers make the determination.

(2) Where the Scottish Ministers consider that in all the circumstances it would be unjust not to do so, they may, when making their determination, set a later date for the purposes of paragraph (1)(b), (c), (d) or (e).

PART 10

DETERMINATION OF ENTITLEMENT TO PENSION AGE DISABILITY PAYMENT WITHOUT APPLICATION

Consideration of entitlement after specified period

39. The Scottish Ministers must make a determination of an individual's entitlement to Pension Age Disability Payment, without receiving an application, after the end of the period specified (if any) in— 1.128

(a) the individual's notice of determination under section 40 or notice of re-determination under section 44 (as the case may be), or

(b) a determination made by the First-tier Tribunal for Scotland under section 49,

of the 2018 Act.

Determination following change of circumstances etc.

1.129 **40.** The Scottish Ministers must make a determination of an individual's entitlement to Pension Age Disability Payment, without receiving an application, where the individual has an ongoing entitlement to Pension Age Disability Payment and they become aware—

(a) of a change of circumstances, whether or not notified by the individual in accordance with section 56 of the 2018 Act, or where the Scottish Ministers become aware that a determination of an individual's entitlement was made in ignorance of a material fact, which would possibly result in an alteration to the rate of Pension Age Disability Payment payable to the individual or which is likely to mean that the individual is no longer entitled to Pension Age Disability Payment,

(b) that the individual has died,

(c) of an alteration of the rate of award of Attendance Allowance which the individual was entitled to immediately before the date of transfer to Pension Age Disability Payment in accordance with Part 3 of the schedule (Transfer from Attendance Allowance to Pension Age Disability Payment) as a result of a decision made pursuant to—

(i) a revision under regulation 3 of the Social Security and Child Support (Decisions and Appeals) Regulations 1999 ("the 1999 Regulations"),

(ii) a supersession under regulation 6 of the 1999 Regulations,

(iii) an appeal under section 12 of the Social Security Act 1998 ("the 1998 Act"),

(iv) a re-consideration under section 13 of the 1998 Act,

(v) an appeal to the Upper Tribunal under section 14 of the 1998 Act,

(vi) a revision under article 10 of the Social Security (Northern Ireland) Order 1998 ("the 1998 Order"),

(vii) a supersession under article 11 of the 1998 Order,

(viii) an appeal under article 13 of the 1998 Order, or

(ix) an appeal to the Commissioner under article 15 of the 1998 Order,

(d) of an alteration of the rate of award of Attendance Allowance which the individual was entitled to immediately before moving to Scotland in circumstances in which regulation 44 (individuals in respect of whom Attendance Allowance is paid in another part of the United Kingdom immediately before moving to Scotland) applies, as a result of a decision made pursuant to—

(i) a revision under regulation 3 of the 1999 Regulations,

(ii) a supersession under regulation 6 of the 1999 Regulations,

(iii) an appeal under section 12 of the 1998 Act,

(iv) a re-consideration under section 13 of the 1998 Act,

(v) an appeal to the Upper Tribunal under section 14 of the 1998 Act,

(vi) a revision under article 10 of the 1998 Order,

(vii) a supersession under article 11 of the 1998 Order,

(viii) an appeal under article 13 of the 1998 Order, or

(ix) an appeal to the Commissioner under article 15 of the 1998 Order.

Determination following official error – underpayments

41.—(1) The Scottish Ministers are to make a determination of an individual's entitlement to Pension Age Disability Payment, without receiving an application, where— 1.130

(a) they have previously made a determination of the individual's entitlement to Pension Age Disability Payment ("the original determination"),

(b) they establish that, due to an official error, the original determination was incorrect resulting in the individual—

(i) not being given an award of Pension Age Disability Payment, or

(ii) being given a lower award than that,

to which the individual was entitled,

(c) the Scottish Ministers are not considering a request for a re-determination of the individual's entitlement to Pension Age Disability Payment, and

(d) the individual has not appealed to the First-tier Tribunal for Scotland against the Scottish Ministers' determination of the individual's entitlement to Pension Age Disability Payment.

(2) In making a determination required by paragraph (1) the Scottish Ministers are to use—

(a) the information—

(i) provided in the application that led to the original determination,

(ii) they have obtained in connection with that application, and

(b) any other information they have obtained in connection with the individual's entitlement to Pension Age Disability Payment.

(3) In this regulation, "official error" means an error made by someone acting on behalf of the Scottish Ministers or on behalf of a Minister of the Crown that was not materially contributed to by anyone else.

Determination following error – overpayments

42.—(1) The Scottish Ministers are to make a determination of an individual's entitlement to Pension Age Disability Payment, without receiving an application, where— 1.131

(a) they have previously made a determination of the individual's entitlement to Pension Age Disability Payment ("the original determination"),

(b) they establish that, due to an error, the original determination was incorrect resulting in the individual being given—

(i) an award of Pension Age Disability Payment to which the individual was not entitled, or

(ii) a higher award than that to which the individual was entitled,

(c) the Scottish Ministers are not considering a request for a re-determination of the individual's entitlement to Pension Age Disability Payment, and

(d) the individual has not made an appeal to the First-tier Tribunal for Scotland or Upper Tribunal against the Scottish Ministers' determination of the individual's entitlement to Pension Age Disability Payment, that has not yet been determined.

(2) In making a determination required by paragraph (1) the Scottish Ministers are to use—

(a) the information—
(i) provided in the application that led to the original determination, and
(ii) they have obtained in connection with that application,
(b) any other information they have obtained in connection with the individual's entitlement to Pension Age Disability Payment, and
(c) any other information available to them that is relevant to their consideration of whether the individual is entitled to Pension Age Disability Payment.

(3) In this regulation references to an "error" are to—
(a) an error in the performance of a function conferred by these Regulations or the 2018 Act, including a determination being made—
(i) wrongly, or
(ii) correctly but on the basis of—
(aa) incorrect information, or
(bb) an assumption which proves to be wrong, or
(b) a new determination having not been made after an assumption on the basis of which an earlier determination was made has proven to be wrong.

Determination to effect a deduction decision

1.132 **43.**—(1) The Scottish Ministers are to make a determination of an individual's entitlement to Pension Age Disability Payment, without receiving an application, where the circumstances in paragraphs (2) and (3) apply.

(2) This paragraph applies where—
(a) regulation 36 (form of payment – giving Pension Age Disability Payment by way of deduction) allows Pension Age Disability Payment to be given to the individual by way of deduction, or
(b) Pension Age Disability Payment is being given to the individual by way of deduction, and the Scottish Ministers consider that may no longer be appropriate.

(3) This paragraph applies where the Scottish Ministers have decided to—
(a) vary the amount of Pension Age Disability Payment to be given by way of deduction (including introducing a deduction, where the full amount of Pension Age Disability Payment was previously given as money),
(b) vary any period for which the individual's Pension Age Disability Payment is to be given by way of deduction, that may have been specified in a previous determination of the individual's entitlement, or
(c) cease making deductions, and instead give the individual's Pension Age Disability Payment in the form of money.

(4) The Scottish Ministers are to make a determination, without receiving an application, where an individual who is receiving Pension Age Disability Payment by way of deduction under a previous determination of entitlement notifies the Scottish Ministers that the individual—
(a) withdraws their agreement to their Pension Age Disability Payment being given by way of deduction,

(b) wishes the Scottish Ministers to increase the amount of their Pension Age Disability Payment that is given by way of deduction,
(c) wishes the Scottish Ministers to decrease the amount of their Pension Age Disability Payment that is given by way of deduction (including ceasing the deduction), or
(d) wishes the Scottish Ministers to amend the length of any period referred to in paragraph (3)(b).

PART 11

MOVEMENT OF INDIVIDUALS BETWEEN SCOTLAND AND THE REST OF THE UNITED KINGDOM

Individuals in respect of whom Attendance Allowance is paid in another part of the United Kingdom immediately before moving to Scotland

44.—(1) Where an individual— 1.133
(a) becomes resident in Scotland,
(b) was resident in another part of the United Kingdom, and
(c) was entitled to Attendance Allowance immediately before the date of the move,

the Scottish Ministers are to make a determination without application of the individual's entitlement to Pension Age Disability Payment.

(2) Entitlement to Pension Age Disability Payment under paragraph (1) begins on the day after the day on which the individual's entitlement to Attendance Allowance ends.

(3) In this regulation, "the date of the move" is the date when the individual becomes resident in Scotland, as notified by the individual or otherwise communicated to the Scottish Ministers (whether the notification takes place before or after the date of the move).

Individuals in respect of whom Pension Age Disability Payment is paid at the time of moving to another part of the United Kingdom

45.—(1) Where the Scottish Ministers become aware that an individual 1.134
who is entitled to Pension Age Disability Payment has moved or is to move to become resident in another part of the United Kingdom, the individual is to be treated as though the individual meets the condition under regulation 9(1)(a) of being ordinarily resident in Scotland for a period of 13 weeks beginning in accordance with paragraph (4).

(2) Subject to Part 8 (effect of time spent in care homes, hospital and legal detention), where the Scottish Ministers become aware that an individual has moved or is to move to another part of the United Kingdom mentioned in paragraph (1), they are to make a determination without application at the end of the 13-week period mentioned in paragraph (1) that the individual's entitlement to Pension Age Disability Payment is to terminate.

(3) Where before the end of the 13-week period, the Scottish Ministers become aware that the individual is no longer to move to become resident

in another part of the United Kingdom, the duty in paragraph (2) does not apply.

(4) The 13-week period mentioned in paragraph (1) begins on the date the individual ceases to be ordinarily resident in Scotland.

(5) On the day after the 13-week period specified in paragraph (4) ends—

(a) entitlement to Pension Age Disability Payment ceases, and

(b) regulation 42 (determination following error – overpayments) applies to any Pension Age Disability Payment paid to an individual in relation to a period after the end of that 13-week period.

PART 12

PERIODS IN RESPECT OF A RE-DETERMINATION REQUEST

Periods in respect of a re-determination request

1.135 **46.**—(1) The period for requesting a re-determination of entitlement to Pension Age Disability Payment under section 41 of the 2018 Act (right to request re-determination) is 42 days beginning with the day that the individual is informed, in accordance with section 40 of the 2018 Act (notice of determination), of the right to make the request.

(2) In relation to determining entitlement to Pension Age Disability Payment, the period allowed for re-determination (within the meaning of section 43 of the 2018 Act (duty to re-determine)) is 56 days beginning with—

(a) the day that the request for a re-determination is received by the Scottish Ministers,

(b) in a case where the request for a re-determination is received by the Scottish Ministers outwith the period prescribed in paragraph (1), the day on which it is decided by the Scottish Ministers or (as the case may be) the First-tier Tribunal for Scotland that the individual in question has a good reason for not requesting a re-determination sooner, or

(c) in a case where the Scottish Ministers have informed the individual of their decision that the request for re-determination was not made in such form as the Scottish Ministers require, the day on which it is subsequently decided by the First-Tier Tribunal for Scotland that the individual in question has made the request in such form as the Scottish Ministers require.

PART 13

SHORT-TERM ASSISTANCE

Entitlement to short-term assistance

1.136 **47.** Part 1 of the schedule makes provision about short-term assistance.

PART 14

INITIAL PERIOD FOR APPLICATIONS

Initial period for applications

48. Part 2 of the schedule makes provision about the initial period for applications. 1.137

PART 15

TRANSFER FROM ATTENDANCE ALLOWANCE TO PENSION AGE DISABILITY PAYMENT

Transfer from Attendance Allowance to Pension Age Disability Payment

49. Part 3 of the schedule makes provision about transferring from Attendance Allowance to Pension Age Disability Payment. 1.138

PART 16

TRANSITORY PROVISION

Transitory provision – initial period for applications

50.—(1) During the initial period for applications, in addition to meeting the residence and presence conditions in Part 5, an individual must be resident in one of the local authority areas specified in relation to the relevant phase of that period in paragraph 6 of Part 2 of the schedule on the date their application is received by the Scottish Ministers. 1.139

(2) In this regulation and in Part 2 of the schedule, "initial period for applications" means the period beginning with 21 October 2024 and ending with 21 April 2025.

(3) The initial period for applications comprises two phases—

(a) phase 1, beginning with 21 October 2024 and ending with 23 March 2025, and

(b) phase 2, beginning with 24 March 2025 and ending with 21 April 2025.

Exclusion to transitory provision

51.—(1) An individual who has made a claim for Attendance Allowance prior to 21 October 2024 which has not yet been decided is not entitled to be paid Pension Age Disability Payment during the initial period for applications. 1.140

(2) In paragraph (1) a claim for Attendance Allowance is decided if it has—

(a) been decided by the Secretary of State under section 8 (decisions by Secretary of State) of the Social Security Act 1998,

(b) been withdrawn in accordance with regulation 5(2) of the Social Security (Claims and Payments) Regulations 1987, or

(c) otherwise is no longer to be decided by the Secretary of State as mentioned in sub-paragraph (a).

PART 17

CONSEQUENTIAL AMENDMENT

Consequential amendment

1.141 **52.** The amendment specified in Part 4 of the schedule has effect.

PART 18

MISCELLANEOUS AMENDMENTS

1.142 **53.** The amendments specified in Part 5 of the schedule have effect.

SCHEDULE

Regulation 47

PART 1

SHORT-TERM ASSISTANCE

Entitlement to short-term assistance

1.143 **1.**—(1) Subject to sub-paragraph (5) and (6), an individual who is, or was, entitled to Pension Age Disability Payment under a determination made on the basis that the individual has ongoing entitlement is entitled to short-term assistance where—

(a) that determination of the individual's entitlement to Pension Age Disability Payment ("the earlier determination") has been superseded by—

(i) a determination under section 37 (duty to make a determination) of the 2018 Act, or

(ii) if the earlier determination is a determination—

(aa) of an application for Pension Age Disability Payment,

(bb) without application of an individual's entitlement to Pension Age Disability Payment under paragraph 9 of Part 3 of this schedule (determination without application of entitlement to Pension Age Disability Payment), or

(cc) without application of an individual's entitlement to Pension Age Disability Payment under regulation 44(individuals to whom Attendance Allowance is paid moving to Scotland),

a determination under section 43 (Scottish Ministers' duty to re-determine) or section 49 (First-tier Tribunal's power to determine entitlement on appeal) of the 2018 Act,

(b) as a result of—

(i) the earlier determination being superseded as mentioned in sub-paragraph (1)(a), or

(ii) a later determination under section 43 or section 49 of the 2018 Act in relation to the individual's entitlement to Pension Age Disability Payment for the period to which the determination mentioned in sub-paragraph (1)(a)(i), or the earlier determination in sub-paragraph (1)(a)(ii), relates,
the individual—
(iii) is no longer entitled to Pension Age Disability Payment, or
(iv) is entitled to less Pension Age Disability Payment than they were under the earlier determination,

(c) the individual's entitlement to Pension Age Disability Payment is under review within the meaning of—
(i) paragraph 1(2) of schedule 10 of the 2018 Act, or
(ii) sub-paragraph (2), and

(d) the individual—
(i) continues to meet the conditions as to residence and presence set out in Part 5, or
(ii) has transferred to become resident in another part of the United Kingdom, and the matter under review is the determination of entitlement for the 13-week period beginning in accordance with regulation 45 (individuals in respect of whom Pension Age Disability Payment is paid at the time of moving to another part of the United Kingdom).

(2) An individual's entitlement to Pension Age Disability Payment is under review in terms of sub-paragraph (1)(c)(ii) if—

(a) a decision of the First-tier Tribunal for Scotland under section 49 of the 2018 Act, in relation to the individual's entitlement to Pension Age Disability Payment for the period to which the determination mentioned in sub-paragraph (1)(a)(i) or the earlier determination mentioned in sub-paragraph (1)(a)(ii) relates, is set aside after a review under section 43(2) of the Tribunals (Scotland) Act 2014 ("the 2014 Act"), and

(b) the First-tier Tribunal for Scotland decide not to uphold a determination of an individual's entitlement to Pension Age Disability Payment in an appeal under section 46 of the 2018 Act and the First-tier Tribunal for Scotland are to make a determination of the individual's entitlement to Pension Age Disability Payment under section 49 of the 2018 Act.

(3) Where—

(a) an individual's entitlement to Pension Age Disability Payment is set aside after a review in terms of sub-paragraph (2)(a), and

(b) the individual had previously been awarded short-term assistance on the basis that their entitlement to Pension Age Disability Payment was under review by the First-tier Tribunal prior to it making the decision that has been set aside,

the Scottish Ministers are to make a determination without application of the individual's entitlement to short-term assistance.

(4) Where—

(a) the First-tier Tribunal for Scotland set aside a decision by the Scottish Ministers not to accept a request for a re-determination of the individual's entitlement to Pension Age Disability Payment under the determination mentioned in sub-paragraph (1)(a)(i), and

(b) the Scottish Ministers had previously determined, pursuant to an application made by the individual, that the individual was not entitled to short-term assistance on the basis that the determination referred to in sub-paragraph (1)(a)(i) was not under review,

the Scottish Ministers are to make a determination without application of the individual's entitlement to short-term assistance.

(5) An individual is not entitled to short-term assistance where the individual is no longer entitled to Pension Age Disability Payment as a result of a subsequent determination made under regulation 40(b) (determination following change of circumstances etc.).

(6) An individual to whom regulation 19(2) (effect of admission to a care home on ongoing entitlement to Pension Age Disability Payment), regulation 20(2) (effect of admission to hospital on ongoing entitlement to Pension Age Disability Payment), regulation 22(3) (effect of legal detention on ongoing entitlement to Pension Age Disability Payment), or 24(2) (entitlement beginning while in alternative accommodation) applies is not entitled to short-term assistance in respect of Pension Age Disability Payment for which the value is to be £0 under those regulations.

(7) Where the Scottish Ministers have made a determination under section 37 of the 2018 Act (duty to make determination) that an individual is entitled to short-term assistance, entitlement to short-term assistance begins—

(a) where a request is made under section 41 of the 2018 Act (right to request re-determination) for a re-determination of the individual's entitlement to Pension Age Disability Payment for the period to which the determination mentioned in sub-paragraph (1)(a)(i) relates, on the day that request is made,

(b) where a notice of appeal is submitted under section 47 of the 2018 Act (initiating an appeal) against a determination of the individual's entitlement to Pension Age Disability Payment for the period to which the determination mentioned in sub-paragraph (1)(a)(i) or the earlier determination mentioned in sub-paragraph (1)(a)(ii) relates, on the day that request is made,

(c) where a decision of the Scottish Ministers is made not to accept a request for a re-determination of the individual's entitlement to Pension Age Disability Payment for the period to which the determination mentioned in sub-paragraph (1)(a)(i) relates, on the day that decision is set aside by the First-tier Tribunal for Scotland,

(d) where a request is made under section 48(1)(b) of the 2018 Act (deadline for appealing) for permission to appeal a determination of the individual's entitlement to Pension Age Disability Payment for the period to which the determination mentioned in sub-paragraph (1)(a)(i) or the earlier determination mentioned in sub-paragraph (1)(a)(ii) relates, on the day that request is made, or

(e) where a decision of the First-tier Tribunal for Scotland under section 49 of the 2018 Act, in relation to a determination of the individual's entitlement to Pension Age Disability Payment for the period to which the determination mentioned in sub-paragraph (1)(a)(i) or the earlier determination mentioned in sub-paragraph (1)(a)(ii) relates, is set aside after a review under section 43(2) of the 2014 Act (review of decisions) and the First-tier Tribunal for Scotland are to make a decision about the individual's entitlement to Pension Age Disability Payment under section 49 of the 2018 Act, on the day that the decision is set aside.

(8) Regulation 46 (periods in respect of a re-determination request) applies to short-term assistance in the same way as it applies to Pension Age Disability Payment.

(9) In this Part of the schedule "the earlier determination" has the meaning given in sub-paragraph (1)(a).

Value and form

1.144 **2.**—(1) The value of short-term assistance payable for any period is equal to V1-V2 where—

(a) V1 is the value of the Pension Age Disability Payment the individual would have been given in respect of the period under the earlier determination had the earlier determination not been superseded, and

(b) V2 is the value of the Pension Age Disability Payment that the individual is to be given in respect of the period under what is, at the time the individual becomes eligible for short-term assistance in respect of the period, the most recent determination of the individual's entitlement to Pension Age Disability Payment.

(2) The form in which the short-term assistance is to be given is to be the same as the form in which Pension Age Disability Payment was given under the earlier determination.

(3) Regulations 36 (form of payment - giving Pension Age Disability Payment by way of deduction), 41 (determination following official error – underpayments), 42 (determination following error – overpayments) and 43 (determination to effect a deduction decision) apply to short-term assistance in the same way as they apply to Pension Age Disability Payment.

End of entitlement

3.—(1) When an individual's entitlement to short-term assistance is to end under sub-paragraph (2), the Scottish Ministers are to make a determination without application.

(2) Entitlement to short-term assistance ends on the day—

(a) a determination of an individual's entitlement to short-term assistance is cancelled under section 26(2) of the 2018 Act (individual's right to stop receiving assistance),

(b) a re-determination of an individual's entitlement to Pension Age Disability Payment is made by the Scottish Ministers under section 43 of the 2018 Act (duty to re-determine),

(c) the First-tier Tribunal for Scotland makes a determination under section 49 of the 2018 Act (First-tier Tribunal's power to determine entitlement) in relation to the individual's entitlement to Pension Age Disability Payment for the period to which the determination mentioned in paragraph 1(1)(a)(i) or the earlier determination mentioned in paragraph 1(1)(a)(ii) relates,

(d) that the First-tier Tribunal for Scotland makes a determination to refuse permission under section 48(1)(b) of the 2018 Act (deadline for appealing) to bring an appeal against the determination of the individual's entitlement to Pension Age Disability

Payment for the period to which the determination mentioned in paragraph 1(1)(a)(i) or the earlier determination mentioned in paragraph 1(1)(a)(ii)(aa relates, or

(e) where the individual withdraws their application to bring an appeal against the determination of the individual's entitlement to Pension Age Disability Payment for the period to which the determination mentioned in paragraph 1(1)(a)(i) or the earlier determination mentioned in paragraph 1(1)(a)(ii) relates, on that day.

Reduction of Pension Age Disability Payment where short-term assistance is paid

4. Where an individual has received short-term assistance for a period and a determination is subsequently made that the individual is entitled to Pension Age Disability Payment for the same period, any payment of Pension Age Disability Payment to be made as a result of the subsequent determination for that period—

(a) where the individual is to be paid Pension Age Disability Payment at the same rate as or a lower rate than any short-term assistance and any Pension Age Disability Payment already paid to that individual for that period, is to be reduced to £0, and

(b) in any other case, is to be reduced by any short-term assistance and any Pension Age Disability Payment already paid to that individual for that period.

PART 2 — Regulation 48

INITIAL PERIOD FOR APPLICATIONS

Initial period for applications

5.—(1) These Regulations apply to an individual who is resident in one of the local authority areas mentioned in paragraph 6 when the individual makes an application for Pension Age Disability Payment during the initial period for applications. **1.145**

(2) An individual who is awarded Pension Age Disability Payment pursuant to an application made during the initial period for applications will continue to be entitled if that person moves to another local authority area in Scotland.

Local authority areas for initial period for applications

6. The local authority areas specified for the purposes of regulation 50 are—

(a) in phase 1, Argyll and Bute, Highland, Orkney Islands, City of Aberdeen, and Shetland Islands,

(b) in phase 2, Argyll and Bute, Highland, Orkney Islands, City of Aberdeen, Shetland Islands, Moray, Aberdeenshire, East Ayrshire, North Ayrshire, South Ayrshire, Western Isles, Stirling, Clackmannan, Falkirk, Fife, Angus, City of Dundee, and Perthshire and Kinross.

PART 3 — Regulation 49

TRANSFER FROM ATTENDANCE ALLOWANCE TO PENSION AGE DISABILITY PAYMENT

Interpretation

7. In this Part of the schedule— **1.146**

"date of transfer" means the date when a transferring individual's entitlement to Pension Age Disability Payment begins by virtue of a determination made under paragraph 9(1),

"relevant individual" means an individual—

(a) who has an award of Attendance Allowance who appears to the Scottish Ministers to be likely to be eligible for Pension Age Disability Payment,

(b) who is—

(i) ordinarily resident in Scotland, or

(ii) someone to whom regulation 9(4) (residence and presence conditions) or 14(2) (persons residing outside the United Kingdom to whom a relevant EU regulation applies) applies,

"sufficient" means a link to Scotland that is sufficiently close that regulations 9(4) or 14(2) would be incompatible with the applicable agreement mentioned in that regulation, if the relevant individual were not entitled to Pension Age Disability Payment, and

"transferring individual" means an individual on whom the Scottish Ministers have served a notice of intention to transfer in accordance with paragraph 8.

Notice of intention to transfer to Pension Age Disability Payment

8.—(1) The Scottish Ministers are to notify each relevant individual of their intention to transfer that individual's entitlement to disability assistance from an entitlement to Attendance Allowance to an entitlement to Pension Age Disability Payment.

(2) Notice under sub-paragraph (1) must—

(a) be given in a way that leaves the relevant individual with a record of the information which they can show to, or otherwise share with, others,

(b) inform the relevant individual that—

(i) they have been identified as a relevant individual for the purposes of transfer to Pension Age Disability Payment,

(ii) the Scottish Ministers will make a determination without application to transfer the individual's entitlement to Attendance Allowance to an entitlement to Pension Age Disability Payment within a period to be specified within the notice (the individual will be notified when the determination is made and informed about their award and start date of Pension Age Disability Payment), and

(iii) the individual's award of Attendance Allowance will cease—

(aa) immediately before the award of Pension Age Disability Payment begins, or

(bb) where a transferring individual was paid Attendance Allowance one week in advance and 3 weekly in arrears, the date one week after the date their entitlement to Pension Age Disability Payment begins.

(3) Where a notice under sub-paragraph (1) is given—

(a) to a transferring individual who, before a determination is made under paragraph 9(1), ceases to be ordinarily resident in Scotland, or

(b) in error where the individual is neither—

(i) ordinarily resident in Scotland, nor

(ii) an individual who is habitually resident in an EEA state, Gibraltar or Switzerland and has a genuine and sufficient link to Scotland,

the duty on the Scottish Ministers in paragraph 9(1) does not apply.

(4) Where sub-paragraph (3) applies in respect of an individual and a determination under paragraph 9(1) has not been made, the Scottish Ministers are to notify the individual that the duty on the Scottish Ministers in paragraph 9(1) does not apply.

Determination without application of entitlement to Pension Age Disability Payment

1.147 **9.**—(1) The Scottish Ministers are to make a determination without application in respect of a transferring individual of that individual's entitlement to Pension Age Disability Payment.

(2) Entitlement to Pension Age Disability Payment under a determination under sub-paragraph (1) begins on the date specified in the notice of determination given to the transferring individual in accordance with section 40 of the 2018 Act.

(3) The determination under sub-paragraph (1) is to be made on the basis of—

(a) such information as the Scottish Ministers have received from the Secretary of State for Work and Pensions in respect of the transferring individual's entitlement to Attendance Allowance, and

(b) any other information available to the Scottish Ministers that appears to them to be relevant.

(4) Subject to paragraph 11, a determination under sub-paragraph (1) must be made on the basis that the transferring individual is entitled to the rate of Pension Age Disability Payment that is equivalent to the rate of Attendance Allowance to which the individual was entitled immediately before the date of transfer.

(5) A determination under sub-paragraph (1)—

(a) may be made on the assumption that whatever can be discerned about the transferring individual's circumstances from the information mentioned in sub-paragraph (3) remains accurate on the date on which the determination is made,

(b) notwithstanding the generality of head (a), is to be made on the assumption that the conditions relating to residence and presence set out in regulations 9 to 16 (residence and presence conditions) are satisfied in the individual's case, and

(c) must be made not later than the end of the period specified within the notice under paragraph 8(1) unless the Scottish Ministers have—

(i) good reason to extend that period,

(ii) agreed the period for extension with the Secretary of State for Work and Pensions, and

(iii) notified the transferring individual of the extension and the reason for it.

Effect of determination on entitlement to Attendance Allowance

10.—(1) Where a determination is made under paragraph 9 that the transferring individual is entitled to Pension Age Disability Payment, the transferring individual's entitlement to Attendance Allowance will cease on—

(a) the date their entitlement to Pension Age Disability Payment begins, or
(b) where a transferring individual was paid Attendance Allowance one week in advance and 3 weekly in arrears, the date one week after the date their entitlement to Pension Age Disability Payment begins, or
(c) where paragraph 11 applies, the date their entitlement to Pension Age Disability Payment would have begun had paragraph 11(2) not applied to set an earlier date of entitlement.

(2) Where paragraph (1)(b) applies—
(a) section 64(1A) of the Social Security Contributions and Benefits Act 1992, and
(b) regulation 4(b) of these Regulations (entitlement to other benefits),

do not apply in respect of the first week of entitlement to Pension Age Disability Payment.

Exceptions to paragraph 9(4)

11.—(1) Where the Scottish Ministers have— **1.148**
(a) received information from the Secretary of State for Work and Pensions that the transferring individual is terminally ill in terms of section 82 of the Welfare Reform Act 2012 immediately before the date of transfer, or
(b) not received information from the Secretary of State for Work and Pensions that the transferring individual is terminally ill in terms of section 82 of the Welfare Reform Act 2012, but become aware, before they have made a determination under paragraph 9(1), that the individual has a terminal illness in terms of regulation 18(6) (entitlement under special rules for terminal illness),

the determination made under paragraph 9(1) must be made on the basis that the transferring individual satisfies the conditions for the higher rate of Pension Age Disability Payment.

(2) Where sub-paragraph (1) applies—
(a) paragraphs (3) to (5) of regulation 18 do not apply, and
(b) the transferring individual's entitlement to Pension Age Disability Payment will commence on whichever is the later of—
 (i) the date that these Regulations come into force,
 (ii) the day that the clinical judgement was made in accordance with regulation 18(6), or
 (iii) the day one year before the determination was made in accordance with paragraph 9(1).

(3) Where sub-paragraph (1)(a) applies, paragraphs (7), (8) and (9) of regulation 18 (entitlement under special rules for terminal illness) are to be treated as satisfied for the individual.

(4) Where sub-paragraph 2(b) applies—
(a) section 64(1A) of the Social Security Contributions and Benefits Act 1992, and
(b) regulation 4(b) of these Regulations (entitlement to other benefits),

do not apply in respect of the period between commencement of entitlement to Pension Age Disability Payment and cessation of entitlement to Attendance Allowance.

Modification of these Regulations: transferring individuals

12. These Regulations apply to a transferring individual on and after the date of transfer with the following modifications—
(a) regulation 10 (temporary absence from the common travel area) is to be read as if—
 (i) after paragraph (2) there is inserted—
  "(3) Where an individual is temporarily absent from the common travel area on the date of transfer, the period at paragraph (1)(a) or (b) is to commence on the date Scottish Ministers identify as the commencement of the temporary absence from the common travel area";
(b) regulation 18 (entitlement under special rules for terminal illness) is to be read as if paragraph (10) reads "Where an individual has previously received Pension Age Disability Payment or a benefit listed in paragraph (11)(a) for a period (during which period any payment of attendance allowance paid by virtue of paragraph 10(1)(b) of the schedule is disregarded) and a determination is subsequently made that the same individual is entitled to Pension Age Disability Payment at a higher rate for that period by virtue of paragraph 9(1) of the schedule, that individual will be entitled to the difference between the value of entitlement to Pension Age Disability Payment under the subsequent determination and the value of Pension Age Disability Payment or a benefit listed in paragraph (11)(a) to which that individual was previously entitled for that period.",
(c) regulation 24 (entitlement beginning while in alternative accommodation) is to be read as if—

(i) where a transferring individual is resident in legal detention on the date of transfer—
(aa) paragraph (1) reads "This regulation applies where an individual is in legal detention on the day on which their entitlement to Pension Age Disability Payment begins by virtue of a determination made under paragraph 9 of Part 3 of the schedule",
(bb) in paragraph (2) for "that day" reads "the day after the day on which the individual has been entitled to Pension Age Disability Payment for 28 days", and
(cc) in paragraph (2), sub-paragraphs (a), (b) and (c) are treated as omitted, and
(dd) paragraph (3) is treated as omitted,
(ee) after paragraph (2) there is inserted—
"(3) For the purposes of this regulation, an individual is to be treated as though they are not in legal detention on any day on which they are an in-patient in a hospital or in a hospice.",
(ii) where a transferring individual is resident in a care home or is undergoing medical or other treatment as an in-patient at a hospital or similar institution and any of the costs of the treatment, accommodation and any related services provided for them are borne out of public funds—
(aa) in paragraph (1)—
(bb) after "begins" there are the words "by virtue of a determination made under paragraph 9 of Part 3 of the schedule", and
(cc) after "similar institution", omit ", or in legal detention",
(dd) in paragraph (2)—
(ee) for "On and after that day" substitute "On the day after the day on which the individual has been resident in a care home or an in-patient in a hospital or similar institution for 28 days (which period of 28 days includes days before the date of transfer and is calculated in accordance with regulation 19(3) or 20(3))",
(ff) in head (ii) of sub-paragraph (b), after "of regulation 3(4)" for ", or" substitute ".", and
(gg) sub-paragraph (c) is treated as omitted,
(d) regulation 27 (when an application is to be treated as made and beginning of entitlement to assistance) is treated as omitted,
(e) in regulation 28 (time of payment), for sub-paragraph (b), substitute—
"(b) any subsequent payment—
(i) 4 weekly in arrears,
(ii) weekly in advance, or
(iii) where the Scottish Ministers consider that it would be unjust not to do so, at such intervals as may be specified in the notice of determination.",
(f) in regulation 37 (when an increase in level of entitlement takes effect)—
(i) paragraph (4) is to be read as if after "Where an individual has previously received" and "the subsequent determination and the value of" there is inserted "Attendance Allowance or", and
(ii) after paragraph (4) there is inserted—
"(5) Where paragraph (4) applies—
(a) section 64(1A) of the Social Security Contributions and Benefits Act 1992, and
(b) regulation 4(b) of these Regulations (entitlement to other benefits),

do not apply in respect of the period between commencement of entitlement to Pension Age Disability Payment and cessation of entitlement to Attendance Allowance.".

Appointees

13.—(1) A person appointed by the Secretary of State for Work and Pensions under regulation 33 of the Social Security (Claims and Payments) Regulations 1987 to receive Attendance Allowance on behalf of a transferring individual is to be treated on and after the date of transfer as though appointed by the Scottish Ministers to act on behalf of that transferring individual under section 85B of the 2018 Act.

(2) As soon as reasonably practicable after the date of transfer, the Scottish Ministers must—

(a) consider whether the conditions for making an appointment in respect of the transferring individual are met (having regard to section 85B(3) of the 2018 Act),

(b) consider whether to terminate the appointment that is treated as having been made by virtue of sub-paragraph (1) and terminate it if they consider it appropriate, and

(c) if they have terminated an appointment in pursuance of head (b), appoint under section 85B of the 2018 Act another person to act on the transferring individual's behalf if they consider it appropriate to do so.

(3) The duty in sub-paragraph (2) does not apply where the Scottish Ministers have already appointed the person mentioned in sub-paragraph (1) to act on behalf of that transferring individual under section 85B of the 2018 Act.

PART 4 Regulation 52

CONSEQUENTIAL AMENDMENT

14.—(1) The Social Security Contributions and Benefits Act 1992 is amended in accordance with paragraph (2). **1.149**

(2) In section 70(2) (carer's allowance), after "child disability payment by virtue of entitlement to the care component at the middle or highest rate" insert "or pension age disability payment".

PART 5 Regulation 53

MISCELLANEOUS AMENDMENTS

15.—(1) The Disability Assistance for Children and Young People (Scotland) Regulations are amended as follows. **1.150**

(2) In regulation 2 (interpretation - general) in the definition of "hospice" after paragraph (c) insert—

"(ca) a hospital or similar institution under the Health and Personal Social Services (Northern Ireland) Order 1972 or the Health and Personal Services (Northern Ireland) Order 1991,".

(3) In paragraph 1 of the schedule (entitlement to short-term assistance)—

(a) for sub-paragraph (1) substitute—

"(1) Subject to sub-paragraph (2) or (3), an individual who is, or was, entitled to Child Disability Payment under a determination made on the basis that the individual has ongoing entitlement is entitled to short-term assistance where—

(a) that determination of the individual's entitlement to Child Disability Payment ("the earlier determination") has been superseded by—

(i) a determination under section 37 (duty to make a determination) of the 2018 Act, or

(ii) if the earlier determination is a determination—

(aa) of an application for Child Disability Payment,

(bb) without application of an individual's entitlement to Child Disability Payment under paragraph 9 of this schedule (determination without application of entitlement to Child Disability Payment),

(cc) without application of an individual's entitlement to Child Disability Payment under regulation 35 (individuals in respect of whom Disability Living Allowance is paid in another part of the United Kingdom immediately before moving to Scotland),

a determination under section 43 (Scottish Ministers' duty to re-determine) or section 49 (First-tier Tribunal's power to determine entitlement on appeal) of the 2018 Act

(b) as a result of—

(i) the earlier determination being superseded as mentioned in sub-paragraph (1)(a), or

(ii) a later determination under section 43 or section 49 of the 2018 Act in relation to the individual's entitlement to Child Disability Payment for the period to which the determination mentioned in sub-paragraph (1)(a)(i), or the earlier determination mentioned in sub-paragraph (1)(a)(ii), relates,

the individual—

(iii) is no longer entitled to Child Disability Payment, or

(iv) is entitled to less Child Disability Payment than they were under the earlier determination,

(c) the individual's entitlement to Child Disability Payment is under review within the meaning of—

(i) paragraph 1(2) of schedule 10 of the 2018 Act, or
(ii) sub-paragraph (1A), and
(d) the individual—
(i) continues to meet the conditions as to residence and presence set out in regulations 5 to 9A, or
(ii) has transferred to become resident in another part of the United Kingdom, and the matter under review is the determination of entitlement for the 13-week period beginning in accordance with regulation 36 (individuals in respect of whom Child Disability Payment is paid at the time of moving to another part of the United Kingdom).",
(b) in sub-paragraph (1A) for "(1)(b)(ii)" substitute "(1)(c)(ii)",
(c) in sub-paragraph (1A)(a) for "subsequent determination of the individual's entitlement to Child Disability Payment mentioned in paragraph 1(1)(a)" substitute "individual's entitlement to Child Disability Payment for the period to which the determination mentioned in sub-paragraph (1)(a)(i) or the earlier determination mentioned in sub-paragraph (1)(a)(ii) relates",
(d) in sub-paragraph (1C) for "the subsequent determination of the individual's entitlement to Child Disability Payment mentioned in sub-paragraph (1)(a)" substitute "the individuals' entitlement to Child Disability Payment for the period to which the determination mentioned in sub-paragraph (1)(a)(i) relates",
(e) in sub-paragraph (1C) for "subsequent determination" as it appears in the second instance substitute "individual's entitlement to Child Disability Payment for the period to which the determination mentioned in sub-paragraph (1)(a)(i) relates",
(f) in sub-paragraphs (4)(a) to (e), after "Payment" insert "for the period to which the determination",
(g) in sub-paragraphs (4)(a) and (c), after "(1)(a)" insert "(i) relates",
(h) in sub-paragraphs (4)(b) and (d), for "the determination" as it appears in the first instance substitute "a determination",
(i) in sub-paragraphs (4)(b), (d) and (e) after "(1)(a)" insert "(i) or the earlier determination mentioned in sub-paragraph (1)(a)(ii) relates",
(j) in sub-paragraph (4)(e), for "the subsequent" substitute "a" and for "make a determination of" substitute "make a decision about",
(k) After sub-paragraph (5) insert—
"(6) In this part of the schedule "the earlier determination" has the meaning given in sub-paragraph (1)(a).".

(4) In paragraph 2 of the schedule (value and form) for sub-paragraph (1) substitute—
"(1) The value of short-term assistance payable for any period is equal to V1-V2 where—
(a) V1 is the value of the Child Disability Payment the individual would have been given in respect of the period under the earlier determination had the earlier determination not been superseded, and
(b) V2 is the value of the Child Disability Payment that the individual is to be given in respect of the period under what is, at the time the individual becomes eligible for short-term assistance in respect of the period, the most recent determination of the individual's entitlement to Child Disability Payment.".

(5) In paragraph 3 of the schedule (end of entitlement)—
(a) in sub-paragraph (1)(c) omit "the subsequent determination of",
(b) in sub-paragraphs (1)(c), (d) and (e),
(i) after "Payment" insert "for the period to which the determination",
(ii) after "1(1)(a)" insert "(i) or the earlier determination mentioned in paragraph 1(1)(a)(ii) relates,
(c) in sub-paragraphs (1)(d) and (e), for "the subsequent" substitute "a".

16.—(1) The Disability Assistance for Working Age People (Scotland) Regulations 2022 are amended as follows.

(2) In regulation 28 (effect of admission to hospital on ongoing entitlement to Adult Disability Payment), in paragraph (4)(a)—
(a) at the end of head (ii) omit "or",
(b) after head (iii) insert—
"(iv) a hospital or similar institution under the Health and Personal Social Services (Northern Ireland) Order 1972 or the Health and Personal Social Services (Northern Ireland) Order 1991,".

(3) In regulation 29 (exception: hospices), after paragraph (2)(c) insert—

"(ca) a hospital or similar institution under the Health and Personal Social Services (Northern Ireland) Order 1972 or the Health and Personal Social Services (Northern Ireland) Order 1991,".

(4) In paragraph 1 of schedule 2 (entitlement to short-term assistance)—

(a) for sub-paragraph (1) substitute—

"(1) Subject to sub-paragraph (5) and (6), an individual who is, or was, entitled to Disability Payment under a determination made on the basis that the individual has ongoing entitlement is entitled to short-term assistance where—

(a) that determination of the individual's entitlement to Adult Disability Payment ("the earlier determination") has been superseded by—

(i) a determination under section 37 of the 2018 Act, or

(ii) if the earlier determination is a determination—

(aa) of an application for Adult Disability Payment,

(bb) without application of an individual's entitlement to Adult Disability Payment under paragraph 9 of this schedule (determination without application of entitlement to Adult Disability Payment),

(cc) without application of an individual's entitlement to Adult Disability Payment under regulation 52 (individuals in respect of whom Personal Independence Payment is paid in another part of the United Kingdom immediately before moving to Scotland),

(dd) without application of an individual's entitlement to Adult Disability payment under regulation 4 (transfer determination without application of entitlement to Adult Disability Payment) of the Disability Assistance for Working Age People (Transitional Provisions and Miscellaneous Amendment) (Scotland) Regulations 2022,

a determination under section 43 (Scottish Ministers' duty to re-determine) or section 49 (First-tier Tribunal's power to determine entitlement on appeal) of the 2018 Act,

(b) as a result of—

(i) the earlier determination being superseded as mentioned in sub-paragraph (1)(a), or

(ii) a later determination under section 43 or section 49 of the 2018 Act in relation to the individual's entitlement to Adult Disability Payment for the period to which the determination mentioned in sub-paragraph (1)(a)(i) or the earlier determination mentioned in sub-paragraph (1)(a)(ii) relates,

the individual—

(iii) is no longer entitled to Adult Disability Payment, or

(iv) is entitled to less Adult Disability Payment than they were under the earlier determination,

(c) the individual's entitlement to Adult Disability Payment is under review within the meaning of—

(i) paragraph 1(2) of schedule 10 of the 2018 Act, or

(ii) sub-paragraph (2), and

(d) the individual—

(i) continues to meet the conditions as to residence and presence set out in Part 5, or

(ii) has transferred to become resident in another part of the United Kingdom, and the matter under review is the determination of entitlement for the 13-week period beginning in accordance with regulation 53 (individuals in respect of whom Adult Disability Payment is paid at the time of moving to another part of the United Kingdom).",

(b) in sub-paragraph (2) for "(1)(b)(ii)" substitute "(1)(c)(ii)",

(c) in sub-paragraph (2)(a) for "subsequent determination of the individual's entitlement to Adult Disability Payment mentioned in sub-paragraph (1)(a)" substitute "individual's entitlement to Adult Disability Payment for the period to which the determination mentioned in sub-paragraph (1)(a)(i) or the earlier determination mentioned in sub-paragraph (1)(a)(ii) relates",

(d) in sub-paragraph (4)(a) after "(1)(a)" insert "(i)",

(e) in sub-paragraph (4)(b) for "subsequent determination referred to in sub-paragraph (1)(a)" substitute "determination mentioned in sub-paragraph (1)(a)(i)",

(f) in sub-paragraphs (7)(a) to (e), after "Payment" insert "for the period to which the determination",

(g) in sub-paragraphs (7)(a) and (c), after "(1)(a)" insert "(i) relates",

(h) in sub-paragraphs (7)(b) and (d), for "the determination" as it appears in the first instance substitute "a determination"
(i) in sub-paragraphs (7)(b), (d) and (e), after "(1)(a)" insert "(i) or the earlier determination mentioned in sub-paragraph (1)(a)(ii) relates",
(j) in sub-paragraph (7)(e), for "the subsequent" substitute "a" and for "make a determination of" substitute "make a decision about", and
(k) after sub-paragraph (5) insert—
"(6) In this part of the schedule "the earlier determination" has the meaning given in sub-paragraph (1)(a).".

(5) In paragraph 2 of schedule 2 (value and form) for sub-paragraph (1) substitute—
"(1) The value of short-term assistance payable for any period is equal to V1-V2 where—
(a) V1 is the value of the Adult Disability Payment the individual would have been given in respect of the period under the earlier determination had the earlier determination not been superseded, and
(b) V2 is the value of the Adult Disability Payment that the individual is to be given in respect of the period under what is, at the time the individual becomes eligible for short-term assistance in respect of the period, the most recent determination of the individual's entitlement to Adult Disability Payment.".

(6) In paragraph 3 of the schedule (end of entitlement)—
(a) in sub-paragraph (2)(c) omit "the subsequent determination of",
(b) in sub-paragraphs (2)(c), (d) and (e),
   (i) after "1(1)(a)" insert "(i) or the earlier determination mentioned in paragraph 1(1)(a)(ii) relates", and
   (ii) after "Payment" insert "for the period to which the determination",
(c) in sub-paragraphs (2)(d) and (e), omit "subsequent".

PART II

UPDATING MATERIAL

VOLUME I
NON MEANS TESTED BENEFITS

Commentary by

Ian Hooker

John Mesher

Edward Mitchell

Christopher Ward

Nick Wikeley

p.28, *amendment to the Social Security Contributions and Benefits Act 1992 s.1(6) (Outline of contributory system)*

With effect from April 6, 2024, reg.5(1) of the Social Security (Class 2 National Insurance Contributions) (Consequential Amendments and Savings) Regulations 2024 (SI 2024/377) amended s.1(6) by inserting after sub-para.(a) the following new sub-paragraph: **2.001**

"(aa) be treated under section 11(5B) as having actually paid Class 2 contributions unless he fulfils such conditions;".

p.103, *amendment to the Social Security Contributions and Benefits Act 1992 s.64(1A) (attendance allowance) (entitlement)*

With effect from October 21, 2024, art.2(2) of the Social Security (Scotland) Act 2018 (Disability Assistance) (Consequential Modifications) Order 2024 (SI 2024/1048) amended s.64(1A) by inserting after para. (b) the following (note this amendment applies to England & Wales and Scotland): **2.002**

"(c) pension age disability payment."

p.112, *amendment to the Social Security Contributions and Benefits Act 1992 s.70(2) (carer's allowance)*

With effect from October 21, 2024, art.4 of the Social Security (Scotland) Act 2018 (Disability Assistance) (Consequential Modifications) Order 2024 (SI 2024/1048) amended s.70(2) by inserting "or pension age disability payment" after the words "middle or highest rate". Note this regulation applies only to England & Wales. The same amendment and from the same date is effected for Scotland by Pt 4 of the Schedule to the Disability Assistance for Older People (Scotland) Regulations 2024 (SSI 2024/166). **2.003**

p.122, *amendment to the Social Security Contributions and Benefits Act 1992 s.71(7) (disability living allowance)*

With effect from October 21, 2024, art.2(3) of the Social Security (Scotland) Act 2018 (Disability Assistance) (Consequential Modifications) Order 2024 (SI 2024/1048) amended s.71(7) by inserting "pension age disability payment," after the words "they are entitled to". Note this amendment applies to England & Wales and Scotland. **2.004**

pp.231–233, *General Note on Reciprocal agreements*

The Social Security (Gibraltar) Order 2024 (SI 2024/149) introduced a new reciprocal agreement with Gibraltar, which became effective from June 1, 2024. **2.005**

p.241, *amendment to the Social Security Contributions and Benefits Act 1992 s.122 (Interpretation of Parts I to VI and supplementary provisions)*

With effect from October 21, 2024, art.2(4) of the Social Security (Scotland) Act 2018 (Disability Assistance) (Consequential Modifications) **2.006**

Order 2024 (SI 2024/1048) inserted after the definition of "payments by way of occupational or personal pension" the following definition (note this amendment applies to England & Wales and Scotland):

""pension age disability payment" means disability assistance given in accordance with the Disability Assistance for Older People (Scotland) Regulations 2024);".

p.247, *amendment to the Social Security Contributions and Benefits Act 1992 s.150(2) (interpretation of Part X)*

2.007 With effect from October 21, 2024, art.2(5) of the Social Security (Scotland) Act 2018 (Disability Assistance) (Consequential Modifications) Order 2024 (SI 2024/1048) amended s.150(2) by inserting after para.(g) in the definition of "attendance allowance" the following—

"(h) pension age disability payment given in accordance with the Disability Assistance for Older People (Scotland) Regulations 2024;".

Note this amendment applies to England & Wales and Scotland.

pp.366–367, *annotation to the Jobseekers Act 1995 s.6F (Imposition of work-related requirements)*

2.008 Note, in relation to what must be done for a requirement to be imposed, the endorsement and application in *SB v SSWP (ESA)* [2024] UKUT 372 (AAC) of the general principles set out by Judge Poynter in paras 76 and 77 of *PPE v SSWP (ESA)* [2020] UKUT 59, that for the Secretary of State to impose a legal obligation on a claimant to do something they must use "the language of clear and unambiguous mandatory requirement", not merely that of inviting, advising or encouraging. In *SB* the claimant was invited to a medical examination in a letter that warned that a consequence of failing without good cause to attend could be loss of his ESA award, but failed to warn that that consequence could also follow under the relevant regulation from a failure without good cause to "submit to" the examination. Judge Wikeley accepted the Secretary of State's submission that the letter accordingly did not meet the *PPE* principles. That approach is plainly relevant where the legal provision is not merely to attend an interview or course, but to participate in it.

p.527, *amendment to the Welfare Reform Act 2012 s.77(4) (personal independence payment)*

2.009 With effect from October 21, 2024, art.3(2) of the Social Security (Scotland) Act 2018 (Disability Assistance) (Consequential Modifications) Order 2024 (SI 2024/1048) amended s.77(4) by inserting "pension age disability payment," after the words "they are entitled to". Note this amendment applies to England & Wales and Scotland.

p.540, *amendment to the Welfare Reform Act 2012 s.95 (interpretation of Part 4)*

2.010 With effect from October 21, 2024, art.3(3) of the Social Security (Scotland) Act 2018 (Disability Assistance) (Consequential Modifications)

Order 2024 (SI 2024/1048) amended s.95 by inserting after the definition of "mobility component" the following—

> ""pension age disability payment" means disability assistance given in accordance with the Disability Assistance for Older People (Scotland) Regulations 2024;".

Note this amendment applies to England & Wales and Scotland.

p.569, *annotation to the Pensions Act 2014 s.30 (Bereavement support payment)*

An appeal against the decision of Judge Ward in *HM v SSWP (BB); MK v SSWP (BB)* [2023] UKUT 15 (AAC) has been dismissed by the Court of Appeal though for slightly different reasons—see *Margaret Kelly v SSWP* [2024] EWCA Civ 613. **2.011**

p.643, *amendment to the Social Security (Crediting and Treatment of Contributions, and National Insurance Numbers) Regulations 2001 (SI 2001/769) reg.1 (Citation, commencement and interpretation)*

With effect from April 6, 2024, reg.2(2) of the Social Security (Class 2 National Insurance Contributions) (Consequential Amendments and Savings) Regulations 2024 (SI 2024/377) amended para.(b) of the definition of "due date" by inserting "or is treated as having actually paid as a result of s.11(5B) of the Act" after "entitled to pay". **2.012**

p.645, *amendment to the Social Security (Crediting and Treatment of Contributions, and National Insurance Numbers) Regulations 2001 (SI 2001/769) reg.4 (Treatment for the purpose of any contributory benefit of late paid contributions)*

With effect from April 6, 2024, reg.2(3) of the Social Security (Class 2 National Insurance Contributions) (Consequential Amendments and Savings) Regulations 2024 (SI 2024/377) amended reg.4 by inserting "4A and" after "provisions of regulations" in para.(1), omitting the "or" at the end of para.(1) and inserting after para.(3)(a)(ii) the following new sub-paragraph: **2.013**

> "(iii) following the year in respect of which the person is treated as having actually paid the contribution (as a result of section 11(5B) of the Act)."

p.647, *amendment to the Social Security (Crediting and Treatment of Contributions, and National Insurance Numbers) Regulations 2001 (SI 2001/769) by insertion of new reg.4A (Treatment for the purpose of any contributory benefit of Class 2 contributions treated as paid where relevant profits notified late)*

With effect from April 6, 2024, reg.2(4) of the Social Security (Class 2 National Insurance Contributions) (Consequential Amendments and Savings) Regulations 2024 (SI 2024/377) inserted after reg.4 a new reg.4A as follows: **2.014**

Treatment for the purpose of any contributory benefit of Class 2 contributions treated as paid where relevant profits notified late

4A.—(1) For the purposes of entitlement to any contributory benefit, this regulation applies to a person if—

(a) the person has relevant profits for a tax year of, or exceeding, the small profits threshold, and

(b) the person has not made a relevant profits return for that tax year by the date on which the return is required to be made.

(2) The Class 2 contributions that the person is treated as having actually paid for the tax year (as a result of section 11(5B) of the Act) are to be treated as having been paid on the day on which a relevant profits return for the tax year is made.

(3) For the purposes of this regulation—

"relevant profits" has the meaning given by section 11(3) of the Act;

"relevant profits return" in relation to a tax year means—

(a) a return under section 8 of the Taxes Management Act 1970 that includes relevant profits for that tax year, or

(b) a notification to His Majesty's Revenue and Customs of relevant profits for that tax year that is required by, and made in accordance with, any other enactment."

pp.675–678, *annotation to the Social Security Benefit (Computation of Earnings) Regulations 1996 (SI 1996/2745)—General Note*

2.015 The FTT is not confined to reviewing the rationality of SSWP's exercise of the discretion under reg.8(3) but must itself consider whether the discretion under reg.8(3) should be exercised: *SL v SSWP (CA)* [2024] UKUT 228 (AAC).

pp.744–745, *amendments to the Social Security Benefit (Persons Abroad) Regulations 1975 (SI 1975/563) reg.2 (Modification of the Act in relation to incapacity benefit, severe disablement allowance, unemployability supplement and maternity allowance)*

2.016 With effect from October 21, 2024, art.3 of the Social Security (Scotland) Act 2018 (Disability Assistance) (Consequential Amendments) Order 2024 (SI 2024/919) made the following amendments:

(a) in paragraph (1A)—

(i) for "or personal independence payment" substitute ", personal independence payment";

(ii) after "2012" insert "or Scottish disability assistance";

(b) at the end of paragraph (5)(b) omit "and";

(c) after paragraph (5)(b) insert—

"(ba) "Scottish disability assistance" means disability assistance given in accordance with regulations made under section 31 of the Social Security (Scotland) Act 2018; and".

p.782, *annotation to the Social Security (Attendance Allowance) Regulations 1991 (SI 1991/2740) reg.2 (Conditions as to residence and presence in Great Britain)*

2.017 Note that following the introduction of disability assistance for working age people in Scotland, a person in receipt of that benefit who has moved to England & Wales cannot apply for attendance allowance for a period of 13 weeks during which he is deemed to remain in Scotland.

Note too that following the introduction of pension age disability payment in Scotland, a person who qualifies for that benefit will not be able to claim attendance allowance. (See reg.14 of the Disability Assistance for Older People (Consequential Amendment and Transitional Provision) (Scotland) Regulations (SSI 2024/141)). And a person in receipt of that benefit in Scotland who moves to live in England or Wales will be treated as remaining in Scotland for the same 13-week period. (See Disability for Older People (Scotland) Regulations 2024 Pt 11 (SSI 2024/166)).

p.782, *amendment to the Social Security (Attendance Allowance) Regulations 1991 (SI 1991/2740) reg.2A (Persons residing in Great Britain to whom a relevant EU Regulation applies)*

With effect from November 7, 2024, reg.3(2) of Social Security (Genuine and Sufficient Link to the United Kingdom) (Amendment) Regulations (SI 2024/936) amended reg.2A by omitting the words "social security system" in para.(1)(c). Note that this regulation applies only to England & Wales. The same amendment with effect from the same date is made in respect of Scotland by reg.3(2) of the Social Security (Genuine and Sufficient Link to the United Kingdom) (Miscellaneous Amendment) (Scotland) Regulations 2024 (SSI 2024/241). **2.018**

p.783, *amendment to the Social Security (Attendance Allowance) Regulations 1991 (SI 1991/2740) reg.2B (Persons residing in an EEA state or in Switzerland to whom a relevant EU Regulation applies)*

With effect from November 7, 2024, reg.3(3) of Social Security (Genuine and Sufficient Link to the United Kingdom) (Amendment) Regulations (SI 2024/936) amended reg.2B by omitting the words "social security system" in para.(c). Note that this regulation applies only to England & Wales. The same amendment with effect from the same date is made in respect of Scotland by reg.3(3) of the Social Security (Genuine and Sufficient Link to the United Kingdom) (Miscellaneous Amendment) (Scotland) Regulations 2024 (SSI 2024/241). **2.019**

p.805, *amendment to the Social Security (Disability Living Allowance) Regulations 1991 (SI 1991/2890) reg.2A (Persons residing in Great Britain to whom a relevant EU Regulation applies)*

With effect from November 7, 2024, reg.4(2) of Social Security (Genuine and Sufficient Link to the United Kingdom) (Amendment) Regulations (SI 2024/936) amended reg.2A by omitting the words "social security system" in para.(1)(c). Note that this regulation applies only to England & Wales. The same amendment with effect from the same date is made in respect of Scotland by reg.4(2) of the Social Security (Genuine and Sufficient Link to the United Kingdom) (Miscellaneous Amendment) (Scotland) Regulations 2024 (SSI 2024/241). **2.020**

p.806, *amendment to the Social Security (Disability Living Allowance) Regulations 1991 (SI 1991/2890) reg.2B (Persons residing in an EEA state or in Switzerland to whom a relevant EU Regulation applies)*

2.021 With effect from November 7, 2024, reg.4(3) of Social Security (Genuine and Sufficient Link to the United Kingdom) (Amendment) Regulations (SI 2024/936) amended reg.2B by omitting the words "social security system" in para.(c). Note that this regulation applies only to England & Wales. The same amendment with effect from the same date is made in respect of Scotland by reg.4(3) of the Social Security (Genuine and Sufficient Link to the United Kingdom) (Miscellaneous Amendment) (Scotland) Regulations 2024 (SSI 2024/241).

p.854, *annotation to the Social Security (Disability Living Allowance) Regulations 1991 (SI 1991/2890) reg.12 (Entitlement to the mobility component)*

2.022 The requirements of reg.12(6) have been considered again by a Social Security Commissioner in Northern Ireland. An appeal was allowed on the ground that the FTT had failed to consider all of the evidence relating to the test of severe behavioural problems. See *CC v Dept. for Communities (DLA)* [2024] NI Com 18.

p.873, *correction to the Social Security (Invalid Care Allowance) Regulations 1976 (SI 1976/409 reg.7 (Manner of electing the person entitled to a carer's allowance in respect of a severely disabled person for the purposes of s.70 of the Contributions and Benefits Act)*

2.023 Amendments were made to reg.7 in consequence of the introduction of Carer Support Payment in Scotland by two sets of regulations in 2023. The first (made by the Scottish Parliament's Carer's Assistance (Carer Support Payment) (Consequential and Miscellaneous Amendments and Transitional Provision) (Scotland) Regulations (SSI 2023/258) apparently applied only to Scotland (though no "extent" is expressed in the regulations). The second, the Carer's Assistance (Carer Support Payment) (Scotland) Regulations 2023 (SI 2023/1218), applied only to England & Wales.

The consequence of this is that reg.7 now has two different forms in each jurisdiction. The version that appears in the current edition of Volume I is a combination of those in both jurisdictions. Although the numbering of paragraphs in the amendments would suggest that the amendments made by each of these regulations were intended to be cumulative, for the present it appears that reg.7 has been amended to a separate extent in each jurisdiction.

To make the current position clear both versions are expressed below.

England and Wales

[5 Manner of electing the person entitled to a carer's allowance in respect of a severely disabled person for the purposes of section 70 of the Contributions and Benefits Act]

7.—(1) For the purposes of the provision in [2 [5 section 70(7ZA)]] of the Contributions and Benefits Act] which provides that where, apart from that section, two or more persons would [3 have a relevant entitlement for the same day] in respect of the same severely disabled person one of them only [3 shall have that entitlement], being such one of them as they may jointly elect in the prescribed manner, an election shall be made by giving the Secretary of State a notice in writing signed by the persons who but for the said provision would [3 have a relevant entitlement] in respect of the same severely disabled person specifying one of them as the person [3 to have that entitlement].

[5 (1C) For the purposes of section 70(7ZB) and (7ZC) of the Contributions and Benefits Act, which provides that where, apart from those subsections, one person (A) would have an entitlement mentioned in subsection (7ZB) and another person (B) would have a relevant entitlement for the same day in respect of the same severely disabled person, persons A and B may jointly elect in the prescribed manner that B shall have the relevant entitlement and that A shall not have an entitlement mentioned in subsection (7ZB), an election shall be made by giving the Secretary of State a notice in writing signed by both A and B specifying that B shall have the relevant entitlement and A shall not have an entitlement mentioned in subsection (7ZB).]

(2) An election under [5 paragraph (1) or (1C)] of this regulation shall not be effective to confer [3 a relevant entitlement] either for the day on which the election is made or for any earlier day if such day is one for which [3 a carer's allowance or the care element of universal credit] has been paid in respect of the severely disabled person in question and has not been repaid or recovered.

[3 (3) In paragraph (2) "the carer element of universal credit" means an amount included in an award of universal credit in respect of the fact that a person has regular and substantial caring responsibilities for a severely disabled person.]

[5 (5) In paragraph (2), "carer support payment" means carer's assistance given in accordance with the Carer's Assistance (Carer Support Payment) (Scotland) Regulations 2023.]

AMENDMENTS

1. Social Security Amendment (Carer's Allowance) Regulations 2002 (SI 2002/2497) reg.3 (April 1, 2003).

2. Social Security (Invalid Care Allowance) Amendment Regulations 1996 (SI 1996/2744), reg.2 (November 25, 1996).

3. Universal Credit and Miscellaneous Amendment Regulations (SI 2015/1754) reg.12 (November 5, 2015).

4. *[omitted]*

5. Carer's Assistance (Care Support Payment) (Scotland) Regulations 2023 (Consequential Amendments) Order 2023 (SI 2023/1218) art.2 (November 19, 2023).

Note that paragraph (7) of art.(2) provides that the manner of election specified in regulation 7(1C), of this regulation, is to be regarded as being "the prescribed manner" within the meaning of section 70(7ZC)(a) of the Social Security Contributions and Benefits Act 1992. **2.024**

Scotland

[4 Manner of electing the person entitled to a carer's allowance in respect of a severely disabled person where more than one person would be entitled]

7.—(1) For the purposes of the provision in [2 [4 section 70(7ZA)]] of the Contributions and Benefits Act] which provides that where, apart from that section, two or more persons would [3 have a relevant entitlement for the same day] in respect of the same severely disabled person one of them only [3 shall have that entitlement], being such one of them as they may jointly elect in the prescribed manner, an election shall be made by giving the Secretary of State a notice in writing signed by the persons who but for the said provision would [3 have a relevant entitlement] in respect of the same severely disabled person specifying one of them as the person [3 to have that entitlement].

[4 (1A) For the purposes of section 70(7ZC) of the Contributions and Benefits Act which provides that where, apart from that section, one person (A) would have an entitlement mentioned in subsection (7ZB) and another person (B) would have an entitlement to carer's allowance for the same day in respect of the same severely disabled person, A and B may jointly elect in the prescribed manner which of them shall have such entitlement, an election shall be made by giving the Scottish Ministers a notice in writing signed by both A and B specifying that B shall have entitlement to carer's allowance and A shall not have an entitlement mentioned in subsection (7ZB).

(1B) For the purposes of section 70(7ZE) of the Contributions and Benefits Act which provides that where, apart from that section, one person (A) has, or would have an entitlement to universal credit carer element and another person (B) would have an entitlement to carer's allowance for the same day in respect of the same severely disabled person, A and B may jointly elect in the prescribed manner which of them shall have such entitlement, an election shall be made by giving the Scottish Ministers a notice in writing signed by both A and B specifying that B shall have an entitlement to carer's allowance and A shall not have entitlement to universal credit carer element.]

(2) An election under [4 paragraphs (1), (1A) or (1B)] of this regulation shall not be effective to confer [3 a relevant entitlement] either for the day on which the election is made or for any earlier day if such day is one for which [3 a carer's allowance or the care element of universal credit] has been paid in respect of the severely disabled person in question and has not been repaid or recovered.

[3 (3) In paragraph (2) "the carer element of universal credit" means an amount included in an award of universal credit in respect of the fact that a person has regular and substantial caring responsibilities for a severely disabled person.]

[4 (4) In paragraph (2), "carer support payment" means a payment made under the Carer's Assistance (Carer Support Payment) (Scotland) Regulations 2023.]

AMENDMENTS

1. Social Security Amendment (Carer's Allowance) Regulations 2002 (SI 2002/2497) reg.3 (April 1, 2003).

2. Social Security (Invalid Care Allowance) Amendment Regulations 1996 (SI 1996/2744), reg.2 (November 25, 1996).
3. Universal Credit and Miscellaneous Amendment Regulations (SI 2015/1754) reg.12 (November 5, 2015).
4. Carer's Assistance (Carer Support Payment) (Consequential and Miscellaneous Amendments and Transitional Provision) (Scotland) Regulations 2023 (SSI 2023/258) reg.2 (November 19, 2023).

p.877, *amendments to the Social Security (Invalid Care Allowance) Regulations 1976 (SI 1976/409) reg.9 (Conditions relating to residence and presence in Great Britain)*

With effect from October 21, 2024, reg.9(2) was amended by art.2 of the Social Security ((Scotland) Act 2018 (Disability Assistance) (Consequential Amendments) Order (SI 2024/919) by inserting after para. (2)(b)(i) the following: **2.025**

"(ia) pension age disability payment given in accordance with the Disability Assistance for Older People (Scotland) Regulations 2024,"

Note that this regulation applies only to England & Wales.

With effect from March 21, 2025, reg.9(2) was amended by reg.2 of the Disability Assistance (Scottish Adult Disability Living Allowance) (Consequential Amendment, Revocation and Saving Provision) Regulations 2024 (SSI 2024/311) by inserting after head (ii)—

"(iia) the care component of Scottish adult disability living allowance at the highest or middle rate in accordance with regulation 6(4)(a) or (b) of the Disability Assistance (Scottish Adult Disability Living Allowance) Regulations 2025;".

With effect from October 24, 2024, reg.9(2)(b) was amended by reg.2 of the Disability Assistance for Older People (Consequential Amendment and Transitional Provision) (Scotland) Regulations 2024 (SSI 2024/141) by omitting "or" at the end of head (v) and inserting at the end of head (vi)—

"or,
(vii) pension age disability payment in accordance with the Disability Assistance for Older People (Scotland) Regulations 2024."

p.879, *amendment to the Social Security (Invalid Care Allowance) Regulations 1976 (SI 1976/409) reg.9A (Persons residing in Great Britain to whom a relevant EU Regulation applies)*

With effect from November 7, 2024, reg.2(2) of Social Security (Genuine and Sufficient Link to the United Kingdom) (Amendment) Regulations (SI 2024/936) amended reg.9A by omitting the words "social security system" in para.(1)(c). Note that this regulation applies only to England & Wales. The same amendment with effect from the same date is made in respect of Scotland by reg.2(2) of the Social Security (Genuine and Sufficient Link to the United Kingdom) (Miscellaneous Amendment) (Scotland) Regulations 2024 (SSI 2024/241). **2.026**

p.879, *amendment to the Social Security (Invalid Care Allowance) Regulations 1976 (SI 1976/409) reg. 9B (Persons residing in an EEA state or in Switzerland to whom a relevant EU Regulation applies)*

2.027 With effect from November 7, 2024, reg.2(3) of Social Security (Genuine and Sufficient Link to the United Kingdom) (Amendment) Regulations (SI 2024/936) amended reg.9B by omitting the words "social security system" in para.(c). Note that this regulation applies only to England & Wales. The same amendment with effect from the same date is made in respect of Scotland by reg.2(3) of the Social Security (Genuine and Sufficient Link to the United Kingdom) (Miscellaneous Amendment) (Scotland) Regulations 2024 (SSI 2024/241).

p.887, *annotation to the Social Security (Personal Independence Payment) Regulations 2013 (SI 2013/377) reg.2 (Interpretation)*

2.028 In *AB v SSWP (PIP)* [2024] UKUT 376 (AAC) the Upper Tribunal decided that a bone anchored hearing aid (BAHA), which consists of a surgical implant and a separate external (removeable) sound processor, both of which are integral to its functioning, qualified as an "aid or appliance" for the purposes of daily living Descriptor 7(b) in Sch.1. As UTJ Wikeley noted (at para.10):

> "My understanding is that cochlear implants comprise both an implanted device and an external detachable element (the microphone and processor). If that is right, and both the internal and external parts need to be operational for the implant to work, then a cochlear implant should presumably be treated in the same way as a BAHA for present purposes."

p.892, *annotation to the Social Security (Personal Independence Payment) Regulations 2013 (SI 2013/377) (Daily living activities and mobility activities)*

2.029 The treatment of a concession made before the hearing of an appeal by the FTT has been considered again in *TL v SSWP (PIP)* [2024] UKUT 282 (AAC). Responding to the appeal, the response writer had recommended changing the points awarded by adding points for taking nutrition and for managing therapy, but the effect of doing so was to increase the claimant's score to only 7 points for the daily living component. On appeal the FTT had added points on other activities but declined to add the points suggested above and the claimant's score remained as 7 points. The FTT said in their statement of reasons that they did not accept the concession made and they gave their reasons for not doing so, but they did not refer to the decision in *DO v SSWP (PIP)* [2021] UKUT 161 (AAC) above. On appeal, UTJ Butler accepted a submission made on behalf of the Secretary of State that this was an error of law. Although in the *DO* case the claimant had been given an award of benefit and was appealing for a higher award, whereas in this the claimant had no award, Judge Butler held that the principles outlined by Judge Wright at paras 45 and 46 of the *DO* decision still applied. She held that although the FTT could still identify an issue of their own in accordance with s.12(8)(a) of the SSA 1998 if they were choosing to do that (and in doing so to reject the binding authority of the *DO* case) they must do so consciously and explain their reasons for that.

p.896, *annotation to the Social Security (Personal Independence Payment) Regulations 2013 (2013/377) reg.4 (assessment of ability to carry out activities)*

When hearing an appeal, the function of the FTT is to assess the claimant's ability to carry out the activities prescribed in the schedule and to do so as required in paragraph (2A). In doing this, s.12(8)(b) of the Social Security Act 1998 requires that they have regard only to the circumstances as they exist between the time the claim is made and the time of the decision under appeal. This does not mean, however, that the FTT cannot have regard to evidence that arises, or is generated, after that date if it may be relevant to show the claimant's ability at the earlier time. There is a distinction to be made between the circumstances obtaining at that time and evidence of those circumstances. In *JS v SSWP (PIP)* [2024] UKUT 90 (AAC) the claimant had been diagnosed several years earlier with epilepsy, but it appears that at the time her claim was made and when it was decided, she retained her licence to drive. At the time her appeal was heard she had suffered more severe epileptic episodes, and a doctor had written a letter that reviewed the claimant's condition going back over a longer period. In the UT Judge Fitzpatrick held that this evidence must be considered and its relevance to the claimant's ability to undertake activities, and to do so safely, during the period in question assessed. Their reasons for decision should explain what information they took from the evidence and their reasons for accepting or for rejecting such information. In doing so she followed several earlier decisions in the context of other benefits. 2.030

p.899, *annotation to the Social Security (Personal Independence Payment) Regulations (SI 2013/377) reg.4 (Assessment of ability to carry out activities)*

The relationship between doing something safely so as to satisfy para. (2A) and the 50 per cent rule (need to require an aid on more that 50 per cent of the days under reg.7) is explained clearly for the benefit of FTTs by Judge Fitzpatrick in *JT v SSWP (PIP)* [2024] UKUT 211 (AAC). The claimant suffered muscle spasms in his legs which made it difficult for him to use the toilet without an aid in the form of a grab handle to avoid falling. The FTT had found that the spasms occurred "occasionally" but appeared to have found that this meant that he did not require the aid "for the majority of the time" and hence did not qualify for points under Activity 5. In the UT, Judge Fitzpatrick points out that this appears to be conflating the requirements of "safely" under para.(4A) with those of reg. 7 which requires that claimants satisfy a Descriptor on more than 50 per cent of the days of the required period. But, unless the claimant has forewarning of a condition that makes an activity unsafe, the fact that it may occur for less than the majority of days is irrelevant. An activity may be unsafe whenever there is a substantial risk of the harm occurring. 2.031

p.900, *annotation to the Social Security Personal Independence Payment Regulations (SI 2013/377) reg.4 (Assessment of ability to carry out activities—safely)*

In *AM v SSWP (PIP)* [2024] UKUT 289 (AAC) Judge Church has provided guidance for FTTs as to the correct approach when considering whether a claimant can carry out activities safely when they have seizures. 2.032

The claimant, who had a number of other medical conditions, had developed a condition that caused her to lose consciousness. The nature of her condition was uncertain, but it was thought not to be epilepsy. The claimant had some limited forewarning of these events and most of the episodes were of a short duration. The claimant had appealed against a decision refusing the mobility component. The FTT had found that she could travel safely on her own because the seizures were brief, she had forewarning of them and being non-epileptic were less likely to occur without warning than if they were epileptic. Judge Church found this was an inadequate finding of facts and failure to give adequate reasons for their decision. What he thought to be necessary in such cases was as follows:

> "46. While the claimant's case was that she experienced a loss of consciousness lasting 10 minutes on one occasion, and she denied having "warning signs" of seizures, the Tribunal found that:
> a. the claimant's episodes of loss of consciousness lasted "only 5–10 seconds";
> b. the episodes were non-epileptic seizures; and
> c. non-epileptic seizures are "less likely" to occur without warning when a person is doing a potentially dangerous activity.
>
> 47. However, it didn't make any finding as to:
> a. how likely it was that the claimant might have a non-epileptic seizure involving loss of consciousness without warning;
> b. what "warning signs" (prodromal/pre-ictal symptoms) the claimant experiences, and how long before a seizure these symptoms occur;
> c. what harm could occur were the claimant to experience a non-epileptic seizure while carrying out mobility activity 1; or
> d. what post-ictal symptoms the claimant experiences, how long these last, and what risks they might pose to the claimant's safety and the safety of other persons.
>
> 48. Neither has the Tribunal explained what the claimant could be expected to do were she to experience "warning signs" of an approaching non-epileptic seizure to reduce the risk that she may herself suffer, or cause another, harm. Clear findings on such matters are necessary if such "warning signs" are to be relied upon as reducing the risk of harm.
>
> ...
>
> 51. Neither did the Tribunal explain what significance it attached to the short duration of the claimant's non-epileptic seizures. Even a short episode could potentially give rise to risk of harm depending on the circumstances in which the claimant experiences them. Were she to find herself on an escalator, crossing a busy road, or standing on a railway platform, for instance, a loss of consciousness (or indeed a seizure which doesn't involve a loss of consciousness but includes other disabling features) for 5 seconds might have very serious consequences. The Tribunal was not entitled simply to assume that because it found the episodes to be short that they were insignificant: it needed to conduct a proper assessment in line with the approach in *RJ*."

2.033 One unusual feature of this case was that the claimant had continued to drive a car even after one of her medical advisers, a consultant neurologist, had advised that she must inform the DVLA of her condition and that she must stop driving. Judge Church says that even though the FTT was clearly entitled to find that the claimant was still driving, and to attach significance to that evidence, the fact that she did drive, did not mean that it was wise, responsible or safe for her to do so. The FTT had found that it was still safe for her to drive because in their view the consultant was "being cautious rather than being of the view that there was a genuine risk". Judge Church thought that, given the stark nature of the neurologist's statement, a greater explanation was required.

This case relates to the effect that seizures may have upon Activities of the mobility component, but similar issues may arise in relation to some of the daily living Activities, for example, those involved in preparing food, taking medication and washing and bathing.

p.901, *annotation to the Social Security Personal Independence Payment Regulations 2013 (SI 2013/377) reg.4 (Assessment of ability to carry out activities)*

The problem presented by a claimant who can perform an activity with or without an aid or assistance but cannot do so timeously has been considered again by Judge Wikeley in *MS v SSWP (PIP)* [2024] UKUT 185 (AAC). The claimant suffered from multiple sclerosis and as a result was doubly incontinent. He was employed as a travelling serviceman, working on his own, from a van in which he was able to carry extra equipment and a change of clothes with which he was able to clean himself and dress as necessary after leakages. He had been awarded only 2 points for Descriptor 5(b) in relation to Activity 5 (managing toilet needs or continence) on the basis that he required aids in the form of incontinence pads. His appeal to FTT having failed, he appealed to the UT where Judge Wikeley accepted a submission from the representative of the Secretary of State that the tribunal had failed to find sufficient facts as to the claimant's ability to deal with his toileting needs and to give sufficient reasons for the conclusion that they reached. As Judge Wikeley pointed out when granting leave to appeal, no regard had been had to the matter of the time taken by the claimant to clean himself and when necessary, change his clothing. As the judge surmised it was unlikely to be less than twice the time taken by an able person to complete their toileting needs. He thought that by analogy to the decision reached by Judge Gray in *GP v SSWP (PIP)* [2016] UKUT 444 (AAC), where a claimant could not satisfy an Activity timeously, that it was reasonable to award the highest points available. Given the concession made by the Secretary of State and the evidence provided by the claimant, he was able to substitute his own decision awarding 8 points under Descriptor 5(f) which in this case would mean that the claimant needed assistance to manage double incontinence though no assistance was available or, given time, was necessary for him. 2.034

p.905, *annotation to the Social Security Personal Independence Payment Regulations 2013 (SI2013/377) reg.7 (Scoring: further provision)*

Note that the test prescribed in para.(1)(a) is for the Descriptor to be satisfied on over 50% of the days of the required period. This is not the same as "50% of the time" or of "the majority of the time" as it may be expressed in the decisions of FTTs. In *QWH v SSWP (PIP)* [2024] UKUT 339 (AAC) Judge Perez finds that it can be an error of law to express their findings in that way. 2.035

"47. The First-tier Tribunal materially erred in law in misciting the test in regulation 7 and in applying the wrong test. The test is not "for more than 50% of the time" (as the First tier Tribunal said at paragraph 13), or "for the majority of the time" (as the tribunal said at paragraph 44), or "for a majority of the time" (as the tribunal said at paragraph 50). It is "on over 50% of the days of the required period". While some First-tier Tribunal panels do sometimes miscite regulation 7 in this way (a hangover from previous legislation), it is not always a material miscitation. Here, however, it appears that the First-tier Tribunal's application of "for more than 50% of the time" and of "for the/a majority of the time" could well have led it to reject any needs for activity 1 by imposing too high a bar: "on" a day is a lower test; it can be satisfied even if the descriptor is satisfied for less (indeed much less) than 51% of the day."

No doubt a tribunal can make clear in their reasons that when they use general expressions such as most of the time, or seldom or infrequently that they are doing so in a context of the number of days on which that event occurs, but probably the easiest way to do that is to make use of the statutory formula.

p.920, *amendment to the Social Security (Personal Independence Payment) Regulations 2013 (SI 2013/377) reg.22 (Persons residing in Great Britain to whom a relevant EU Regulation applies)*

2.036 With effect from November 7, 2024, reg.5(2) of Social Security (Genuine and Sufficient Link to the United Kingdom) (Amendment) Regulations (SI 2024/936) amended reg.22 by omitting the words "social security system" in para.(c). Note that this regulation applies only to England & Wales. The same amendment with effect from the same date is made in respect of Scotland by reg.5(2) of the Social Security (Genuine and Sufficient Link to the United Kingdom) (Miscellaneous Amendment) (Scotland) Regulations 2024 (SSI 2024/241).

p.920, *annotation to the Social Security (Personal Independence Payment) Regulations 2013 (SI 2013/377) reg.22 (Persons residing in Great Britain to whom a relevant EU Regulation applies)*

2.037 The relevant EU regulation that is specified in s.84 of WRA 2012 is (EC) No 883/2004. The operation of reg.22 following the exit of the United Kingdom from the EU has been considered by Judge Jacobs in *ES v SSWP (PIP)* [2024] UKUT 97 (AAC). He decides that although Regulation 883/2004 does not apply directly, the effect of that regulation does still apply through the *Agreement on the withdrawal of the United Kingdom of Great Britain and Northern Ireland from the European Union and the European Atomic Energy Community* (2019/C 384 I/01). Article 31 of that Agreement provides that "The rules and objectives set out in ... Regulation (EC) 883/2004 ... shall apply to persons covered by this title." In this case the claimant was an EU national living with her daughter in Scotland, but on visiting her family in Poland had been detained there during the Covid crisis. The Secretary of State had accepted that she was habitually resident in this country, and that she formed part of her daughter's family.

The "rules and objectives" of Regulation (EC) 883/2004 applied to her and hence reg.16(b) requiring her presence for a sufficient period in this country was disapplied by reg.22.

p.921, *amendment to the Social Security (Personal Independence Payment) Regulations 2013, (SI 2013/377) reg.23 (Persons residing in an EEA state or in Switzerland to whom a relevant EU Regulation applies)*

With effect from November 7, 2024, reg.5(3) of Social Security (Genuine and Sufficient Link to the United Kingdom) (Amendment) Regulations (SI 2024/936) amended reg.23 by omitting the words "social security system" in para.(c). Note that this regulation applies only to England & Wales. The same amendment with effect from the same date is made in respect of Scotland by reg.5(3) of the Social Security (Genuine and Sufficient Link to the United Kingdom) (Miscellaneous Amendment) (Scotland) Regulations 2024 (SSI 2024/241). 2.038

p.927, *annotation to the Social Security (Personal Independence Payment) Regulations (SI 2013/377) reg.27 (Revision and supersession of an award after a person has reached the relevant age)*

The operation of reg.27 has been considered again by Judge Jacobs in *MM v SSWP (PIP)* [2024] UKUT 288 (AAC). The claimant had an award of benefit for the daily living component only on the day before she reached the relevant age—in her case 65. Four years later that decision was superseded. The decision letter sent to her stated, correctly, that she could not then qualify for the mobility component but for a period of about 2 years she was paid that component in error. The claimant applied for a revised award on the ground that her condition had deteriorated and on appeal she was awarded the daily living component at the enhanced rate, but not the mobility component. That decision is upheld by Judge Jacobs because neither of the exceptions allowed for in para.(2) applied to her, but in doing so, he says that the "original" award referred to must mean, and can only mean, the award by which the claimant qualified before her 65th birthday. (In fact, in this case, the claimant never had any award by which she qualified for the mobility component). 2.039

p.943, *annotation to the Social Security (Personal Independence Payment) Regulations 2013 (SI 2013/377) Schedule 1—Interpretation—Personal Independence Payment assessment)*

Many of the Descriptors that are used to assess the claimant's degree of disablement are expressed in terms of "need". It is important to note that, as with the benefits that PIP replaced, what is in question is the claimant's need for an aid or for assistance and not whether he actually uses an aid or gets assistance, though clearly, if he does so will be evidence of his need, and if he does not, may be a reason for an FTT to conclude that he has no need. For an example of a case where the need was clear though the assistance was not available, see *MS v SSWP (PIP)* [2024] UKUT 185 (AAC). The claimant suffered from double incontinence, but was able to work on his own as a service engineer from a van in which he could carry extra supplies of incontinence pads, personal cleaning items and a change of clothes 2.040

if that became necessary. The claimant had been awarded 2 points on the basis that he required aids in the form of the pads to manage his toileting needs, but in the UT, as a result of a concession made by the representative of the Secretary of State, together with a detailed account from the claimant of how he managed those needs, Judge Wikeley was able to find that he qualified for the highest level of 8 points. This meant that he was effectively finding that the claimant required assistance to manage incontinence of both bowel and bladder, though in fact the claimant never had that assistance available to him. In fact what the claimant needed was more time rather than any assistance.

p.957, *annotation to the Social Security (Personal Independence Payment) Regulations 2013 (SI 2013/377) Activity 3 (Managing therapy or monitoring a health condition)*

2.041 The use of prescribed compression stockings as treatment for lymphoedema in the legs was accepted as a form of therapy by Judge Stout in *CF v SSWP* [2024] UKUT 244 (AAC). The claimant needed help in putting the stockings on and could therefore qualify for 2 points under Descriptor c. Judge Stout gives helpful guidance on the distinction between medication and therapy as follows:

> "29 ... Whether something that is prescribed by a relevant professional is "medication" or "therapy" within the meaning of the regulations will need in each case to be determined by the Tribunal by reference to case law and by reference to the ordinary meaning of the words "medication" and "therapy" as those words are not otherwise defined in the Regulations. In this case, I am content that compression stockings can properly be described as "therapy", as (with reference to the Shorter Oxford English Dictionary definitions), the normal meaning of medication relates to treatment with a "medicinal substance" or "drug", whereas "therapy" refers to "treatment" more generally including by "systems of activities" and by action taken to "alleviate" as well as "cure" symptoms (see further *AS v SSWP* [2017] AACR 31 at [7] per Judge Bano for consideration of the meaning of "therapy"). It seems to me that the wearing of compression stockings to aid in lymphatic drainage and reduce swelling in the legs falls comfortably within the ordinary meaning of the word "therapy".

Judge Stout went on to hold, as well, that the claimant could not qualify also for points under Activity 6 (Dressing and undressing) in relation to the help that she needed in putting on the compression stockings. To award points under both Activities would, she said, be double counting. Although the legislation does not expressly preclude points under more than one Activity in respect of the same disability, where, as here, the assistance was needed in respect of an item that was specifically defined so as to qualify, it could not, by implication, be regarded as qualifying under a more general heading such as dressing. See also the decisions of Judge Bano in *AS v SSWP (PIP)* [2016] UKUT 554 (AAC); [2017] AACR 31 and of Judge Mesher in *SSWP v KS (PIP)* [2018] UKUT 102 (AAC) to the same effect.

p.963, *annotation to the Social Security (Personal Independence Payment) Regulations 2013 (SI 2013/377) Activity 5—(Managing toilet needs or incontinence)*

Note that if the claimant's disability means that he cannot manage toilet needs safely, to an acceptable standard, repeatedly and within a reasonable time (see reg.4(2A)) it may mean that he cannot manage toilet needs at all and consequently may qualify under Descriptor 5(f) as needing assistance to manage toilet and incontinence needs. See *MS v SSWP (PIP)* [2024] UKUT 185 (AAC) discussed in the notes to reg.4 above. **2.042**

p.967, *annotation to the Social Security (Personal Independence Payment) Regulations 2013 (SI 2013/377) Activity 6 (Dressing and undressing)*

Note that in *CF v SSWP (PIP)* [2024] UKUT 244 Judge Stout has held that a claim which succeeded under Activity 3 (managing therapy), in respect of assistance needed to put on prescribed compression stockings, could not also succeed under this heading. To award points under both Activities would, she said, be double counting. Although the legislation does not expressly preclude points under more than one Activity in respect of the same disability where, as here, the assistance was needed in respect of an item that was specifically defined so as to qualify, it could not, by implication, be regarded as qualifying under a more general heading such as dressing. See also the decisions of Judge Bano in *AS v SSWP (PIP)* [2016] UKUT 554 (AAC); [2017] AACR 31 and of Judge Mesher in *SSWP v KS (PIP)* [2018] UKUT 102 (AAC) to the same effect. The Judge does, however, go on to point out that a claim under Activity 6 might still succeed if the claimant needs help when dressing in other respects including, if she needed assistance to put on non-compression stockings. **2.043**

p.970, *annotation to the Social Security (Personal Independence Payment) Regulations 2013 (SI 2013/377) Activity 8 (Reading and understanding signs symbols and words)*

In *JM v SSWP (PIP)* [2024] UKUT 283 (AAC) the claimant was able to read words on her laptop computer without assistance, though not words written or printed on paper. Judge Fitzpatrick suggests (though she did not find it necessary to decide) that the words in Sch.1 defining both basic and complex written information as signs, symbols and dates "written or printed" should be read disjunctively as had been done by Judge Rowley in relation to the words "bath or shower" in Activity 4 (washing and bathing). Here then, it would mean that the claim would succeed if she were unable to read either written words or printed words; and, depending upon how a tribunal interpreted the words written and printed, the evidence that she could read words on a computer might possibly satisfy the latter but not the former or, perhaps, neither. **2.044**

p.972, *annotation to the Social Security (Personal Independence Payment) Regulations 2013 (SI 2013/377) Article 9 (Engaging with other people face to face)*

The relevance of a claimant's ability to engage with others face to face in other than social circumstances has been considered again by Judge Stout **2.045** in *CF v SSWP (PIP)* [2024] UKUT 244 (AAC). In granting leave to appeal the judge had said that the claimant's ability to relate to others at her job was not relevant to the test in Activity 9 (though she did moderate that by saying "or at any rate not determinative"). At the hearing of the appeal the parties agreed with a submission made on behalf of the Secretary of State that such evidence was not irrelevant relying on a statement of Judge Rowland in an unreported case *(CPIP/1203/2016)*. What Judge Rowland had said was this:

> "I am also satisfied that the First-tier Tribunal did not err in law in its consideration of Activity 9. As has been noted before, the term "engage socially" is defined in Part 1 of Schedule 1 to the Social Security (Personal Independence Payment) Regulations 2013 (SI 2013/377) and is then not used anywhere in the Schedule but, even assuming that it defines "engage with other people" for the purpose of Activity 9, there is no need for the term "social" in the phrase "socially appropriate manner" to imply that, in considering whether any of the descriptors in Activity 9 is satisfied, regard should be had only to contact in a social, as opposed to a business or professional, context. The reasoning in *JC v Secretary of State for Work and Pensions (ESA)* [2014] UKUT 352 (AAC); [2015] AACR 6 at [24] to [35] applies to personal independence payment as much as to employment and support allowance. Accordingly, the reasoning of the First-tier Tribunal in paragraph 21 of its statement of reasons was quite adequate against the background of the evidence in the case."

In this case, however, it was clear that the FTT had misapplied the test as described above and, in remitting the case to a new FTT, Judge Stout reiterated that they must follow the guidance supplied in *HA* case from which she quoted as follows:

> "13. It is now widely accepted that the definition of "engage socially" in Part 1 of Schedule 1 to the Social Security (Personal Independence Payments) Regulations 2013 applies to daily living activity 9, even though the expression does not actually appear within the terms of the activity or its descriptors. The expression is defined as meaning: "(a) interact with others in a contextually and socially appropriate manner; (b) understand body language; and (c) establish relationships". If a claimant is unable to satisfy these criteria, it follows that (s)he is unable to engage with other people "to an acceptable standard" (regulation 4(2A)(b)).
> 14. For completeness, Part 1 of Schedule 1 defines "prompting" as meaning "reminding, encouraging or explaining by another person", and "psychological distress" as meaning "distress related to an enduring mental health condition or an intellectual or cognitive impairment".
> 15. It is implicit from the tribunal's conclusion—that the claimant needed prompting to engage with other people—that it considered that he was able to engage with other people without social support, without overwhelming psychological distress and without exhibiting behaviour which would result in a substantial risk of harm to the claimant or another person.
> 16. In my judgment it was incumbent on the tribunal to consider the claimant's ability to satisfy the three components of the phrase "engage socially", and to make adequate findings of fact as to the nature and quality of his interactions with other people (*HJ v SSWP* [2016] UKUT

0487 (AAC)). However, the tribunal simply listed those with whom it said the claimant could engage, without investigating or making findings in relation to what actually happened during his interactions with them. In the light of the evidence as to (for example) his selective mutism, his inability to make eye contact and read facial expressions, his inability to understand body language and his tendency to bite himself or lash out during communication, it did not necessarily follow that – without more – the claimant was able to "engage socially" even with those people listed by the tribunal, for the purposes of daily living activity 9, at least on over 50% of days (regulation 7).

17. In any event, all of the "other people" in the tribunal's examples were, as the tribunal stated, of the claimant's age (16). They would not, therefore, generally be regarded as adults. Just as Upper Tribunal Judge Jacobs was of the view that a claimant's inability to engage with men (albeit having an ability to engage with women) was of such a magnitude as to satisfy the descriptors (*RC v Secretary of State for Work and Pensions* [2017] UKUT 0352 (AAC)), equally, in my judgment, a claimant's inability to engage with adults falls into the same category, irrespective of his or her ability to engage with children and young people. There was ample evidence before the tribunal to indicate that the claimant had considerable difficulties engaging with adults due to his anxiety. In my judgment the tribunal did not adequately explain why it considered that he would be able to engage with adults if he simply had another person "reminding, encouraging or explaining" and why it considered that the higher point-scoring descriptors of daily living activity 9 were not satisfied.

18. Further, the "other people" relied upon by the tribunal were all people known to the claimant. However, the term "engage socially" is not limited to such people. Rather, a tribunal must consider a claimant's ability to engage with people generally, and not just those people they know well (*HJ v SSWP* [2016] UKUT 0487 (AAC)). The tribunal did not address whether the claimant's ability to engage with those listed by it showed that he was able to engage with people generally, rather than just those whom he knew well. That, also, constituted an error of law.

19. Finally, the tribunal's reliance on the claimant's ability to use a phone to engage with others was misplaced and amounted to a further error of law. The tribunal did not explain in what way it considered that the claimant could use a phone to engage with other people. In fact, the evidence was that he would send texts by phone. The description of the activity is "engaging with other people face to face" (my emphasis). I am quite unable to see how a claimant's ability to use a phone to send texts could possibly demonstrate an ability to engage with other people "face to face", not least because one of the requisite criteria of an ability to "engage socially" is an ability to understand body language."

p.980, *annotation to the Social Security (Personal Independence Payment) Regulations (SI 2013/377) (The mobility component—Activities and Descriptors)*

As with all Activities the claimant must be able to accomplish this activity safely—see reg.4(2A) above. The relevance of this for a claimant who has seizures has been considered in *AM v SSWP (PIP)* [2024] UKUT 289 **2.046**

(AAC) by Judge Church. The judge found that it was necessary for the FTT to have made findings of fact as to the likelihood of the claimant having episodes of unconsciousness, whether the claimant had warning signs of such events, what actions the claimant might be able to take after warning signs, what dangers might be incurred and what risks might arise following the seizures. For a fuller discussion of this case see the notes following reg. 4 above.

p.988, *annotation to the Social Security (Personal Independence Payment) Regulations 2013 (SI 2013/377) (The mobility component—Activity 2—moving around)*

2.047 The relationship between this Activity and the tests required in reg. 4(2A) has been examined further by Judge Perez in *LB v SSWP (PIP)* [2024] UKUT 338 (AAC). The claimant had told the FTT that he could walk the length of two aisles with a shopping trolley when he went to the supermarket with his wife. He said that he walked slowly and in pain. Judge Perez allowed an appeal to the UT because there had been no finding as to the length of the aisles, nor as to how long it took the claimant to complete them, both of which would be necessary to determine whether he could accomplish that distance in a reasonable time. Further, she held that it was necessary too, for there to be findings as to whether he could do that repeatedly if he was required to do so, whether he could do so before he had to stop and rest, and finally whether he could do any of this with an acceptable level of pain. The FTT had made no finding as to the level of pain that the claimant experienced while walking. The judge finds that even if the claimant can walk the specified distance and do so repeatedly and safely and within a reasonable time, to do so only in pain may not be doing it to an acceptable standard.

> "19. Third, the First-tier Tribunal made no finding as to the level of pain the claimant is in while walking. The First-tier Tribunal needed to make such a finding in order to be satisfied that the walking was – even if able to be done safely, repeatedly and within a reasonable time period – able to be done to an acceptable standard. This applied even to the first round of walking two supermarket aisles. Walking despite pain is not to an acceptable standard."

p.1003, *annotation to the Social Security (Personal Independence Payment) Regulations 2013 (SI 2013/377) reg.17 (Procedure following and consequences of determination of claim for personal independence payment)*

2.048 The operation of reg.17 and of reg.13(1) has been explained by Judge Wikeley in *SR v SSWP (PIP)* [2024] UKUT 308 (AAC). Although the general rule is that on transfer cases entitlement to PIP begins the day after a claimant's entitlement to DLA ends in accordance with para.(1) of reg.17, there is a special case that applies where the claimant has had a negative determination under reg.13(1) above, and that determination is subsequently reversed by the Secretary of State or on appeal by an FTT. In that case the entitlement to PIP is provided for by para.(2)(b) of reg.17 and entitlement is backdated to the date that DLA terminated under the negative determination.

p.1032, *amendment to the Social Security (Deferral of Retirement Pensions) Regulations 2005 (SI 2005/453) reg.3 (Amount of retirement pension not included in the calculation of the lump sum)*

With effect from June 8, 2024, reg.3 was amended by reg.7(2) of the Social Security (State Pension Age Claimants: Closure of Tax Credits) (Amendment) Regulations (SI 2024/611) by inserting at the end of para. (1)(a) the following: **2.049**

"(vi) universal credit under part 1 of the Welfare Reform Act 2012,"

p.1073, *amendment to the Social Security (Widow's Benefit and Retirement Pensions) Regulations 1979 (SI 1979/642) reg.4 (Days to be treated as days of increment)*

With effect from June 8, 2024, reg.7(1) of the Social Security (State Pension Age Claimants: Closure of Tax Credits) (Amendment) Regulations 2024 (SI 2024/611) amended reg. 4 by deleting the word "and" at the end of para.(1)(b) and substituting: **2.050**

"or
(vi) universal credit, and"

p.1136, *amendment to the State Pension Regulations 2015 (SI 2015/173) reg.37 (Credits for persons engaged in caring)*

With effect from October 21, 2024, art.18 of the Social Security (Scotland) Act 2018 (Disability Assistance) (Consequential Amendments) Order 2024 (SI 2024/919) amended reg.37(4) by inserting after sub-paragraph (a) the following sub-paragraph "(aa) pension age disability payment in accordance with the Disability Assistance for Older People (Scotland) Regulations 2024;". **2.051**

p.1228, *amendments to the Jobseeker's Allowance Regulations 2013 (SI 2013/378), reg.42(3) and (4) (Remunerative work)*

With effect from October 21, 2024, art.15 of the Social Security (Scotland) Act 2018 (Disability Assistance) (Consequential Amendments) Order 2024 (SI 2024/919) amended reg.42(3)(c)(i), (ii) and (iv) by inserting ", pension age disability payment" after "attendance allowance" in each place where that occurs and amended reg.42(4) by inserting the following definition after the definition of "daily living component": **2.052**

""pension age disability payment" has the meaning given in regulation 2 of the Disability Assistance for Older People (Scotland) Regulations 2024;"

Those Scottish Regulations are SSI 2024/166 (see Part I of this Supplement).

p.1271, *amendments to the Jobseeker's Allowance Regulations 2013 (SI 2013/378) reg.62 (Deduction of tax and contributions for self-employed earners)*

With effect from April 6, 2024 (omitted in error from the main volume), reg.8(20)(a) of the Social Security (Class 2 National Insurance **2.053**

Contributions) (Consequential Amendments and Savings) Regulations 2024 (SI 2024/377) amended reg.62 by omitting sub-para.(a) of both para.(3) and para.(4).

p.1280, *amendment to the Jobseeker's Allowance Regulations 2013 (SI 2013/378) reg.73(4)(d) (Calculation of earnings of share fishermen)*

2.054 With effect from April 6, 2024 (omitted in error from the main volume), reg.8(20)(b) of the Social Security (Class 2 National Insurance Contributions) (Consequential Amendments and Savings) Regulations 2024 (SI 2024/377) amended reg.73(4)(d) by omitting the words "the amount specified in section 11(4)(a) of the Benefits Act" from the text of the added reg.62(6).

PART III

UPDATING MATERIAL

VOLUME II
UNIVERSAL CREDIT, STATE PENSION CREDIT AND THE SOCIAL FUND

Commentary by

John Mesher

Tom Royston

Nick Wikeley

p.49, *GENERAL NOTE to the Welfare Reform Act 2012 (Challenges of transition)*

The General Note details the (frequently amended) official schedule for transition from legacy benefits to universal credit. The latest instalment is in HM Treasury, *Autumn Budget 2024* (HC 295, October 30, 2024) §4.113: **3.001**

> "An additional £90 million is allocated to accelerate the move of employment and support allowance claimants onto universal credit, which will now start from September 2024 instead of 2028. This will allow DWP to complete the rollout of universal credit in 2026, with all working age benefit claimants brought onto one system, enabling the decommissioning of the remaining legacy benefits."

There has however still been no public announcement of what arrangements are proposed for claimants receiving housing benefit for temporary or supported accommodation, that now being the sole part of the system in which new claims for any 'legacy benefit' remain possible. Those housing costs are not currently receivable through universal credit.

p.69, *annotation to the Welfare Reform Act 2012 s.4 (Basic conditions)*

The General Note observes that there is no authority on the direct point of whether s.4(5) WRA 2012 confers the vires to make the restrictions which reg.9 Universal Credit Regulations 2013 does on the entitlement to UC of migrants who have a grant of leave to be in the UK, and are not excluded from access to public funds under the terms of their leave. That remains the case. However, note that in *GA v SSWP* [2024] UKUT 380 (AAC), the Upper Tribunal (in the course of allowing an appeal) records that it had refused permission to appeal on the ground that the FTT misdirected itself in law by failing to hold that reg.9(3)(c)(i) of the Universal Credit Regulations 2013 is ultra vires s.4(5)(a) of the Welfare Reform Act 2012. The UT held that "there is no realistic prospect of success in arguing that the ratio of *Sarwar and Getachew* [*R v Secretary of State for Social Security ex p Sarwar and Getachew* [1997] CMLR 648 (CA)], by which the Upper Tribunal is bound, is not equally applicable to reg.9(3)(c)(i)." **3.002**

pp.90–93, *annotation to the Welfare Reform Act 2012 s.15 (Work-focused interview requirement)*

In relation to what must be done for a requirement to participate in an interview to be imposed, see *SB v SSWP (ESA)* [2024] UKUT 372 (AAC) in the entry for pp.114-116. **3.003**

p.106, *annotation to the Welfare Reform Act 2012 s.19(2)(a) (Claimants subject to no work-related requirements—limited capability for work and work-related activity)*

Note, now that managed migration to universal credit of claimants of old style income-related ESA is in full swing, the effect of reg.19 of the Universal Credit (Transitional Provisions) Regulations 2014 (p.760 of the main volume). Under s.40, the meaning of "limited capability for work and **3.004** work-related activity" is set out in s.37(1) and (2). Section 37(3) and (4) provide that the question of whether a claimant has such limited capability is to be determined in accordance with regulations that must provide for the determination to be on the basis of an assessment. Regulation 40 of the Universal Credit Regulations provides that a claimant has such limited capability if that has been determined on the basis of an assessment (or limited deeming) under those regulations or under the ESA Regulations 2013, that govern new style ESA. Thus, an assessment under the ESA Regulations 2008, governing old style ESA, does not count under those provisions to bring a migrating claimant within s.19(2)(a). Regulation 19(4)(b) of the Transitional Provisions Regulations, in cases where a claimant was entitled to old style ESA on the date of a claim for universal credit that leads to an award, provides that, where it had been determined that the claimant had or was deemed to have limited capability for work-related activity for the purposes of old style ESA, they are to be treated as having limited capability for work and work-related activity for the purposes of s.19(2)(a). If the migration process works and the universal credit claim is made before the deadline involved, those conditions will be met.

There were initially some serious problems in the effect of that rule being picked up at the beginning of the universal credit award, with the result that work-related requirements were purportedly applied to migrating old style ESA claimants on the basis that there had not yet been an assessment under universal credit or they were required to provide fit notes. An automatic "feature fix", following earlier manual fixes, was put in place from November 25, 2024, designed to avoid such results (for further details see the news story dated November 27, 2024 on the Rightsnet website).

Note also, more generally, that s.19(2)(a) applies from the first date that the determination relates to. There is no basis for applying the three-month waiting period for the inclusion of the LCWRA element (see reg.28 of the Universal Credit Regulations) in this context.

p.108, *annotation to the Welfare Reform Act 2012 s.20 (Claimants subject to work-focused interview requirement only)*

3.005 According to the Office for Budget Responsibility report *Economic and fiscal outlook – October 2024* (CP 1169), para.3.59, the rate of appointments offered to responsible carers of children aged one or two remained well below the original assumptions of the 2023 policy on meetings with work coaches.

p.110, *annotation to the Welfare Reform Act 2012 s.21 (Claimants subject to work preparation requirement)*

3.006 According to the Office for Budget Responsibility report *Economic and fiscal outlook—October 2024* (CP 1169), para.3.59, the rate of appointments offered to responsible carers of children aged one or two remained well below the original assumptions of the 2023 policy on meetings with work coaches.

pp.112–114, *annotation to the Welfare Reform Act 2012 s.23 (Connected requirements)*

3.007 In relation to what must be done for a requirement to participate in an interview to be imposed, see *SB v SSWP (ESA)* [2024] UKUT 372 (AAC) in the entry for pp.114–116.

pp.114–116, *annotation to the Welfare Reform Act 2012 s.24 (Imposition of requirements)*

Note, in relation to what must be done for a requirement to be imposed, the endorsement and application in *SB v SSWP (ESA)* [2024] UKUT 372 (AAC) of the general principles set out by Judge Poynter in paras 76 and 77 of *PPE v SSWP (ESA)* [2020] UKUT 59, that for the Secretary of State to impose a legal obligation on a claimant to do something they must use "the language of clear and unambiguous mandatory requirement", not merely that of inviting, advising or encouraging. In *SB* the claimant was invited to a medical examination in a letter that warned that a consequence of failing without good cause to attend could be loss of his ESA award, but failed to warn that that consequence could also follow under the relevant regulation from a failure without good cause to "submit to" the examination. Judge Wikeley accepted the Secretary of State's submission that the letter accordingly did not meet the *PPE* principles. That approach is plainly relevant where the legal provision is not merely to attend an interview or course, but to participate in it. **3.008**

p.236, *annotation to the Universal Credit Regulations 2013 (SI 2013/376) reg.9 (Persons treated as not being in Great Britain)*

The General Note observes that definitive judicial determination is still awaited on a number of issues relating to reg.9(3)(c)(i). Three recent developments are: **3.009**

- *on whether reg.9(3)(c)(i) is incompatible with art.23 Withdrawal Agreement*, the Court of Appeal has now granted permission to appeal against the decision of the High Court in *Fertre v Vale of White Horse District Council* [2024] EWHC 1754 (KB), which rejected that argument. A hearing is listed for 14–16 May 2025;
- *on whether reg.9(3)(c)(i) discriminates unlawfully against EEA nationals in comparison with third country nationals, contrary to art.14 ECHR and s.3 HRA 1998*, in *GA v SSWP* [2024] UKUT 380 (AAC), a claimant with PSS argued that she was is in a comparable position to a foreign national who could have made use of the Destitution Domestic Violence Concession due to having leave under Appendix FM of the Immigration Rules, and would in those circumstances have been able to gain access to means tested benefit; that she was refused benefit as a person with PSS; and that the differential treatment was unjustified. The Secretary of State conceded that the differential treatment was unlawful, the UT accepted that concession, and the appeal was allowed. But that concession turned on the particular factual matrix. In other types of case, whether there is art.14 discrimination against people with PSS may be much more contentious.
- *on whether s.4(5) Welfare Reform Act 2012 confers the vires to make reg.9(3)(c)(i)*, in *GA v SSWP* [2024] UKUT 380 (AAC), the Upper Tribunal (in the course of allowing the appeal) records that it had refused permission to appeal on the ground that the FTT misdirected itself in law by failing to hold that reg.9(3)(c)(i) of the

Universal Credit Regulations 2013 is ultra vires s.4(5)(a) of the Welfare Reform Act 2012. The UT held that "there is no realistic prospect of success in arguing that the ratio of *Sarwar and Getachew* [*R v Secretary of State for Social Security Ex p. Sarwar and Getachew* [1997] CMLR 648 (CA)], by which the Upper Tribunal is bound, is not equally applicable to reg 9(3)(c)(i)."

p.236, *annotation to the Universal Credit Regulations 2013 (SI 2013/376) reg.11 (Temporary absence from Great Britain)*

3.010 Regulation 11(3)(a)(i) permits disregard of absences up to 6 months where that is "solely in connection with the person undergoing... treatment for an illness or physical or mental impairment by, or under the supervision of, a qualified practitioner". That is similar (not identical) wording to the exception prescribed under reg.153 of the Employment and Support Allowance Regulations 2008 (SI 2004/798). Regulation 153 ESA Regs is considered in *SSWP v NJ* [2024] UKUT 194 (AAC). The Upper Tribunal finds that the FTT did not err where it decided a person whose mental illness was improved by sunshine was "undergoing treatment" when she spent time at her holiday home in Spain (there being some medical support for the proposition that the sunshine improved her mental health); that it was "solely" for the purpose of that treatment ("solely" relating to the overall purpose of the visit, not the question of whether the claimant did anything else while there, given that almost no treatment regime would last 24 hours per day); and that it was being "supervised" by her "qualified" husband, a retired doctor.

p.271, *annotation to the Universal Credit Regulations 2013 (SI 2013/376) reg.24 (The child element)*

3.011 The General Note discusses the case of *SSWP v MS (UC)* [2023] UKUT 44 (AAC) in which the Upper Tribunal decided that the child element of universal credit is not a social security family benefit under Regulation (EC) 883/2004. In *Simkova v Secretary of State for Work and Pensions* [2024] EWCA Civ 419 the Court of Appeal dismissed an appeal from that decision of the UT; the Supreme Court has however subsequently granted permission to appeal (UKSC 2024/0093, October 8, 2024), so the point remains live.

p.273, *annotation to the Universal Credit Regulations 2013 (SI 2013/376) reg.24A (Availability of the child element where maximum exceeded)*

3.012 The General Note discusses the case of *AT v SSWP* [2023] UKUT 148 (AAC), in which the Upper Tribunal rejected a HRA challenge to the 'ordering' rule from a woman who had conceived two children non-consensually, followed by a third consensually, but commented (at §30) that [a] 'judicial review challenge, alleging irrationality in the terms of the ordering provision, might well have a more promising prospect of success'. In *R. (LMN and EFG) v Secretary of State for Work and Pensions* [2024] EWHC 2577 (Admin) two claimants have brought such a challenge (on rationality grounds, and also on HRA grounds), and have been given permission to apply for judicial review. A hearing is listed for 17–18 June 2025.

pp.307–309, *annotation to the Universal Credit Regulations 2013 (SI 2013/376) reg.46 (What is included in capital?)*

On September 11, 2024, the Property (Digital Assets etc) Bill was introduced into the House of Lords, aimed at implementing the Law Commission's recommendation for legislation. Clause 1, as currently drafted, provides that a thing (including a thing that is digital or electronic in nature) is not prevented from being the object of personal property rights merely because it is neither a thing in possession nor a thing in action. It is far from clear how such a provision, when finally enacted, would affect the calculation of capital for social security purposes, which is more concerned with whether there is a market for assets, for sale or by use as security in raising money etc, than with personal property rights. However, it might be taken to strengthen the argument for treating cryptoassets as "things" capable of having such a market value. 3.013

Another example of a case where claimants may not have capital that may seem to be available to them beyond those mentioned on pp.308–309 is where they are a shareholder in a company, as illustrated in *ZA v London Borough of Barnet (HB)* [2024] UKUT 222 (AAC). There the claimant and her husband (H) were shareholders (H 50 shares, claimant 15, their children 35) in a company of which H was the sole director. At the relevant date the company's net assets after liabilities were valued in the accounts at £284,000 and described as retained profits or shareholders' funds. In a very confused process of decision-making the local authority rejected entitlement to housing benefit on the ground of possession of capital over £16,000, but without invoking any of the provisions allowing a claimant to be treated as possessing capital. That decision and reasoning, or lack of it, was upheld by a First-tier Tribunal, that thus obviously went wrong in law. Judge Butler, in considering the options available to a decision-maker in such circumstances, stated in paras 68 to 70 that the categorisation of funds as retained profits or shareholders' funds does not mean that they cease to be the company's assets and become something else that could be viewed as capital actually held by a shareholder. Generally, shareholders only get access to such funds if the company, as a separate legal person, decides to declare dividends, which is not guaranteed as a company may decide to retain profits. The judge also stated in paras 82 to 89 that *Prest v Petrodel Resources Ltd* [2013] UKSC 34; [2013] 2 A.C. 415, bandied about by the local authority at some stages but not in the end relied on before the Upper Tribunal, was not relevant to the case. The principles on which the properties owned by the companies in that case were found by the Supreme Court to be held on resulting trust for the husband in matrimonial proceedings were highly fact-specific and there was no justification for looking further into the assets of the company in *ZA* than allowed by the complete legislative system for dealing with capital provided in the Housing Benefit Regulations. The case was sent back to a new tribunal to investigate whether the provisions equivalent to reg.77 of the UC Regulations (but with some crucial differences) applied. See the entry in this Supplement for pp.473–475.

p.337, *annotation to the Universal Credit Regulations 2013 (SI 2013/376) reg.55 (Employed earnings)*

In *SSWP v NC (ESA)* [2024] UKUT 251 (AAC) the claimant agreed to a salary sacrifice arrangement with his employer under which his weekly 3.014

wage was reduced by £6.55 and the employer made contributions to its occupational pension of that weekly amount. If his earnings as calculated under the ESA Regulations 2008 included the amount sacrificed, they would have exceeded the level to allow him to benefit from the "permitted work" rules and retain entitlement to ESA. If they did not, they would not have exceeded the limit. The Secretary of State took the view that his gross earnings were the larger amount subject only to the deduction of half the pension contribution as a contribution made by him. The claimant's appeal to the First-tier Tribunal was allowed and the Secretary of State on their appeal to the Upper Tribunal put forward the same view. That view was rejected by Judge Church in dismissing the appeal as a misunderstanding of the essential nature of salary sacrifice pension arrangements as explained in Commissioner's decision *R(CS) 9/08*. By regarding the claimant as receiving the larger amount that view did not acknowledge the legal reality of the sacrifice of £6.55 of contractual earnings. The effect of that correct analysis is much easier to work out for universal credit than for other means-tested benefits (on which see the entry for pp.382–385 of Vol.V in Pt VI of this Supplement). That is because, whether or not the contribution made by the employer would be regarded as remuneration or profit derived from employment or as part of "general earnings" as defined in s.62 of the Income Tax (Earnings and Pensions) Act 2003 (ITEPA), such a contribution is exempted from income tax in respect of earnings by s.308 of ITEPA. Accordingly, the amount would be excluded from employed earnings by reg.55(2)(b).

However, there is an issue that might well reduce the impact of the decision in *NC* in other cases of the same kind that could affect universal credit. It was probably right, when the Secretary of State had not put forward any further arguments or suggestions of other relevant provisions, to dismiss their appeal. As a result, there was no consideration in *NC* of the effect of reg.108(3) of the ESA Regulations 2008 on notional income where a claimant is paid less than the rate for comparable employment in the area (although there is a pointer to the issue in the parts of *R(CS) 9/08* subsequent to that specifically followed in *NC*). Regulation 60(3) of the Universal Credit Regulations supplies substantially the same rule. The application of the rule is subject to no discretion if the initial condition is met and the means of the person to whom the services were provided are sufficient to pay more. It then requires the Secretary of State to treat the claimant as having received the remuneration that would be reasonable for the provision of the comparable services. In the circumstances of *NC* there would seem to be no way out of concluding that the initial condition was met, because someone doing the same job who did not make the salary sacrifice arrangement would have been paid £6.55 a week more and the employer plainly had the means to pay that amount by way of remuneration rather than as a pension contribution. So notional earned income would have to be assessed, the question of reasonableness arising only in relation to the amount, not the initial application of the rule. An extra £6.55 a week would not seem unreasonable. Regulation 60 says nothing about any permissible deductions from such notional earned income, but reg.55(5)(a) requires the deduction from "the amount of general earnings or benefits specified in paragraphs (2) to (4)" of any relievable pension contributions (defined in reg.53(1)) made by the claimant. Could that provision possibly be interpreted to include the contribution actually made by the employer? The argument is much more difficult than for other means-tested benefits, first because of the lack of express mention of reg.55 in reg.60, or of reg.60 and notional earned income in reg.55. Further, the use of the words "contributions made", not "payable", in para.(5)(a) and the express mention of what is specified in paras (2) to (4) make it hard to interpret the provision as covering a contribution that could/would have been made by the claimant if he had not made the salary sacrifice arrangement.

p.368, *annotation to the Universal Credit Regulations 2013 (SI 2013/376) reg.54A (Surplus earnings)*

It was announced in the *Autumn Budget 2024*, para.5.135, that the amount of the "relevant threshold", or de minimis amount, for surplus earnings purposes would be maintained at £2,500 until March 2026. **3.015**

pp.401–404, *annotation to the Universal Credit Regulations 2013 (SI 2013/376) reg.60(3) and (4) (Notional earned income)*

See the entry above for p.337 for the argument that on facts similar to those of *SSWP v NC (ESA)* [2024] UKUT 251 (AAC) (salary sacrifice pension arrangement) the rule in reg.60(3) would have to be applied to treat a claimant as having received the remuneration foregone to enable the employer to make a pension contribution of the same amount. See that entry also for the severe obstacles in the way of an argument that there could be a deduction of the amount of the pension contribution under reg.55(5)(a). **3.016**

pp.409–410, *annotation to the Universal Credit Regulations 2013 (SI 2013/376) reg.61(2) (Information for calculating earned income—real time information etc.)*

In the discussion of the decision in *SK and DK v SSWP (UC)* [2023] UKUT 21 (AAC), reported as [2023] AACR 5, note first that the decision was concerned with the form of reg.61 in force before November 16, 2020 and also that in the last paragraph on p.409 the reference to reg.55(4) should be to reg.55(4A). **3.017**

Doubts have been raised about the reasoning in paras 47 and 48 of the decision, as set out in the main volume, and the conclusion that the repayment of income tax made by the employer under the PAYE system constituted employed earnings in the assessment period in which it was reported. A full discussion will be included in the next main volume, but two points raised are that the repayment could not properly be regarded as employed earnings as defined in reg.55 as they would not constitute general earnings that would be subject to income tax and that the PAYE Regulations and system required the reporting of such repayments separately from ordinary earnings. It can then be argued that reg.61(2) cannot convert something that is not employed earnings into such earnings, especially if not reported as such on the employer's report to HMRC under the PAYE Regulations.

p.443, *annotation to the Universal Credit Regulations 2013 (SI 2013/376) reg.66(1)(h) (What is included in unearned income?—income protection insurance)*

Although the text of reg.66(1)(h) was belatedly corrected in the 2024/25 edition to take account of the revocation of head (ii) with effect from April 6, 2018, the notes to that provision were not corrected. The references there to head (ii) should be ignored. **3.018**

The income protection insurance covered by head (i) is often called permanent health insurance, but it is necessary to distinguish between individual policies, that provide payments for loss of income to the individual insured, and group income protection policies that pay funds to employers to cover the costs of paying sick pay. The former come within head (i). The latter result in payments of earnings by the employer that are taxable under ss.62 or 221 of the Income Tax (Earnings and Pensions) Act 2003 (ITEPA) and so are employed earnings within reg.55. There might be a question of attribution if an individual policy provided for payments direct to a mortgage lender or to a landlord to meet housing costs. Arguably, if the claimant had no say in whether such direct payment was made or not, the amount would not be part of their income. It would appear that critical illness insurance would not fall within head (i) because it typically provides a lump sum on diagnosis of specified serious illnesses or conditions and is thus not linked to the risk of losing income.

p.453, *annotation to the Universal Credit Regulations 2013 (SI 2013/376) reg.68 (Person treated as having student income)*

3.019 *SO v SSWP (UC)* [2024] UKUT 305 (AAC) contains detailed discussion of the structure of student support in Wales and of the terminology used, at least as it stood in 2021/22, although the system does not seem to have changed since. It also points out convincingly in paras 56–58 that the test of whether a person could acquire a student loan by taking reasonable steps to do so applies slightly differently in reg.68(5) and in reg.69(1). In reg.68(5) the focus is on the reasonableness of the actions taken by the particular person (as in *IB v Gravesham BC and SSWP (HC)* [2023] UKUT 193 (AAC), discussed in detail in the notes to reg.69 in the main volume). See the entry below for pp.454–456 for the slightly different focus necessary in the circumstances of *SO* under reg.69 and for the particular interaction of reg.68(3) and reg.69(2) where a person receives both a student loan and a grant.

The amount of a postgraduate loan in England for courses beginning on or after August 1, 2024 is £12,471.

pp.454–456, *annotation to the Universal Credit Regulations 2013 (SI 2013/376) reg.69 (Calculation of student income—student loans and postgraduate loans)*

3.020 In *SO v SSWP (UC)* [2024] UKUT 305 (AAC), the claimant was a full-time student who for the academic year 2021/22 received a student loan of £5,350 for maintenance from the Welsh Government. That amount was reduced under the Government's rules from the maximum loan amount of £8,289 by £2,939 because she was also entitled to a Welsh Government Learning Grant (WGLG) of that amount. Her universal credit was calculated taking into account income of £8,289. A First-tier Tribunal rejected the claimant's contention that only £5,350 should have been taken into account. Although there was a good deal of confusion in the approach both at first instance and by the tribunal about how the income should be distributed among the legislative categories, Judge Mitchell dismissed the claimant's appeal as the substance of the result was correct.

The proper analysis was that, as the claimant had a student loan (so that the deeming of having one under reg.68(5) was not necessary), her student income was to be based on the amount of her student loan (reg.68(2)).

Accordingly, the amount of the WGLG was to be disregarded (reg.68(3)), as it did not include any amounts excepted from that rule. However, the amount of student loan to be taken into account under reg.69 was to be the maximum student loan that the claimant would be able to acquire by taking reasonable steps to do so (reg.69(1)) on the assumption that there had been no reduction on account of any grant (defined in wide terms in reg.68(7)) made to the claimant (reg.69(2)(b)). The judge found the most difficult question to be whether it had to be found that some reasonable steps had not been taken in order for student income to include an amount of student loan that exceeded what had actually been received. The claimant plainly had taken all reasonable steps open to her, but the judge held that the different language in reg.69(2) as compared with that in reg.68(5), in particular "would be able", meant that the issue was intended to be approached on a notional basis, not on the basis of the individual claimant's actions. The question was what was the maximum amount a notional student, whose material circumstances matched those of the claimant, would be able to acquire by taking reasonable steps. With the requirement to ignore any reduction on account of receipt of a grant, the answer to that question was £8,289. Note that in paras 30 and 53 of the decision the terms of reg.69(2) are misdescribed.

p.462, *annotation to the Universal Credit Regulations 2013 (SI 2013/376) reg.74 (Notional unearned income)*

See reg.60B of the UC Transitional Regulations in the entry below for p.591, as inserted with effect from June 8, 2024, where a tax credit beneficiary who has reached the qualifying age for SPC has become entitled to universal credit under managed migration and has not applied for retirement pension income to which they might expect to be entitled. The effect of reg.74 is lifted for the first 12 assessment periods. **3.021**

p.465, *annotation to the Universal Credit Regulations 2013 (SI 2013/376) reg.75 (Compensation for personal injury)*

In *DR v SSWP (UC)* [2024] UKUT 196 (AAC), the claimant received some £27,000 under an ACAS settlement of employment tribunal proceedings, comprising elements for loss of employment (£6,411.60), statutory redundancy pay (£6,945.90) and compensation for injury to feelings arising from alleged discrimination (£14,142.50). An immediate claim for universal credit was refused on the ground that she had capital exceeding £16,000 and a later claim, when her capital had reduced to £10,700, was allowed subject to the taking into account of an assumed yield from capital of £82.65 per assessment period. The tribunal had rejected the claimant's argument that the whole payment should have been disregarded as it was not taxable. On further appeal, Judge Wikeley held that it had been right to do so. Liability or otherwise to tax was not relevant. There was nothing in the universal credit legislation allowing a disregard as capital of the elements of the sum for loss of employment or for statutory redundancy. Nor could the element for injury to feelings be disregarded under reg.75, as compensation for injury to feelings is distinct from a payment "for actual injury to physical or mental health (by way of, for instance, psychiatric injury)". It was therefore not necessary to decide whether the first decision was within the jurisdiction of the tribunal as well as the second. **3.022**

The inclusion of the category of psychiatric injury has been further supported by the decision of the Court of Appeal in *Shehabi v Kingdom of Bahrain* [2024] EWCA Civ 1158, in the context of the application of a statutory exception to the principle of State immunity from legal action, holding that "personal injury" includes a standalone psychiatric injury.

p.472, *annotation to the Universal Credit Regulations 2013 (SI 2013/376) reg.76(3) (Special schemes for compensation etc—disregards for claimants other than the diagnosed or infected person)*

3.023 With effect from October 10, 2024, the scope of para.(3) has been extended by the insertion of sub-para.(5B) in para.15 of Sch.V to the State Pension Credit Regulations 2022 (see the entry for p.929 for that amendment, which extends the capital disregard to any "payment out of the estate of a person which derives from a payment made under or by the Scottish Infected Blood Support Scheme or an approved blood scheme to the estate of the person as a result of that person having been infected from contaminated blood product"). Thus, it no longer matters who the person is who receives the payment from the infected person's estate. It is enough that they receive the payment from the estate. The Social Security Advisory Committee at its meeting of September 11, 2024 decided not to take the proposal to make the amending regulations on formal reference, but helpfully (in view of the common delays in the publication of SSAC meeting minutes) published on the SSAC website the letter of September 18, 2024 from the chair to the Secretary of State expressing a number of concerns. The holding reply from the Minister for Social Security and Disability (Sir Stephen Timms) of September 19, 2024 has also been published, as well as the minutes of the meeting of September 11, 2024 and a further letter from the Minister dated December 5, 2024. The immediate concerns included possible problems stemming from the use of the concept of the estate, such as in identifying who is an eligible recipient and in such recipients knowing of or being able to evidence such receipt on claiming a means-tested benefit possibly many years down the line, and in working out the amount of income or interest from the disregarded capital also to be disregarded, for instance if the money had been used to buy some investment or been mixed with other capital. The latter point seems unlikely to be problematic in universal credit because income from capital is not as such listed in reg.66(1) as unearned income to be taken into account. However, there might be problems stemming from the use of the concept of the estate, as explored more generally in the next two paragraphs.

Imagine an estate made up of the value of a matrimonial home (say, £250,000), in an infected person's sole name, and some savings (say, £50,000), to which an interim payment of £100,000 is made from the infected blood compensation scheme, and the infected person's will leaving the home to their spouse absolutely with the residue to be divided equally between the spouse and their two adult children. If one or more of the survivors is in receipt of or needs to claim universal credit, how will their £50,000 share of the residue (once distributed: see below for the position while the estate remains unadministered) be treated as capital? There is no problem with the home because its value will be disregarded if it remains the spouse's home. But how much of each actual share of the residue should be regarded as derived from the compensation payment and so to be disregarded under reg.76(3)? Should one just look at the ratio of the amount of the payment to the value of the residue and say that two thirds is to be disregarded from each share or should one look at the ratio to the overall value of the estate, including the home, and say that only a quarter of each share should be disregarded as capital? Who knows? And can there be a disregard from the capital value of the beneficiaries' chose in action in the form of the right to have the estate properly administered (see para.2.161 of the main volume) before any payment is actually made from the estate?

The structure of para.15 of Sch.V to the SPC Regulations is somewhat unwieldy (a point also raised in the letter of September 18, 2024). In relation to infected blood payments, including under the Scottish scheme, sub-para.(1) appears to cover the person to whom the payment is made by the scheme. Sub-paragraph (2) covers payments by a living infected person derived from a scheme payment to a partner or some former partners (and sub-para.(3) vice versa). Sub-paragraph (4) appears to cover some payments by a living infected person to a parent and sub-para.(5) some payments to parents from the estate of such a recipient. Then, sub-para.(5A) was introduced in August 2023 specifically to cover the particular recommendation of the Infected Blood Inquiry to extend the making of interim payments to making payments to the infected person's estate when that person had died before the payment could be made to them, disregarding payments out of the estate to the person's sons or daughters.

The new sub-para.(5B) uses the same structure as (5A), requiring that the payment from the scheme be made to the infected person's estate as well as a further payment deriving from the first payment being made out of the estate to anyone. However, that appears to leave out of the protection of the disregard cases where the infected person receives a payment from the scheme during life and then, after their death, a payment is made out of their estate, except in the very limited circumstances of sub-para.(5). It seems odd, in view of the overall aim to avoid amounts deriving from scheme payments affecting means-tested benefits, if such cases are not covered. In the ordinary use of language a scheme payment to an infected person during life could not be said to be to their estate, which only has any meaningful existence after death. So it appears that such a payment cannot give access to the disregard under sub-para.(5A) or (5B) if a payment is later made out of the person's estate after their death. There is though evidence in the recommendations of the Infected Blood Inquiry that that is what was intended.

The development of the compensation scheme for directly and indirectly infected persons and affected persons (e.g. family and carers) that was the primary recommendation of the Inquiry was still unfolding as at December 2024. The Victims and Prisoners Act 2024, passed on May 24, 2024, set up the Infected Blood Compensation Authority and required (s.49(1)) that a compensation scheme be established within three months. The Infected Blood Compensation Scheme Regulations 2024 (SI 2024/872), set out in Part I of this Supplement, came into force on August 23, 2024. They deal with compensation for infected persons. That part of the scheme became open to very small numbers of invitees in October 2024. Applications for further interim payments to estates from existing support schemes also opened in October 2024, although there have been administrative problems in processing claims. Further regulations are to be made dealing with affected persons with a view to applications starting in 2025. There is an excellent analysis of the development of the scheme as at September 24, 2024 in the House of Commons Library Briefing *Infected Blood Inquiry: compensation* (CBP 10099), with many references to more detailed sources, and some further background in the SSAC minutes of September 11, 2024. The *Government Response to the Infected Blood Inquiry* (CP 1224), published on December 17, 2024, contains updates on progress in implementing the Inquiry's recommendations.

pp.473–475, *annotation to the Universal Credit Regulations 2013 (SI 2013/376) reg.77 (Company analogous to a partnership or one-person business)*

3.024 *ZA v London Borough of Barnet (HB)* [2024] UKUT 222 (AAC) (see the entry for pp.307–309 for details) discusses the terms of the provisions of the Housing Benefit Regulations 2006 (reg.49(5) and (6)) equivalent to reg.77, but with the important difference that there is a discretion whether or not the provision should be applied if the basic condition for its application is met, whereas under reg.77(1) the rules in reg.77 must be applied if the claimant's position in relation to the company is analogous to that of a sole owner or partner in a trade or a property business. Thus, the judge's analysis of the options available is not directly relevant to universal credit.

p.519, *amendments to the Universal Credit Regulations 2013 (SI 2013/376) reg.99(6) (Circumstances in which requirements must not be imposed—administrative earnings threshold)*

3.025 As foreshadowed in the notes at pp.528–529 of the main volume, with effect from May 6, 2024, reg.2 of the Universal Credit (Administrative Earnings Threshold) (Amendment) Regulations 2024 (SI 2024/529) amended reg.99(6) by substituting "18 hours" for "15 hours" in sub-para.(a) and "29 hours" for "24 hours" in sub-para.(b). With effect from May 13, 2024, the Universal Credit (Administrative Earnings Threshold) (Amendment) (No.2) Regulations 2024 (SI 2024/529) revoked SI 2024/529 and by reg.2 made the identical amendments. See the notes to pp.528-529 and the entry for those pages below for critiques of that process and of the development of policy.

Note that, where a claimant (A) is a member of a couple and the other member, also of course a claimant, is for whatever reason not subject to the work search or work availability requirements and so does not need the protection of reg.99(6), A is entitled to that protection on meeting the threshold in reg.99(6)(a) (whose terms do not limit its application to single claimants). A does not need also to meet the alternative higher threshold in reg.99(6)(b) for couples.

pp.528–529, *annotation to the Universal Credit Regulations 2013 (SI 2013/376) reg.99(6) (Circumstances in which requirements must not be imposed—administrative earnings threshold)*

3.026 These notes were mistaken in suggesting that the absence from the preambles to SI 2024/529 and SI 2024/536 of a mention of the SSAC's report on the proposal to make the regulations was unusual. It is not yet known whether the proposal to abandon the higher threshold for couples is still extant under the new Labour administration.

p.580, *erratum in the Universal Credit Regulations 2013 (SI 2013/376) Sch.4 (Housing costs elements for renters) para.14 (Amount of housing cost contributions)*

In para.14(1) the relevant figure should read £91.47 not £291.47. 3.027

pp.629 and 632, *annotations to the Universal Credit Regulations 2013 (SI 2013/376) Sch.10, paras 18 and 18A (Capital to be disregarded—arrears of certain benefits and local welfare provision)*

It was announced in the Autumn Budget 2024 that the Household Support Fund and Discretionary Housing Payments were to be extended into the 2025/26 financial year. 3.028

p.730, *amendment to the Universal Credit (Transitional Provisions) Regulations 2014 (SI 2014/1230) reg.2 (Interpretation)*

With effect from June 8, 2024, reg.2(2) of the Social Security (State Pension Age Claimants: Closure of Tax Credits) (Amendment) Regulations 2024 (SI 2024/611) amended reg.2 by inserting after the definition of "tax credit" the following new definition: 3.029

> ""tax credit closure notice" means a notice issued under article 3A (tax credit closure notice) of the Welfare Reform Act 2012 (Commencement No. 32 and Savings and Transitional Provisions) Order 2019;".

p.791, *amendment to the Universal Credit (Transitional Provisions) Regulations 2014 (SI 2014/1230) reg.44 (Migration notice)*

With effect from June 8, 2024, reg.2(3)(a) of the Social Security (State Pension Age Claimants: Closure of Tax Credits) (Amendment) Regulations 2024 (SI 2024/611) amended reg.44 by inserting after para.(3) a new para (3A): 3.030

> "(3A) But where a migration notice is issued after cancellation of a previous migration notice or after cancellation of a tax credit closure notice the deadline day may be within such shorter period as the Secretary of State considers appropriate."

p.791, *amendment to the Universal Credit (Transitional Provisions) Regulations 2014 (SI 2014/1230) reg.44 (Migration notice)*

With effect from June 8, 2024, reg.2(3)(b) of the Social Security (State Pension Age Claimants: Closure of Tax Credits) (Amendment) Regulations 2024 (SI 2024/611) amended reg.44 by inserting after para.(5) a new para (5A): 3.031

> "(5A) In a case referred to in paragraph (5)(a) the Secretary of State may, instead of cancelling the migration notice, treat that notice as if it were a tax credit closure notice issued to that person and may treat the deadline day in the migration notice as if it were the deadline day in a tax credit closure notice."

p.807, *amendment to the Universal Credit (Transitional Provisions) Regulations 2014 (SI 2014/1230) reg.56(1) (Circumstances in which transitional protection ceases)*

3.032 With effect from June 8, 2024, reg.2(4)(a) of the Social Security (State Pension Age Claimants: Closure of Tax Credits) (Amendment) Regulations 2024 (SI 2024/611) amended reg.56(1) by inserting ", (3A)" after "paragraph (2)".

p.808, *amendment to the Universal Credit (Transitional Provisions) Regulations 2014 (SI 2014/1230) reg.56(2) (Circumstances in which transitional protection ceases)*

3.033 With effect from June 8, 2024, reg.2(4)(b) of the Social Security (State Pension Age Claimants: Closure of Tax Credits) (Amendment) Regulations 2024 (SI 2024/611) amended reg.56(2) by inserting "other than an assessment period in relation to an award of universal credit mentioned in regulation 60A(1) (waiver of upper age limit for claimants migrated from tax credits)" after "assessment period" where it is first mentioned.

p.808, *amendment to the Universal Credit (Transitional Provisions) Regulations 2014 (SI 2014/1230) reg.56 (Circumstances in which transitional protection ceases)*

3.034 With effect from June 8, 2024, reg.2(4)(c) of the Social Security (State Pension Age Claimants: Closure of Tax Credits) (Amendment) Regulations 2024 (SI 2024/611) amended reg.56 by inserting after para.(3) a new para. (3A):

"(3A) This paragraph applies to an assessment period in relation to an award of universal credit mentioned in regulation 60A(1) (waiver of upper age limit for claimants migrated from tax credits) which—

(a) is not one of the first 12 assessment periods; and
(b) is the assessment period after the third consecutive assessment period in which the claimant's earned income, (or, if the claimant is a member of a couple the couple's combined earned income) is less than the amount that a person would be paid at the hourly rate set out in regulation 4 of the National Minimum Wage Regulations for 16 hours a week converted to a monthly amount by multiplying by 52 and dividing by 12."

p.811, *amendment to the Universal Credit (Transitional Provisions) Regulations 2014 (SI 2014/1230) by insertion of new regs.60A–60C*

3.035 With effect from June 8, 2024, reg.2(5) of the Social Security (State Pension Age Claimants: Closure of Tax Credits) (Amendment) Regulations 2024 (SI 2024/611) inserted after reg.60 the following new regs 60A, 60B and 60C:

"Waiver of upper age limit for claimants migrated from tax credits

60A.—(1) Where a qualifying claim is made by—

(a) a single claimant who, at the time the migration notice is issued—

(i) has reached the qualifying age for state pension credit;
(ii) is entitled to an award of working tax credit; and
(iii) is not entitled to an award of state pension credit; or
(b) joint claimants both of whom satisfy the criteria in sub-paragraph (a)(i) to (iii) at the time the migration notice is issued,

then, subject to paragraphs (2) and (3), the condition in section 4(1)(b) of the Act (claimant has not reached the qualifying age for state pension credit) is not to apply for the purposes of determining entitlement to universal credit in respect of the qualifying claim or any award made in respect of that claim.

(2) The reference in paragraph (1) to a person who is entitled to an award of working tax credit includes a person who meets the entitlement conditions for both that credit and child tax credit.

(3) Paragraph (1) ceases to apply in respect of an award of universal credit mentioned in paragraph (1) in an assessment period in which—
(a) a transitional element or transitional capital disregard would cease to apply by virtue of regulation 56 (circumstances in which transitional protection ceases) or regulation 57 (application of transitional protection to a subsequent award); or
(b) a person who is entitled to an award of universal credit by virtue of paragraph (1) makes a claim for state pension credit.

Deferral of retirement pension income

60B.—(1) Where, at the time a migration notice is issued, the notified person—
(a) has reached the qualifying age for state pension credit;
(b) is entitled to an award of a tax credit; and
(c) has not made an application for retirement pension income to which they might expect to be entitled,

regulation 74 (notional unearned income) of the Universal Credit Regulations is not, subject to paragraph (2), to apply in relation to that person for the purpose of calculating the amount of an award of universal credit (including the indicative UC amount) until the assessment period following the first 12 assessment periods of an award made in respect of a claim by that person.

(2) This regulation ceases to apply in an assessment period in which a transitional element or transitional capital disregard would cease to apply by virtue of regulation 56 (circumstances in which transitional protection ceases) or regulation 57 (application of transitional protection to a subsequent award).

(3) In this regulation "retirement pension income" has the same meaning as in regulation 67 of the Universal Credit Regulations.

Exemption from the benefit cap

60C. Where a qualifying claim is made by a single claimant who has, or joint claimants both of whom have, reached the qualifying age for state pension credit, regulation 79 (circumstances where the benefit cap applies) of the Universal Credit Regulations is not to apply for the purpose of calculating the amount of an award of universal credit (including the indicative UC amount)."

p.817, *erratum in the Universal Credit (Transitional Provisions) Regulations 2014 (SI 2014/1230) Sch.1 para.16 (Modification of tax credits legislation (Finalisation of tax credits))*

3.036 The modification involving the insertion by para.16 of a new para.(3) has been included twice in error.

p.833, *amendment to the State Pension Credit Regulations 2002 (SI 2002/1792) reg.1 (Citation, commencement and interpretation)*

3.037 With effect from April 6, 2010, reg.3(2) of the Social Security (Miscellaneous Amendments) (No. 6) Regulations 2009 (SI 2009/3229) substituted for the definition of "benefit week" the following new definition:

""benefit week" means—
(a) where state pension credit is paid in advance, the period of 7 days beginning on the day on which, in the claimant's case, that benefit is payable;
(b) where state pension credit is paid in arrears, the period of 7 days ending on the day on which, in the claimant's case, that benefit is payable.".

p.838, *amendment to the State Pension Credit Regulations 2002 (SI 2002/1792) reg.1 (Citation, commencement and interpretation)*

3.038 With effect from June 8, 2024, reg.4(2) of the Social Security (State Pension Age Claimants: Closure of Tax Credits) (Amendment) Regulations 2024 (SI 2024/611) inserted the following new definition before the definition of "universal credit":

""tax credit closure notice" means a notice issued under article 3A (tax credit closure notice) of the Welfare Reform Act 2012 (Commencement No. 32 and Savings and Transitional Provisions) Order 2019;".

p.857, *amendment to the State Pension Credit Regulations 2002 (SI 2002/1792) reg.6 (Amount of the guarantee credit)*

3.039 With effect from June 8, 2024, reg.4(3) of the Social Security (State Pension Age Claimants: Closure of Tax Credits) (Amendment) Regulations 2024 (SI 2024/611) amended reg.6(6) by omitting "or" at the end of para.(6)(c) and inserting after para.(6)(d) the following:

"or
(e) in accordance with Schedule IIB (transitional protection on closure of tax credits).".

p.870, *amendment to the State Pension Credit Regulations 2002 (SI 2002/1792) reg.13A (Part-weeks)*

3.040 With effect from April 6, 2010, reg.3(3) of the Social Security (Miscellaneous Amendments) (No. 6) Regulations 2009 (SI 2009/3229) amended reg.13A by omitting para.(2), omitting the phrase ", taking into account the requirements of paragraph (2)," in para.(3)(a) and also omitting the words from "any fraction" to the end of para.(3).

p.870, *amendment to the State Pension Credit Regulations 2002 (SI 2002/1792) reg.13B (Date on which benefits are treated as paid)*

With effect from April 6, 2010, reg.3(4) of the Social Security (Miscellaneous Amendments) (No. 6) Regulations 2009 (SI 2009/3229) amended reg.13B by substituting for para.(2) the following: **3.041**

"(2) All benefits except those mentioned in paragraph (1) shall be treated as paid—
(a) where the benefit is paid in advance, on the first day of the benefit week in which the benefit is payable;
(b) where the benefit is paid in arrears, on the last day of the benefit week in which the benefit is payable."

p.887, *amendment to the State Pension Credit Regulations 2002 (SI 2002/1792) reg.18(1A) (Notional income)*

With effect from June 8, 2024, reg.4(4)(a) of the Social Security (State Pension Age Claimants: Closure of Tax Credits) (Amendment) Regulations 2024 (SI 2024/611) amended para.(1A) by substituting ", (1CB) and (5A)" for "and (1CB)". **3.042**

pp.887–888, *amendments to the State Pension Credit Regulations 2002 (SI 2002/1792) reg.18(1D) and (2) (Notional income)*

With effect from June 8, 2024, reg.4(4)(b) of the Social Security (State Pension Age Claimants: Closure of Tax Credits) (Amendment) Regulations 2024 (SI 2024/611) amended paras (1D) and (2) by inserting at the beginning of each paragraph "Subject to paragraph (5A),". **3.043**

p.888, *amendment to the State Pension Credit Regulations 2002 (SI 2002/1792) reg.18 (Notional income)*

With effect from June 8, 2024, reg.4(4)(c) of the Social Security (State Pension Age Claimants: Closure of Tax Credits) (Amendment) Regulations 2024 (SI 2024/611) amended reg.18 by inserting after para.(5): **3.044**

"(5A) Where a person—
(a) makes a claim for state pension credit on or after the issue of a tax credit closure notice and before the expiry of one month beginning with the deadline day specified in that notice; and
(b) has not, at the time the notice is issued, made an application for retirement pension income to which they might expect to be entitled,

paragraphs (1), (1D) and (2) are not to apply for a period beginning with the first day on which the person is entitled to an award of state pension credit as a consequence of that claim and ending after 52 weeks or, if sooner, on the day the person ceases to be entitled to state pension credit."

p.919, *amendment to the State Pension Credit Regulations 2002 (SI 2002/1792) by insertion of new Sch.IIB (Transitional Protection on Closure of Tax Credits)*

3.045 With effect from June 8, 2024, reg.4(5) of the Social Security (State Pension Age Claimants: Closure of Tax Credits) (Amendment) Regulations 2024 (SI 2024/611) inserted after Sch.IIA the following new Schedule:

"SCHEDULE IIB regulation 6(6)

TRANSITIONAL PROTECTION ON CLOSURE OF TAX CREDITS

Interpretation

1. In this Schedule—

"HMRC" means His Majesty's Revenue and Customs;

"indicative SPC amount" has the meaning given in paragraph 5;

"migration day" in relation to a claimant means the day before the day specified in paragraph (1) of article 3B (saving to cease following issue of tax credit closure notice) of the No. 32 Order;

"the No. 32 Order" means the Welfare Reform Act 2012 (Commencement No. 32 and Savings and Transitional Provisions) Order 2019;

"tax credit", "child tax credit" and "working tax credit" have the same meaning as in the Tax Credits Act 2002.

Claimants eligible for protection

2.—(1) This Schedule applies where the claimant has been issued with a tax credit closure notice and—

(a) the claimant was entitled to an award of child tax credit on the migration day; and

(b) either—

(i) the claimant was entitled to an award of state pension credit when the tax credit closure notice was issued; or

(ii) the claimant made a claim for state pension credit on or after the issue of the tax credit closure notice and before the expiry of one month beginning with the deadline day specified in that notice.

(2) This Schedule does not apply where—

(a) the claimant was a member of a couple for the purposes of the child tax credit award when the tax credit closure notice was issued but is a single person or a member of a different couple for the purposes of state pension credit on the migration day; or

(b) the claimant was a single person for the purposes of the child tax credit award when the tax credit closure notice was issued but is a member of a couple for the purposes of state pension credit on the migration day.

Transitional additional amount

3. An additional amount of the appropriate minimum guarantee ("the transitional additional amount") applies in accordance with regulation 6(6)(e) if the weekly amount determined in accordance with paragraph 4 (representative weekly amount of child tax credit), combined with the weekly amount of state pension credit (if any) to which the claimant was entitled on the migration day, is greater than the weekly amount determined in accordance with paragraph 5 (indicative SPC amount).

Representative weekly amount of child tax credit

4.—(1) To calculate the representative weekly amount of an award of child tax credit—

(a) take the figure for the daily rate of the award on the migration day provided by HMRC and calculated on the basis of the information as to the claimant's circumstances held by HMRC on that day; and

(b) convert to a weekly figure by multiplying by 7.

(2) For the purposes of sub-paragraph (1)(a) "the daily rate" is—

(a) in a case where section 13(1) of the Tax Credit Act 2002 (relevant income does not exceed the income threshold or the claimant is entitled to a prescribed social security benefit) applies, the maximum rate of each element to which the claimant is entitled on the migration day divided by 365; and

(b) in any other case, the rate that would be produced by applying regulations 6 to 9 of the Tax Credits (Income Thresholds and Determination of Rates) Regulations 2002 as if the migration day were a relevant period of one day.

Indicative SPC amount

5.—(1) The indicative SPC amount is the weekly amount to which a claimant would be entitled if an award of state pension credit were calculated in accordance with the Act and these Regulations by reference to the claimant's circumstances on the migration day—

(a) disregarding any amount of working tax credit to which the person may be entitled on that day;

(b) including an additional amount in accordance with Schedule IIA (additional amount applicable for claimants responsible for a child or qualifying young person); and

(c) applying the assumptions in sub-paragraph (2).

(2) The assumptions are—

(a) the claimant is responsible for any child or qualifying young person in respect of whom the individual element of child tax credit is payable;

(b) the amount of the claimant's earned income is the annual amount of any employment income or trading income, as defined by regulation 4 or 6 respectively of the Tax Credits (Definition and Calculation of Income) Regulations 2002, by reference to which the representative weekly rate of that tax credit is calculated for the purposes of paragraph 4(1) converted to a net weekly amount by—

(i) dividing by 52; and

(ii) deducting such amount for income tax and national insurance contributions as the Secretary of State considers appropriate.

(3) If the claimant would not satisfy the condition in section 2(1) (guarantee credit) of the Act because the claimant has income which exceeds the appropriate minimum guarantee, the claimant is to be treated for the purposes of calculating the indicative SPC amount as if they were entitled to a guarantee credit of a nil amount.

Initial calculation of the transitional additional amount

6. The initial amount of the transitional additional amount is—

(a) if the amount of the guarantee credit in the indicative SPC amount is greater than nil, the amount by which the representative weekly amount of child tax credit combined with the weekly amount of state pension credit (if any) to which the claimant was entitled on the migration day, exceeds the weekly amount of the indicative SPC amount;

(b) if the amount of the guarantee credit in the indicative SPC amount is nil—

(i) the sum of the representative weekly amount of child tax credit and the amount, if any, by which the income deducted in the calculation of the indicative SPC amount exceeds the amount of the appropriate minimum guarantee; minus

(ii) the amount of the maximum saving credit, but only if the indicative SPC amount includes a savings credit or would do but for the claimant's income being such that the condition in section 3(2)(b) of the Act is not met.

Reduction of the transitional additional amount

7.—(1) Whenever there is a relevant increase after the first day on which the transitional additional amount applies, the transitional additional amount is to be reduced by an amount equal to that increase.

(2) A relevant increase is an increase in the standard minimum guarantee or in any additional amount prescribed under section 2(3) of the Act, including where that additional amount is applied for the first time or reapplied following a change of circumstances.

Circumstances in which the transitional additional amount ceases

8.—(1) A transitional additional amount is no longer applicable if—

(a) the transitional additional amount is reduced to nil in accordance with paragraph 7;

(b) the claimant was a member of a couple and ceases to be a member of that couple or becomes a member of a different couple;

(c) the claimant was single and becomes a member of a couple; or

(d) the claimant is no longer responsible for any child or qualifying young person for whom they were responsible at the time the tax credit closure notice was issued.

(2) Where the claimant ceases to be entitled to state pension credit, the transitional additional amount is not, subject to sub-paragraph (3), to apply to a subsequent award to the claimant or, if the claimant is a member of a couple, their partner.

(3) Where an award ("the subsequent award") is made to a person who moves from Northern Ireland when they are entitled to an award of state pension credit that includes a transitional additional amount then, provided their circumstances are otherwise unchanged,

the subsequent award is to include a transitional additional amount calculated as if the subsequent award were a continuation of the award made in Northern Ireland.

Effect of revision, appeal etc. of an award of a tax credit

9.—(1) Nothing in paragraph 4 or 5 requiring a calculation in relation to the transitional additional amount to be made on the basis of information held by HMRC on the migration day prevents the Secretary of State from revising or superseding a decision in relation to a claim for, or an award of, state pension credit where—

(a) in the opinion of the Secretary of State, the information held on that day was inaccurate or incomplete in some material respect because of—
  (i) a misrepresentation by a claimant;
  (ii) a failure to report information that a claimant was required to report where that failure was advantageous to the claimant; or
  (iii) an official error; or
(b) a decision has been made on or after the migration day on—
  (i) an application made before the migration day to revise a decision in relation to an award of a tax credit (including the report of a change of circumstances); or
  (ii) an appeal in relation to such an application.

(2) In this paragraph "official error" means an error that—
(a) was made by an officer of, or an employee of a body acting on behalf of, the Department for Work and Pensions or HMRC; and
(b) was not caused, or materially contributed to, by any person outside that body or outside the Department or HMRC,

but excludes any error of law which is shown to have been such by a subsequent decision of the Upper Tribunal or of a court as defined in section 27(7) of the Social Security Act 1998."

Note also that reg.5 of the Social Security (State Pension Age Claimants: Closure of Tax Credits) (Amendment) Regulations 2024 (SI 2024/611) provides as follows:

Supplementary provision relating to persons moving to state pension credit: time for claiming and part-week payments

5.—(1) Where a person who is not entitled to an award of state pension credit is issued with a tax credit closure notice then, notwithstanding anything in regulation 19(2) (time for claiming benefit) of the Social Security (Claims and Payments) Regulations 1987, the prescribed times for making a claim for state pension credit are as follows—
(a) if the person is claiming in respect of a period that begins before the deadline day specified in that notice, the first day of that period;
(b) if the person is claiming in respect of a period that begins on the deadline day, within three months beginning with the deadline day.

(2) Where, by virtue of paragraph (1), state pension credit is awarded from a day which is not the first day of a benefit week then, notwithstanding anything in regulation 16A of those Regulations, entitlement shall begin on the first day of the award and the amount payable in respect of that part-week shall be determined by—
(a) dividing by 7 the weekly amount which would be payable in respect of the full week; and then
(b) multiplying the resulting figure by the number of days in the part-week.

(3) But paragraph (2) does not apply if the claimant's entitlement to state pension credit is unlikely to continue throughout the first full benefit week that follows the part-week.

(4) In this regulation—

"benefit week" means—
(a) where state pension credit is paid in advance, the period of 7 days beginning on the day on which, in the claimant's case, that benefit would (if not for paragraph (2)) be payable;
(b) where state pension credit is paid in arrears, the period of 7 days ending on the day on which, in the claimant's case, that benefit would (if not for paragraph (2)) be payable; and

"tax credit closure notice" means a notice issued under article 3A (tax credit closure notice) of the Welfare Reform Act 2012 (Commencement No. 32 and Savings and Transitional Provisions) Order 2019.

p.929, *amendment to the State Pension Credit Regulations 2002 (SI 2002/1792) Sch.V para.15 (Income from capital—Capital disregarded for the purpose of calculating income)*

With effect from October 10. 2024, reg.2(1)(c) and 2(2) of the Social Security (Infected Blood Capital Disregard) (Amendment) Regulations 2024 (SI 2024/964) amended para.15 by inserting after sub-para.(5A) the following: 3.046

> "(5B) Any payment out of the estate of a person, which derives from a payment made under or by the Scottish Infected Blood Support Scheme or an approved blood scheme to the estate of the person as a result of that person having been infected from contaminated blood products."

p.957, *revocation of the Social Fund Winter Fuel Payment Regulations 2000 (SI 2000/729); making of the Social Fund Winter Fuel Payment Regulations 2024 (SI 2024/869)*

The existing regulatory scheme for making winter fuel payments is revoked, with effect from September 16, 2024, by reg.7(1) and Sch.2 of the Social Fund Winter Fuel Payment Regulations 2024 (SI 2024/869). The 2024 regulations establish a new scheme: see Part I above. 3.047

p.969, *errata in the Social Fund Maternity and Funeral Expenses (General) Regulations 2005 (SI 2005/3061) reg.3 (Interpretation)*

In paragraph 1: 3.048

- in the definition of "family", sub-paragraph (c) contains an error. The amendment showing to that provision should feature at the beginning, not the end, of the sub-paragraph.
- The definition of "residence order" should be replaced with an ellipsis.
- After the ellipsis replacing the "residence order" definition, the following definition should appear: ""responsible person" has the meaning given in regulation 7(1);"

p.986, *erratum in the Social Fund Maternity and Funeral Expenses (General) Regulations 2005 (SI 2005/3061) reg.6 (Persons affected by a trade dispute)*

The words "the "relevant claim" was made before the beginning of the trade dispute." should appear at the end of reg.6(1)(b). 3.049

p.1005, *erratum in the Social Fund Maternity and Funeral Expenses (General) Regulations 2005 (SI 2005/3061) reg.10 (Deductions from an award of a funeral payment)*

Paragraph 1A(b) should read: "[(b) bereavement support payment under section 30 of the Pensions Act 2014;]". The substitution of that provision for the original reg.10(1A)(b) was made with effect from April 6, 2017 by the Pensions Act 2014 (Consequential, Supplementary and Incidental Amendments) Order 2017 (SI 2017/422), arts 1(2) and 24. 3.050

PART IV

UPDATING MATERIAL

VOLUME III
ADMINISTRATION, ADJUDICATION AND THE EUROPEAN DIMENSION

Commentary by

Will Rolt

Christopher Ward

pp.20–23, *annotation to the Social Security Administration Act 1992 s.1 (Entitlement to benefit dependent on claim)—General Note*

In *PHC v SSWP (UC)* [2024] UKUT 340 (AAC) among numerous possible interpretations of less than coherent decision-making on behalf of the Secretary of State was whether a claimant who failed to provide evidence of identity following a change of name had failed to comply with s.1(1)(a). Dicta in *ED v SSWP* (a case with very different facts) had alluded to this possibility, which Judge Wikeley at [39]–[47] declined to adopt, accepting a submission from SSWP's representative that 4.001

> "26 ... the requirements that make up a prescribed manner of claiming merely require the claimant to set out in a particular way *the case for benefit* he wishes to make. Once that has been done, a claim in the prescribed manner is made, and the truthfulness and merits of the case that has been presented are separately and subsequently considered as part of an outcome decision as to the claimant's entitlement to benefit under the claim. In my submission, this approach is more consistent not just with well-established conceptions of decision making but also with the existence of a condition of entitlement (in sections 1(1A)–(1B) of the Administration Act) that quite obviously has to do with the claimant's identity."

Rather (at [52]), the correct approach to questions of a claimant's identity in relation to new claims for universal credit is via sub-sections (1A) and (1B). As to how the FTT should approach such a case, Judge Wikeley adopts a submission on behalf of SSWP that:

> "39. On appeal against a decision that a claimant is not entitled to benefit because he or she does not satisfy section 1(1A) of the Administration Act, a FTT is not confined to considering whether the Secretary of State's decision – and thus his approach to section 1(1B)" – was reasonable on the evidence before him and consistent with the relevant law. Rather, the FTT is engaged in a rehearing of the question of whether the claimant satisfies the requirements of section 1(1B) (*R(IB) 2/04* at paragraphs 13–15 and 19–33). In effect, it must apply *for itself* the tests in section 1(1B) in the light of the evidence that is *now* available to it, which could in principle include any evidence of identity that was brought to light by the claimant or the Secretary of State after the date of the decision under appeal (cf. *R(DLA) 3/01* at paragraph 58).
>
> 40. On appeal, a FTT should establish precisely what steps the Secretary of State has taken in relation to section 1(1B). In particular, it should ensure that it is provided with (a) copies of all information and evidence that the claimant provided when claiming and during the Secretary of State's subsequent investigations (including proper accounts of any interviews that have been conducted), and (b) an informative summary of what has been fed into what tools with what results. However, the tribunal is not, in my submission, bound to follow in the Secretary of State's footsteps. It will be up to it to decide for itself how to approach and apply the tests in section 1(1B). For example, where, as here, the Secretary of State has found that section 1(1B) is not satisfied without determining whether the specialist tools available to a NiNo allocation officer can trace a NiNo for a person with the claimant's alleged details,

but the tribunal is of the view that it would be best to establish whether a NiNo exists for such a person and then consider whether the claimant and that person are one and the same with the benefit of the information relating to the NiNo-holder that DWP's records contain, then it is entitled to direct the Secretary of State to carry out this investigation and provide it with an account of its methods and findings. In the end, it will be for the tribunal to decide whether a NiNo allocated to the claimant has been identified and (if not) whether the claimant has established his identity to such a degree of confidence that a NiNo can properly to be allocated to him. In short, in my submission, one way or another, it will fall to the tribunal to make a fresh, evidence-based appraisal of whether the claimant is who [she] says [she] is."

Subsections (1A) and (1B) do not apply to a child or qualifying young person in respect of whom universal credit is claimed: see the Universal Credit, Personal Independence Payment, Jobseeker's Allowance and Employment and Support Allowance (Claims and Payments) Regulations 2013 (SI 213/380), reg.5.

pp.97–98, *annotation to the Social Security Administration Act 1992 s.78—Recovery of social fund awards—General Note*

4.002 In *Houston v Secretary of State for Work and Pensions* [2024] CSOH 79 the claimant was unsuccessful in challenging the recovery of a loan from his award of state pension credit. Section 78(2) and the 1988 Regulations provided statutory authority for the recovery. The attempt to recover was not made out of time, nor was there any mistake of fact capable of amounting to an error of law. Nor could he rely on s.187 of the 1992 Act, which is concerned with the voluntary transfer of the right to receive benefit.

pp.157–158, *annotation to the Social Security Administration Act 1992 s.187 (Certain benefit to be inalienable)—General Note*

4.003 An attempt to rely on this section to defeat recovery of a social fund loan from an award of state pension credit failed in *Houston v Secretary of State for Work and Pensions* [2024] CSOH 79. Section 187 concerns the voluntary transfer of the right to receive benefit; recovery of the loan was permitted by s.78(2) and associated regulations.

p.257, *annotation to the Social Security Act 1998 s.12 (Appeal to the First-tier Tribunal)*

4.004 However, it is suggested that the decision in *AO* has been superseded by the Court of Appeal's decision in *Williamson v Bishop of London* [2023] EWCA Civ 379 in which it was noted at para.8 that: "The term "any court" in section 42(1A) SCA 1981 has been held to extend to all inferior courts including tribunals." Whilst the Court of Appeal was dealing with a case concerning appeals from the Employment Tribunal, and *AO* was not referred to, it appears clear that the Court of Appeal is of the view that a section 42 order applies to appeals to Tribunals and as such this would include social security cases.

p.328, *the Welfare Reform and Pensions Act 1999 s.68 (Certain overpayments of benefit not to be recoverable)—erratum*

Subsection (4) should be replaced by the following text: **4.005**

"(4) For the purposes of this section "qualifying benefit" means—
(a) attendance allowance;
(b) disability living allowance;
(c) any benefit awarded wholly or partly by reason of a person being (or being treated as being) in receipt of a component (at any rate) of disability living allowance or in receipt of attendance allowance;
(d) incapacity benefit;
(e) any benefit (other than incapacity benefit) awarded wholly or party by reason of a person being (or being treated as being) incapable of work; or
(f) any benefit awarded wholly or partly by reason of a person being (or being treated as being) in receipt of any benefit falling within paragraph (c), (d) or (e)."

p.391, *amendment to the Social Security (Claims and Payments) Regulations 1987 (SI 1987/1968) reg.4 (Making a claim for benefit)*

With effect from September 16, 2024, reg.6 of the Social Fund Winter Fuel Payment Regulations 2024 (SI 2024/869) amended reg.4(6A) by substituting "regulation 4(1)(c) of the Social Fund Winter Fuel Payment Regulations 2024" for "regulation 3(1)(b) of the Social Fund Winter Fuel Payment Regulations 2000". **4.006**

p.420, *amendment to the Social Security (Claims and Payments) Regulations 1987 (SI 1987/1968) reg.6 (Date of claim)*

With effect from October 21, 2024, art.5 of the Social Security (Scotland) Act 2018 (Disability Assistance) (Consequential Amendments) Order 2024 (SI 2024/936) made the following amendments: **4.007**

(a) in paragraph (20)(c)—
  (i) at the end of sub-paragraph (iii) omit "or";
  (ii) after sub-paragraph (iv) insert—
  ", or
  (v) regulation 19 (effect of admission to a care home on ongoing entitlement to daily living component), or as the case may be, regulation 20 (effect of admission to hospital on ongoing entitlement to Pension Age Disability Payment) of the Disability Assistance for Older People (Scotland) Regulations 2024 because the claimant is, respectively, a resident of a care home or undergoing treatment in a hospital.";
(b) in paragraph (38)(b)—
  (i) for "either" substitute "any";
  (ii) at the end of paragraph (i) omit "and";
  (iii) after paragraph (ii) insert—
  "; or
  (iii) pension age disability payment within the meaning of regulation 2 of the Disability Assistance for Older People (Scotland) Regulations 2024.".

p.432, *the Social Security (Claims and Payments) Regulations 1987 (SI 1987/1968) reg.7 (Evidence and information)—erratum*

4.008 In para.4, the words "is aged not less than 60" were replaced with effect from April 6, 2010 by the words "has attained the qualifying age". The amending legislation was the Social Security (Miscellaneous Amendments) (No.2) Regulations 2010 (SI 2010/641) reg.3. "Qualifying age" is defined, via reg.2 and the State Pension Credit Act 2002, s.1(6) as referring to pensionable age.

General Note

4.009 It may be thought curious that this amendment, which as pensionable age increases reduces the number of those subject to the duty in reg.7(4), does not appear to have been made to reg.32(4), which imposes a similar duty on those "aged not less than 60".

pp.458–459, *annotation to the Social Security (Claims and Payments) Regulations 1987 (SI 1987/1968) reg.19(2) (Time for claiming benefit)—General Note*

4.010 Regulation 5 of the Social Security (State Pension Age Claimants: Closure of Tax Credits) (Amendment) Regulations 2024 (SI 2024/611) makes specific provision for the situation where a person who is not entitled to an award of state pension credit is issued with a tax credit closure notice "notwithstanding anything in regulation 19(2)".

pp.489–490, *the Social Security (Claims and Payments) Regulations 1987 (SI 1987/1968) reg.31 – erratum*

4.011 The purported subsection (1A) was included in error and it and its associated footnote are deleted.

p.502, *amendment to the Social Security (Claims and Payments) Regulations 1987 (SI 1987/1968) reg.36 (Payment to a partner as alternative payee)*

4.012 With effect from September 16, 2024, reg.6 of the Social Fund Winter Fuel Payment Regulations 2024 (SI 2024/869) omitted paragraph (2).

pp.569–570, *annotation to the Universal Credit, Personal Independence Payment, Jobseeker's Allowance and Employment and Support Allowance (Claims and Payments) Regulations 2013 (SI 2013/380) reg.33 (Advance claim for and award of personal independence payment)*

4.013 The application of reg.33 is well illustrated by *SR v SSWP (PIP)* [2024] UKUT 198 (AAC). The claimant had sustained his disabling injuries in an accident on September 5, 2021 and claimed on November 15, 2021. The FTT erred in law by disallowing the claim on the basis that the period of less than 3 months between the accident and the claim meant that he had not satisfied the 3 month qualifying period for PIP. Reg.33(1) means that an advance award could be made if the claimant were found to meet the conditions for a 3 month period that was completed only later.

pp.571–572, *annotation to the Universal Credit, Personal Independence Payment, Jobseeker's Allowance and Employment and Support Allowance (Claims and Payments) Regulations 2013 (SI 2013/380) s.37 (Evidence and information in connection with a claim)—General Note*

Failure to provide evidence required by the Secretary of State under reg.37(2) does not, in and of itself, provide justification for refusing a claim. It may however result in adverse inferences being drawn, leading to the claim being disallowed: see *PHC v SSWP (UC)* [2024] UKUT 340 (AAC) at [29]–[33]. **4.014**

pp.572–574, *annotation to the Universal Credit, Personal Independence Payment, Jobseeker's Allowance and Employment and Support Allowance (Claims and Payments) Regulations 2013 (SI 2013/380) s.38 (Evidence and information in connection with an award)—General Note*

If authority be needed that this section can only apply where there is an existing award and not in relation to a new claim, it is to be found in *PHC v SSWP* (above). **4.015**

pp.595–596, *annotation to the Universal Credit, Personal Independence Payment, Jobseeker's Allowance and Employment and Support Allowance (Claims and Payments) Regulations 2013 (SI 2013/380) Sch.2 (Use of electronic communications)*

Where a claimant successfully completes the online claim process but is then required by the Secretary of State to provide evidence of identity and fails to do so, that cannot be categorised as a failure to comply with para.2(3)(a) of the Schedule. The process for making an online claim in the case did not include a requirement that a prospective claimant prove their identity: see *PHC v SSWP (UC)* [2024] UKUT 340 (AAC) at [34]–[38]. **4.016**

p.684, *annotation to the Social Security and Child Support (Decisions and Appeals) Regulations 1999 (SI 1999/991) reg.7 (Date from which a decision superseded under section 10 takes effect)*

Regulation 7(2)(c)(ii) was further considered in *SS v SSWP (DLA)* [2024] UKUT 327 (AAC). The requirements of the regulation must be considered specifically by a First-tier Tribunal which must provide reasoned findings as to each of its conditions. However, the weight to give to each piece of evidence bearing on a decision on each condition is a matter for the First-tier Tribunal's judgement. In particular, it is not the case that actual or constructive knowledge of an obligation to report a change in circumstance can only arise from a claimant having been expressly told that they were so obliged. Nor is it necessary for the claimant to know (or be in a position where they could reasonably be expected to know) that the obligation to report was a legal obligation: what is required is that they know (or could reasonably be expected to know) that the obligation exists, not its nature. **4.017**

p.1061, *annotation to the Tribunals, Courts and Enforcement Act 2007 s.3 (The First-tier Tribunal and Upper Tribunal)*

4.018 In *CB v SSWP* [2024] UKUT 257 (AAC) a presenting officer had stated at the hearing that further evidence might available and had not been provided. The First-tier Tribunal erred in law in (i) piecing together a matter without evidence when evidence of it might have been available; and (ii) failing to explore whether such evidence was available and adjourning the appeal for that evidence to be obtained.

p.1062, *annotation to the Tribunals, Courts and Enforcement Act 2007 s.3 (The First-tier Tribunal and Upper Tribunal)*

4.019 The decision of the Court of Appeal in *Hima v SSHD* [2024] EWCA Civ 680 is a reminder that a Tribunal Judge must exercise caution when exercising the inquisitorial role. It is not the same as cross-examination. The Court of Appeal concluded that the First-tier Tribunal judge's cross-examination of the applicant was not a minor departure from ideal practice. It demonstrated that the judge had entered the arena to an impermissible extent, and his treatment of the applicant's legal representative when he objected to such questioning also impacted on the overall fairness of the hearing. Questions of procedural fairness depended on context and were fact and case-specific, *Elmi Abdi v Entry Clearance Officer* [2023] EWCA Civ 1455, [2023] 12 WLUK 66 followed. Any suggestion that First-tier Tribunal judges were not subject to the same requirement to act fairly as other judges was misconceived. The concept of acting fairly was implicit in the judicial oath.

p.1067, *annotation to the Tribunals, Courts and Enforcement Act 2007 s.3 (The First-tier Tribunal and Upper Tribunal)*

4.020 The well-established principle that, when a tribunal uses its specialist knowledge or expertise to decide an issue, fairness will normally require it to give the parties an opportunity to comment was discussed in the case of *NH v SSWP* [2024] UKUT 173 (AAC), where information from a website was used by the First-tier Tribunal. The Upper Tribunal highlighted the relevant case law (*R. (L) v London Borough of Waltham Forest* [2003] EWHC 2907 (Admin), *MB v Department for Social Development* (II) [2010] NICom 133, at [14] and *Harrow LBC v AM* [2013] UKUT 0157 (AAC)) and concluded that tribunal was not truly using its own expertise but material from a website that it had not shared with the appellant. The fact that the tribunal made selective use of the website material, ignoring the passages from the website that supported the appellants' case, increased the unfairness.

p.1068, *annotation to the Tribunals, Courts and Enforcement Act 2007 s.3 (The First-tier Tribunal and Upper Tribunal)*

4.021 However, *MB v SSWP* [2024] UKUT 271 (AAC) comments that it is important for the First-tier Tribunal to consider the totality of the evidence in a holistic manner, make sufficient findings of fact to resolve conflicts in the evidence and state which evidence it prefers and why, in its written reasons. Observations made on the day of hearing should be considered carefully given this will usually be some months after the date of decision and consideration should be given to whether, in the interests of natural justice, the claimant should be afforded the opportunity to comment on these observations particularly when they are material to the Tribunal's findings of fact.

p.1084, *annotation to the Tribunals, Courts and Enforcement Act 2007 s.3 (The First-tier Tribunal and Upper Tribunal)*

However, it is suggested that the decision in *AO* has been superseded by the Court of Appeal's decision in *Williamson v Bishop of London* [2023] EWCA Civ 379 in which it was noted at para. 8 that; "The term "any court" in section 42(1A) SCA 1981 has been held to extend to all inferior courts including tribunals." Whilst the Court of Appeal was dealing with a case concerning appeals from the Employment Tribunal, and *AO* was not referred to, it appears clear that the Court of Appeal is of the view that a section 42 order applies to appeals to Tribunals and as such this would include First-tier Tribunals. **4.022**

p.1086, *annotation to the Tribunals, Courts and Enforcement Act 2007 s.7 (The First-tier Tribunal and Upper Tribunal)*

The First-tier Tribunal and Upper Tribunal (Chambers) (Amendment No. 2) Order 2024 (SI 2024/1285) has amended the functions (with effect from December 26, 2024) to include appeals under s.49(1) of the Victims and Prisoners Act 2024 and, specifically, the Infected Blood Compensation Scheme Regulations 2024 (SI 2024/872), which came into force on August 23, 2024. **4.023**

p.1190, *annotation to the First-tier Tribunal and Upper Tribunal (Composition of Tribunal) Order 2008 (SI 2008/2835) r.2 (Number of members of the First-tier Tribunal)*

An example of the application of the delegated powers afforded by the Practice Direction can be seen in *SSWP v NJ* [2024] UKUT 194 (AAC). This appeal was dealing with what was then referred to as a Practice Statement but the same provisions have been carried over into the Practice Direction. The issue was whether the First-tier Tribunal was in error in proceeding with a panel consisting of a Judge sitting alone, as opposed to sitting with a specialist medical member. The case concerned the interpretation of the Employment and Support Allowance Regulations 2008 reg.153, temporary absence from Great Britain for medical treatment provisions. The Upper Tribunal found that deciding whether reg.153 applies will not normally require a Tribunal to have any particular medical expertise. Therefore; **4.024**

> "68. As such, it was not an error of law for the Tribunal to fail to consider (or to fail to consider requesting that the Regional Judge or Chamber President consider) reconstituting the Tribunal as a two-person panel with a medical member. In any event, even if this had been a case involving a complex medical issue, it would still have been a matter of discretion, to be exercised by the Chamber President, Regional Tribunal Judge

or District Tribunal Judge in accordance with … the Practice Statement, susceptible to challenge on appeal only on rationality grounds."

p.1221, *annotation to the Tribunal Procedure (First-tier Tribunal) (SEC) Rules 2008 (SI 2008/2685) r.8(3) (Striking out a party's case)*

4.025 In *Farnsworth v Information Commissioner* [2024] UKUT 206 (AAC) the Upper Tribunal considered the decision in *HMRC v Fairford* and commented that a litigant in person in person "will not be across the ins and outs of the law". What appellants will therefore often do is simply "throw before the tribunal" all the reasons they believe the challenged decision is wrong. At para.20:

> "In such cases it is for the tribunal, on an application to strike out under rule 8(3)(c), to look at those reasons, reasonably and realistically and with fairness and justice firmly in mind, and decide whether they disclose a realistic case…."

p.1222, *annotation to the Tribunal Procedure (First-tier Tribunal) (SEC) Rules 2008 (SI 2008/2685) r.8(5) (Striking out a party's case)*

4.026 However, in a decision of the Upper Tribunal Lands Chamber *Siraj Deane v LB Newham* [2024] UKUT 00300 (LC) LC-2024-185, the Upper Tribunal recognised the close alignment approach stated in *BPP Holdings* but pointed out that it is important to recognise that the Tribunal Procedure Rules, and specifically the First-tier Tribunal Rules, are not a carbon copy of the Civil Procedure Rules. In particular the overriding objectives identified in the two sets of rules are not identical and contain differences of emphasis and nuance which reflect the different characteristics of dispute resolution in courts and tribunals. The case concerned an application for reinstatement after strike out. The strike out arose from lack of action by the appellant in a financial penalty appeal. The Upper Tribunal considered that the First-tier Tribunal was too draconian and failed to give sufficient consideration to the Tribunal's overriding objective and more flexible rules. The Upper Tribunal found that the First-tier Tribunal misdirected itself in its application of the First-tier Tribunal procedural rules by relying on the Civil Procedural Rules. The Lands Chamber rules are broadly similar to the SEC Rules in this regard.

p.1245, *amendment to the Tribunal Procedure (First-tier Tribunal) (Social Entitlement Chamber) Rules 2008 (SI 2008/2685) r.22 (Cases in which the notice of appeal is to be sent to the Tribunal)*

4.027 With effect from December 27, 2024, art.2(2) of the Tribunal Procedure (Amendment No.2) Rules 2024 (SI 2024/1283) amended the Tribunal Procedure (First-tier Tribunal) (Social Entitlement Chamber) Rules 2008 as follows:

> In rule 22 (cases in which the notice of appeal is to be sent to the Tribunal)—
>
> (a) in paragraph (2) after sub-paragraph (c) insert—
>
> "(ca) in appeals under a scheme established under section 49(1) of the Victims and Prisoners Act 2024 (infected blood compensation

scheme), within 1 month after the date on which the appellant was sent written notice of the decision being challenged;"

(b) in paragraph (7)(b) after "in all other" insert "cases";

(c) in paragraph (8)(a) omit "not more than";

(d) in paragraph (9)(b) after "the appeal" insert ", other than an appeal under section 38(1) of the Tax Credits Act 2002,".

p.1270, *annotation to the Tribunal Procedure (First-tier Tribunal) (SEC) Rules 2008 (SI 2008/2685) r.27 (Decisions with or without a hearing)*

However, in *MR v SSWP* [2024] UKUT 199 (AAC) the Upper Tribunal found that the First-tier Tribunal had erred in law by failing to adjourn the paper determination to an oral hearing in order to allow the claimant an opportunity to respond to its concerns about his credibility. It was not enough, as the Upper Tribunal found in *JP v SSWP* [2011] UKUT 459 (AAC), for the First-tier Tribunal merely to state that it had considered the rules and case law and was satisfied that it was able to proceed to determine the appeal on the papers. The First-tier Tribunal had to provide an adequate explanation as to why it has decided to proceed in this way. In addition, the First-tier Tribunal also failed to keep the question of whether or not to proceed on the papers under review up to the point of decision (referring to *MH v Pembrokeshire County Council* (paragraphs [11]–[13]). 4.028

p.1274, *annotation to the Tribunal Procedure (First-tier Tribunal) (SEC) Rules 2008 (SI 2008/2685) r.27 (Decisions with or without a hearing)*

By r.1(3) of the Tribunal rules, telephone hearings are a form of oral hearing. Therefore, as observed in *CF v SSWP* [2024] UKUT 244 (AAC), the authorities on Tribunals continuing with decisions on the papers when fairness required an oral hearing (such as *JP v SSWP* [2011] UKUT 459 (AAC)) are not directly relevant. However, the Tribunal has a continuing responsibility to ensure that a hearing is conducted fairly and in accordance with the overriding objective. In *JP* the First-tier Tribunal had stated in its decision that the appellant had requested an oral hearing, that an oral hearing was supposed to have been listed if possible, and also that it had not had the 'benefit' of seeing the appellant in person in a case where the appellant sought to dispute the content of a face-to-face assessment with the Healthcare Practitioner. In such circumstances the Upper Tribunal found that; 4.029

> "43 ... it was ... incumbent on the Tribunal in this case to consider of its own motion whether it was fair to continue with the hearing by telephone and, if it concluded that it was, to explain why it had reached that decision."

The Upper Tribunal was not satisfied that the First-tier Tribunal "even addressed its mind to the question of fairness, or to its power to adjourn of its own motion if need be to ensure that the hearing was fair." The error was material given that the First-tier Tribunal's own remarks indicated the a face-to-face hearing could have had an impact on its assessment of the evidence.

p.1285, *amendment to the Tribunal Procedure (First-tier Tribunal) (Social Entitlement Chamber) Rules 2008 (SI 2008/2685) r.30 (Public and private hearings)*

4.030 With effect from December 24, 2024, art.2 of Tribunal Procedure (Amendment No. 2) Rules 2024 (SI 2024/1283 amended the Tribunal Procedure (First-tier Tribunal) (Social Entitlement Chamber) Rules 2008 by omitting para.(2) in r.30 (public and private hearings).

p.1292, *annotation to the Tribunal Procedure (First-tier Tribunal) (SEC) Rules 2008 (SI 2008/2685) r.31 (Hearings in a party's absence)*

4.031 In *GMcA [Appointee] v Department for Communities (PIP)* [2024] NICom 23 (C7/24-25 (PIP) the claimant's mother was the appointee and the claimant had requested an oral hearing. On the day of hearing, the appointee phoned the tribunal venue to explain that her daughter was unable to attend owing to anxiety. The chair of the tribunal encouraged attendance but the appointee said she thought that the claimant would be unwilling to attend on another occasion, and asked the tribunal to proceed in the absence of either her or her daughter. Accordingly, the tribunal heard the case on the papers and the appeal was refused. The Commissioner found that the tribunal (unwittingly) compromised the claimant's right to a fair hearing.

> "During, or following, the appointee's telephone call to the venue there was material failure on the part of the tribunal to consider, and communicate to the appointee, any alternative to the conventional format, given her view that the claimant would not be prepared to attend the venue at a later date. This is particularly so considering that online and telephone hearings had been normalised during the pandemic. The appointee's request that the tribunal proceed in their absence must be seen as an election made while uninformed of the ambit of possibilities" (para.28).

The tribunal's failure to explore other forms of hearing gave rise to injustice. The appointee's position as an unrepresented litigant is of significance "because a representative would have known or been capable of asking about a different form of hearing, but the appointee would not be expected to anticipate these" (para.30). A further aspect is that the tribunal did not consider facilitating the participation in the hearing of the appointee herself. It could have raised the possibility of her attending and giving oral evidence of her daughter's difficulties and her ways of managing the activities under consideration. The appointee "has a right to tell the tribunal what she observes, both as a party to the proceedings and as a representative".

p.1301, *annotation to the Tribunal Procedure (First-tier Tribunal) (SEC) Rules 2008 (SI 2008/2685) r.34(5) (Reason for decisions)*

4.032 The wording of r.34(5) makes it clear that if a party makes an application for a written statement of reasons the First-tier Tribunal <u>must</u> provide the statement. In *OU v SSWP* [2024] UKUT 223 (AAC) the First-tier Tribunal Judge's direction, that the appellant should make a second request for a statement of reasons after an in-time first request, with a strike out warning for a lack of timely compliance, was found to be misconceived. In giving such directions the Judge appeared to try and dissuade the appellant from seeking a statement of reasons and placed conditions on the entitlement conferred by r.34(5) beyond the condition already contained in that rule.

p.1317, *annotation to the Tribunal Procedure (First-tier Tribunal) (SEC) Rules 2008 (SI 2008/2685) r.37(2)(c) (Setting aside a decision which disposes of proceedings)*

How r.37 applies to paper determinations has been the subject of some discussion, especially as regard to r.37(2)(c), the issue being whether r.37(2)(c) can be used to set aside a paper determination. In *JG v SSWP* [2024] UKUT 329 (AAC), the appellant had asked for the appeal to be determined on the papers. The First-tier Tribunal refused the appeal. The appellant then applied for a statement of reasons and for the decision to be set aside. The application was considered by a salaried judge who granted the application and set aside the decision. The Upper Tribunal commented [obiter] that it was open to a salaried judge to make a decision to set aside a paper determination using r.37(2)(c)—see para.20. However, the issue had previously been considered by the Upper Tribunal in *JC v SSWP (DLA)* [2013] UKUT 171 (AAC)—a case not previously included in Vol. III of this series. The Upper Tribunal concluded in *JC* that, in circumstances where there has been an election for the appeal to be determined on the papers, r.37(2)(c) cannot be used to set aside the paper determination because there has been no "hearing" as such. This is the case whether or not the Tribunal panel consisted of one or more members. This decision is binding on the First-tier Tribunal. **4.033**

However, there has been commentary in some publications that the question is not just about whether the definition of a "hearing" means an "oral hearing", rather whether a party can be "present" at an oral hearing which does not take place. It has been suggested that the salaried judge to whom an application is referred must ask themselves: "Was the relevant party or representative present at a hearing related to the proceedings?". If no hearing has taken place, the answer to that question would be no, in which case r.37(2)(c) would apply.

It is suggested that such a broad construction of para.2(c) is not supportable when applying the Tribunal Rules, as clearly set out in *JC v SSWP (DLA)* [2013] UKUT. What constitutes a hearing is defined by r.1, which specifically states that a "hearing" means an "oral hearing". Therefore, a determination of an appeal on the papers is not a hearing as such. The suggested question for the salaried judge would appear to be in error. There has been no hearing so it is irrelevant to ask if a person has been present at a hearing. No one can be present at something that does not exist.

That is not to say that r.37 does not have relevance to all applications to set aside decisions which dispose of proceedings. Clearly para.(2)(a) or (b) could apply, depending on the facts. However, note *McCalla v Secretary of State for Defence* [2024] EWCA Civ 1467, a decision regarding the parallel Upper Tribunal r.43, which holds that the relevant document would need to be in existence before the Tribunal determined the appeal. The parties are not told the date that the case will be dealt with on the papers. It is perhaps understandable therefore that a party might not provide documents relevant to the appeal in time.

4.034 It could also be open for a judge to set aside a paper determination by reference to r.37(2)(d), "procedural irregularity". However, providing the parties have clearly elected a paper determination, what is the "procedural irregularity"? How can it be procedurally irregular to determine the appeal without a hearing when that was what was requested? One possibility could be that there was a problem with the SSCS1 appeal form which might be considered to lack clarity or might have been incorrectly or misleadingly completed by the appellant and this was not noted by the administration when processing the appeal. There have been issues with the on-line SSCS1 forms which might not explain clearly the various options that an appellant can chose when stating how they want their appeal to be decided. If an appellant is given the option of a paper or oral appeal, but the types of oral hearing are not visible, then the appellant might not opt for a telephone or video hearing if they think that the only type of oral hearing is face to face at a venue. Such a problem might be considered in an appropriate case to be a procedural error.

It is suggested that where application to set aside under r.37 does not apply then r.27 might become relevant. The rule makes it clear that the default position (save as specified) is that there must be a hearing before a decision is made which disposes of proceedings, unless (a) each party has consented to, or has not objected to, the matter being decided without a hearing, and (b) the Tribunal considered that it is able to decide the matters without a hearing. Failure to give due consideration to r.27 would be an error of law. A decision to set aside would need to be dealt with under rr.39–40. The appellant would need to apply for a statement of reasons and then seek permission to appeal, arguing that the Tribunal were in error of law having regard to r.27. This is a much more lengthy and complicated process for an appellant.

p.1318, *annotation to the Tribunal Procedure (First-tier Tribunal) (SEC) Rules 2008 (SI 2008/2685) r.37(1) (Setting aside a decision which disposes of proceedings)*

4.035 However, as confirmed in *JG v SSWP* [2024] UKUT 329 (AAC), the power to set aside in r.37(1) applies only to decisions disposing of proceedings. It cannot be used to set aside an earlier set aside decision. Neither do the case management powers in r.5 assist.

p.1324, *annotation to the Tribunal Procedure (First-tier Tribunal) (SEC) Rules 2008 (SI 2008/2685) r.39(2) (Tribunal's consideration of application for permission to appeal)*

4.036 In *CD v SSWP (UC)* [2024] UKUT 256 (AAC) it was commented that, unless it is clear there is an issue on which the guidance of the Upper Tribunal is needed then permission should not be granted. Given that the First-tier Tribunal considered that decision of the Secretary of State under appeal was "correct under the current law", it was not apparent why the First-tier Tribunal considered it may arguably have erred in law in upholding that decision so as to merit giving permission to appeal to the Upper Tribunal. The Upper Tribunal suggested that the First-tier Tribunal should not have given permission unless it could also indicate on what basis the Upper Tribunal might find that the "current law" is either wrong in law or can be distinguished.

pp.1334 and 1357, *amendments to the Tribunal Procedure (Upper Tribunal) Rules 2008 (SI 2008/2685) rr.1 (Citation, commencement, application and interpretation) and 11 (Representatives)*

With effect from May 1, 2024, art.2(2) and (3) of the Tribunal Procedure (Upper Tribunal) (Immigration and Asylum Chamber) (Amendment) Rules 2024 (SI 2024/588) amended the Tribunal Procedure (Upper Tribunal) Rules 2008 as follows: 4.037

In r.1 (citation, commencement, application and interpretation)—
(a) after paragraph (2) insert—
"(2A) The Suspensive Claims Rules apply to proceedings before the Upper Tribunal in the circumstances and in the manner specified in those Rules.";
(b) in paragraph (3)—
(i) in the appropriate place insert—
""the 2023 Act" means the Illegal Migration Act 2023;"
""suspensive claim" has the meaning given in section 38(2) of the 2023 Act;"
""the Suspensive Claims Rules" means the rules set out in Schedule 5,";
(ii) in the definition of "applicant"—
(aa) at the end of paragraph (a) omit "or";
(bb) at the end of paragraph (b) insert "or";
(cc) after paragraph (b) insert—
(c) "a person who applies to the Upper Tribunal under rule 19 (application for a declaration) of the Suspensive Claims Rules for a declaration;".

In r.11(1) (representatives) for "in an asylum or immigration case" substitute "in an asylum case, immigration case or suspensive claim case".

p.1404, *annotation to the Tribunal Procedure (Upper Tribunal) Rules 2008 (SI 2008/2698) r.43 (Application for permission to appeal)*

The decision in *Plescan* was followed by the Court of Appeal in *McCalla v Secretary of State for Defence* [2024] EWCA Civ 1467. The appellant appealed against the refusal of the Upper Tribunal to set aside its decision refusing him permission to appeal against a First-tier Tribunal decision. As stated in *Plescan*, the power to set aside under r.43 can only be exercised in limited circumstances: the appellant has to show a procedural error in the Upper Tribunal permission to appeal proceedings, and that it was in the interests of justice to set aside the decision. Rule 43 does not enable an appellant to challenge the Upper Tribunal decision to refuse permission to appeal, or the reasons on which that decision was based. Rule 43 is concerned only with how the Upper Tribunal had handled the permission to appeal application. An Upper Tribunal decision not to set aside a refusal of permission did not merge with, or become part of, the actual refusal of permission. Rule 43 was a procedural rule, designed to provide a safeguard for Upper Tribunal proceedings. 4.038

Rule 43(2)(b) can therefore only apply to a document relating to the proceedings disposed of by the decision which the appellant sought to have set aside, namely the application for permission to appeal to the Upper Tribunal. An appellant would have to show that there had been a procedural irregularity in the UT proceedings because a document had not been sent to it at an appropriate time. While the Rules did not define "appropriate time", that had to refer to a time appropriate to the determination of the permission to appeal application. That would have to be before the application was refused, and a document could only have been sent to the Upper Tribunal before that determination if it existed at the time. In *McCalla* the document concerned did not exist before the refusal of permission. The judge's reasoning had therefore been correct, and there had been no procedural error in the Upper Tribunal's handling of the application for permission. Rule 43(2)(b) did not enable an unsuccessful applicant for permission to appeal to rely on a document created after the refusal of permission (or other decision sought to be set aside) (paras 52–56).

p.1500, *National authorities on art.14 read with art.1 of Protocol 1 in relation to specific benefits—(e) Family issues*

4.039 A challenge by a father with equal shared care, claiming he had been unlawfully discriminated against under the universal credit rules in not being entitled to an amount of universal credit to enable his son to have a bedroom when living with him, failed in *CD v SSWP (UC)* [2024] UKUT 256 (AAC). There was insufficient evidence to raise a strong prima facie case of indirect discrimination (and so nothing to be explained by SSWP) and even if there had been any discrimination, a number of other cases had demonstrated that discrimination in similar contexts could be justified.

p.1524, *United Kingdom Withdrawal from the European Union*

4.040 The Court of Appeal has given permission to appeal against the decision in *Fertré*.

p.1529, *European Union (Withdrawal) Act 2018, s.3 (Incorporation of direct EU legislation)*

4.041 The Supreme Court has given judgment in *Lipton v BA City Flyer Limited* [2024] UKSC 24. The judgment contains a lengthy survey of the legislation concerning the UK's withdrawal from the European Union, but expressly excludes consideration of the impact of the Retained EU Law (Revocation and Reform) Act 2023.

pp.1531–1535, *European Union (Withdrawal) Act 2018 s.6 (Interpretation of assimilated law)—General Note*

4.042 Sections 6A–6C, provided for by REULRRA s.6, remain not in force. SI 2024/714 has been revoked by the Retained EU Law (Revocation and Reform) Act 2023 (Commencement No. 2 and Saving Provisions) (Revocation) Regulations (SI 2024/976).

pp.1566–1567, *European Union (Withdrawal Agreement) Act 2020, s.38 (Parliamentary sovereignty)*

General Note

With effect from February 20, 2024, the text of this section was amended, in ways outside the scope of the present work, by the Windsor Framework (Constitutional Status of Northern Ireland) Regulations 2024 (SI 2024/164). **4.043**

pp.1567–1568, *European Union (Withdrawal Agreement) Act 2020, s.39 (Interpretation)*

General Note

With effect from February 20, 2024, the text of this section was amended, in ways outside the scope of the present work, by the Windsor Framework (Constitutional Status of Northern Ireland) Regulations 2024 (SI 2024/164). **4.044**

p.1575, *annotation to the European Union (Future Relationship) Act 2020, s.26—General Note*

In the main volume it was suggested that the views expressed by Green LJ in relation to s.29 of the Act in *Lipton v BA City Flyer Ltd* [2021] EWCA Civ 454 at [77]–[82] might be of assistance in relation to s.26 also. The Supreme Court has now given its judgment in *Lipton* [2024] UKSC 24 and at [80] expressly distances itself from Green LJ's analysis on the point, which it suggests will need to be looked at afresh in a case in which the point arises. The General Note in the main volume should therefore be disregarded. **4.045**

p.1575, *annotation to the Retained EU Law (Revocation and Reform) Act 2023—General Note*

As to amendments made by s.6, certain of which remain not in force, see the note to pp.1531–1535. **4.046**

pp.1585–1588, *amendments to The Cessation of EU Law Relating to Prohibitions on Grounds of Nationality and Free Movement of Persons Regulations 2022 (SI 2022/1240)*

With effect from March 1, 2024, the Retained EU Law (Revocation and Reform) Act 2023 (Consequential Provision) Regulations 2024 (SI 2024/80) reg.2 and Sch., para.17 amended the 2022 Regulations by omitting: **4.047**

In regulation 1 (citation, commencement and interpretation), paragraph (3) and, in paragraph (4), by omitting sub-paragraphs (a) and (b) (including "or" at the end); and

regulations 2 (cessation of prohibitions on the grounds of nationality) and 3 (cessation of free movement of persons).

p.1599, *annotation to the Agreement on the withdrawal of the United Kingdom, art.10—General Note*

4.048 Although in *R. (Ali) v SSHD* [2023] EWHC 1615 (Admin), the judge observed that the expression "continue to reside thereafter" in art.10(1)(e)(i) referred to residence in accordance with Union law after the end of the transition period, the Court of Appeal has subsequently allowed an appeal: [2024] EWCA Civ 1546. The Court of Appeal did not need to address the effect of the phrase quoted above because of view it took of the CJEU's decision in *Reyes v Migrationsverket* C-423/12.

pp.1600–1601, *annotation to the Agreement on the withdrawal of the United Kingdom, art.13—General Note*

The Court of Appeal has given permission to appeal against the decision in *Fertré*.

p.1602, *annotation to the Agreement on the withdrawal of the United Kingdom, art.17—General Note*

4.049 Article 17(2) does not however assist a person whose dependency ended before the end of the transition period: *R. (Ali) v SSHD* [2023] EWHC 1615. This point was not challenged on appeal to the Court of Appeal: see [2024] EWCA Civ 1546 at [151].

pp.1606–1607, *annotation to the Agreement on the withdrawal of the United Kingdom, art.18—General Note*

4.050 The Court of Appeal has given permission to appeal against the decision in *Fertré*.

p.1608, *annotation to the Agreement on the withdrawal of the United Kingdom, art.23—General Note*

4.051 The Court of Appeal has given permission to appeal against the decision in *Fertré*.

p.1627, *Updating commentary on the Treaty on the Functioning of the European Union, art.49*

4.052 In *SSWP v VB and AD* [2024] UKUT 212 (UC), the Upper Tribunal addressed the question of when, and what, preliminary steps would bring a nascent business within art.49, concluding that *R(IS) 6/00* remained good law after the decision in C-268/99 *Jany v Staatssecretaris van Justitie* which required a business to be genuine and effective. Accordingly, concrete steps towards setting up a genuine and effective business – but not a mere intention – were sufficient.

p.1628, *Updating commentary to Charter of Fundamental Rights "Art.1 – Human dignity"*

4.053 In a revised version of circular ADM Memo 06/24 (published February 2025) *SSWP* appears to accept that the decision in *SSWP v AT* is potentially applicable to third country national family members of EU citizens, if they had pre-settled status at the end of the transition period.

p.1631, *Updating commentary to Directive 2004/38/EC, art.2(2)(d)—family members*

The Advocate General's Opinion in *XXX v État belge* (C-607/21) was delivered on September 19, 2024. The CJEU's judgment is awaited at the time of writing. The reference in *ZK and MS v Minister for Justice and Equality* (C-248/22) has been withdrawn. 4.054

p.1631, *Updating commentary to Directive 2004/38/EC, art.2(2)(d)—family members*

3.241	*Reyes v Migrationsverket* (C-423/12) was applied by the Court of Appeal in *R. (Ali) v SSHD* [2024] EWCA Civ 1546.

p.1632, *Updating commentary to Directive 2004/38/EC, art.7—right of residence for more than three months—self-sufficiency*

In *SSWP v Versnick* [2024] EWCA Civ 1454, the Court of Appeal dismissed SSWP's appeal, emphasising the critical feature that there had been no increase in the burden on the UK social assistance system as a result of the claimant joining his wife's household. There has to be a causal link between the exercise of free movement rights by an EU national and the imposition of a burden on the social assistance system of the host State (at [69]). 4.055

The requirement imposed by art.7(1)(b) for a person to have sufficient resources for themselves and their family members not to become a burden on the social assistance system of the host Member State does not mean that that person, as well as having sufficient resources to support themselves, "must also have resources to support a family member who is a British citizen, who is already here and is entitled to UK social assistance benefits in her own right" (at [83]).

In the circumstances of the case, the claimant, having previously been self-sufficient, was therefore entitled to a *Brey*-style evaluation of the burden which awarding him universal credit would impose. The Upper Tribunal had assessed the burden up to when the claimant would be awarded settled status. The Court of Appeal agreed, observing (at [99]) that from the point in time when he attained settled status, his entitlement would be derived from his own rights in this country rather than being a burden on the social assistance system of the UK as a result of his exercise of free movement rights.

p.1638, *Updating commentary on Regulation (EC) 883/2004, art.67.*

The Supreme Court has given permission to appeal against the decision in *Michaela Simkova v SSWP* [2024] EWCA Civ 419. 4.056

For a case giving effect to art.67 and exploring the associated part of the implementing Regulation (EC) 987/2009, see the note to p.1644.

p.1644, *Updating commentary on Regulation (EC) 987/2009, art.60.*

4.057

3.637	Art.60(1) (in particular the second sentence) and (2) was relied upon by Commissioner Stockman in *HMRC v MG (TC)* [2024] NiCom 14 to sort out the situation where the Polish claimant of child tax credit (CTC) and working tax credit (WTC) had failed to mention in his claim form that he had a wife in Poland with whom his three children were living (although he did mention his wife at a subsequent stage, before a decision was given on his claim.) His claim was treated as a single claim by HMRC, but this was reversed by the Appeal Tribunal. There is no provision under domestic law enabling a single claim to be treated as a joint claim.
	On HMRC's appeal, the Commissioner held that while WTC is not a family benefit, CTC is. As such, art.67 of Regulation (EC) 883/2004 means that CTC can be claimed, including in respect of those resident in another Member State. So far only as CTC was concerned, Tax Credits Act 2002, s.3(3)(a), which precludes a joint claim for tax credits unless those claiming are in the United Kingdom, had to yield to EU law in the form of art.67 of reg.883/2004 and art.60 of the implementing regulation. It followed that the correct approach was to treat the claim as being a joint claim for CTC but a single claim for WTC.

p.1686–1691, *amendment of the Trade and Cooperation Agreement, Annex SSC.1*

4.058 Decision 1/2024 of the Specialised Committee on Social Security Coordination (November 8, 2024) has amended Part 1 of Annex SCC.1 to include the mobility component of Child Disability Payment and Adult Disability Payment and Part 2 of that Annex to include Carer Support Payment, the care component of Child Disability Payment and the Daily Living Component of Adult Disability Payment. Further amendments are made in respect of other States.

PART V

UPDATING MATERIAL

VOLUME IV
HMRC-ADMINISTERED SOCIAL SECURITY BENEFITS AND SCOTLAND

Commentary by

Ian Hooker

Edward Mitchell

Nick Wikeley

p.322, *amendment to the Income Tax (Earnings and Pensions) Act 2003 s.677 (UK social security benefits wholly exempt from tax: Table B)*

With effect from October 21, 2024, reg.2 of the Income Tax (Exemption of Social Security Benefits) (No. 2) Regulations 2024 (SI 2024/901) amended Table B-Part 1 in s.677(1) by inserting the following entry at the appropriate alphabetical place: **5.001**

"Pension Age Disability Payment SS(S)A 2018 Sections 24 and 31"

p.551, *annotation to the Welfare Reform Act 2012 (Commencement No.32) Order 2019 (SI 2019/167) art.3A (Tax credit closure notice)*

Article 3A provides a mechanism for the issue of tax credit closure notices and the closure of tax credit awards for claimants moving to, or in receipt of, pension credit. **5.002**

p.561, *amendment to the Universal Credit (Transitional Provisions) Regulations 2014 (SI 2014/1230) reg.2 (Interpretation)*

With effect from June 8, 2024, reg.2(2) of the Social Security (State Pension Age Claimants: Closure of Tax Credits) (Amendment) Regulations 2024 (SI 2024/611) amended reg.2 by inserting after the definition of "tax credit" the following new definition: **5.003**

""tax credit closure notice" means a notice issued under article 3A (tax credit closure notice) of the Welfare Reform Act 2012 (Commencement No. 32 and Savings and Transitional Provisions) Order 2019;".

p.578, *amendment to the Universal Credit (Transitional Provisions) Regulations 2014 (SI 2014/1230) reg.44 (Migration notice)*

With effect from June 8, 2024, reg.2(3)(a) of the Social Security (State Pension Age Claimants: Closure of Tax Credits) (Amendment) Regulations 2024 (SI 2024/611) amended reg.44 by inserting after para.(3) a new para. (3A): **5.004**

"(3A) But where a migration notice is issued after cancellation of a previous migration notice or after cancellation of a tax credit closure notice the deadline day may be within such shorter period as the Secretary of State considers appropriate."

p.578, *amendment to the Universal Credit (Transitional Provisions) Regulations 2014 (SI 2014/1230) reg.44 (Migration notice)*

With effect from June 8, 2024, reg.2(3)(b) of the Social Security (State Pension Age Claimants: Closure of Tax Credits) (Amendment) Regulations 2024 (SI 2024/611) amended reg.44 by inserting after para.(5) a new para. (5A): **5.005**

"(5A) In a case referred to in paragraph (5)(a) the Secretary of State may, instead of cancelling the migration notice, treat that notice as if it were a tax credit closure notice issued to that person and may treat the deadline day in the migration notice as if it were the deadline day in a tax credit closure notice."

p.579, *annotation to the Universal Credit (Transitional Provisions) Regulations 2014 (SI 2014/123) reg.44 (Migration notice)*

5.006 Regulation 44(3) normally means that claimants will have at least three months to claim universal credit from the date of issue of the migration notice. However, under reg.44(3A) the Secretary of State may impose such shorter period as considered appropriate where a migration notice is issued after cancellation of a previous migration notice or after cancellation of a tax credit closure notice. The Explanatory Memorandum to SI 2024/611 states that "this may be needed in some cases to ensure migration can be completed before the tax credit service closes on 6 April 2025".

p.588, *amendment to the Universal Credit (Transitional Provisions) Regulations 2014 (SI 2014/1230) reg.56(1) (Circumstances in which transitional protection ceases)*

5.007 With effect from June 8, 2024, reg.2(4)(a) of the Social Security (State Pension Age Claimants: Closure of Tax Credits) (Amendment) Regulations 2024 (SI 2024/611) amended reg.56(1) by inserting ", (3A)" after "paragraph (2)".

p.588, *amendment to the Universal Credit (Transitional Provisions) Regulations 2014 (SI 2014/1230) reg.56(2) (Circumstances in which transitional protection ceases)*

5.008 With effect from June 8, 2024, reg.2(4)(b) of the Social Security (State Pension Age Claimants: Closure of Tax Credits) (Amendment) Regulations 2024 (SI 2024/611) amended reg.56(2) by inserting "other than an assessment period in relation to an award of universal credit mentioned in regulation 60A(1) (waiver of upper age limit for claimants migrated from tax credits)" after "assessment period" where it is first mentioned.

p.589, *amendment to the Universal Credit (Transitional Provisions) Regulations 2014 (SI 2014/1230) reg.56 (Circumstances in which transitional protection ceases)*

5.009 With effect from June 8, 2024, reg.2(4)(c) of the Social Security (State Pension Age Claimants: Closure of Tax Credits) (Amendment) Regulations 2024 (SI 2024/611) amended reg.56 by inserting after para.(3) a new para. (3A):

"(3A) This paragraph applies to an assessment period in relation to an award of universal credit mentioned in regulation 60A(1) (waiver of upper age limit for claimants migrated from tax credits) which—

(a) is not one of the first 12 assessment periods; and
(b) is the assessment period after the third consecutive assessment period in which the claimant's earned income, (or, if the claimant is a member of a couple the couple's combined earned income) is less than the amount that a person would be paid at the hourly rate set

out in regulation 4 of the National Minimum Wage Regulations for 16 hours a week converted to a monthly amount by multiplying by 52 and dividing by 12."

p.591, *amendment to the Universal Credit (Transitional Provisions) Regulations 2014 (SI 2014/1230) by insertion of new regs 60A–60C*

With effect from June 8, 2024, reg.2(5) of the Social Security (State Pension Age Claimants: Closure of Tax Credits) (Amendment) Regulations 2024 (SI 2024/611) inserted after reg.60 the following new regs 60A, 60B and 60C: 5.010

"Waiver of upper age limit for claimants migrated from tax credits

60A.—(1) Where a qualifying claim is made by—

(a) a single claimant who, at the time the migration notice is issued—

(i) has reached the qualifying age for state pension credit;

(ii) is entitled to an award of working tax credit; and

(iii) is not entitled to an award of state pension credit; or

(b) joint claimants both of whom satisfy the criteria in sub-paragraph (a)(i) to (iii) at the time the migration notice is issued,

then, subject to paragraphs (2) and (3), the condition in section 4(1)(b) of the Act (claimant has not reached the qualifying age for state pension credit) is not to apply for the purposes of determining entitlement to universal credit in respect of the qualifying claim or any award made in respect of that claim.

(2) The reference in paragraph (1) to a person who is entitled to an award of working tax credit includes a person who meets the entitlement conditions for both that credit and child tax credit.

(3) Paragraph (1) ceases to apply in respect of an award of universal credit mentioned in paragraph (1) in an assessment period in which—

(a) a transitional element or transitional capital disregard would cease to apply by virtue of regulation 56 (circumstances in which transitional protection ceases) or regulation 57 (application of transitional protection to a subsequent award); or

(b) a person who is entitled to an award of universal credit by virtue of paragraph (1) makes a claim for state pension credit.

Deferral of retirement pension income

60B.—(1) Where, at the time a migration notice is issued, the notified person—

(a) has reached the qualifying age for state pension credit;

(b) is entitled to an award of a tax credit; and

(c) has not made an application for retirement pension income to which they might expect to be entitled,

regulation 74 (notional unearned income) of the Universal Credit Regulations is not, subject to paragraph (2), to apply in relation to that person for the purpose of calculating the amount of an award of universal credit (including the indicative UC amount) until the assessment period following the first 12 assessment periods of an award made in respect of a claim by that person.

(2) This regulation ceases to apply in an assessment period in which a transitional element or transitional capital disregard would cease to apply by virtue of regulation 56 (circumstances in which transitional protection ceases) or regulation 57 (application of transitional protection to a subsequent award).

(3) In this regulation "retirement pension income" has the same meaning as in regulation 67 of the Universal Credit Regulations.

Exemption from the benefit cap

60C. Where a qualifying claim is made by a single claimant who has, or joint claimants both of whom have, reached the qualifying age for state pension credit, regulation 79 (circumstances where the benefit cap applies) of the Universal Credit Regulations is not to apply for the purpose of calculating the amount of an award of universal credit (including the indicative UC amount)."

p.591, *annotation to the Universal Credit (Transitional Provisions) Regulations 2014 (SI 2014/123) reg.60A (Waiver of upper age limit for claimants migrated from tax credits)*

5.011 Regulation 60A removes the prohibition on a person qualifying for universal credit if they have reached state pension age but are not a member of a mixed-age couple. However, the prohibition reapplies in the circumstances set out in regulation 60A(3).

p.677, *amendment to the Tax Credits (Definition and Calculation of Income) Regulations 2002 (SI 2002/2006) reg.5(1) (Pension income)*

5.012 With effect from April 6, 2024, reg.5 of the Pensions (Abolition of Lifetime Allowance Charge etc) Regulations 2024 (SI 2024/356) amended reg.5 by substituting "637G or 637N" for "636B or 636C" in para.(1)(o).

p.678, *amendment to the Tax Credits (Definition and Calculation of Income) Regulations 2002 (SI 2002/2006) reg.5(2) (Pension income), Table 2*

5.013 With effect from April 6, 2024, reg.5 of the Pensions (Abolition of Lifetime Allowance Charge etc) Regulations 2024 (SI 2024/356) amended reg.5 by substituting "any provision of Chapter 15A of Part 9 of ITEPA (lump sums under registered pension schemes) apart from sections 637G and 637N" for "section 636A of ITEPA" in para. (2), in Table 2, in entry 10, in the first column.

p.761, *amendment to the Tax Credits (Income Thresholds and Determination of Rates) Regulations 2002 (SI 2002/2006) reg.7(3) (Determination of rate of working tax credit)*

5.014 With effect from April 16, 2024, reg.2(2) of the Tax Credits (Income Thresholds and Determination of Rates) (Amendment) Regulations 2024 (SI 2024/510) amended reg.7(3) by substituting "£7,955" for "£7,995" in Step 4.

p.1145, *amendment to the Statutory Paternity Pay and Statutory Adoption Pay (Parental Orders and Prospective Adopters) Regulations 2014 (SI 2014/2934) reg.11 (Application of the Pay Regulations to intended parents and parental order parents)*

With effect from August 26, 2024, reg.4 of the Statutory Paternity Pay and Statutory Adoption Pay (Parental Orders and Prospective Adopters) (Amendment) Regulations 2024 (SI 2024/843) omitted para.(b) from reg.11. **5.015**

p.1147, *amendment to the Statutory Paternity Pay and Statutory Adoption Pay (Parental Orders and Prospective Adopters) Regulations 2014 (SI 2014/2934) reg.14 (Application of the Pay Regulations to intended parents and parental order parents)*

With effect from August 26, 2024, reg.5(2) of the Statutory Paternity Pay and Statutory Adoption Pay (Parental Orders and Prospective Adopters) (Amendment) Regulations 2024 (SI 2024/843) substituted for para.(ca) the following: **5.016**

"(ca) paragraph (5) shall apply as if—
(i) in the opening words, after "statutory paternity pay (adoption)" the words "at least 28 days before" were inserted;
(ii) sub-paragraphs (a) and (b) were omitted and replaced by—
"(a) the first day of the expected week of the child's birth, where the option in regulation 12(1)(a) is chosen;
(b) the date falling the specified number of days after the first day of the expected week of the child's birth, where the option in regulation 12(1)(b) is chosen;
(c) the predetermined date, where the option in regulation 12(1)(c) is chosen;
or, in a case where it was not reasonably practicable for the person to provide it in that period, as soon as is reasonably practicable."

In addition, reg.5(3) substituted "the date provided under paragraph (2)(c) above as the date on which the child is expected to be placed for adoption" for "the date referred to in paragraph (5)(a)" in para.(cb) and reg.5(4) inserted "child's" before "birth" in para.(d).

p.1289, *amendments to the Child Trust Funds Regulations 2004 (SI 2004/1450) reg.8(2) (General requirements for accounts)*

With effect from November 4, 2024, reg.3(a) of the Child Trust Funds (Amendment) (No. 2) Regulations 2024 (SI 2024/1023) inserted after para.(2)(a) the following new sub-paragraph: **5.017**

"(aa) where the account investments are fractional interests—
(i) the requirement under sub-paragraph (a) applies in relation to the beneficial ownership of the whole share in which the named child holds a fractional interest, and
(ii) the beneficial interest held by the named child shall be in proportion to the fractional interest in the whole share;".

With effect from November 4, 2024, reg.3(b) of the Child Trust Funds (Amendment) (No. 2) Regulations 2024 (SI 2024/1023) inserted "in relation to a fractional interest and" after "except" in para.(2)(b).

With effect from November 4, 2024, reg.3(c) of the Child Trust Funds (Amendment) (No. 2) Regulations 2024 (SI 2024/1023) inserted after para.(2)(b) the following new sub-paragraph:

> "(ba) investments in fractional interests are treated as meeting the requirements of sub-paragraph (b) if (and only if) the title to the whole share in which the named child holds a fractional interest meets the requirements of that sub-paragraph;".

p.1290, *amendment to the Child Trust Funds Regulations 2004 (SI 2004/1450) reg.8(2) (General requirements for accounts)*

5.018 With effect from November 4, 2024, reg.3(d) of the Child Trust Funds (Amendment) (No. 2) Regulations 2024 (SI 2024/1023) inserted after para.(2)(e) the following new sub-paragraph:

> "(ea) in relation to investments in fractional interests, where the named child holds more than one fractional interest in relation to the same investment, the aggregated value of which amounts to at least one whole share (an "aggregated whole share")—
> (i) the obligations under sub-paragraphs (d) and (e) apply to the manager in relation to the named child who holds the aggregated whole share, and
> (ii) the aggregated whole share is subject to the requirements in sub-paragraphs (b) and (c);".

p.1294, *amendment to the Child Trust Funds Regulations 2004 (SI 2004/1450) reg.11 (General investment rules)*

5.019 With effect from November 4, 2024, reg.4 of the Child Trust Funds (Amendment) (No. 2) Regulations 2024 (SI 2024/1023) substituted for para.(3) the following:

> "(3) All other transactions by way of sale or otherwise by an account provider in investments under account, and all transactions by way of trade or otherwise of an investment in fractional interests—
> (a) shall be made at the price for which those investments might reasonably be expected to be sold or otherwise transacted, as the case may be, in the open market, and
> (b) in the case of transactions in fractional interests, the price shall be proportionate to the size of the fraction relative to the whole share."

p.1296, *amendments to the Child Trust Funds Regulations 2004 (SI 2004/1450) reg.12(2) (Qualifying investments for an account)*

5.020 With effect from November 4, 2024, reg.5(a) of the Child Trust Funds (Amendment) (No. 2) Regulations 2024 (SI 2024/1023) made the following amendments to reg.12(2):

(i) in sub-paragraph (a), before the word "shares" (where it first appears) insert "subject to paragraphs (2B) and (2C),";

(ii) in sub-paragraph (f), before the word "shares" insert "subject to paragraphs (2B) and (2C),".

(iii) after sub-paragraph (q) insert—

"(qa) subject to paragraphs (2B) and (2C), shares of a UK UCITS, a recognised UCITS or non-UCITS retail scheme that are listed on or admitted to trading on a recognised stock exchange;";

With effect from November 4, 2024, reg.5(b) of the Child Trust Funds (Amendment) (No. 2) Regulations 2024 (SI 2024/1023) inserted after para (2)(r) the following:

"(s) an interest in a fraction of a share where the named child holds the beneficial interest in a fraction that is less than one whole share under terms which are contained in a contractual arrangement between the named child and the manager ("fractional interest")."

p.1297, *amendment to the Child Trust Funds Regulations 2004 (SI 2004/1450) reg.12 (Qualifying investments for an account)*

With effect from November 4, 2024, reg.5(c) of the Child Trust Funds (Amendment) (No. 2) Regulations 2024 (SI 2024/1023) inserted after para.(2A) the following: **5.021**

"(2B) An interest in a fraction of a qualifying investment falling within any of sub-paragraphs (a) to (j) of paragraph (2) is not a qualifying interest for an account unless it is a fractional interest within the meaning of sub-paragraph (s) of that paragraph.

(2C) In sub-paragraph (s) of paragraph (2), "shares" means shares which are qualifying investments in accordance with sub-paragraphs (a), (f) or (qa) of that paragraph."

p.1331, *amendments to the Child Trust Funds Regulations 2004 (SI 2004/1450) Sch. para.2 (Stakeholder accounts)*

With effect from November 4, 2024, reg.6(2) of the Child Trust Funds (Amendment) (No. 2) Regulations 2024 (SI 2024/1023) inserted after para 2(2)(a)(vii) the following: **5.022**

"(viii) fractional interests in shares in an investment trust (shares in an investment trust are specified in regulation 12(2)(f));

(ix) interests in a fraction of a share (as specified in regulation 12(2)(a));.

(x) shares specified in regulation 12(2)(qa), unless it is a requirement of the scheme in which the shares are held that the purchase and sale price of the shares shall, at any given time, not differ from each other and that the price must be available to the public on a daily basis."

p.1392, *amendment to the Childcare (Free of Charge for Working Parents) (England) Regulations 2022 (SI 2022/1134) reg.7 (Meaning of "employee")*

With effect from May 12, 2024, reg.2(2) of the Childcare (Free of Charge for Working Parents) (England) (Amendment) (No. 2) Regulations 2024 (SI 2024/527) amended reg.7(1)(a) by omitting "who is not on unpaid leave" and by substituting "the applicable period." in reg.7(1)(d) for "31 **5.023** days" to the end. Regulation 2(2) also inserted in reg.7(2) before the definition of "office" the following—

""applicable period" means, in relation to a person ("P") who expects to become a person mentioned in any of paragraph (1)(a) to (c) on a date in the period specified in the first column of the table, the period specified in the corresponding second column of the table.

P expects to become a person mentioned in any of paragraph (1)(a) to (c) in the period—	*Applicable period—*
(i) beginning with 1st February and ending with the next 30th April	begins with 1st January immediately preceding the start of the period specified in the first column and ends with the next 30th April
(ii) beginning with 1st May and ending with the next 30th September	begins with 1st April immediately preceding the start of the period specified in the first column and ends with the next 30th September
(iii) beginning with 1st October and ending with the next 31st January	begins with 1st September immediately preceding the start of period specified in the first column and ends with the next 31st January;"

p.1398, *amendment to the Childcare (Free of Charge for Working Parents) (England) Regulations 2022 (SI 2022/1134) reg.16 (Qualifying paid work requirement: employee)*

5.024 With effect from April 6, 2024, reg.2(2)(a)-(d) of the Childcare (Free of Charge for Working Parents) (England) (Amendment) Regulations 2024 (SI 2024/369) amended reg.16(3) as follows:

(a) in sub-paragraph (a)(i), after "foster parent," insert "or";
(b) for sub-paragraph (a)(ii) to (iv), substitute—
"(ii) on specified leave other than leave of the kind mentioned in sub-paragraph (b);";
(c) for sub-paragraph (b), substitute—
"(b) in the case of a person on specified leave that—
(i) is not specified leave of the kind mentioned in sub-paragraph (a)(vi), (a)(vii), (b)(iv) or (b)(vii) of the definition in paragraph (4), and
(ii) was started because of the birth or adoption of a child in respect of whom a declaration is being made,
the period of 31 days ending with the day before the day on which the person returns to work.";
(d) omit sub-paragraph (c).

With effect from April 6, 2024, reg.2(3) of the same amending regulations inserted the following after reg.16(3):

"(3A) In the case of a person in an EEA State or Switzerland, the references in paragraph (3)(a) and (b) to a person on specified leave of a particular kind mean any period the person is, under the law of that EEA State or Switzerland, on leave of a kind substantially similar to that kind of specified leave."

With effect from April 6, 2024, reg.2(4) of the same amending regulations inserted "(vii) carer's leave" in reg.16(4) in the definition of "specified leave", after sub-paragraph (a)(vi).

p.1398, *amendment to the Childcare (Free of Charge for Working Parents) (England) Regulations 2022 (SI 2022/1134) reg.16 (Qualifying paid work requirement: employee)*

With effect from May 12, 2024, reg.2(3) of the Childcare (Free of Charge for Working Parents) (England) (Amendment) (No. 2) Regulations 2024 (SI 2024/527) substituted "the applicable period" for the words after paragraph (ii) in reg.16(3)(b) and inserted in reg.16(4) before the definition of "employment rights enactment", the following— 5.025

""applicable period" means, in relation to a person ("P") who returns to work from specified leave on a date in the period specified in the first column of the table, the period beginning with the date specified in the corresponding second column of the table and ending with the day before the day on which P returns to work.

P returns to work from specified leave on a date in the period—	*Applicable period begins with—*
(i) beginning with 1st February and ending with the next 30th April	1st January immediately preceding the start of the period specified in the first column
(ii) beginning with 1st May and ending with the next 30th September	1st April immediately preceding the start of the period specified in the first column
(iii) beginning with 1st October and ending with the next 31st January	1st September immediately preceding the start of the period specified in the first column;"

p.1401, *amendment to the Childcare (Free of Charge for Working Parents) (England) Regulations 2022 (SI 2022/1134) reg.20 (When a declaration may be made)*

With effect from April 6, 2024, reg.2(5)(a) of the Childcare (Free of Charge for Working Parents) (England) (Amendment) Regulations 2024 (SI 2024/369) amended reg.20 by substituting for sub-para.(a) the following: 5.026

"(a) in the period of 16 weeks ending with the day before the day on which the child will meet the description in regulation 13 (if known), or".

p.1402, *amendment to the Childcare (Free of Charge for Working Parents) (England) Regulations 2022 (SI 2022/1134) reg.20 (When a declaration may be made)*

With effect from April 6, 2024, reg.2(5)(b) of the Childcare (Free of Charge for Working Parents) (England) (Amendment) Regulations 2024 5.027

(SI 2024/369) amended reg.20 by inserting "with the day" after "ending" in sub-para.(b)(ii).

p.1404, *amendment to the Childcare (Free of Charge for Working Parents) (England) Regulations 2022 (SI 2022/1134) reg.27 (Period of eligibility for childcare)*

5.028 With effect from May 12, 2024, reg.2(4) of the Childcare (Free of Charge for Working Parents) (England) (Amendment) (No. 2) Regulations 2024 (SI 2024/527) amended reg.27(1)(a) by omitting "on or" before "after" and amended reg.27(1)(b) by inserting "with the day" after "ending".

p.1459, *annotation to the Social Security (Scotland) Act 2018 s.41 (Right to request re-determination)*

5.029 See further *Social Security Scotland v MW* 2024 UT 70.

p.1528, *amendments to the Funeral Expense Assistance (Scotland) Regulations 2019 (SSI 2019/292) reg.2 (Interpretation)*

5.030 With effect from December 2, 2024, reg.2(2) of the Funeral Expense Assistance (Scotland) Amendment Regulations 2024 (SSI 2024/363) amended reg.2 by substituting or adding the following definitions:

(a) for the definition of "burial", substitute—
""burial" does not include—
(a) burial of ashes, where a person's remains have been cremated,
(b) burial of powder,",
(b) after the definition of "determination" insert—
""disposal by way of alkaline hydrolysis" means the disposal of human remains using hot water with the addition of—
(a) potassium hydroxide,
(b) sodium hydroxide, or
(c) a mix of both components mentioned in paragraphs (a) and (b),
in a pressurised chamber in accordance with applicable laws and procedures,",
(c) for the definition of "funeral" substitute—
""funeral" means a burial, cremation or disposal by way of alkaline hydrolysis of a deceased person or still-born child,",
(d) after the definition of "partner" insert—
""powder" means the residual matter following the disposal by way of alkaline hydrolysis,"

p.1529, *amendments to the Funeral Expense Assistance (Scotland) Regulations 2019 (SSI 2019/292) reg.3(5) (Applications)*

5.031 With effect from December 2, 2024, reg.2(3) of the Funeral Expense Assistance (Scotland) Amendment Regulations 2024 (SSI 2024/363) amended reg.3(5) by substituting "Regulation 10 describes" for "Regulations 10 and 11 describe" and by omitting ", and of the estate of the deceased person". Note that applications made before December 2, 2024, but decided on or after that date, are to be determined by reference to the original regulations in their pre-amended form: see the transitional provision in SSI 2024/363 reg.3.

p.1532, *amendments to the Funeral Expense Assistance (Scotland) Regulations 2019 (SSI 2019/292) reg.9 (Residence conditions, place of funeral and status)*

With effect from December 2, 2024, reg.2(4)(a) of the Funeral Expense Assistance (Scotland) Amendment Regulations 2024 (SSI 2024/363) amended reg.9(2) by substituting for sub-para.(b) the following: 5.032

"(b) the place of the funeral is—
(i) in the United Kingdom,
(ii) in a member state of the EU, Iceland, Liechtenstein, Norway or Switzerland and paragraph (3) applies,
(iii) outside the United Kingdom and paragraph (3B) applies."

In addition, reg.2(4)(b) substituted for reg.9(3) the following paragraphs:

"(3) This paragraph applies where the applicant or, where the applicant has a partner, the applicant's partner—
(a) was prior to IP completion day—
(i) a qualified person within the meaning of regulation 6(1)(b) (worker) or (c) (self-employed person) of the EEA Regulations,
(ii) a person who retained the status referred to in head (i) pursuant to regulation 6(2) or (4) of the EEA Regulations,
(iii) a person who is a family member of a person referred to in head (i) or (ii) within the meaning of regulation 7(1) of the EEA Regulations,
(iv) a person who had a right to reside permanently in the United Kingdom by virtue of regulation 15(1)(c), (d) or (e) of the EEA Regulations,
(b) is a person granted indefinite or limited leave to enter, or remain in, the United Kingdom under the Immigration Act 1971 by virtue of Appendix EU to the immigration rules made under section 3(2) of that Act ("the EU Settlement Scheme"),
(c) is a person who has made a valid application for indefinite or limited leave to enter, or remain in, the United Kingdom under the EU Settlement Scheme and that application is pending a final decision,
(d) is a person who is a family member within the meaning of Article 9 of the EU withdrawal agreement.
(3A) In paragraph (3) "EEA Regulations" means the Immigration (European Economic Area) Regulations 2016, as in force on 30 December 2020.
(3B) This paragraph applies where the Scottish Ministers consider that there are exceptional circumstances which merit entitlement to assistance for a funeral outside the United Kingdom.".

p.1534, *revocation of the Funeral Expense Assistance (Scotland) Regulations 2019 (SSI 2019/292) reg.11 (Estate of deceased person)*

With effect from December 2, 2024, reg.2(5) of the Funeral Expense Assistance (Scotland) Amendment Regulations 2024 (SSI 2024/363) omitted reg.11. 5.033

pp.1534–1536, *amendments to the Funeral Expense Assistance (Scotland) Regulations 2019 (SSI 2019/292) reg.13 (Amount of funeral expense assistance)*

5.034 With effect from December 2, 2024, reg.2(6) of the Funeral Expense Assistance (Scotland) Amendment Regulations 2024 (SSI 2024/363) made the following amendments to reg.13:

(a) in paragraph (1)(a) for "(4)" substitute "(4A)",
(b) in paragraph (2)(a), for "or cremation (see paragraph 4)" substitute ", cremation (see paragraph 4) or disposal by way of alkaline hydrolysis (see paragraph (4A)),",
(c) after paragraph (4), insert—
"(4A) For the disposal by way of alkaline hydrolysis, the costs are fees levied by the local authority or person responsible for the operation of disposals by way of alkaline hydrolysis in the area where the disposal takes place.",
(d) for paragraph (5) substitute—
"(5) Where the place of the funeral is outside the United Kingdom and the cost of the funeral (including transport costs) exceeds those that would have applied had the funeral taken place in the local authority area where the deceased was ordinarily resident, no assistance is to be given for those additional costs.",
(e) in paragraph (6)(a) for "pre-paid funeral plan" substitute "pre-paid funeral plan or analogous arrangement paid for in full prior to the death of the deceased",
(f) in paragraph (7)(c) for "burial or cremation" substitute "the funeral",
(g) in paragraph (8), for "burial or cremation" substitute "funeral".

p.1536, *amendments to the Funeral Expense Assistance (Scotland) Regulations 2019 (SSI 2019/292) reg.14 (Deductions from an award of funeral expense assistance)*

5.035 With effect from December 2, 2024, reg.2(7) of the Funeral Expense Assistance (Scotland) Amendment Regulations 2024 (SSI 2024/363) amended reg.14 by omitting "which are available without confirmation having been granted, or (elsewhere in the United Kingdom) without probate or letters of administration" in sub-para.(a) and inserting after sub-para.(c) the following:

"(d) a pre-paid funeral plan or analogous arrangement—
(i) where the plan or arrangement has not been paid in full prior to the death of the deceased, the amount of any sum payable under that plan or arrangement, or
(ii) where the plan or arrangement has been paid for in full prior to the death of the deceased, the amount of any sum payable under that plan or arrangement for the types of costs described in regulation 13".

p.1582, *amendments to the Social Security Co-ordination (EU Exit) (Scotland) (Amendments etc.) Regulations 2020 (SSI 2020/399) reg.6 (Savings for Gibraltar)*

5.036 With effect from January 1, 2024, para.38(2), (3) and (4)(a) of Sch.2 of the Retained EU Law (Revocation and Reform) Act 2023 (Consequential

Amendments) (Scotland) Regulations 2023 (SSI 2023/374) amended reg.6(1), (2) and (4) by substituting "assimilated direct legislation" for "RDEUL". Paragraph 38(4)(b) also substituted "assimilated direct" for "retained direct EU" in reg.6(4).

p.1582, *amendments to the Social Security Co-ordination (EU Exit) (Scotland) (Amendments etc.) Regulations 2020 (SSI 2020/399) reg.7 (Revocation of retained direct EU legislation)*

With effect from January 1, 2024, para.38(5) and (6) of Sch.2 of the Retained EU Law (Revocation and Reform) Act 2023 (Consequential Amendments) (Scotland) Regulations 2023 (SSI 2023/374) amended the heading to reg.7 and reg.7 itself by substituting "assimilated direct" for "retained direct EU". **5.037**

p.1597, *amendment to the Disability Assistance for Children and Young People (Scotland) Regulations 2021 (SSI 2021/174) reg.2 (Interpretation—general)*

With effect from June 7, 2024, reg.53 and para.15(2) of Part 5 of the Sch. to the Disability Assistance for Older People (Scotland) Regulations 2024 (SSI 2024/166) amended reg.2 by inserting after para.(c) the following: **5.038**

> "(ca) a hospital or similar institution under the Health and Personal Social Services (Northern Ireland) Order 1972 or the health and Personal Services (Northern Ireland) Order 1991,".

pp.1632–1634, *amendments to the Disability Assistance for Children and Young People (Scotland) Regulations 2021 (SSI 2021/174) Sch. Part 1 (Short-term assistance)*

With effect from June 7, 2024, reg.53 and para.15(3)-(5) of Part 5 of the Sch. to the Disability Assistance for Older People (Scotland) Regulations 2024 (SSI 2024/166) made multiple amendments to Part 1 of the Schedule to SSI 2021/174. For the full text of these amendments see Part I (New Legislation) above in this Supplement. **5.039**

pp.1648–1704, *correction to the running headers for the Disability Assistance for Working Age People (Scotland) Regulations 2022 (SI 2022/54)*

On pp.1648—1704 the left-hand page running headers should read "The Disability Assistance for Working Age People (Scotland) Regulations 2022". **5.040**

p.1651, *amendment to the Disability Assistance for Working Age People (Scotland) Regulations 2022 (SI 2022/54) reg.2 (Interpretation)*

With effect from October 21, 2024, reg.12(2) of the Disability Assistance for Older People (Consequential Amendment and Transitional Provision) (Scotland) Regulations 2024 (SSI 2024/141) inserted the following new definition after the definition of "needs": **5.041**

> ""Pension Age Disability Payment" means disability assistance for older people given in accordance with the Disability Assistance for Older People (Scotland) Regulations 2024,".

p.1653, *amendment to the Disability Assistance for Working Age People (Scotland) Regulations 2022 (SI 2022/54) reg.4 (Entitlement to other benefits)*

5.042 With effect from October 21, 2024, reg.12(3) of the Disability Assistance for Older People (Consequential Amendment and Transitional Provision) (Scotland) Regulations 2024 (SSI 2024/141) amended reg.4 by inserting "(ba) Pension Age Disability Payment," after para.(b).

p.1653, *annotation to the Disability Assistance for Working Age People (Scotland) Regulations 2022 (SI 2022/54) reg.4 (Entitlement to other benefits)*

General Note

5.043 See *Social Security Scotland v IR* 2024 UT 69.

p.1653, *erratum in the Disability Assistance for Working Age People (Scotland) Regulations 2022 (SI 2022/54) reg.5 (Daily Living Component)*

5.044 This regulation has been wrongly numbered as regulation 4.

p.1654, *annotation to the Disability Assistance for Working Age People (Scotland) Regulations 2022 (SI 2022/54) reg.5 (Daily Living Component)*

General Note

5.045 The parallels with PIP are obvious. In *Social Security Scotland v AM* 2024 UT 46 Lord Fairley held as follows:

> "22. These decisions under the PIP Regulations provide useful guidance as to how the 2022 Regulations ought to be interpreted. Before points can be awarded under the Regulations 5 and 6 of the 2022 Regulations and the relative schedule 1, there must be an effect on the claimant which falls within the terms of the descriptor in question. There must also be a causal link between that effect and a physical or mental condition experienced by the claimant. ...
> 23. The requirement for there to be "mental condition" for these purposes means no more than there must be a physical or mental cause of the relevant effect. In other words, the claimant must lack the physical or mental power or capability to perform the activity in question. It is not essential that the absence of power or capability should arise from a clinically recognised illness, disease or other health condition."

See also *Social Security Scotland v BM* 2024 UT 58.

p.1654, *annotation to the Disability Assistance for Working Age People (Scotland) Regulations 2022 (SI 2022/54) reg.6 (Mobility Component)*

General Note

5.046 Again, there are clear parallels with PIP. In *Social Security Scotland v SS; Social Security Scotland v GA* 2024 UT 63 Lady Carmichael confirmed that mobility activity 1 had to be interpreted in the same way as the equivalent PIP rules (see *MH v SSWP (PIP)* [2016] UKUT 531 (AAC); [2018] AACR 12).

p.1670, *amendment to the Disability Assistance for Working Age People (Scotland) Regulations 2022 (SI 2022/54) reg.26 (Entitlement under special rules for terminal illness)*

5.047 With effect from October 21, 2024, reg.12(4) of the Disability Assistance for Older People (Consequential Amendment and Transitional Provision)

(Scotland) Regulations 2024 (SSI 2024/141) amended reg.26 by inserting "(iia) Pension Age Disability Payment," after para.(12)(a)(ii).

p.1671, *amendments to the Disability Assistance for Working Age People (Scotland) Regulations 2022 (SI 2022/54) reg.28 (Effect of admission to hospital on ongoing entitlement to Adult Disability Payment)*

With effect from June 7, 2024, reg.53 and para.16(2) of Part 5 of the Sch. to the Disability Assistance for Older People (Scotland) Regulations 2024 (SSI 2024/166) amended reg.28 by omitting "or" at the end of para.(4)(a)(ii) and inserting after head (iii) the following: 5.048

"(iv) a hospital or similar institution under the Health and Personal Social Services (Northern Ireland) Order 1972 or the Health and Personal Social Services (Northern Ireland) Order 1991,".

p.1672, *amendments to the Disability Assistance for Working Age People (Scotland) Regulations 2022 (SI 2022/54) reg.29 (Exception: hospices)*

With effect from June 7, 2024, reg.53 and para.16(3) of Part 5 of the Sch. to the Disability Assistance for Older People (Scotland) Regulations 2024 (SSI 2024/166) amended reg.29 by inserting after para.(2)(c) the following: 5.049

"(ca) a hospital or similar institution under the Health and Personal Social Services (Northern Ireland) Order 1972 or the Health and Personal Social Services (Northern Ireland) Order 1991,".

p.1677, *annotation to the Disability Assistance for Working Age People (Scotland) Regulations 2022 (SI 2022/54) reg.37 (Continuing eligibility)*

General Note

See *Social Security Scotland v BM* 2024 UT 58, confirming that a tribunal must state whether an award is for a fixed or indefinite period. 5.050

pp.1698–1700, *amendments to the Disability Assistance for Working Age People (Scotland) Regulations 2022 (SI 2022/54) Sch.2 Part 1 (Short-term assistance)*

With effect from June 7, 2024, reg.53 and paras 15(4)–(6) of Part 5 of the Sch. to the Disability Assistance for Older People (Scotland) Regulations 2024 (SSI 2024/166) made multiple amendments to Part 1 of Sch.2 to SSI 2022/54. For the full text of these amendments see Part I (New Legislation) above in this Supplement. 5.051

pp.1706–1714, *correction to the running headers for the Disability Assistance for Working Age People (Transitional Provisions and Miscellaneous Amendment) (Scotland) Regulations 2022 (SI 2022/217)*

On pp.1706–1714 the left-hand page running headers should read "The Disability Assistance for Working Age People (Transitional Provisions and Miscellaneous Amendment) (Scotland) Regulations 2022". 5.052

p.1720, *Carer's Assistance (Carer Support Payment) (Consequential and Miscellaneous Amendments and Transitional Provision) (Scotland) Regulations 2023 (SSI 2023/258) reg.9 (Transitional provision—extinguishment of right to apply for Carer's Allowance)*

5.053 The following standalone provision should be inserted on p.1720 immediately before the Carer's Assistance Carer Support Payment) (Scotland) Regulations 2023 (SSI 2023/302):

The Carer's Assistance (Carer Support Payment) (Consequential and Miscellaneous Amendments and Transitional Provision) (Scotland) Regulations 2023

(SSI 2023/258)

Made	*13th September 2023*
Laid before the Scottish Parliament	*14th September 2023*
Coming into force	*19th November 2023*

The Scottish Ministers make the following Regulations in exercise of the powers conferred by section 95 of the Social Security (Scotland) Act 2018, section 70 of the Social Security Contributions and Benefits Act 1992 and all other powers enabling them to do so.

1.–8. *[Omitted (amendments incorporated in other Regulations in this volume)]*

Transitional provision – extinguishment of right to apply for Carer's Allowance

9.—(1) No person may claim carer's allowance under section 70 of the Social Security Contributions and Benefits Act 1992 who—

[[1](a) during the initial period for applications for carer support payment—
(i) in phase 1 is resident in the local authority area of Perthshire and Kinross, City of Dundee or Western Isles,
(ii) in phase 2 is resident in the local authority area of Perthshire and Kinross, City of Dundee, Western Isles, Angus, North Lanarkshire or South Lanarkshire,
(iii) in phase 3 is resident in the local authority area of Perthshire and Kinross, City of Dundee, Western Isles, Angus, North Lanarkshire, South Lanarkshire, Fife, City of Aberdeen, Aberdeenshire, Moray, North Ayrshire, East Ayrshire or South Ayrshire, or]

(b) after the expiry of the initial period for applications—
(i) is resident in Scotland, or
(ii) is a person to whom regulation 6(3) (residence and presence conditions), regulation 8 (serving members of His Majesty's forces, civil servants and their family members) or regulation 11 (persons residing outside the United Kingdom to whom a relevant EU regulation applies) of the Carer's Assistance (Carer Support Payment) (Scotland) Regulations 2023 applies.

(2) In this regulation—

"carer support payment" means carer's assistance payable under the Carer's Assistance (Carer Support Payment) (Scotland) Regulations 2023,

"carer's allowance" means assistance payable under the Social Security Contributions and Benefits Act 1992, and

"initial period for applications" means the period referred to in regulation 46 (transitory provision – initial period for applications) of the Carer's Assistance (Carer Support Payment) (Scotland) Regulations 2023, beginning with 19 November 2023 and ending with [1 3 November 2024, and references to phases of that period are to be construed in accordance with regulation 46(3) of those Regulations].

AMENDMENTS

1. Carer's Assistance (Carer Support Payment) (Scotland) Amendment Regulations 2024 (SSI 2024/173) reg.3(2) and (3) (June 23, 2024).

p.1723, *amendment to the Carer's Assistance (Carer Support Payment) (Scotland) Regulations 2023 (SSI 2023/302) reg.1 (Citation and commencement)*

With effect from June 23, 2024, reg.2(2) of the Carer's Assistance (Carer Support Payment) (Scotland) Amendment Regulations 2024 (SSI 2024/173) amended reg.1(3) by substituting "23 June 2024" for "1 October 2024". **5.054**

p.1724, *amendments to the Carer's Assistance (Carer Support Payment) (Scotland) Regulations 2023 (SSI 2023/302) reg.2 (Interpretation)*

With effect from October 21, 2024, reg.13(2) of the Disability Assistance for Older People (Consequential Amendment and Transitional Provision) (Scotland) Regulations 2024 (SSI 2024/141) amended reg.2 by inserting after the definition of "legal detention" the following: **5.055**

"Pension Age Disability Payment" means disability assistance for older people given in accordance with the Disability Assistance for Older People (Scotland) Regulations 2024,",

and by inserting in the definition of "qualifying disability benefit" after para.(d) the following:

"(da) Pension Age Disability Payment,".

p.1726, *amendment to the Carer's Assistance (Carer Support Payment) (Scotland) Regulations 2023 (SSI 2023/302) reg.5 (Provision of care to a cared for person)*

With effect from June 23, 2024, reg.2(3) of the Carer's Assistance (Carer Support Payment) (Scotland) Amendment Regulations 2024 (SSI 2024/173) amended reg.5(6) by substituting for para.(6) the following: **5.056**

"(6) A period during which an individual fails to satisfy the requirement of paragraph (2) is to be treated as a temporary break in care within the meaning of regulation 40 (temporary break in care), provided the individual satisfies the requirements set out in regulation 40."

p.1727, *amendments to the Carer's Assistance (Carer Support Payment) (Scotland) Regulations 2023 (SSI 2023/302) reg.6 (Residence and presence conditions)*

5.057 With effect from October 21, 2024, reg.13(3) of the Disability Assistance for Older People (Consequential Amendment and Transitional Provision) (Scotland) Regulations 2024 (SSI 2024/141) amended reg.6 by omitting the "or" at the end of para.(6)(b)(iii)(ee) and inserting after para.(6)(b)(iii)(ff) the following:

", or
(gg) regulation 9(7), 11(2), 12 or 13 of the Disability Assistance for Older People (Scotland) Regulations 2024".

With effect from October 21, 2024 the same amending regulation inserted after para.(7)(d) the following:

"(da) Pension Age Disability Payment by virtue of regulation 18 of the Disability Assistance for Older People (Scotland) Regulations 2024,".

p.1740, *amendment to the Carer's Assistance (Carer Support Payment) (Scotland) Regulations 2023 (SSI 2023/302) by insertion of new reg.18A (Entitlement beginning before individual satisfied the residence requirements in regulation 46) and reg.18B (Entitlement beginning before individual satisfied the residence requirements in regulation 46—individuals in education mentioned in regulation 13(2))*

5.058 With effect from June 23, 2024, reg.2(4) of the Carer's Assistance (Carer Support Payment) (Scotland) Amendment Regulations 2024 (SSI 2024/173) inserted after reg.18 the following new regulations:

Entitlement beginning before individual satisfied the residence requirements in regulation 46

18A.—(1) This paragraph applies where an individual—
(a) is undertaking—
  (i) a course of full-time advanced education,
  (ii) a course of full-time education which is provided by virtue of their employment or any office held by them, or
  (iii) a course of full-time education and has reached the age of 20,
(b) is exempt from fulfilling the past presence test in regulation 6(1)(e) (residence and presence) by virtue of an exception mentioned in regulation 6(6), or
(c) would not satisfy the past presence test in regulation 9(1)(c) (residence and presence in Great Britain) of the Social Security (Invalid Care Allowance) Regulations 1976 at any point between 19 November 2023 and the date on which they first satisfied the eligibility criteria prescribed in these regulations (including those prescribed in regulation 46 (transitory provision – initial period for applications), insofar as it applies).

(2) Where, on the basis of an application, a determination is made that an individual to whom paragraph (1) applies is entitled to Carer Support Payment, entitlement to assistance is to begin—

(a) on the first day of the award week in which the application is treated as made in accordance with regulation 18(1) (when an application is to be treated as made and beginning of entitlement to assistance), or

(b) where the individual has notified the Scottish Ministers that they wish their entitlement to assistance to begin on a date prior to the day on which their application is treated as made, on the first day of the award week in which that chosen date falls, provided that—

(i) the date chosen by the individual is no earlier than 19 November 2023,

(ii) the individual's application is received by the Scottish Ministers—

(aa) on or before the relevant date, or

(bb) after the relevant date, provided the Scottish Ministers consider that the individual has good reason for not making their application on or before the relevant date, and

(iii) the individual satisfied the eligibility requirements set out in Part 3 of these Regulations on that chosen date.

(3) For the purposes of this regulation—

"advanced education" has the same meaning as in regulation 13(4),

"full-time education" has the same meaning as in regulation 13(4),

"the relevant date" means the date specified paragraph 2A of schedule 1.

Entitlement beginning before individual satisfied the residence requirements in regulation 46 – individuals in education mentioned in regulation 13(2)

18B.—(1) This paragraph applies to any individual—

(i) who has not reached the age of 20, and

(ii) to whom regulation 13(2) (individuals in education) applies.

(2) Where, on the basis of an application, a determination is made that an individual to whom paragraph (1) applies is entitled to Carer Support Payment, entitlement to assistance is to begin—

(a) on the first day of the award week in which the application is treated as made in accordance with regulation 18(1) (when an application is to be treated as made and beginning of entitlement to assistance), or

(b) where the individual has notified the Scottish Ministers that they wish their entitlement to assistance to begin on a date prior to the day on which their application is treated as made, on the first day of the award week in which that chosen date falls, provided that—

(i) the date chosen by the individual is no earlier than 23 June 2024,

(ii) the individual's application is received by the Scottish Ministers—

(aa) on or before the relevant date, or

(bb) after the relevant date, provided the Scottish Ministers consider that the individual has good reason for not making their application on or before the relevant date, and

(iii) the individual satisfied the eligibility requirements set out in Part 3 of these Regulations on that chosen date.

(3) For the purposes of this regulation—

"advanced education" has the same meaning as in regulation 13(4),

"full-time education" has the same meaning as in regulation 13(4),

"the relevant date" means the date specified in paragraph 2B of schedule 1."

p.1742, *amendments to the Carer's Assistance (Carer Support Payment) (Scotland) Regulations 2023 (SSI 2023/302) reg.23 (Temporary stop in entitlement)*

5.059 With effect from October 21, 2024, reg.13(4) of the Disability Assistance for Older People (Consequential Amendment and Transitional Provision) (Scotland) Regulations 2024 (SSI 2024/141) amended reg.23 by omitting the "or" at the end of para.(4)(c)(i)(aa) and inserting after sub-head (bb) the following:

", or

(cc) regulation 30(3)(a) of the Disability Assistance for Older People (Scotland) Regulations 2024,".

p.1747, *amendment to the Carer's Assistance (Carer Support Payment) (Scotland) Regulations 2023 (SSI 2023/302) reg.27 (When a decrease in amount or cessation of entitlement takes effect)*

5.060 With effect from June 23, 2024, reg.2(5) of the Carer's Assistance (Carer Support Payment) (Scotland) Amendment Regulations 2024 (SSI 2024/173) amended reg.27 by substituting a new para.(1)(b) as follows:

"(b) in the case of an earlier determination which was based on error within the meaning of regulation 37 (determination following official error – underpayments) or regulation 38 (determination following error – overpayments), on the first day of the award week in which the earlier determination took effect,".

p.1747, *amendment to the Carer's Assistance (Carer Support Payment) (Scotland) Regulations 2023 (SSI 2023/302) reg.28 (When an increase in amount of entitlement takes effect)*

5.061 With effect from June 23, 2024, reg.2(6) of the Carer's Assistance (Carer Support Payment) (Scotland) Amendment Regulations 2024 (SSI 2024/173) amended reg.28 by substituting a new para.(1)(b) as follows:

"(b) in the case of an earlier determination which was based on error within the meaning of regulation 37 (determination following official error – underpayments) or regulation 38 (determination following error – overpayments), on the first day of the award week in which the earlier determination took effect,".

p.1753, *amendment to the Carer's Assistance (Carer Support Payment) (Scotland) Regulations 2023 (SSI 2023/302) reg.40 (Temporary break in care)*

With effect from June 23, 2024, reg.2(7) of the Carer's Assistance (Carer Support Payment) (Scotland) Amendment Regulations 2024 (SSI 2024/173) amended reg.40 by inserting a new para.(3) as follows: **5.062**

"(3) Paragraph (1) applies to an individual who fails to satisfy the requirement of regulation 5(2) because they are in legal detention, provided the individual satisfies the requirements of this regulation."

p.1756, *amendments to the Carer's Assistance (Carer Support Payment) (Scotland) Regulations 2023 (SSI 2023/302) reg.46 (Transitory provision—initial period for applications)*

With effect from June 23, 2024, reg.2(8) of the Carer's Assistance (Carer Support Payment) (Scotland) Amendment Regulations 2024 (SSI 2024/173) amended reg.46(2) by substituting "3 November 2024" for "30 September 2024" and inserting a new para.(3) as follows: **5.063**

"(3) The initial period for applications comprises three phases—
(a) phase 1, beginning with 19 November 2023 and ending with 23 June 2024,
(b) phase 2, beginning with 24 June 2024 and ending with 18 August 2024, and
(c) phase 3, beginning with 19 August 2024 and ending with 3 November 2024."

p.1756, *amendment to the Carer's Assistance (Carer Support Payment) (Scotland) Regulations 2023 (SSI 2023/302) Sch.1 para.2 (Local authority areas for initial period for applications)*

With effect from June 23, 2024, reg.2(9) of the Carer's Assistance (Carer Support Payment) (Scotland) Amendment Regulations 2024 (SSI 2024/173) amended para.2 by substituting the following for sub-paras (a)-(c): **5.064**

"(a) in phase 1, Perthshire and Kinross, City of Dundee and Western Isles,
(b) in phase 2, Perthshire and Kinross, City of Dundee, Western Isles, Angus, North Lanarkshire and South Lanarkshire
(c) in phase 3, Perthshire and Kinross, City of Dundee, Western Isles, Angus, North Lanarkshire, South Lanarkshire, Fife, City of Aberdeen, Aberdeenshire, Moray, North Ayrshire, East Ayrshire and South Ayrshire."

p.1756, *amendment to the Carer's Assistance (Carer Support Payment) (Scotland) Regulations 2023 (SSI 2023/302) Sch.1 (Initial period for applications)*

With effect from June 23, 2024, reg.2(10) of the Carer's Assistance (Carer Support Payment) (Scotland) Amendment Regulations 2024 (SSI 2024/173) amended Sch.1 by inserting after Part I the following Part 1A: **5.065**

"PART 1A

RELEVANT DATE

2A. For the purposes of regulation 18A (entitlement beginning before individual satisfied residence requirements), the "relevant date" in respect of an individual who is resident in a local authority area listed in column 1 of table 1, is the date specified in the corresponding entry of column 2.

Table 1

Column 1: local authority area	*Column 2: relevant date*
Angus, North Lanarkshire or South Lanarkshire,	22 September 2024
Fife, City of Aberdeen, Aberdeenshire, Moray, North Ayrshire, East Ayrshire or South Ayrshire,	17 November 2024
Argyll and Bute, Clackmannanshire, Dumfries and Galloway, East Dunbartonshire, East Lothian, East Renfrewshire, City of Edinburgh, Falkirk, Glasgow City, Highlands, Inverclyde, Midlothian, Orkney Islands, Renfrewshire, Scottish Borders, Shetland Islands, Stirling, West Dunbartonshire or West Lothian	2 February 2025

2B. For the purposes of regulation 18B (entitlement beginning before individual satisfied residence requirements – education), the "relevant date" in respect of an individual who is resident in a local authority area listed in column 1 of table 2, is the date specified in the corresponding entry of column 2.

Table 2

Column 1: local authority area	*Column 2: relevant date*
Perthshire and Kinross, City of Dundee, Western Isles, Angus, North Lanarkshire or South Lanarkshire	22 September 2024
Fife, City of Aberdeen, Aberdeenshire, Moray, North Ayrshire, East Ayrshire or South Ayrshire	17 November 2024
Argyll and Bute, Clackmannanshire, Dumfries and Galloway, East Dunbartonshire, East Lothian, East Renfrewshire, City of Edinburgh, Falkirk, Glasgow City, Highlands, Inverclyde, Midlothian, Orkney Islands, Renfrewshire, Scottish Borders, Shetland Islands, Stirling, West Dunbartonshire or West Lothian	2 February 2025".

p.1762, *amendment to the Carer's Assistance (Carer Support Payment) (Scotland) Regulations 2023 (SSI 2023/302) Sch.2 para.5 (Calculation of earnings of employed earners)*

5.066 With effect from June 23, 2024, reg.2(11) of the Carer's Assistance (Carer Support Payment) (Scotland) Amendment Regulations 2024 (SSI

2024/173) amended Sch.2 by substituting for the formula in para.5(2)(b) the following—

$$“\frac{P}{Q + R}”$$

p.1765, *amendment to the Carer's Assistance (Carer Support Payment) (Scotland) Regulations 2023 (SSI 2023/302) Sch.2 para.10 (Calculation of earnings of self-employed earners)*

With effect from June 23, 2024, reg.2(12) of the Carer's Assistance (Carer Support Payment) (Scotland) Amendment Regulations 2024 (SSI 2024/173) amended Sch.2 by substituting for the formula in para.10(2) the following— **5.067**

$$“\frac{S}{T + U}”$$

pp.1767–1768, *amendment to the Carer's Assistance (Carer Support Payment) (Scotland) Regulations 2023 (SSI 2023/302) Sch.2 para.13 (Deduction of tax and contributions for self-employed earners)*

With effect from June 23, 2024, reg.2(13) of the Carer's Assistance (Carer Support Payment) (Scotland) Amendment Regulations 2024 (SSI 2024/173) amended Sch.2 by substituting “determination for “decision” in heads (a) and (b). **5.068**

p.1768, *amendment to the Carer's Assistance (Carer Support Payment) (Scotland) Regulations 2023 (SSI 2023/302) Sch.2 para.14 (Sums to be disregarded in the calculation of earnings and profits)*

With effect from June 23, 2024, reg.2(14) of the Carer's Assistance (Carer Support Payment) (Scotland) Amendment Regulations 2024 (SSI 2024/173) amended para.14 of Sch.2 by substituting “NHS England” for “the National Health Service Commissioning Board” in sub-para.(g) and substituting for sub-para.(d) the following: **5.069**

> “(d) except in the case of an individual who is absent from the United Kingdom and to whom regulation 11 (persons residing outside the United Kingdom to whom a relevant EU regulation applies) applies—
> (i) any earnings derived from employment which are payable in a country outside the United Kingdom for such period during which there is a prohibition against transfer to the United Kingdom of those earnings,
> (ii) where a payment of earnings is made in a currency other than sterling, any banking charge or commission payable in converting that payment into sterling,”.

PART VI

CUMULATIVE UPDATING MATERIAL

VOLUME V 2021/22
INCOME SUPPORT AND THE LEGACY BENEFITS

Commentary by

John Mesher

Tom Royston

Nick Wikeley

Replace Vol II 2024/25 pp.1067–1215 with the following:

Part I

Social Security Statutes

p.15, *amendment to the Social Security Contributions and Benefits Act 1992 s.126(7) (Trade disputes)*

With effect from April 8, 2024, art.22 of the Social Security Benefits Up-rating Order 2024 (SI 2024/242) substituted "£50.00" for "£47.00" (as had been in effect from April 10, 2023) in subs.(7). 6.001

p.18, *annotation to the Social Security Contributions and Benefits Act 1992 s.126(5)(b) (Trade disputes—relevant sum)*

Note that the amount of the "relevant sum" for the purposes of s.126(5)(b) is specified in subs.(7), not (6). With effect from April 8, 2024 the sum was increased to £50 (see the entry for p.15). 6.002

pp.19–20, *annotation to the Social Security Contributions and Benefits Act 1992 s.134(1) (Exclusions from benefit)*

In the Institute for Government and the Social Security Advisory Committee's 2021 joint report *Jobs and benefits: The Covid-19 challenge* it was noted that if the capital limit had risen in line with prices since 2006 it would be close to £23,500 (or £25,000: different figures are given) and recommended that the limit should be increased to £25,000 and subsequently automatically indexed to maintain its real value (pp.22 and 31). That recommendation was summarily rejected in the Government's response of March 22, 2022. 6.003

p.33, *annotation to the old style Jobseekers Act 1995 GENERAL NOTE*

The two remaining prohibitions on claiming universal credit have now been removed. The former exception for "frontier workers" was removed with effect from March 30, 2022 by the Welfare Reform Act 2012 (Commencement No.34 and Commencement No.9, 21, 23, 31 and 32 and Transitional Provisions (Amendment)) Order 2022 (SI 2022/302) and the discretion given to the Secretary of State under reg.4 of the Transitional Provisions Regulations 2014 (SI 2014/1230) to determine (for the safeguarding of efficient administration or ensuring the efficient testing of administrative systems) that no claims for universal credit were to be accepted in an area or category of case was removed with effect from July 25, 2022 by reg.2 of the Universal Credit (Transitional Provisions) Amendment Regulations 2022 (SI 2022/752). There is thus now no exception, however remote, to the proposition that any new claim for JSA can only be for new style JSA. 6.004

p.72, *annotation to the Jobseekers Act 1995 s.13(1) (Income and capital: income-based jobseeker's allowance)*

6.005 In the Institute for Government and the Social Security Advisory Committee's 2021 joint report *Jobs and benefits: The Covid-19 challenge* it was noted that if the capital limit had risen in line with prices since 2006 it would be close to £23,500 (or £25,000: different figures are given) and recommended that the limit should be increased to £25,000 and subsequently automatically indexed to maintain its real value (pp.22 and 31). That recommendation was summarily rejected in the Government's response of March 22, 2022.

p.81, *annotation to the old style Jobseekers Act 1995 s.15(2) (Effect on other claimants—trade disputes)*

6.006 With effect from April 8, 2024 the "prescribed sum" for the purposes of s.15(2)(d) was increased to £50 (see the entry for p.1086).

p.124, *correction to the old style Jobseekers Act 1995 s.20E (Contracting out)*

6.007 The text in s.20E(1)–(3) should be replaced with the following:

"(1) The following functions of the Secretary of State may be exercised by, or by employees of, such person (if any) as the Secretary of State may authorise for the purpose, namely—

(a) [2...]
(b) [2...]
(c) [2...]
(d) [3...]
(e) [3...]
(f) [3...]

(2) The following functions of officers of the Secretary of State may be exercised by, or by employees of, such person (if any) as the Secretary of State may authorise for the purpose, namely—

(a) specifying places and times, and being contacted, under section 8;
(b) entering into or varying any jobseeker's agreement under section 9 or 10 and referring any proposed agreement or variation to the Secretary of State under section 9 or 10;
(c) giving notifications under section 16[2...];
(d) [2...].

(3) Regulations may provide for any of the following functions of the Secretary of State to be exercisable by, or by employees of, such person (if any) as the Secretary of State may authorise for the purpose—

(a) any function under regulations under section 8,[2...] 17A[2...][3...], except the making of an excluded decision (see subsection (4));
(b) the function under section 9(1) of the 1998 Act (revision of decisions) so far as relating to decisions (other than excluded decisions) that relate to any matter arising under any such regulations;
(c) the function under section 10(1) of the 1998 Act (superseding of decisions) so far as relating to decisions (other than excluded decisions) of the Secretary of State that relate to any matter arising under any such regulations;

(d) any function under Chapter 2 of Part 1 of the 1998 Act (social security decisions), except section 25(2) and (3) (decisions involving issues arising on appeal in other cases), which relates to the exercise of any of the functions within paragraphs (a) to (c)."

p.133, *annotation to the old style Jobseekers Act 1995 s.35 (Interpretation—definition of "employment officer")*

Note in relation to the schemes whose providers have been designated as employment officers that the Work Programme has ceased to operate and that reg.8(3) of the SAPOE Regulations has been revoked with effect from March 22, 2022 (see the entry for p.1187). **6.008**

PART II

INCOME SUPPORT REGULATIONS

p.226, *amendments to list of regulations for the Income Support (General) Regulations 1987 (SI 1987/1967)*

Insert the following entries between the entries for regs 66B and 67: **6.009**

"66C. Treatment of fee loans
66D. Treatment of loans for specific purposes"

p.229, *amendments to the Income Support (General) Regulations 1987 (SI 1987/1967) reg.2 (Interpretation)*

With effect from July 26, 2021, Sch.1 para.2 of the Social Security (Scotland) Act 2018 (Disability Assistance for Children and Young People) (Consequential Modifications) Order 2021 (SI 2021/786) inserts the following definitions: **6.010**

"child disability payment" has the meaning given in regulation 2 of the DACYP Regulations;
"DACYP Regulations" means the Disability Assistance for Children and Young People (Scotland) Regulations 2021;

With effect from January 1, 2022, reg.2(2) of the Social Security (Income and Capital Disregards) (Amendment) Regulations 2021 (SI 2021/1405) inserts the following definitions:

"child abuse payment" means a payment from a scheme established or approved by the Secretary of State for the purpose of providing compensation in respect of historic institutional child abuse in the United Kingdom;"
"Windrush payment" means a payment made under the Windrush Compensation Scheme (Expenditure) Act 2020;"

With effect from January 1, 2022, reg.2(2) of the Social Security (Income and Capital Disregards) (Amendment) Regulations 2021 (SI 2021/1405) inserts ", a child abuse payment or a Windrush payment" into the definition of "qualifying person", after "Grenfell Tower payment".

With effect from March 21, 2022, art.2(2) of the Social Security (Disability Assistance for Working Age People) (Consequential Amendments) Order 2022 (SI 2022/177) inserts the following definition:

"adult disability payment" has the meaning given in regulation 2 of the Disability Assistance for Working Age People (Scotland) Regulations 2022;

With effect from July 9, 2023, reg.2 of the Social Security (Income and Capital Disregards) (Amendment) Regulations 2023 (SI 2023/640) amends reg.2 as follows:

- for the definition of "Grenfell Tower payment" substitute— ""Grenfell Tower payment" means a payment made for the purpose of providing compensation or support in respect of the fire on 14th June 2017 at Grenfell Tower;";
- insert the following definitions:
  - "the Horizon system" means any version of the computer system used by the Post Office known as Horizon, Horizon Legacy, Horizon Online or HNG-X;
  - "the Post Office" means Post Office Limited (registered number 02154540);
  - "Post Office compensation payment" means a payment made by the Post Office or the Secretary of State for the purpose of providing compensation or support which is—
    (a) in connection with the failings of the Horizon system; or
    (b) otherwise payable following the judgment in Bates and Others v Post Office Ltd ((No. 3) "Common Issues")(10);
  - "vaccine damage payment" means a payment made under the Vaccine Damage Payments Act 1979(11);";
- in the definition of "qualifying person", for "or a Windrush payment" substitute ", a Windrush payment, a Post Office compensation payment or a vaccine damage payment".

With effect from October 27, 2023, reg.3 of the Social Security (Habitual Residence and Past Presence, and Capital Disregards) (Amendment) Regulations 2023 (SI 2023/1144) amends reg.2 as follows:

- in the definition of "qualifying person", after "the National Emergencies Trust" insert ", the Victims of Overseas Terrorism Compensation Scheme";
- insert the following definition:

  "the Victims of Overseas Terrorism Compensation Scheme" means the scheme of that name established by the Ministry of Justice in 2012 under section 47 of the Crime and Security Act 2010;

With effect from November 19, 2023, art.5 of the Carer's Assistance (Carer Support Payment) (Scotland) Regulations 2023 (Consequential Amendments) Order 2023 (SI 2023/1218) amends reg.2 as follows:

after the definition of "care home" insert—

""carer support payment" means carer's assistance given in accordance with the Carer's Assistance (Carer Support Payment) (Scotland) Regulations 2023;".

p.275, *amendments to the Income Support (General) Regulations 1987 (SI 1987/1967) reg.4 (Temporary absence from Great Britain)*

With effect from July 26, 2021, Sch.1 para.3 of the Social Security (Scotland) Act 2018 (Disability Assistance for Children and Young People) (Consequential Modifications) Order 2021 (SI 2021/786) makes the following amendment: 6.011

In reg.4(2)(c)(v)(aa) after "allowance", insert ", the care component of child disability payment at the highest rate in accordance with the DACYP Regulations (see regulation 11(5) of those Regulations)".

With effect from March 21, 2022, art.2(3) of the Social Security (Disability Assistance for Working Age People) (Consequential Amendments) Order 2022 (SI 2022/177) makes the following amendment:

In reg.4(2)(c)(v)(aa) (temporary absence from Great Britain):
(a) for "or" after "armed forces independence payment" substitute ",";
(b) after "personal independence payment" insert "or the enhanced rate of the daily living component of adult disability payment".

p.314, *annotation to the Income Support (General) Regulations 1987 (SI 1987/1967) reg.17 (Applicable amounts)*

The Social Security (Coronavirus) (Further Measures) Regulations 2020 (SI 2020/371), followed by the Universal Credit (Extension of Coronavirus Measures) Regulations 2021 (SI 2021/313), had the effect that for the 18 months to October 2021, the standard allowances of UC were uplifted by £20 per week. Similar measures were employed for working tax credit: the Coronavirus Act 2020 s.77, followed by the Coronavirus Act 2020 Functions of Her Majesty's Revenue and Customs (Covid-19 support scheme: working households receiving tax credits) Direction (7 April 2021). 6.012

Recipients of IS, ESA and JSA did not receive an uplift. In *R(T) v Secretary of State for Work and Pensions*, the legality of this differential treatment was challenged (unsuccessfully) as being unlawfully discriminatory contrary to the ECHR.

In [2022] EWHC 351 (Admin) (18 February 2022) the High Court: (i) rejected the claim that there was unlawful discrimination against people with the status of being a legacy benefit claimant, on the basis that being a legacy benefit claimant was not a status within the scope of ECHR art.14 (paras 22–24); and (ii) rejected the claim that there was unlawful discrimination against disabled people, on the basis that the discrimination was justified (paras 30–38). Permission to appeal to the Court of Appeal was refused on point (i) but given on point (ii). In [2023] EWCA Civ 24 (17 January 2023), the Court of Appeal confirmed that the disability discrimination was justified. The Secretary of State's focus was on prioritising people likely to be facing a recent reduction in income, and on adopting an approach she considered technically practicable (paras 53–54). In that context, the High Court did not err by deciding that the limitation of uplift to UC and WTC was a proportionate means of achieving a legitimate aim.

pp.329–331, *amendment to the Income Support (General) Regulations 1987 (SI 1987/1967) reg.21AA (Special cases: supplemental—persons from abroad)*

6.013 The text in the main volume at para.2.167 should be replaced with the following:

"[1 Special cases: supplemental—persons from abroad

21AA.—(1) "Person from abroad" means, subject to the following provisions of this regulation, a claimant who is not habitually resident in the United Kingdom, the Channel Islands, the Isle of Man or the Republic of Ireland.

(2) No claimant shall be treated as habitually resident in the United Kingdom, the Channel Islands, the Isle of Man or the Republic of Ireland unless he has a right to reside in (as the case may be) the United Kingdom, the Channel Islands, the Isle of Man or the Republic of Ireland other than a right to reside which falls within paragraph (3) [12 or (3A)].

(3) A right to reside falls within this paragraph if it is one which exists by virtue of, or in accordance with, one or more of the following—

(a) regulation 13 of the [12 Immigration (European Economic Area) Regulations 2016];

(b) regulation 14 of those Regulations, but only in a case where the right exists under that regulation because the claimant is—

(i) a jobseeker for the purpose of the definition of "qualified person" in regulation 6(1) of those Regulations, or

(ii) a family member (within the meaning of regulation 7 of those Regulations) of such a jobseeker; [14 or]

[7 [12(bb) regulation 16 of those Regulations, but only in a case where the right exists under that regulation because the claimant satisfies the criteria in paragraph (5) of that regulation;]]

[14 (c)–(e) . . .]

[12 (3A) A right to reside falls within this paragraph if it exists by virtue of a claimant having been granted limited leave to enter, or remain in, the United Kingdom under the Immigration Act 1971 by virtue of—

(a) Appendix EU to the immigration rules made under section 3(2) of that Act; [15 . . .]

(b) being a person with a Zambrano right to reside as defined in Annex 1 of Appendix EU to the immigration rules made under section 3(2) of that Act.] [15; or

(c) having arrived in the United Kingdom with an entry clearance that was granted under Appendix EU (Family Permit) to the immigration rules made under section 3(2) of that Act.]

[13 (3B) Paragraph (3A)(a) does not apply to a person who—

(a) has a right to reside granted by virtue of being a family member of a relevant person of Northern Ireland; and

(b) would have a right to reside under the [12 Immigration (European Economic Area) Regulations 2016] if the relevant person of Northern Ireland were an EEA national, provided that the right to reside does not fall within paragraph (3).]

(4) A claimant is not a person from abroad if he is—

[17(zza) a person granted leave in accordance with the immigration rules made under section 3(2) of the Immigration Act 1971, where such leave is granted by virtue of—

(i) the Afghan Relocations and Assistance Policy; or
(ii) the previous scheme for locally-employed staff in Afghanistan (sometimes referred to as the ex-gratia scheme);

(zzb) a person in Great Britain not coming within sub-paragraph (zza) or [18 (h)] who left Afghanistan in connection with the collapse of the Afghan government that took place on 15th August 2021;]

[18(zzc) a person in Great Britain who was residing in Ukraine immediately before 1st January 2022, left Ukraine in connection with the Russian invasion which took place on 24th February 2022 and—
(i) has been granted leave in accordance with immigration rules made under section 3(2) of the Immigration Act 1971; [19 . . .]
(ii) has a right of abode in the United Kingdom within the meaning given in section 2 of that Act;] [19 or
(iii) does not require leave to enter or remain in the United Kingdom in accordance with section 3ZA of that Act;]

[20(zzd) a person who was residing in Sudan before 15th April 2023, left Sudan in connection with the violence which rapidly escalated on 15th April 2023 in Khartoum and across Sudan and—
(i) has been granted leave in accordance with immigration rules made under section 3(2) of the Immigration Act 1971;
(ii) has a right of abode in the United Kingdom within the meaning given in section 2 of that Act; or
(iii) does not require leave to enter or remain in the United Kingdom in accordance with section 3ZA of that Act;]

[21(zze) a person who was residing in Israel, the West Bank, the Gaza Strip, East Jerusalem, the Golan Heights or Lebanon immediately before 7th October 2023, who left Israel, the West Bank, the Gaza Strip, East Jerusalem, the Golan Heights or Lebanon in connection with the Hamas terrorist attack in Israel on 7th October 2023 or the violence which rapidly escalated in the region following the attack and—
(i) has been granted leave in accordance with immigration rules made under section 3(2) of the Immigration Act 1971;
(ii) has a right of abode in the United Kingdom within the meaning given in section 2 of that Act; or
(iii) does not require leave to enter or remain in the United Kingdom in accordance with section 3ZA of that Act;]

[10(za) a qualified person for the purposes of [16 regulation 6 of the Immigration (European Economic Area) Regulations 2016] as a worker or a self-employed person;

(zb) a family member of a person referred to in sub-paragraph (za) [13 . . .];

(zc) a person who has a right to reside permanently in the United Kingdom by virtue of regulation 15(1)(c), (d) or (e) of those Regulations;]

[13(zd) a family member of a relevant person of Northern Ireland, with a right to reside which falls within paragraph (3A)(a), provided that the relevant person of Northern Ireland falls within sub-paragraph (za), or would do so but for the fact that they are not an EEA national;]

[14(ze) a frontier worker within the meaning of regulation 3 of the Citizens' Rights (Frontier Workers) (EU Exit) Regulations 2020;

(zf) a family member, of a person referred to in sub-paragraph (ze), who has been granted limited leave to enter, or remain in, the United

Kingdom by virtue of Appendix EU to the immigration rules made under section 3(2) of the Immigration Act 1971;]

(g) a refugee within the definition in Article 1 of the Convention relating to the Status of Refugees done at Geneva on 28th July 1951, as extended by Article 1(2) of the Protocol relating to the Status of Refugees done at New York on 31st January 1967;

[3[9(h) a person who has been granted leave or who is deemed to have been granted leave outside the rules made under section 3(2) of the Immigration Act 1971 [18 . . .];

(hh) a person who has humanitarian protection granted under those rules;] [9 or]

(i) a person who is not a person subject to immigration control within the meaning of section 115(9) of the Immigration and Asylum Act and who is in the United Kingdom as a result of his deportation, expulsion or other removal by compulsion of law from another country to the United Kingdom; [5 . . .] [9 . . .]

[13 (5) In this regulation—

"EEA national" has the meaning given in regulation 2(1) of the Immigration (European Economic Area) Regulations 2016;

"family member" has the meaning given in regulation 7(1)(a), (b) or (c) of the Immigration (European Economic Area) Regulations 2016 except that regulation 7(4) of those Regulations does not apply for the purposes of paragraphs (3B) and (4)(zd);

"relevant person of Northern Ireland" has the meaning given in Annex 1 of Appendix EU to the immigration rules made under section 3(2) of the Immigration Act 1971.]

[14 (6) In this regulation references to the Immigration (European Economic Area) Regulations 2016 are to be read with Schedule 4 to the Immigration and Social Security Co-ordination (EU Withdrawal) Act 2020 (Consequential, Saving, Transitional and Transitory Provisions) Regulations 2020.]"

Amendments

1. Social Security (Persons from Abroad) Amendment Regulations 2006 (SI 1026/2006) reg.6(3) (April 30, 2006).

2. Social Security (Lebanon) Amendment Regulations 2006 (SI 2006/1981) reg.2 (July 25, 2006). The amendment ceased to have effect from January 31, 2007.

3. Social Security (Persons from Abroad) Amendment (No. 2) Regulations 2006 (SI 2006/2528) reg.2 (October 9, 2006).

4. Social Security (Bulgaria and Romania) Amendment Regulations 2006 (SI 2006/3341) reg.2 (January 1, 2007).

5. Social Security (Habitual Residence) (Amendment) Regulations 2009 (SI 2009/362) reg.2 (March 18, 2009).

6. Social Security (Miscellaneous Amendments) (No. 3) Regulations 2011 (SI 2011/2425) reg.7(1) and (3) (October 31, 2011).

7. Social Security (Habitual Residence) (Amendment) Regulations 2012 (SI 2012/2587) reg.2 (November 8, 2012).

8. Social Security (Croatia) Amendment Regulations 2013 (SI 2013/1474) reg.2 (July 1, 2013).

9. Social Security (Miscellaneous Amendments) (No. 3) Regulations 2013 (SI 2013/2536) reg.4(1) and (5) (October 29, 2013).

10. Social Security (Habitual Residence) (Amendment) Regulations 2014 (SI 2014/902) reg.2(1) (May 31, 2014).

11. Social Security (Updating of EU References) (Amendment) Regulations 2018 (SI 2018/1084) reg.4 and Sch. para.6 (November 15, 2018).
12. Social Security (Income-related Benefits) (Updating and Amendment) (EU Exit) Regulations 2019 (SI 2019/872) reg.2 (May 7, 2019).
13. Social Security (Income-Related Benefits) (Persons of Northern Ireland—Family Members) (Amendment) Regulations 2020 (SI 2020/683) reg.2 (August 24, 2020).
14. Immigration and Social Security Co-ordination (EU Withdrawal) Act 2020 (Consequential, Saving, Transitional and Transitory Provisions) (EU Exit) Regulations 2020 (SI 2020/1309) reg.53 (December 31, 2020 at 11.00pm).
15. Immigration (Citizens' Rights etc.) (EU Exit) Regulations 2020 (SI 2020/1372) reg.8 (December 31, 2020 at 11.00 pm).
16. Social Security (Income-related Benefits) (Updating and Amendment) (EU Exit) Regulations (SI 2019/872) reg.2 (May 7, 2019).
17. Social Security (Habitual Residence and Past Presence) (Amendment) Regulations 2021 (SI 2021/1034) reg.2 (September 15, 2021).
18. Social Security (Habitual Residence and Past Presence) (Amendment) Regulations 2022 (SI 2022/344) reg.2 (March 22, 2022).
19. Social Security (Habitual Residence and Past Presence) (Amendment) (No. 2) Regulations 2022 (SI 2022/990) reg.2 (October 18, 2022).
20. Social Security (Habitual Residence and Past Presence) (Amendment) Regulations 2023 (SI 2023/532), reg.2 (May 15, 2023).
21. Social Security (Habitual Residence and Past Presence, and Capital Disregards) (Amendment) Regulations 2023, reg.2 (SI 2023/1144) (October 27, 2023).

p.355, *annotation to the Income Support (General) Regulations 1987 (SI 1987/1967) reg.23 (Calculation of the income and capital of members of claimant's family and of a polygamous marriage)*

In line 4 of p.355, for "on the exclusion of", substitute "so as to exclude" and in line 5 for "s.11", substitute "ss.11 and 12". **6.014**

pp.382–385, *annotation to the Income Support (General) Regulations 1987 (SI 1987/1967) reg.35(1) (Earnings of employed earners)*

In *SSWP v NC (ESA)* [2024] UKUT 251 (AAC) the claimant agreed to a salary sacrifice arrangement with his employer under which his weekly wage was reduced by £6.55 and the employer made contributions to its occupational pension of that weekly amount. If his earnings as calculated under the Employment Support Allowance Regulations 2008 included the amount sacrificed, they would have exceeded the level to allow him to benefit from the "permitted work" rules and retain entitlement to ESA. If they did not, they would not have exceeded the limit. The Secretary of State took the view that his gross earnings were the larger amount subject only to the deduction of half the pension contribution as a contribution made by him. The claimant's appeal to the First-tier Tribunal was allowed and the Secretary of State on their appeal to the Upper Tribunal put forward the same view. That view was rejected by Judge Church in dismissing the appeal as a misunderstanding of the essential nature of salary sacrifice pension arrangements as explained in Commissioner's decision *R(CS) 9/08*. By regarding the claimant as receiving the larger amount that view did not acknowledge the legal reality of the sacrifice of £6.55 of contractual earnings. There was no danger of an irrational extra deduction of half of the sum **6.015** paid by the claimant by way of a pension contribution, because the contribution was made by the employer, not the claimant. The judge suggests that the employer's contribution did not count as earnings because it was a payment in kind (reg.95(2)(a) of the ESA Regulations, the equivalent of reg.35(2)(a) of the Income Support Regulations) and thus excluded. It may be doubted whether in the ordinary use of language the contribution could be said to be a payment in kind to the claimant (and note that the phrase in the legislation is not benefit in kind, as used in some other contexts). But that does not matter, as in any event the employer's contribution, like any employer's contribution to an occupational or personal pension scheme, would not be regarded as remuneration or profit derived from employment under reg.95(1) (reg.35(1)).

However, there is an issue that might well reduce the impact of the decision in *NC* in other cases of the same kind. It was probably right, when the Secretary of State had not put forward any further arguments or suggestions of other relevant provisions, to dismiss their appeal. As a result, there was no consideration in *NC* of the effect of reg.108(3) of the ESA Regulations 2008 (the equivalent of reg.42(6) of the Income Support Regulations) on notional income where a claimant is paid less than the rate for comparable employment in the area (although there is a pointer to the issue in the parts of *R(CS) 9/08* subsequent to that specifically followed in *NC*). In both provisions the application of the rule is subject to no discretion if that condition is met and requires the Secretary of State to treat the claimant as possessing such earnings as are reasonable for the comparable employment unless the employer has insufficient means to pay more. In the circumstances of *NC* there would seem to be no way out of concluding that the initial condition was met, because someone doing the same job who did not make the salary sacrifice arrangement would have been paid £6.55 a week more. Then notional earnings would have to be assessed, the question of reasonableness arising only in relation to the amount, not the initial application of the rule. An extra £6.55 a week of notional income would not seem unreasonable and the employer could not be said to have insufficient means because there were sufficient means to make the actual pension contribution. Regulation 109(2)(d) of the ESA Regulations 2008 (reg.42(8)(c) of the Income Support Regulations) requires the deduction of half of any sum payable by the claimant by way of a pension contribution. Could that provision possibly be interpreted to include the contribution actually made by the employer, so as at least to allow that element of protection? Possibly yes, because in context it is very difficult to give reg.109(2)(d) (42(8)(c)) any practical application if interpreted literally when it requires the claimant to be treated as if they had actually received the income notionally attributed. So "payable" could possibly be interpreted as meaning "would have been payable by the claimant if they had received the notional income as actual earnings".

p.385, *annotation to the Income Support (General) Regulations 1987 (SI 1987/1967) reg.35(1)(d) (Earnings of employed earners—holiday pay)*

Replace the second paragraph of 2.265 (starting "Holiday pay") with the following:

6.016 Holiday pay outside this sub-paragraph is to be treated as capital (reg.48(3)), with no disregard. It then appears that it cannot be taken into account as actual income, whether it would in the absence of reg.48(3) be regarded as earnings under the general meaning in reg.35(1) or as income other than earnings. In either case there is also a disregard (Sch.8, paras 1–2, and Sch.9, para.32).

pp.393–396, *annotation to the Income Support (General) Regulations 1987 (SI 1987/1967) reg.37 (Earnings of self-employed earners)*

SSWP v MA (ESA) [2024] UKUT 131 (AAC) decides that the fact that the claimant's income was derived from the criminal enterprise of buying and selling stolen bikes on an industrial scale did not prevent it counting as earnings from self-employment. If for some reason that did not work, it would count as income other than earnings. Although the main point in the case was whether the claimant's activity constituted "work", so as to cause him to be treated as not entitled to ESA under reg.40 of the ESA Regulations 2008 (which it did), it was possible that there were some weeks in which he did not work in which the self-employed earnings would be relevant. **6.017**

The two Business Interruption Loan Schemes and the Bounce Back Loan Scheme ceased to operate on March 31, 2021, to be replaced by the Recovery Loan Scheme.

p.403, *amendment to the Income Support (General) Regulations 1987 (SI 1987/1967) reg.39(2) (Deduction of tax and contributions for self-employed earners)*

With effect from April 6, 2024, reg.8(3) of the Social Security (Class 2 National Insurance Contributions) (Consequential Amendments and Savings) Regulations 2024 (SI 2024/377) amended reg.39(2) by omitting sub-para.(a). **6.018**

p.412, *annotation to the Income Support (General) Regulations 1987 (SI 1987/1967) reg.40(1) (Calculation of income other than earnings)*

Add to the non-exhaustive list of benefits disregarded as income under Sch.9, various Scottish benefits (paras 81–85 of Sch.9). **6.019**

p.421, *amendment to the Income Support (General) Regulations 1987 (SI 1987/1967) reg.42(4ZB) (Notional income—exceptions)*

With effect from January 1, 2022, reg.2(3) of the Social Security (Income and Capital Disregards) (Amendment) Regulations 2021 (SI 2021/1405) amended para.(4ZB) by substituting the following for "a payment of income which is a Grenfell Tower payment": **6.020**

"any of the following payments of income—
(a) a Grenfell Tower payment;
(b) a child abuse payment;
(c) a Windrush payment."

All of those payments are defined in reg.2(1). See the entry for p.684 for discussion of the nature of child abuse and Windrush payments.

With effect from July 9, 2023, reg.2(3) of the Social Security (Income and Capital Disregards) (Amendment) Regulations 2023 (SI 2023/640) amended reg.42(4ZA) by inserting the following after sub-para.(c):

"(d) a Post Office compensation payment."

Such payments are newly defined in reg.2(1), where there is now also an expanded definition of Grenfell Tower payments. See the entry for pp.684–685 for the background.

pp.431–433, *annotation to the Income Support (General) Regulations 1987 (SI 1987/1967) reg.42(4) and (4ZA) (Notional income—third parties)*

6.021 Note the extended exception to the operation of para.(4) (see the entry for p.421).

pp.433–436, *annotation to the Income Support (General) Regulations 1987 (SI 1987/1967) reg.42(6), (6A) and (8) (Notional income—earnings below going rate)*

6.022 See the discussion of *SSWP v NC (ESA)* [2024] UKUT 251 (AAC) in cases of salary sacrifice pension arrangements in the entry for pp.382–385.

p.438, *annotation to the Income Support (General) Regulations 1987 (SI 1987/967) reg.45 (Capital limit)*

6.023 In the Institute for Government and the Social Security Advisory Committee's 2021 joint report *Jobs and benefits: The Covid-19 challenge* it was noted that if the capital limit of £16,000 had risen in line with prices since 2006 it would be close to £23,500 (or £25,000: different figures are given) and recommended that the limit should be increased to £25,000 and subsequently automatically indexed to maintain its real value (pp.22 and 31). That recommendation was summarily rejected in the Government's response of March 22, 2022.

p.439, *annotation to the Income Support (General) Regulations 1987 (SI 1987/1967) reg.46 (Calculation of capital)*

6.024 At some point, the valuation of digital assets, such as non-fungible tokens, cryptocurrency etc., may have to be addressed, including how they fit into the notions of capital and of personal possessions. There is extensive discussion of the existing legal framework in the Law Commission's *Digital Assets: Consultation Paper* (Law Com. No.256, July 28, 2022). Now see *Digital Assets: Final report* (Law Com. No.412, June 27, 2023). The DWP universal credit guidance on the treatment of capital deposited in the House of Commons library (as collected in the Resources section of the Rightsnet website) suggests that cryptoassets, including cryptocurrency, be treated as investments, with a 10% deduction from valuation for expenses of sale. If cryptocurrency were to be treated like any other money, para.21 of Sch.10 on commission or banking charges for conversion into sterling would need consideration.

On September 11, 2024, the Property (Digital Assets etc) Bill was introduced into the House of Lords, aimed at implementing the Law Commission's recommendation for legislation. Clause 1, as currently drafted, provides that a thing (including a thing that is digital or electronic in nature) is not prevented from being the object of personal property rights merely because it is neither a thing in possession nor a thing in action. It is far from clear how such a provision, when finally enacted, would affect the calculation of capital for social security purposes, which is more concerned with whether there is a market for assets, for sale or by use as security in raising money etc, than with personal property rights. However, it might be taken to strengthen the argument for treating cryptoassets as "things" capable of having such a market value.

pp.440–441, *annotation to the Income Support (General) Regulations 1987 (SI 1987/1967) reg.46 (Calculation of capital)*

Another example of a case where a claimant may not have capital that may seem to be available to them is where they are a shareholder in a company, as illustrated in *ZA v London Borough of Barnet (HB)* [2024] UKUT 222 (AAC). There the claimant and her husband (H) were shareholders (H 50 shares, claimant 15, their children 35) in a company of which H was the sole director. At the relevant date the company's net assets after liabilities were valued in the accounts at £284,000 and described as retained profits or shareholders' funds. In a very confused process of decision-making the local authority rejected entitlement to housing benefit on the ground of possession of capital over £16,000, but without invoking any of the provisions allowing a claimant to be treated as possessing capital. That decision and reasoning, or lack of it, was upheld by a First-tier Tribunal, that thus obviously went wrong in law. Judge Butler, in considering the options available to a decision-maker in such circumstances, stated in paras 68 to 70 that the categorisation of funds as retained profits or shareholders' funds does not mean that they cease to be the company's assets and become something else that could be viewed as capital actually held by a shareholder. Generally, shareholders only get access to such funds if the company, as a separate legal person, decides to declare dividends, which is not guaranteed as a company may decide to retain profits. The judge also stated in paras 82 to 89 that *Prest v Petrodel Resources Ltd* [2013] UKSC 34; [2013] 2 A.C. 415, bandied about by the local authority at some stages but not in the end relied on before the Upper Tribunal, was not relevant to the case. The principles on which the properties owned by the companies in that case that were found by the Supreme Court to be held on resulting trust for the husband in matrimonial proceedings were highly fact-specific and there was no justification for looking further into the assets of the company in *ZA* than allowed by the complete legislative system for dealing with capital provided in the Housing Benefit Regulations. The case was sent back to a new tribunal to investigate whether the provisions equivalent to reg.50(4) and (5) of the Income Support Regulations (but with an important difference) applied. See the entry below for pp.485–486. 6.025

The text in the paragraph starting "See also" on p.440 to the paragraph ending "had ceased." on p.441 should be deleted.

Insert the following text on p.441 between the paragraph starting "However" and the heading "*Beneficial ownership*":

Interests under a will or intestacy when someone has died

The DMG (paras 29169–29175) contains guidance adopting in para.29174 the general principle that a beneficiary under a will or intestacy has no legal or equitable interest in any specific property while the estate remains unadministered. The personal representative in those circumstances has full ownership of the assets of the estate. That principle was applied by the Tribunal of Commissioners in *R(SB) 5/85*, relying on the foundational Privy Council decision in *Commissioner of Stamp Duties (Queensland) v Livingston* [1965] A.C. 694.

However, there are two important qualifications. The first is that, even where the *Livingston* principle applies, the beneficiary has a right to have the deceased's estate properly administered. That is a chose in action that has a market value. It can be transferred and can be borrowed against. Depending on the particular circumstances, the market value can be considerable and not far off the value that would be put on the asset(s) in question if owned outright. That point was made clearly by Commissioner Howell in para.28 of his decision in *R(IS) 1/01* and nothing to the contrary was said in the Court of Appeal in *Wilkinson v Chief Adjudication Officer*, reported as part of *R(IS) 1/01*, in upholding the Commissioner's decision. Nor is *R(SB) 5/85* to the contrary: the Commissioners there expressly noted that the claimant had a chose in action (para.7). It is submitted that that is the basis on which the later decision of Commissioner Howell in *CIS/1189/2003* is to be supported. The claimant there was the sole residuary beneficiary under her mother's will and the estate, whose main asset was a property that the claimant did not live in, remained unadministered for several years, so that the property had not actually vested in the claimant. In para.11, the Commissioner said that the claimant was beneficially entitled to the property from the date of her mother's death subject only to the formalities needed to perfect her title, so that for all practical purposes she had an entitlement equivalent to full beneficial ownership. That proposition can easily be misinterpreted, but in para.12, the Commissioner noted that as the claimant was the sole *residuary* beneficiary, it was para.28 of *R(IS) 1/01* that was applicable. So the valuation was of the claimant's chose in action, but in the circumstances the difference in value from that of full beneficial ownership was negligible.

The second qualification is that the position may be different where there has been a specific gift of some asset, as was the case in *R(IS) 1/01*, where the will of the claimant's mother gave the claimant and her brother equal shares in some income bonds and other money in a bank account and in a property. The matter was put very strongly by Commissioner Howell in para.27 of his decision, where he said that the *Livingston* principle had:

> "never had any application to property specifically devised or bequeathed by a will. Such property becomes in equity the property of the legatee as soon as the testator dies, subject only to the right of the personal representative to resort to it for payment of debts if the remainder of the estate is insufficient for this purpose [citations omitted]."

No specific comment on that proposition was made in the judgments of the Court of Appeal in *Wilkinson*, but Mummery LJ did note generally that the evidence did not suggest that there was any question of the executors needing to have recourse to the property for payment of debts or that there was any other legal obstacle to the immediate completion of the administration of the estate and to an assent by the executors vesting the property in the names of the claimant and her brother as joint owners. That strongly suggests that what was being considered was a valuation of the claimant's chose in action, rather than of some equitable interest. It is submitted that that is the proper approach. The valuation would therefore be sensitive to the possibilities mentioned by Mummery LJ in the particular case, as well as to the value of the underlying asset. That approach would hold also for personal property or money, although there it should be noted that the process of the personal representative giving an assent, i.e. an indication that a certain asset is not required for administration purposes and may pass under the will or (possibly) an intestacy into the ownership of the beneficiary, does not need to be in writing and may be implied from conduct.

p.443, *annotation to the Income Support (General) Regulations 1987 (SI 1987/967) reg.46 (Calculation of capital—claimant holding as trustee)*

In line 10 of the paragraph starting "One particular", insert the following between "return it" and the full stop: **6.026**

"(a result most recently confirmed by the decision of the Privy Council in the *Prickly Bay* case)"

p.446, *annotation to the Income Support (General) Regulations 1987 (SI 1987/967) reg.46 (Calculation of capital—claimant holding as trustee)*

Note, in relation to the discussion of cases in which the *Quistclose* principle has or has not been applied, that the Privy Council in *Prickly Bay Waterside Ltd v British American Insurance Co Ltd* [2022] UKPC 8; [2022] 1 W.L.R. 2087, while accepting the value of summaries of principles, in particular of those established by the judgment of Lord Millett in *Twinsectra Ltd v Yardley* [2002] 2 A.C. 164, warned against not going back to the "core analysis" in that judgment. It was emphasised again that it is not enough that money is provided for a particular purpose. The question is whether the parties intended that the money should be at the free disposition of the recipient. An intention that it should not be need not be mutual, in the sense of being shared or reciprocated, but could be imposed by one party and acquiesced in by the other. A *Quistclose* trust is a default trust, so can be excluded or moulded by the terms of the parties' express agreements. In the particular case, involving complex commercial transactions in which a sum was loaned to a bank that contracted to guarantee payment of the purchase price of a property on future completion, it was significant to the outcome that a *Quistclose* trust had not been established that there had been no requirement that the sum be segregated by the bank from its other funds. It is submitted that in other contexts, such as family or other relatively informal arrangements more likely to be encountered in the social security context, a lack of segregation, say into a separate account, would not carry nearly such weight. **6.027**

p.449, *annotation to the Income Support (General) Regulations 1987 (SI 1987/1967) reg.46 (Calculation of capital—claimant holding as trustee)*

Note, in relation to the decision in *Marr v Collie*, that the Court of Appeal (*Williams v Williams* [2024] EWCA Civ 42; [2024] 4 W.L.R. 10) has applied what it described as the "long-standing principle of equity that property acquired in joint names for business purposes would be presumed to be held beneficially as tenants in common rather than as joint tenants with the **6.028** accidents of survivorship". There was nothing in *Stack v Dowden* or *Jones v Kermott* relied on in the domestic context to suggest that that principle had been undermined or affected in any way.

p.451, *annotation to the Income Support (General) Regulations 1987 (SI 1987/1967) reg.46 (Calculation of capital—claimant holding as trustee)*

6.029 Note the decision of the Supreme Court, by a majority of three to two, in *Guest v Guest* [2022] UKSC 27; [2024] A.C. 833 on proprietary estoppel and the nature of the remedies available in equity. Lord Briggs, giving the majority judgment, conducted an exhaustive survey of the English and Australian case law, as well as academic debate, and rejected the theory that the aim of the remedy was to compensate the person given a promise or assurance about the acquisition of property for the detriment suffered in reliance on the promise or assurance, rather than primarily to hold the person who had given the promise or assurance to the promise or assurance, which would usually prevent the unconscionability inherent in the repudiation of the promise or assurance that had been detrimentally relied on (paras 71 and 61). However, the remedy was a flexible one dependent on the circumstances. Lord Briggs summarised the principles as follows:

> "74. I consider that, in principle, the court's normal approach should be as follows. The first stage (which is not in issue in this case) is to determine whether the promisor's repudiation of his promise is, in the light of the promisee's detrimental reliance upon it, unconscionable at all. It usually will be, but there may be circumstances (such as the promisor falling on hard times and needing to sell the property to pay his creditors, or to pay for expensive medical treatment or social care for himself or his wife) when it may not be. Or the promisor may have announced or carried out only a partial repudiation of the promise, which may or may not have been unconscionable, depending on the circumstances.
>
> 75. The second (remedy) stage will normally start with the assumption (not presumption) that the simplest way to remedy the unconscionability constituted by the repudiation is to hold the promisor to the promise. The promisee cannot (and probably would not) complain, for example, that his detrimental reliance had cost him more than the value of the promise, were it to be fully performed. But the court may have to listen to many other reasons from the promisor (or his executors) why something less than full performance will negate the unconscionability and therefore satisfy the equity. They may be based on one or more of the real-life problems already outlined. The court may be invited by the promisor to consider one or more proxies for performance of the promise, such as the transfer of less property than promised or the provision of a monetary equivalent in place of it, or a combination of the two.
>
> 76. If the promisor asserts and proves, the burden being on him for this purpose, that specific enforcement of the full promise, or monetary equivalent, would be out of all proportion to the cost of the detriment to the promisee, then the court may be constrained to limit the extent of the remedy. This does not mean that the court will be seeking precisely to compensate for the detriment as its primary task, but simply to put right a disproportionality which is so large as to stand in the way of a full

specific enforcement doing justice between the parties. It will be a very rare case where the detriment is equivalent in value to the expectation, and there is nothing in principle unjust in a full enforcement of the promise being worth more than the cost of the detriment, any more than there is in giving specific performance of a contract for the sale of land merely because it is worth more than the price paid for it. An example of a remedy out of all proportion to the detriment would be the full enforcement of a promise by an elderly lady to leave her carer a particular piece of jewellery if she stayed on at very low wages, which turned out on valuation by her executors to be a Faberge worth millions. Another would be a promise to leave a generous inheritance if the promisee cared for the promisor for the rest of her life, but where she unexpectedly died two months later."

Winter v Winter [2024] EWCA Civ 699, in another farm case, has explored the requirement of detriment in some detail, in particular holding that when deciding whether a claimant has suffered detriment as a result of reliance on an assurance, the court must weigh any nonfinancial disadvantage against any financial benefit even where the disadvantage is not susceptible to quantification, and even though it is a difficult exercise.

Thus, in circumstances where proprietary estoppel might be in play (as would probably now be the case on similar facts to *R(SB) 23/85* and *R(SB) 7/87*), great care would be needed in establishing the primary facts and, outside the clearest cases, in a deeper investigation of the principles of law governing the nature of any remedy available. And would a repudiation of a promise when the promisor would otherwise be forced to rely on a means-tested benefit be unconscionable? However, even if it were to be concluded that the claimant did not hold the property in question on trust for someone else, the possibility of a claim in equity, e.g. for some monetary compensation, may well affect the valuation of the property.

p.457, *amendment to the Income Support (General) Regulations 1987 (SI 1987/1967) reg.48(10) (Income treated as capital—exceptions)*

With effect from January 1, 2022, reg.2(4) of the Social Security (Income and Capital Disregards) (Amendment) Regulations 2021 (SI 2021/1405) amended para.(10) by inserting the following after sub-para.(ab): **6.030**

"(ac) which is a child abuse payment;
(ad) which is a Windrush payment; or"

Both of those payments are defined in reg.2(1). See the entry for p.684 for discussion of their nature. The "or" following sub-para.(ab), omitted in error in the main volume, has also been removed.

With effect from July 9, 2023, reg.2(4) of the Social Security (Income and Capital Disregards) (Amendment) Regulations 2023 (SI 2023/640) amended reg.48(10) by omitting "or" at the end of sub-para.(ad) and inserting the following:

"(ae) which is a Post Office compensation payment."

Such payments are newly defined in reg.2(1), where there is now also an expanded definition of Grenfell Tower payments (see sub-para.(ab)). See the entry for pp.684–685 for the background.

With effect from October 27, 2023, reg.3(3)(a) of the Social Security (Habitual Residence and Past Presence, and Capital Disregards) (Amendment) Regulations 2023 (SI 2023/1144) amended reg.48(10)(c) by inserting ", the Victims of Overseas Terrorism Compensation Scheme" after "the National Emergencies Trust". That scheme is newly defined in reg.2(1). See the entry for pp.684–685 for the background.

p.467, *amendment to the Income Support (General) Regulations 1987 (SI 1987/1967) reg.51(3B) (Notional capital—exceptions)*

6.031 With effect from January 1, 2022, reg.2(5) of the Social Security (Income and Capital Disregards) (Amendment) Regulations 2021 (SI 2021/1405) amended para.(3B) by substituting the following for "a payment of capital which is a Grenfell Tower payment":

"any of the following payments of capital—
(a) a Grenfell Tower payment;
(b) a child abuse payment;
(c) a Windrush payment."

All of those payments are defined in reg.2(1). See the entry for p.684 for discussion of the nature of child abuse and Windrush payments.

With effect from July 9, 2023, reg.2(5) of the Social Security (Income and Capital Disregards) (Amendment) Regulations 2023 (SI 2023/640) amended reg.51(3B) by inserting the following after sub-para.(c):

"(d) a Post Office compensation payment;
(f) a vaccine damage payment."

Such payments are newly defined in reg.2(1), where there is now also an expanded definition of Grenfell Tower payments (see sub-para.(a)). See the entry for pp.684–685 for the background.

With effect from October 27, 2023, reg.3(3)(b) of the Social Security (Habitual Residence and Past Presence, and Capital Disregards) (Amendment) Regulations 2023 (SI 2023/1144) amended reg.51(3A)(a) by inserting ", the Victims of Overseas Terrorism Compensation Scheme" after "the National Emergencies Trust". That scheme is newly defined in reg.2(1). See the entry for pp.684–685 for the background.

p.482, *annotation to the Income Support (General) Regulations 1987 (SI 1987/1967) reg.51(1) (Notional capital—deprivation)*

6.032 See the entry for pp.1029–30 for the acceptance of the position under reg.113(1) of the JSA Regulations 1996 in *DB v DfC (JSA)* [2021] NICom 43. There, it was found that the claimant had deprived herself of capital while in receipt of income-related ESA. It was inherently improbable that when doing so, more than a year before she claimed JSA, she had possible entitlement to JSA or income support in mind. The tribunal had failed to make necessary findings of fact in concluding that her purpose had been the securing of entitlement to JSA. The principle would apply even more so to reg.51(1), where the test of purpose is still restricted to income support (but contrast the position reg.115(1) of the ESA Regulations 2008).

The decision also illustrates that on a new claim neither the decision-maker nor a tribunal on appeal is bound by the findings of fact on capital that have underpinned a decision of non-entitlement on capital grounds. The basis of the ESA decision, that the claimant as at that date still had actual capital of more than £40,000, did not have to be adopted on the JSA claim.

pp.485–486, *annotation to the Income Support (General) Regulations 1987 (SI 1987/1967) reg.51(4) and (5) (Notional income—claimant in position analogous to sole owner or partner in relation to a company)*

ZA v London Borough of Barnet (HB) [2024] UKUT 222 (AAC) (see the entry above for pp.440–441 for details) discusses the terms of the provisions of the Housing Benefit Regulations 2006 (reg.49(5) and (6)) equivalent to reg.51(4) and (5), but with the important difference that there is a discretion whether or not the basic condition for its application is met, whereas under reg.51(4) the rules must be applied if the claimant's position in relation to a company is analogous to that of a sole owner or partner in the business of the company. Thus, the judge's analysis of the options available is not directly relevant to income support (or to old style ESA or JSA). **6.033**

pp.520–523, *annotations to the Income Support (General) Regulations 1987 (SI 1987/1967) reg.61 (Interpretation—students—meaning of "Full-time course")*

The principles derived from the case law, taking into account Court of Appeal decisions not all of which are discussed in the main volume, have recently very helpfully been summarised by Judge Rowley in para.19 of *BK v SSWP (UC)* [2022] UKUT 73 (AAC) (some references added by annotator): **6.034**

"a. Whether or not a person is undertaking a full-time course is a question of fact for the tribunal having regard to the circumstances in each particular case (*R/SB 40/83* at [13]; *R(SB) 41/83* at [12]). Parameters have been set, as appear below:

b. The words 'full-time' relate to the course and not to the student. Specifically, they do not permit the matter to be determined by reference to the amount of time which the student happens to dedicate to their studies (*R/SB 40/83* at [14], [15]; *R(SB) 2/91* at [7]; *R(SB) 41/83* at [11]).

c. Evidence from the educational establishment as to whether or not the course is full-time is not necessarily conclusive, but it ought to be accepted as such unless it is inconclusive on its face, or is challenged by relevant evidence which at least raises the possibility that it ought to be rejected (*R/SB 40/83* at [18]), and any evidence adduced in rebuttal should be weighty in content (*R/SB 41/83* at [12]). See also *Flemming v Secretary of State for Work and Pensions* [2002] EWCA Civ 641; [2002] 1 W.L.R. 2322 [also reported as *R(G) 2/02*] at [21]–[22] and [38]; and *Deane v Secretary of State for Work and Pensions* [2010] EWCA Civ 699; [2011] 1 W.L.R. 743 [also reported at [2010] AACR 42] where the Court of Appeal repeated an earlier statement in *Flemming* that:

> "38 . . . A tribunal of fact should, I think be very slow to accept that a person expects or intends to devote—or does, in fact, devote—significantly less time to the course than those who have

conduct of the course expect of him, and very slow to hold that a person who is attending a course considered by the educational establishment to be a part-time course is to be treated as receiving full-time education because he devotes significantly more time than that which is expected of him . . ."

d. If the course is offered as a full-time course, the presumption is that the recipient is in full-time education. There may be exceptions to the rule, such where a student is granted exemptions from part of the course: *Deane* [51]."

In *BK* itself, the claimant was on a one-year MA course at Goldsmiths, University of London, described by that institution as full-time and involving more than 24 hours of study per week. Letters from the Department concerned confirmed six contact hours of teaching in two terms, with an expectation of at least six hours per week in independent study. A dissertation was to be written in the third term. The First-tier Tribunal rejected the claimant's argument that those letters, and the fact that he could arrange his time to be available for work, showed that the course was not full-time. Judge Rowley held that it did not err in law in doing so and that in saying that Goldsmiths' description was "determinative" of the nature of the course it had not strayed into regarding the description as conclusive, but had applied the test in para.19(c) above.

p.526, *annotation to the Income Support (General) Regulations 1987 (SI 1987/1967) reg.61 (Interpretation—"postgraduate loan")*

6.035 The value of a postgraduate loan under the English scheme described (there are different schemes for other UK countries) has been increased to £11,836 for courses starting on or after August 1, 2022, to £12,167 for courses starting on or after August 1, 2023 and to £12,471 for courses starting on or after August 1, 2024.

p.527, *annotation to the Income Support (General) Regulations 1987 (SI 1987/1967) reg.61 (Interpretation—student loan)*

6.036 See the entry for p.539 below.

p.539, *annotation to the Income Support (General) Regulations 1987 (SI 1987/1967) reg.66A (Treatment of student loans and postgraduate loans)*

6.037 See, in relation to the housing benefit equivalent of the rule in reg.66A(3)(b) and (4) treating students as possessing the maximum student or postgraduate loan in respect of an academic year that they could acquire by taking reasonable steps to do so, the decision of Judge Poynter in *IB v Gravesham BC and SSWP (HB)* [2023] UKUT 193 (AAC); [2024] P.T.S.R. 130 declining to follow *CH/4429/2006*. There, Commissioner Powell had held that "reasonable" qualified only the mechanical steps that had to be taken to acquire a loan and was not concerned with matters such as the motives or religious beliefs of the claimant. The facts of IB were on all fours with those of *CH/4429/2006*, in that the claimant was a devout and observant Muslim, who did not take out student loans otherwise available to him because that would have involved the paying of interest, which he conscientiously believed was forbidden by his religion. Nonetheless, the local authority treated him as possessing income from the loans, so that he failed the housing benefit means test. That decision was upheld by the First-tier Tribunal, considering itself bound by *CH/4429/2006*. The Upper Tribunal substituted the decision that on the particular facts the claimant's entitlement to housing benefit was to be recalculated on the basis that he did not possess any income from the loans that he had not applied for.

The judge's view was that the reasoning in *CH/4429/2006* proceeded on a false basis and contained additional errors of logic. The Commissioner had stated in para.4 that the practical effect of the provision was that a student who was "entitled to a student loan", the use of which words was said to be deliberate, was to suffer a diminution in the amount of housing benefit. That was the apparent basis for the conclusion about the meaning of reasonable steps in para.11 of his decision. The judge points out that those words do not appear anywhere in the applicable Regulations, and that the test actually set out is in terms of what could be acquired by taking reasonable steps and does not assume the making of an application. A straightforward analysis of the steps that would be necessary to acquire a student loan would include scrutinising the terms on which the loan was offered, deciding whether to accept those terms and, if so, completing and submitting the application form and finally signing an agreement accepting the paying of interest. The judge concludes that the steps to be considered under the regulation therefore cannot be restricted to the "mechanical", the particular question of whether to accept the terms being one that would involve issues of judgment for anyone (e.g. about whether to accept the future burden of debt and interest payments). Moreover, while the Commissioner had noted that it was difficult to see how the necessary steps to acquire a loan could in themselves be said to be unreasonable except in the most exceptional cases, Judge Poynter suggests that, if personal circumstances were to be ignored, it would be inconceivable that the mechanics of applying for a student loan could ever require students to take steps that were unreasonable. In order for the words "reasonable steps" to be given some practical application, as must be assumed to have been intended, the interpretation adopted in *CH/4429/2006* could not be correct. For those and other subsidiary reasons, the judge declined to follow that decision.

Judge Poynter formulated the correct test to be applied, without the *CH/4429/2006* limitation and in line with the established approach in other areas of social security law, as follows:

> "139. I therefore conclude that "reasonable steps" means steps that are reasonable in all the circumstances including all the personal characteristics of the individual who was eligible to have applied for the student loan. That includes strong conscientious religious or other objections to the payment of interest.
> 140. I would, however, add that all the circumstances includes the interests of the wider public as represented by the Secretary of State and that assessing reasonableness will need to give those interests weight (see paragraphs 190–191 below). Without being prescriptive, I suggest that an omission to acquire a loan that is based on purely financial considerations is unlikely to outweigh those interests."

He rejected the Secretary of State's submission that that approach would involve direct discrimination against claimants who did not share his particular religious views. That was because (para.142):

> "[t]he line drawn by my interpretation is not between Muslims and non-Muslims nor even between people who have conscientious objections to taking out a student loan and those who don't. Rather it is between, on the one hand, any student whose personal circumstances as a whole are such that—for whatever reason—he cannot take reasonable steps to acquire a student loan and, on the other, all students who are not so circumstanced. Those two groups are not in analogous situations. The latter could reasonably acquire the loan that [the regulation] takes into account as their income. The former cannot."

The judge also rejected the submission that his interpretation would make the housing benefit scheme unworkable and invite numerous, possibly opportunistic, claims, pointing out the limited scope for students to qualify for housing benefit (as for other means-tested benefits, including income support), the fact that to benefit from the rule the claimant would have to turn down the advantages of actually receiving the loan on offer and the difficulties that claimants might have in showing a genuine conscientious religious or other objection to the payment of interest. The latter point might easily be tested by seeing if the particular claimant had any interest-bearing bank or building society accounts, a credit card or a non-Sharia mortgage. Finally, there was the limiting factor of the need to take into account when judging reasonableness the interests of the wider public, in the form of the government policy that the costs of education are usually to be funded from the education budget rather than the social security benefit.

However, in substituting his own decision in IB Judge Poynter had no doubt that the claimant's personal circumstances, in particular his sincere and strongly held religious conviction that it would be a major sin to pay interest, outweighed any loss to public funds or dent in the government's general policy.

The result is that at the moment there are two conflicting decisions of equal authority. A First-tier Tribunal may therefore choose to follow the decision whose reasoning it finds more convincing. In doing so it can give weight to the fact that *IB* contains a detailed review of the reasoning in *CH/4429/2006*.

p.542, *amendment to the Income Support (General) Regulations 1987 (SI 1987/1967) reg.66D (Treatment of special support loans)*

6.038 With effect from April 1, 2024, reg.3 of the Social Security and Universal Credit (Migration of Tax Credit Claimants and Miscellaneous Amendments) Regulations 2024 (SI 2024/341) amended reg.66D by substituting the following for the existing text and heading:

> **"Treatment of loans for specific purposes**
> **66D.** A loan under the Education (Student Support) Regulations 2011 or regulations made under section 73 of the Education (Scotland) Act 1980 that is intended to meet the cost of books, equipment, travel or childcare is to be disregarded as income."

The new form of reg.66D is intended to ensure that special support loans under a scheme to be introduced for full-time students by the Scottish government from the beginning of academic year 2024/25 are to be disregarded as income in same way as special support loans in England and Wales. Although the new form no longer refers to the definition of "special support loan" in reg.68 of the Education (Student Support) Regulations

2011, the restriction to loans intended (i.e., by necessary implication, intended by the awarding authority) to meet the cost of books, equipment, travel or childcare excludes loans under those regulations for other purposes. See reg.62 for the disregard of grants, as opposed to loans, for similar and other purposes.

p.550, *amendments to the Income Support (General) Regulations 1987 (SI 1987/1967) Sch.1B (Prescribed categories of persons)*

With effect from July 26, 2021, Sch.1 para.4 of the Social Security (Scotland) Act 2018 (Disability Assistance for Children and Young People) (Consequential Modifications) Order 2021 (SI 2021/786) makes the following amendments: **6.039**

- In para.4(a) of Sch.1B (persons caring for another person):
  - in para.(i), after "Contributions and Benefits Act" insert ", the care component of child disability payment at the highest or middle rate in accordance with the DACYP Regulations (see regulation 11(5) of those Regulations),";
  - in para.(iii), after "disability living allowance", insert ", child disability payment";
  - after para.(iiia), insert "(iiib) the person being cared for ("P") has claimed entitlement to the care component of child disability payment in accordance with regulation 24 (when an application is to be treated as made and beginning of entitlement to assistance) of the DACYP Regulations, an award at the highest or middle rate has been made in respect of P's claim, and where the period for which the award is payable has begun, P is in receipt of that payment;".

With effect from March 21, 2022, art.2(4)–(5) of the Social Security (Disability Assistance for Working Age People) (Consequential Amendments) Order 2022 (SI 2022/177) makes the following amendments:

- In para.4(a) (persons caring for another person) of Sch.1B (prescribed categories of person):
  - in sub-para.(i):
    - for "or" after "(see regulation 11(5) of those Regulations)," substitute ",";
    - after "2012 Act" insert "or the daily living component of adult disability payment at the standard or enhanced rate in accordance with regulation 5 of the Disability Assistance for Working Age People (Scotland) Regulations 2022";
  - in sub-para.(iii):
    - for "or" after "armed forces independence payment" substitute ",";
    - after "personal independence payment" insert "or adult disability payment";
  - after sub-para.(iv) insert "(v)the person being cared for has claimed entitlement to the daily living component of adult disability payment in accordance with regulation 35 (when an application is to be treated as made and beginning of entitlement to assistance) of the Disability Assistance for Working Age

People (Scotland) Regulations 2022, an award at the standard or enhanced rate has been made in respect of that claim and, where the period for which the award is payable has begun, that person is in receipt of the payment;".

- In para.7A (certain persons in receipt of the daily living component of personal independence payment) of Sch.1B:
  - in the heading, after "personal independence payment" insert "or adult disability payment";
  - after "at the enhanced rate" insert "or the daily living component of adult disability payment at the enhanced rate".

With effect from November 19, 2023, art.5 of the Carer's Assistance (Carer Support Payment) (Scotland) Regulations 2023 (Consequential Amendments) Order 2023 (SI 2023/1218) makes the following amendments to paragraph 4(b) of Schedule 1B:

- after "carer's allowance" insert "or carer support payment";
- for "that allowance" substitute "a carer's allowance".

pp.571–572, *amendments to the Income Support (General) Regulations 1987 (SI 1987/1967) Sch.2 (Applicable amounts)*

6.040 The text in the main volume at paras 2.606–2.626 should be replaced with the following:

Regulations 17 [3 (1)] and 18

"SCHEDULE 2

APPLICABLE AMOUNTS

[35 PART I

PERSONAL ALLOWANCES

2.606 **1.**—The weekly amounts specified in column (2) below in respect of each person or couple specified in column (1) shall be the weekly amounts specified for the purposes of regulations 17(1) and 18(1) (applicable amounts and polygamous marriages).

Column (1) *Person or Couple*	*Column (2)* *Amount*
(1) Single claimant aged—	(1)
(a) except where head (b) or (c) of this sub-paragraph applies, less than 18;	(a) [86 £71.70];
[28(b) less than 18 who falls within any of the circumstances specified in paragraph 1A;]	(b) [86 £71.70];
(c) less than 18 who satisfies the condition in [65 paragraph 11(1)(a)]	(c) [86 £71.70];
(d) not less than 18 but less than 25;	(d) [86 £71.70];
(e) not less than 25.	(e) [86 £90.50].

Column (1) *Person or Couple*	*Column (2)* *Amount*
(2) Lone parent aged— (a) except where head (b) or (c) of this sub-paragraph applies, less than 18; [28(b) less than 18 who falls within any of the circumstances specified in paragraph 1A;] (c) less than 18 who satisfies the condition in [65 paragraph 11(1)(a)] (d) not less than 18.	(2) (a) [86 £71.70]; (b) [86 £71.70]; (c) [86 £67.20]; (d) [86 £90.50].
[28(3) Couple— (a) where both members are aged less than 18 and— (i) at least one of them is treated as responsible fora child; or (ii) had they not been members of a couple, each would have qualified for income support under regulation 4ZA [71 or income-related employment and support allowance]; or (iii) the claimant's partner satisfies the requirement of section 3(1)(f)(iii) of the Jobseekers Act 1995 (prescribed circumstances for persons aged 16 but less than 18); or (iv) there is in force in respect of the claimant's partner a direction under section 16 of the Jobseekers Act 1995 (persons under 18: severe hardship); (b) where both members are aged less than 18 and head (a) does not apply but one member of the couple falls within any of the circumstances specified in paragraph 1A; (c) where both members are aged less than 18 and heads (a) and (b) do not apply; (d) where both members are aged not less than 18; (e) where one member is aged not less than 18 and the other member is a person under 18 who—(2) (i) qualifies for income support under regulation 4ZA [71 or income-related employment and support allowance], or who would so qualify if he were not a member of a couple; or (ii) satisfies the requirements of section 3(1)(f)(iii) of the Jobseekers Act 1995 (prescribed circumstances for persons aged 16 but less than 18); or (iii) is the subject of a direction under section 16 of the Jobseekers Act 1995 (persons under 18: severe hardship); (f) where the claimant is aged not less than 18 but less (f) than 25 and his partner is a person under 18 who— (i) would not qualify for income support under regulation 4ZA [71 or income-related employment and support allowance] if he were not a member of a couple; and (ii) does not satisfy the requirements of section 3(1)(f)(iii) of the Jobseekers Act 1995 (prescribed circumstances for persons aged 16 but less than 18); and (iii) is not the subject of a direction under section 16 of the Jobseekers Act 1995 (persons under 18: severe hardship); (g) where the claimant is aged not less than 25 and his (g) partner is a person under 18 who— (i) would not qualify for income support under regulation 4ZA [71 or income-related employment and support allowance] if he were not a member of a couple; and	(3) (a) [86 £108.30]; (b) [86 £71.70]; (c) [86 £71.70]; (d) [86 £142.25]; (e) [86 £142.25]; (f) [86 £71.70]; (g) [86 £90.50].

Column (1) *Person or Couple*	*Column (2)* *Amount*
(ii) does not satisfy the requirements of section 3(1)(f)(iii) of the Jobseekers Act 1995 (prescribed circumstances for persons aged 16 but less than 18); and (iii) is not the subject of a direction under section 16 of the Jobseekers Act 1995 (persons under 18: severe hardship).]]	

2.607 [28 **1A.**—(1) The circumstances referred to in paragraph 1 are that—

(a) the person has no parents nor any person acting in the place of his parents;

(b) the person—

(i) is not living with his parents nor any person acting in the place of his parents; and

(ii) in England and Wales, was being looked after by a local authority pursuant to a relevant enactment who placed him with some person other than a close relative of his; or in Scotland, was in the care of a local authority under a relevant enactment and whilst in that care was not living with his parents or any close relative, or was in custody in any institution to which the Prison Act 1952 or the Prisons (Scotland) Act 1989 applied immediately before he attained the age of 16;

(c) the person is in accommodation which is other than his parental home, and which is other than the home of a person acting in the place of his parents, who entered that accommodation—

(i) as part of a programme of rehabilitation or resettlement, that programme being under the supervision of the probation service or a local authority; or

(ii) in order to avoid physical or sexual abuse; or

(iii) because of a mental or physical handicap or illness and needs such accommodation because of his handicap or illness;

(d) the person is living away from his parents and any person who is acting in the place of his parents in a case where his parents are or, as the case may be, that person is, unable financially to support him and his parents are, or that person is—

(i) chronically sick or mentally or physically disabled; or

(ii) detained in custody pending trial or sentence upon conviction or under sentence imposed by a court; of

(iii) prohibited from entering or re-entering Great Britain; or

(e) the person of necessity has to live away from his parents and any person acting in the place of his parents because—

(i) he is estranged from his parents and that person; or

(ii) he is in physical or moral danger; or

(iii) there is a serious risk to his physical or mental health.

(2) In this paragraph—

(a) "chronically sick or mentally or physically disabled" has the same meaning it has in regulation 13(3)(b) (circumstances in which persons in relevant education are to be entitled to income support);

(b) in England and Wales, any reference to a person acting in place of a person's parents includes a reference to—

(i) where the person is being looked after by a local authority or voluntary organisation who place him with a family, a relative of his, or some other suitable person, the person with whom the person is placed, whether or not any payment is made to him in connection with the placement; or

(ii) in any other case, any person with parental responsibility for the child, and for this purpose "parental responsibility" has the meaning it has in the Children Act 1989 by virtue of section 3 of that Act;

(c) in Scotland, any reference to a person acting in place of a person's parents includes a reference to a local authority or voluntary organisation where the person is in their care under a relevant enactment, or to a person with whom the person is boarded out by a local authority or voluntary organisation whether or not any payment is made by them.]

2.608 [35 **2.**—[59 . . .]]

2.609 [17 **2A.**—[55 . . .]]

PART II

Regulations 17[3 (1)](c) [3 and 18(1)](d)

FAMILY PREMIUM

3.—[59 . . .] **2.610**

PART III

Regulations 17[3 (1)](d) [3 and 18(1)](e)

PREMIUMS

4.—Except as provided in paragraph 5, the weekly premiums specified in Part IV of this Schedule shall, for the purposes of regulations 17[3(1)](d)[3 and 18(1)](e), be applicable to a claimant who satisfies the condition specified in [42 paragraphs 8A] [10 to 14ZA] in respect of that premium. **2.611**

5.—Subject to paragraph 6, where a claimant satisfies the conditions in respect of more than one premium in this Part of this Schedule, only one premium shall be applicable to him and, if they are different amounts, the higher or highest amount shall apply.

[58 **6.**—(1) Subject to sub-paragraph (2), the following premiums, namely—

(a) a severe disability to which paragraph 13 applies;

(b) an enhanced disability premium to which paragraph 13A applies;

(c) [59 . . .]; and

(d) a carer premium to which paragraph 14ZA applies,

may be applicable in addition to any other premium that may apply under this Schedule.

(2) An enhanced disability premium in respect of a person shall not be applicable in addition to—

(a) a pensioner premium under paragraph 9 or 9A; or

(b) a higher pension premium under paragraph 10.]

7.—[10(1) Subject to sub-paragraph (2)] for the purposes of this Part of this Schedule, once a premium is applicable to a claimant under this Part, a person shall be treated as being in receipt of any benefit—

(a) in the case of a benefit to which the Social Security (Overlapping Benefits) Regulations 1979 applies, for any period during which, apart from the provisions of those Regulations, he would be in receipt of that benefit; [85 . . .]

(b) for any period spent by a claimant in undertaking a course of training or instruction provided or approved by the [12 Secretary of State [68 . . .]] under section 2 of the Employment and Training Act 1973 [11, or by [69 Skills Development Scotland,] Scottish Enterprise or Highlands and Islands Enterprise under section 2 of the Enterprise and New Towns (Scotland) Act 1990,] [7 or for any period during which he is in receipt of a training allowance]. [85 ; and

(c) in the case of carer support payment, for any period during which, apart from regulation 16 of the Carer's Assistance (Carer Support Payment) (Scotland) Regulations 2023, he would be in receipt of that benefit.]

[10(2) For the purposes of the carer premium under paragraph 14ZA, a person shall be treated as being in receipt of [49 carer's allowance] by virtue of sub-paragraph (1)(a) [87 or carer support payment by virtue of sub-paragraph (1)(c)] only if and for so long as the person in respect of whose care the allowance [85 or payment] has been claimed remains in receipt of attendance allowance [15, [75 . . .] the care component of disability living allowance at the highest or middle rate prescribed in accordance with section 37ZB(3) of the Social Security Act [SSCBA, s.72(3)]] [82, the care component of child disability payment at the highest or middle rate prescribed in accordance with the regulation 11(5) of the DACYP Regulations] [75 or the daily living component of personal independence payment at the standard or enhanced rate in accordance with section 78(3) of the 2012 Act] [83, the daily living component of adult disability payment at the standard or enhanced rate in accordance with regulation 5 of the Disability Assistance for Working Age People (Scotland) Regulations 2022] [76 or armed forces independence payment].]

Lone Parent Premium

2.612 **8.**—[29 . . .].

[42 **Bereavement Premium**

2.613 **8A.**—[67 . . .]]

[Pensioner premium for persons under 75

2.614 [54 **9.**—The condition is that the claimant has a partner aged [70 not less than the qualifying age for state pension credit] but less than 75.]

Pensioner premium for persons 75 and over

2.615 [54 **9A.**—The condition is that the claimant has a partner aged not less than 75 but less than 80.]]

Higher Pensioner Premium

2.616 **10.**—[54 (1) [65 Subject to sub-paragraph (6), the] condition is that—
(a) the claimant's partner is aged not less than 80; or
(b) the claimant's partner is aged less than 80 but [70 not less than the qualifying age for state pension credit] and either—
(i) the additional condition specified in [58 paragraph 12(1)(a), (c) or (d)] is satisfied; or
(ii) the claimant was entitled to, or was treated as being in receipt of, income support and—
(aa) the disability premium was or, as the case may be, would have been, applicable to him in respect of a benefit week within eight weeks of [70 the day his partner attained the qualifying age for state pension credit]; and
(bb) he has, subject to sub-paragraph (3), remained continuously entitled to income support since his partner attained [70 the qualifying age for state pension credit].]

(2) [. . .]

(3) For the purposes of this paragraph and paragraph 12—
(a) once the higher pensioner premium is applicable to a claimant, if he then ceases, for a period of eight weeks or less, to be entitled to [41 or treated as entitled to] income support, he shall, on becoming re-entitled to income support, thereafter be treated as having been continuously entitled thereto;
(b) in so far as [54 sub-paragraph (1)(b)(ii) is] concerned, if a claimant ceases to be entitled to [41 or treated as entitled to] income support for a period not exceeding eight weeks which includes [70 the day his partner attained the qualifying age for state pension credit], he shall, on becoming re-entitled to income support, thereafter be treated as having been continuously entitled thereto.

[33 (4) In the case of a claimant who is a welfare to work beneficiary, references in sub-paragraphs (1)(b)(ii) [65 . . .] and (3)(b) to a period of 8 weeks shall be treated as references to a period of [64 104 weeks].]

[41 (5) For the purposes of this paragraph, a claimant shall be treated as having been entitled to and in receipt of income support throughout any period which comprises only days on which he was participating in an employment zone programme and was not entitled to income support because, as a consequence of his participation in that programme, he was engaged in remunerative work or had income in excess of his applicable amount as prescribed in Part IV.]

[65 (6) The condition is not satisfied if the claimant's partner to whom sub-paragraph (1) refers is a long-term patient.]

Disability Premium

2.617 **11.**—[65 (1) Subject to sub-paragraph (2), the] condition is that—
(a) where the claimant is a single claimant or a lone parent, [54 . . .] the additional condition specified in paragraph 12 is satisfied; or
(b) where the claimant has a partner, either—
[54 (i) the claimant satisfies the additional condition specified in paragraph [58 12(1)(a), (b), (c) or (d)]; or]
(ii) his partner [70 has not attained the qualifying age for state pension credit] and the additional condition specified in [58 paragraph 12(1)(a), (c) or (d)] is satisfied by his partner.

[65 (2) The condition is not satisfied if—
(a) the claimant is a single claimant or a lone parent and (in either case) is a long-term patient;

(b) the claimant is a member of a couple or polygamous marriage and each member of the couple or polygamous marriage is a long-term patient; or

(c) the claimant is a member of a couple or a polygamous marriage and a member of that couple or polygamous marriage is—

(i) a long-term patient; and

(ii) the only member of the couple or polygamous marriage to whom sub-paragraph (1)(b) refers.]

Additional condition for the Higher Pensioner and Disability Premiums

12.—(1) Subject to sub-paragraph (2) and paragraph 7 the additional condition referred to in paragraphs 10 and 11 is that either— **2.618**

(a) the claimant or, as the case may be, his partner—

(i) is in receipt of one or more of the following benefits: attendance allowance, [15 disability living allowance, [76 armed forces independence payment,] [75 personal independence payment,] [83 adult disability payment,] [50 the disability element or the severe disability element of working tax credit as specified in regulation 20(1)(b) and (f) of the Working Tax Credit (Entitlement and Maximum Rate) Regulations 2002]], mobility supplement, [25 long-term incapacity benefit] under [22 Part II of the Contributions and Benefits Act or severe disablement allowance under Part III of that Act] [1but, in the case of [25 long-term incapacity benefit] or severe disablement allowance only where it is paid in respect of him]; or

(ii) is provided by the Secretary of State with an invalid carriage or other vehicle under section 5(2) of the National Health Service Act 1977 (other services) or, in Scotland, under section 46 of the National Health Service (Scotland) Act 1978 (provision of vehicles) or receives payments by way of grant from the Secretary of State under paragraph 2 of Schedule 2 to that 1977 Act (additional provisions as to vehicles) or, in Scotland, under that section 46; or

[77 (iii) is certified as severely sight impaired or blind by a consultant ophthalmologist; or]

[26 (b) the claimant—

(i) is entitled to statutory sick pay or [27 is, or is treated as, incapable of work,] in accordance with the provisions of Part XIIA of the Contributions and Benefits Act and the regulations made thereunder (incapacity for work), and

(ii) has been so entitled or so incapable [27, or has been treated as so incapable,] for a continuous period of not less than—

(aa) 196 days in the case of a claimant who is terminally ill within the meaning of section 30B(4) of the Contributions and Benefits Act; or

(bb) [63 subject to [65 paragraph 2A] of Schedule 7] 364 days in any other case; and for these purposes any two or more periods of entitlement or incapacity separated by a break of not more than 56 days shall be treated as one continuous period; or]

[54 (c) the claimant's partner was in receipt of long-term incapacity benefit under Part II of the Contributions and Benefits Act when entitlement to that benefit ceased on account of the payment of a retirement pension under that Act [81 or a state pension under Part 1 of the Pensions Act 2014] and—

(i) the claimant has since remained continuously entitled to income support;

(ii) the higher pensioner premium or disability premium has been applicable to the claimant; and

(iii) the partner is still alive;

(d) except where paragraph [63 2A [65 . . .]] of Schedule 7 (patients) applies, the claimant or, as the case may be, his partner was in receipt of attendance allowance [75, disability living allowance [83, personal independence payment or adult disability payment]]—

(i) but payment of that benefit has been suspended under the [60 Social Security (Attendance Allowance) Regulations 1991 [75, the Social Security (Disability Living Allowance) Regulations 1991 or regulations made under section 86(1) (hospital in-patients) of the 2012 Act]] or otherwise abated as a consequence of the claimant or his partner becoming a patient within the meaning of regulation 21(3); and

(ii) a higher pensioner premium or disability premium has been applicable to the claimant.]

[34 (1A) In the case of a claimant who is a welfare to work beneficiary, the reference in sub-paragraph (1)(b) to a period of 56 days shall be treated as a reference to a period of [64 104 weeks].]

[77 (2) For the purposes of sub-paragraph (1)(a)(iii), a person who has ceased to be certified as severely sight impaired or blind on regaining his eyesight shall nevertheless be treated as severely sight impaired or blind, as the case may be, and as satisfying the additional condition set out in that sub-paragraph for a period of 28 weeks following the date on which he ceased to be so certified.]

(3) [[26] . . .]

(4) For the purpose of [[58] sub-paragraph (1)(c) and (d)], once the higher pensioner premium is applicable to the claimant by virtue of his satisfying the condition specified in that provision, if he then ceases, for a period of eight weeks or less, to be entitled to income support, he shall on again becoming so entitled to income support, immediately thereafter be treated as satisfying the condition in [[58] sub-paragraph (1)(c) and (d)].

[[4] (5) For the purposes of sub-paragraph (1)(b), once the disability premium is applicable to a claimant by virtue of his satisfying the additional condition specified in that provision, he shall continue to be treated as satisfying that condition for any period spent by him in undertaking a course of training provided under section 2 of the Employment and Training Act 1973 [[7] or for any period during which he is in receipt of a training allowance].]

[[25] (6) For the purposes of [[58] sub-paragraph (1)(a)(i) and (c)], a reference to a person in receipt of long-term incapacity benefit includes a person in receipt of short-term incapacity benefit at a rate equal to the long-term rate by virtue of section 30B(4)(a) of the Contributions and Benefits Act (short-term incapacity benefit for a person who is terminally ill), or who would be or would have been in receipt of short-term incapacity benefit at such a rate but for the fact that the rate of short-term incapacity benefit already payable to him is or was equal to or greater than the long-term rate.]

[[40] [[61] . . .]]

Severe Disability Premium

2.619 **13.**—(1) The condition is that the claimant is a severely disabled person.

(2) For the purposes of sub-paragraph (1), a claimant shall be treated as being a severely disabled person if, and only if—

(a) in the case of a single claimant[[19], a lone parent or a claimant who is treated as having no partner in consequence of sub-paragraph (2A)]—

(i) he is in receipt of attendance allowance [[15] [[75] . . .] the care component of disability living allowance at the highest or middle rate prescribed in accordance with section 37ZB(3) of the Social Security Act [SSCBA, s.72(3)]] [[75] or the daily living component of personal independence payment at the standard or enhanced rate in accordance with section 78(3) of the 2012 Act] [[83] , the daily living component of adult disability payment at the standard or enhanced rate in accordance with regulation 5 of the Disability Assistance for Working Age People (Scotland) Regulations 2022] [[76] or armed forces independence payment], and

(ii) subject to sub-paragraph (3), he has no non-dependants aged 18 or over [[23] normally residing with him or with whom he is normally residing,] and

(iii) [[41] no person is entitled to, and in receipt of, [[49] a carer's allowance] under section 70 of the Contributions and Benefits Act [[85] or has an award of universal credit which includes the carer element] in respect of caring for him;]

(b) [[42] in the case of a claimant who] has a partner—

(i) he is in receipt of attendance allowance [[15], [[75] . . .] the care component of disability living allowance at the highest or middle rate prescribed in accordance with section 37ZB(3) of the Social Security Act [SSCBA, s.72(3)]] [[75] or the daily living component of personal independence payment at the standard or enhanced rate in accordance with section 78(3) of the 2012 Act] [[83] , the daily living component of adult disability payment at the standard or enhanced rate in accordance with regulation 5 of the Disability Assistance for Working Age People (Scotland) Regulations 2022] [[76] or armed forces independence payment]; and

(ii) his partner is also in receipt of such an allowance or, if he is a member of a polygamous marriage, all the partners of that marriage are in receipt thereof; and

(iii) subject to sub-paragraph (3), he has no non-dependants aged 18 or over [[23] normally residing with him or with whom he is normally residing,]

and either [[41] a person is entitled to, and in receipt of, [[49] a carer's allowance] [[85] or carer support payment] [[80] or has an award of universal credit which includes the carer element] in respect of caring for only one of the couple or, in the case of a polygamous marriage, for one or more but not all the partners of the marriage or, as the case may be, no person is entitled to, and in receipt of, such an allowance] [[85] or payment] [[80] or has such an award of universal credit] in respect of caring for either member of the couple or any partner of the polygamous marriage.

[19 (2A) Where a claimant has a partner who does not satisfy the condition in sub-paragraph (2)(b)(ii), and that partner is [77 severely sight impaired or blind or treated as severely sight impaired or blind] within the meaning of paragraph 12(1)(a)(iii) and (2), that partner shall be treated for the purposes of sub-paragraph (2) as if he were not a partner of the claimant.]

(3) For the purposes of sub-paragraph (2)(a)(ii) and (2)(b)(iii) no account shall be taken of—

(a) a person receiving attendance allowance [15, [75 . . .] the care component of disability living allowance at the highest or middle rate prescribed in accordance with section 37ZB(3) of the Social Security Act [SSCBA, s.72(3)]] [75 or the daily living component of personal independence payment at the standard or enhanced rate in accordance with section 78(3) of the 2012 Act] [83 , the daily living component of adult disability payment at the standard or enhanced rate in accordance with regulation 5 of the Disability Assistance for Working Age People (Scotland) Regulations 2022] [76 or armed forces independence payment]; or

(b) [21 . . .]

(c) subject to sub-paragraph (4), a person who joins the claimant's household for the first time in order to care for the claimant or his partner and immediately before so joining the claimant or his partner was treated as a severely disabled person; [19 or (d) a person who is [77 severely sight impaired or blind or treated as severely sight impaired or blind] within the meaning of paragraph 12(1)(a)(iii) and (2).]

[1(3A) For the purposes of sub-paragraph (2)(b) a person shall be treated [41 . . .]

(a) [41 as being in receipt of] attendance allowance [15, or the care component of disability living allowance at the highest or middle rate prescribed in accordance with section 37ZB(3) of the Social Security Act [SSCBA, s.72(3)]] if he would, but for his being a patient for a period exceeding 28 days, be so in receipt;

(b) [41 as being entitled to and in receipt of [49 a carer's allowance] [85 or carer support payment] [80 or having an award of universal credit which includes the carer element] if he would, but for the person for whom he was caring being a patient in hospital for a period exceeding 28 days, be so entitled and in receipt [80 of carer's allowance [85 or carer support payment] or have such an award of universal credit].]]

[75 (c) as being in receipt of the daily living component of personal independence payment at the standard or enhanced rate in accordance with section 78(3) of the 2012 Act if he would, but for a suspension of benefit in accordance with regulations under section 86(1) (hospital in-patients) of the 2012 Act, be so in receipt [83 ;

(d) as being in receipt of the daily living component of adult disability payment at the standard or enhanced rate in accordance with regulation 5 of the [84 Disability Assistance for Working Age People (Scotland) Regulations 2022], if they would, but for regulation 28 (effect of admission to hospital on ongoing entitlement to Adult Disability Payment) of those Regulations, be so in receipt.]]

[22 (3ZA) For the purposes of sub-paragraph (2)(a)(iii) and (2)(b), no account shall be taken of an award of [49 a carer's allowance] [85 carer support payment] [80 or universal credit which includes the carer element] to the extent that payment of such an award is back-dated for a period before [66 the date on which the award is first paid].]

(4) Sub-paragraph (3)(c) shall apply only for the first 12 weeks following the date on which the person to whom that provision applies first joins the claimant's household.

[45 (5) In sub-paragraph (2)(a)(iii) and (b), references to a person being in receipt of [49 a carer's allowance] [80 or as having an award of universal credit which includes the carer element] shall include references to a person who would have been in receipt of that allowance [80 or had such an award] but for the application of a restriction under section [72 6B or] 7 of the Social Security Fraud Act 2001 (loss of benefit provisions).]

[80 (6) For the purposes of this paragraph, a person has an award of universal credit which includes the carer element if the person has an award of universal credit which includes an amount which is the carer element under regulation 29 of the Universal Credit Regulations 2013.]

[43 Enhanced disability premium

13A.—[76 (1) Subject to sub-paragraph (2), the condition is that— 2.620

(a) the claimant; or

(b) the claimant's partner, if any, who has not attained the qualifying age for state pension credit, is a person to whom sub-paragraph (1ZA) applies.

(1ZA) This sub-paragraph applies to the person mentioned in sub-paragraph (1) where—

(a) armed forces independence payment is payable to that person;

(b) the care component of disability living allowance is, or would, but for a suspension of benefit in accordance with regulations under section 113(2) of the Contributions and Benefits Act or but for an abatement as a consequence of hospitalization, be payable to that person at the highest rate prescribed under section 72(3) of that Act; [82 . . .

(ba) the care component of child disability payment is payable to that person at the highest rate in accordance with the DACYP Regulations (see regulation 11(5) of those Regulations); [83 . . .]]

(c) the daily living component of personal independence payment is, or would, but for regulations made under section 86(1) (hospital in-patients) of the 2012 Act, be payable to that person at the enhanced rate in accordance with section 78(2) of that Act [83]; or

(d) the daily living component of adult disability payment is, or would, but for regulation 28 (effect of admission to hospital on ongoing entitlement to Adult Disability Payment) of the [84 Disability Assistance for Working Age People (Scotland) Regulations 2022], be payable to that person at the enhanced rate in accordance with regulation 5 of those Regulations.]]

[73 (1A) Where the condition in sub-paragraph (1) ceases to be satisfied because of the death of a child or young person, the condition is that the claimant [74 or partner] is entitled to child benefit in respect of that person under section 145A of the Contributions and Benefits Act (entitlement after death of child or qualifying young person).]

[65 (2) The condition is not satisfied if the person to whom sub-paragraph (1) refers is—

(a) [50 . . .]

(b) a single claimant or a lone parent and (in either case) is a long-term patient;

(c) a member of a couple or polygamous marriage and each member of the couple or polygamous marriage is a long-term patient; or

(d) a member of a couple or polygamous marriage who—

(i) is a long-term patient; and

(ii) is the only member of the couple or polygamous marriage to whom sub-paragraph (1) refers.]

Disabled Child Premium

2.621 **14.**—[59 . . . 65]

[10 Carer premium

2.622 **14ZA.**—(1) [13 Subject to sub-paragraphs (3) and (4),] the condition is that the claimant or his partner is, or both of them are, [41 entitled to [49 a carer's allowance] under section 70 of the Contributions and Benefits Act] [85 or carer support payment].

(2) [57 . . .]

[41 [48 (3) Where a carer premium is awarded but—

(a) the person in respect of whose care the [49 carer's allowance] [85 or carer support payment] has been awarded dies; or

(b) in any other case the person in respect of whom a carer premium has been awarded ceases to be entitled [57 . . .] to [49 a carer's allowance] [85 or carer support payment],

the condition for the award of the premium shall be treated as satisfied for a period of eight weeks from the relevant date specified in sub-paragraph (3A) below.

(3A) The relevant date for the purposes of sub-paragraph (3) above shall be—

(a) [57 where sub-paragraph (3)(a) applies,] the Sunday following the death of the person in respect of whose care [49 a carer's allowance] [85 or carer support payment] has been awarded or the date of death if the death occurred on a Sunday;

(b) [57 . . .]

(c) in any other case, the date on which the person who has been entitled to [46 a carer's allowance] [85 or carer support payment] ceases to be entitled to that allowance [85 or payment].]

(4) Where a person who has been entitled to [49 a carer's allowance] [85 or carer support payment] ceases to be entitled to that allowance [85 or payment] and makes a claim for income support, the condition for the award of the carer premium shall be treated as satisfied for a period of eight weeks from the date on which—

[48 (a) the person in respect of whose care the [49 carer's allowance] [85 or carer support payment] has been awarded dies;

(b) [57 . . .]

[57 (c) in any other case, the person who has been entitled to a carer's allowance [85 or carer support payment] ceased to be entitled to that allowance [85 or payment].]]]]

[3 Persons in receipt of concessionary payments

14A.—For the purpose of determining whether a premium is applicable to a person [12 under paragraphs 12 to 14ZA], any concessionary payment made to compensate that person for the non-payment of any benefit mentioned in those paragraphs shall be treated as if it were a payment of that benefit.] **2.623**

[8 Person in receipt of benefit

14B.—For the purposes of this Part of this Schedule, a person shall be regarded as being in receipt of any benefit if, and only if, it is paid in respect of him and shall be so regarded only for any period in respect of which that benefit is paid.] **2.624**

[37 PART IV

WEEKLY AMOUNTS OF PREMIUMS SPECIFIED IN PART III

2.625

Column (1) *Premium*	*Column (2)* *Amount*
15.—(1) [29 . . .] [42(1A) [67 . . .]] [54(2) Pensioner premium for persons to whom paragraph 9 applies. (2A) Pensioner premium for persons to whom paragraph 9A applies. (3) Higher pensioner premium for persons to whom paragraph 10 applies.]	(1) [29 . . .]. [42 (1A) [67 . . .]] (2) [87 £190.70] (2A) [87 £190.70] (3) [87 £190.70]
(4) Disability Premium— (a) where the claimant satisfies the condition in [65 paragraph 11(1)(a)]; (b) where the claimant satisfies the condition in [65 paragraph 11(1)(b)].	(4) (a) [87 £42.50]. (b) [87 £60.60].
(5) Severe Disability Premium— (a) where the claimant satisfies the condition in paragraph 13(2)(a); (b) where the claimant satisfies the condition in paragraph 13(2)(b). (i) if there is someone in receipt of [49 a carer's allowance] or if he or any partner satisfies that condition only by virtue of paragraph 13(3A); (ii) if no-one is in receipt of such an allowance.	(5) (a) [87 £81.50]; (b) (i) [87 £81.50]; (ii) [87 £163.00];
(6) [59 . . .]	(6) [59 . . .]
(7) Carer Premium—	(7) [87 £45.60] in respect of each person who satisfied the condition specified in paragraph 14ZA.]
[43 (8) Enhanced disability premium where the conditions in paragraph 13A are satisfied—	(8) (a) [59 . . .] (b) [87 £20.85] in respect of each person who is neither— (i) a child or young person; nor (ii) a member of a couple or a polygamous marriage, in respect of whom the conditions specified in paragraph 13A are satisfied:

Column (1) *Premium*	*Column (2)* *Amount*
	(c) [86 £27.90] where the claimant is a member of a couple or a polygamous marriage and the conditions specified in paragraph 13A are satisfied in respect of a member of that couple or polygamous marriage.]

PART V

ROUNDING OF FRACTIONS

2.626 **16.** Where income support is awarded for a period which is not a complete benefit week and the applicable amount in respect of that period results in an amount which includes a fraction of a penny that fraction shall be treated as a penny."

AMENDMENTS

1. Income Support (General) Amendment Regulations 1988 (SI 1988/663) reg.29 (April 11, 1988).
2. Income Support (General) Amendment No. 3 Regulations 1988 (SI 1988/1228) reg.9 (September 12, 1988).
3. Income Support (General) Amendment No. 4 Regulations 1988 (SI 1988/1445) reg.19 (September 12, 1988).
4. Income Support (General) Amendment No. 5 Regulations 1988 (SI 1988/2022) reg.17(*b*) (December 12, 1988).
5. Income Support (General) Amendment No. 5 Regulations 1988 (SI 1988/2022) reg.17(*a*) (April 10, 1989).
6. Income Support (General) Amendment Regulations 1989 (SI 1989/534) reg.5 (October 9, 1989).
7. Income Support (General) Amendment No. 3 Regulations 1989 (SI 1989/1678) reg.6 (October 9, 1989).
8. Income Support (General) Amendment Regulations 1990 (SI 1990/547) reg.17 (April 9, 1990).
9. Income Support (General) Amendment No. 2 Regulations 1990 (SI 1990/1168) reg.2 (July 2, 1990).
10. Income Support (General) Amendment No. 3 Regulations 1990 (SI 1990/1776) reg.8 (October 1, 1990).
11. Enterprise (Scotland) Consequential Amendments Order 1991 (SI 1991/3870) art.9 (April, 1991).
12. Income Support (General) Amendment Regulations 1991 (SI 1991/236) reg.2 (April 8, 1991).
13. Income Support (General) Amendment No. 4 Regulations 1991 (SI 1991/236) reg.15 (August 5, 1991).
14. Income Support (General) Amendment No. 4 Regulations 1991 (SI 1991/1559) reg.15 (October 7, 1991).
15. Disability Living Allowance and Disability Working Allowance (Consequential Provisions) Regulations 1991 (SI 1991/2742) reg.11(4) (April 6, 1992).
16. Income Support (General) Amendment Regulations 1992 (SI 1992/468) reg.6 (April 6, 1992).
17. Social Security Benefits (Amendments Consequential Upon the Introduction of community Care) Regulations 1992 (SI 1992/3147) reg.2 (April 1, 1993).

18. Social Security Benefits (Miscellaneous Amendments) Regulations 1993 (SI 1993/518) reg.5 (April 1, 1993).

19. Income-related Benefits Schemes (Miscellaneous Amendments) (No. 2) Regulations 1993 (SI 1993/1150) reg.3 (May 25, 1993).

[20.]

21. Income-related Benefits Schemes (Miscellaneous Amendments) (No. 4) Regulations 1993 (SI 1993/2119) reg.18 (October 4, 1993).

22. Income-related Benefits Schemes (Miscellaneous Amendments) (No. 5) Regulations 1994 (SI 1994/2139) reg.30 (October 3, 1994).

23. Income-related Benefits Schemes (Miscellaneous Amendments) (No. 6) Regulations 1994 (SI 1994/3061) reg.2(3) (December 2, 1994).

24. Income-related Benefits Schemes (Miscellaneous Amendments) Regulations 1995 (SI 1995/516) reg.24 (April 10, 1995).

25. Disability Working Allowance and Income Support (General) Amendment Regulations 1995 (SI 1995/482) reg.16 (April 13, 1995).

26. Disability Working Allowance and Income Support (General) Amendment Regulations 1995 (SI 1995/482) reg.17 (April 13, 1995).

27. Income-related Benefits Schemes and Social Security (Claims and Payments) (Miscellaneous Amendments) Regulations 1995 (SI 1995/2303) reg.6(8) (October 2, 1995).

28. Income Support (General) (Jobseeker's Allowance Consequential Amendments) Regulations 1996 (SI 1996/206) reg.23 and Sch.2 (October 7, 1996).

29. Child Benefit, Child Support and Social Security (Miscellaneous Amendments) Regulations 1996 (SI 1996/1803) reg.39 (April 7, 1997).

30. Income-related Benefits and Jobseeker's Allowance (Personal Allowances for Children and Young Persons) (Amendment) Regulations 1996 (SI 1996/2545) reg.2 (April 7, 1997).

31. Income-related Benefits and Jobseeker's Allowance (Amendment) (No. 2) Regulations 1997 (SI 1997/2197) regs 7(5) and (6)(a) (October 6, 1997).

32. Social Security Amendment (Lone Parents) Regulations 1998 (SI 1998/766) reg.12 (April 6, 1998).

33. Social Security (Welfare to Work) Regulations 1998 (SI 1998/2231) reg.13(3)(a) (October 5, 1998).

34. Social Security (Welfare to Work) Regulations 1998 (SI 1998/2231) reg.13(3)(b) (October 5, 1998).

35. Social Security Benefits Up-rating Order 1999 (SI 1999/264) art.18(3) and Sch.4 (April 12, 1999).

36. Social Security Benefits Up-rating Order 1999 (SI 1999/264) art.18(4)(b) (April 12, 1999).

37. Social Security Benefits Up-rating Order 1999 (SI 1999/264) art.18(5) and Sch.5 (April 12, 1999).

38. Social Security Amendment (Personal Allowances for Children and Young Persons) Regulations 1999 (SI 1999/2555) reg.2(1)(b) and (2)(April 10, 2000).

39. Social Security and Child Support (Tax Credits) Consequential Amendments Regulations 1999 (SI 1999/2566) reg.2(2) and Sch.2 Pt II (October 5, 1999).

40. Social Security (Miscellaneous Amendments) (No. 2) Regulations 1999 (SI 1999/2556) reg.2(8) (October 4, 1999).

41. Social Security (Miscellaneous Amendments) Regulations 2000 (SI 2000/681) reg.4 (April 3, 2000).

42. Social Security Amendment (Bereavement Benefits) Regulations 2000 (SI 2000/2239) reg.2(3) (April 9, 2001).

43. Social Security Amendment (Enhanced Disability Premium) Regulations 2000 (SI 2629) reg.2(c) (April 9, 2001).

44. Social Security Amendment (Residential Care and Nursing Homes) Regulations 2001 (SI 2001/3767) reg.2 and Sch. Pt I para.14 (April 8, 2002).

45. Social Security (Loss of Benefit) (Consequential Amendments) Regulations 2002 (SI 2002/490) reg.2 (April 1, 2002).

46. Social Security Amendment (Residential Care and Nursing Homes) Regulations 2001 (SI 2001/3767) reg.2 and Sch. Pt I para.14 (as amended by Social Security Amendment (Residential Care and Nursing Homes) Regulations 2002 (SI 2002/398) reg.4(2)) (April 8, 2002).

47. Social Security Amendment (Personal Allowances for Children and Young Persons) Regulations 2002 (SI 2002/2019) reg.2 (October 14, 2002).

48. Social Security Amendment (Carer Premium) Regulations 2002 (SI 2002/2020) reg.2 (October 28, 2002).

49. Social Security Amendment (Carer's allowance) Regulations 2002 (SI 2002/2497) reg.3 and Sch.2 (April 1, 2003).

50. Social Security (Working Tax Credit and Child Tax Credit) (Consequential Amendments) Regulations 2003 (SI 2003/455) regs 1(5) and 2 and Sch.1 para.20(b) (April 7, 2003).

51. Social Security Benefits Up-Rating Order 2003 (SI 2003/526) art.17(3) and Sch.2 (April 7, 2003).

52. Social Security Benefits Up-Rating Order 2003 (SI 2003/526) art.17(5) and Sch.3 (April 7, 2003).

53. Social Security Benefits Up-Rating Order 2003 (SI 2003/526) art.17(4) (April 7, 2003).

54. State Pension Credit (Consequential, Transitional and Miscellaneous Provisions) Regulations 2002 (SI 2002/3019) reg.29(5) (October 6, 2003).

55. Social Security (Removal of Residential Allowance and Miscellaneous Amendments) Regulations 2003 (SI 2003/1121) reg.2 and Sch.1 para.6 (October 6, 2003).

56. Social Security (Hospital In-Patients and Miscellaneous Amendments) Regulations 2003 (SI 2003/1195) reg.3 (May 21, 2003).

57. Social Security (Miscellaneous Amendments) (No. 2) Regulations 2003 (SI 2003/2279) reg.2(3) (October 1, 2003).

58. Income Support (General) Amendment Regulations 2003 (SI 2003/2379) reg.2 (October 6, 2003).

59. Social Security (Working Tax Credit and Child Tax Credit) (Consequential Amendments) Regulations 2003 (SI 2003/455) reg.2 and Sch.1 para.20 (April 6, 2004, except in "transitional cases" and see further the note to reg.17 of the Income Support Regulations).

60. Social Security (Miscellaneous Amendments) (No. 2) Regulations 2004 (SI 2004/1141) reg.6 (May 12, 2004).

61. Social Security (Back to Work Bonus and Lone Parent Run-on) (Amendment and Revocation) Regulations 2003 (SI 2003/1589) reg.2(d) (October 25, 2004).

62. Civil Partnership (Pensions, Social Security and Child Support) (Consequential, etc. Provisions) Order 2005 (SI 2005/2877) art.2(3) and Sch.3 para.13(3) (December 5, 2005).

63. Social Security (Hospital In-Patients) Regulations 2005 (SI 2005/3360) reg.4 (April 10, 2006).

64. Social Security (Miscellaneous Amendments) (No. 4) Regulations 2006 (SI 2006/2378) reg.5(7) (October 2, 2006).

65. Social Security (Miscellaneous Amendments) Regulations 2007 (SI 2007/719) reg.2(7) (April 9, 2007). As it relates to paras 13A(2)(a) and 14, the amendment only affects "transitional cases". See further the note to reg.17 of the Income Support Regulations and the commentary below.

66. Social Security (Miscellaneous Amendments) Regulations 2007 (SI 2007/719) reg.2(7)(e) (April 2, 2007).

67. Social Security (Miscellaneous Amendments) (No. 5) Regulations 2007 (SI 2007/2618) reg.2 and Sch. (October 1, 2007).

68. Social Security (Miscellaneous Amendments) Regulations 2008 (SI 2008/698) reg.2(12) (April 14, 2008).

69. Social Security (Miscellaneous Amendments) Regulations 2009 (SI 2009/583) reg.2(1) and (3) (April 6, 2009).

70. Social Security (Equalisation of State Pension Age) Regulations 2009 (SI 2009/1488) reg.3 (April 6, 2010).
71. Social Security (Miscellaneous Amendments) (No. 2) Regulations 2010 (SI 2010/641) reg.2(1) and (9) (April 13, 2010).
72. Social Security (Loss of Benefit) Amendment Regulations 2010 (SI 2010/1160) reg.10(1) and (3) (April 1, 2010).
73. Social Security (Miscellaneous Amendments) Regulations 2011 (SI 2011/674) reg.3(5) (April 11, 2011).
74. Social Security (Miscellaneous Amendments) (No. 3) Regulations 2011 (SI 2011/2425) reg.7(1) and (7) (October 31, 2011).
75. Personal Independence Payment (Supplementary Provisions and Consequential Amendments) Regulations 2013 (SI 2013/388) reg.8 and Sch. para.11(1) and (5) (April 8, 2013).
76. Armed Forces and Reserve Forces Compensation Scheme (Consequential Provisions: Subordinate Legislation) Order 2013 (SI 2013/591) art.7 and Sch. para.4(1) and (5) (April 8, 2013).
77. Universal Credit and Miscellaneous Amendments (No. 2) Regulations 2014 (SI 2014/2888) reg.3(2)(a) (November 26, 2014).
78. Welfare Benefits Up-rating Order 2015 (SI 2015/30) art.6 and Sch.1 (April 6, 2015).
79. Social Security Benefits Up-rating Order 2015 (SI 2015/457) art.14(5) and Sch.3 (April 6, 2015).
80. Universal Credit and Miscellaneous Amendments Regulations 2015 (SI 2015/1754) reg.14 (October 28, 2015).
81. Pensions Act 2014 (Consequential, Supplementary and Incidental Amendments) Order 2015 (SI 2015/1985) art.8(1) and (3) (April 6, 2016).
82. Social Security (Scotland) Act 2018 (Disability Assistance for Children and Young People) (Consequential Modifications) Order 2021 (SI 2021/786) Sch.1 para.5 (July 26, 2021).
83. Social Security (Disability Assistance for Working Age People) (Consequential Amendments) Order 2022 (SI 2022/177) art.2(6) (March 21, 2022).
84. Social Security (Disability Assistance for Working Age People) (Consequential Amendments) (No. 2) Order 2022 (SI 2022/530) art.2(2) (June 6, 2022).
85. Carers Assistance (Carer Support Payment) (Scotland) Regulations 2023 (Consequential Amendments) Order 2023 (SI 2023/1218) art.5 (November 19, 2023).
86. Social Security Benefits Up-rating Order 2024 (SI 2024/242) art.20(3) and Sch.2 (April 8, 2024).
87. Social Security Benefits Up-rating Order 2024 (SI 2024/242) art.20(5) and Sch.3 (April 8, 2024).

DEFINITIONS

"adult disability payment"—see reg.2(1).
"attendance allowance"—*ibid.*
"benefit week"—*ibid.*
"child"—see SSCBA s.137(1).
"child disability payment"—see reg.2(1).
"claimant"—*ibid.*
"close relative"—*ibid.*
"couple"—*ibid.*
"the DACYP Regulations"—*ibid.*
"disability living allowance"—*ibid.*
"family"—see SSCBA s.137(1).
"invalid carriage or other vehicle"—see reg.2(1).
"lone parent"—*ibid.*
"mobility supplement"—*ibid.*

"non-dependent"—see reg.3.
"partner"—see reg.2(1).
"personal independence payment"—*ibid.*
"polygamous marriage"—*ibid.*
"preserved right"—see reg.2(1) and reg.19.
"single claimant"—see reg.2(1).
"Social Security Act"—*ibid.*
"welfare to work beneficiary"—*ibid.*
"young person"—*ibid.*, reg.14.
For the General Note to Sch.2, see Vol.V paras 2.627–2.650.

p.605, *amendments to the Income Support (General) Regulations 1987 (SI 1987/1967) Sch.3 para.18 (Housing costs—non-dependant deductions)*

6.041 With effect from April 8, 2024, art.20(6) of the Social Security Benefits Up-rating Order 2024 (SI 2024/242) makes the following amendments:

- in sub-paragraph (1)(a) for "£116.75" substitute "£124.55";
- in sub-paragraph (1)(b) for "£18.10" substitute "£19.30";
- in sub-paragraph (2)(a) for "£162.00" substitute "£176.00";
- in sub-paragraph (2)(b)—
  (i) for "£41.60" substitute "£44.40";
  (ii) for "£162.00" substitute "£176.00"; and
  (iii) for "£236.00" substitute "£256.00";
- in sub-paragraph (2)(c)—
  (i) for "£57.10" substitute "£60.95";
  (ii) for "£236.00" substitute "£256.00"; and
  (iii) for "£308.00" substitute "£334.00";
- in sub-paragraph (2)(d)—
  (i) for "£93.40" substitute "£99.65";
  (ii) for "£308.00" substitute "£334.00"; and
  (iii) for "£410.00" substitute "£445.00"; and
- in sub-paragraph (2)(e)—
  (i) for "£106.35" substitute "£113.50";
  (ii) for "£410.00" substitute "£445.00"; and
  (iii) for "£511.00" substitute "£554.00".

p.606, *ERRATUM Income Support (General) Regulations 1987 (SI 1987/1967) Sch.3 para.18 (Housing costs—non-dependant deductions)*

An amendment was made to para.18 by the Social Security (Income and Capital) (Miscellaneous Amendments) Regulations 2020 (SI 2002/618) reg.2(1)(1) (July 15, 2020), adding the words "any Grenfell Tower payment, or". That amendment is incorrectly shown as being to the start of para.18(8)(a). It in fact adds those words at the start of para.18(8)(b).

p.606, *amendments to the Income Support (General) Regulations 1987 (SI 1987/1967) Sch.3 para.18 (Housing costs—non-dependant deductions)*

6.042 With effect from July 26, 2021, para.6 of Sch.1 to the Social Security (Scotland) Act 2018 (Disability Assistance for Children and Young People)

(Consequential Modifications) Order 2021 (SI 2021/786) inserts into sub-paragraph (6)(b), after paragraph (ii), "(iia) the care component of child disability payment;" and inserts into sub-paragraph (8)(a), after "disability living allowance", ", child disability payment".

With effect from January 1, 2022, reg.2(6) of the Social Security (Income and Capital Disregards) (Amendment) Regulations 2021 (SI 2021/1405) inserts into para.18(8)(b), after "Grenfell Tower payment", ", child abuse payment or Windrush payment".

With effect from March 21, 2022, art.2(7) of the Social Security (Disability Assistance for Working Age People) (Consequential Amendments) Order 2022 (SI 2022/177) makes the following amendments:

in para.18(6)(b)(iii) omit "or" at the end;
after para.18(6)(b)(iii) insert "(iiia) the daily living component of adult disability payment; or"; and
in para.18(8)(a), for "or personal independence payment" substitute ", personal independence payment, adult disability payment".

With effect from July 9, 2023, reg.2 of the Social Security (Income and Capital Disregards) (Amendment) Regulations 2023 (SI 2023/640) amends para.18 as follows:

- in paragraph 18(8)(b) (non-dependant deductions), for "or Windrush payment" insert ", Windrush payment or Post Office compensation payment".

p.631, *amendment to the Income Support (General) Regulations 1987 (SI 1987/1967) Sch.8, para.6A (Sums to be disregarded in the calculation of earnings)*

With effect from November 19, 2023, art.5(5) of the Carer's Assistance (Carer Support Payment) (Scotland) Regulations 2023 (Consequential Amendments) Order 2023 (SI 2023/1218) amended para.6A(1) by inserting "or carer support payment" after "carer's allowance" in the first place where that occurs. Carer support payment is newly defined in reg.2(1) by reference to the Scottish legislation (see the entry for p.229). **6.043**

p.642, *amendment to the Income Support (General) Regulations 1987 (SI 1987/1967) Sch.9 paras 6 and 9 (Sums to be disregarded in the calculation of income other than earnings—mobility component and AA, care component and daily living component)*

With effect from March 21, 2022, art.2(8)(a) of the Social Security (Disability Assistance for Working Age People) (Consequential Amendments) Order 2022 (SI 2022/177) amended para.6 to read as follows (square brackets indicate only the present amendment, those indicating previous amendments having been omitted): **6.044**

"**6.**—The mobility component of disability living allowance[,] the mobility component of personal independence payment [or the mobility component of adult disability payment]."

With effect from March 21, 2022, art.2(8)(b) of the same Order amended para.9 to read as follows (square brackets indicate only the present amendment, those indicating previous amendments having been omitted):

> "**9.**—Any attendance allowance, the care component of disability living allowance[,] the daily living component of personal independence payment [or the daily living component of adult disability payment]."

"Adult disability payment" is defined in reg.2(1) by reference to reg.2 of the Disability Assistance for Working Age People (Scotland) Regulations 2022 (SSI 2022/54) (see Vol.IV of this series).

p.644, *amendment to the Income Support (General) Regulations 1987 (SI 1987/1967) Sch.9 para.21(2) (Sums to be disregarded in the calculation of income other than earnings—income in kind)*

6.045 With effect from January 1, 2022, reg.2(7)(a) of the Social Security (Income and Capital Disregards) (Amendment) Regulations 2021 (SI 2021/1405) amended sub-para.(2) by inserting ", a child abuse payment or a Windrush payment" after "Grenfell Tower payment". All of those payments are defined in reg.2(1). See the entry for pp.684–685 for discussion of the nature of child abuse and Windrush payments.

p.646, *amendment to the Income Support (General) Regulations 1987 (SI 1987/1967) Sch.9 para.27 (Sums to be disregarded in the calculation of income other than earnings—payments for persons temporarily in care of claimant)*

6.046 With effect from July 1, 2022, reg.99 of and Sch. to the Health and Care Act 2022 (Consequential and Related Amendments and Transitional Provisions) Regulations 2022 (SI 2022/634) amended para.27(da) by substituting the following for the text after "(da)":

> "an integrated care board established under Chapter A3 of Part 2 of the National Health Service Act 2006;"

With effect from November 6, 2023, reg.2 of the Health and Care Act 2022 (Further Consequential Amendments) (No.2) Regulations 2023 (SI 2023/1071) amended para.27(db) by substituting "NHS England" for "the National Health Service Commissioning Board".

p.648, *amendment to the Income Support (General) Regulations 1987 (SI 1987/1967) Sch.9 para.39 (Sums to be disregarded in the calculation of income other than earnings)*

6.047 With effect from January 1, 2022, reg.2(7)(b) of the Social Security (Income and Capital Disregards) (Amendment) Regulations 2021 (SI 2021/1405) amended para.39 by substituting the following for sub-para.(1A):

> "(1A) Any—
> (a) Grenfell Tower payment;
> (b) child abuse payment;
> (c) Windrush payment."

In addition, reg.2(7)(c) amended sub-paras (2) to (6) by inserting ", a child abuse payment or a Windrush payment" after "Grenfell Tower payment" in each place where those words occur. All of those payments are defined in reg.2(1).

See the entry for p.684–685 (Sch.10 (Capital to be disregarded) para.22) for some technical problems arising from the date of effect of these amendments. Because all the payments so far made from the approved historic institutional child abuse schemes and from the Windrush Compensation Scheme have been in the nature of capital, the question of disregarding income has not yet arisen.

With effect from July 9, 2023, reg.2(7) of the Social Security (Income and Capital Disregards) (Amendment) Regulations 2023 (SI 2023/640) amended para.39(1A) by adding the following after head (c):

"(d) a Post Office compensation payment."

Such payments are newly defined in reg.2(1), where there is now also an expanded definition of Grenfell Tower payments (see head (a)). With effect from the same date, the words substituted in sub-paras (2) to (6) have been further amended by substituting ", a Windrush payment, a Post Office compensation payment or a vaccine damage payment" for "or a Windrush payment". "Vaccine damage payment" is also newly defined in reg.2(1). See the entry for pp.684–685 for the background.

p.651, *amendments to the Income Support (General) Regulations 1987 (SI 1987/1967) Sch.9 (Sums to be disregarded in the calculation of income other than earnings)*

With effect from July 26, 2021, art.11(2) of the Social Security (Scotland) Act 2018 (Disability Assistance, Young Carer Grants, Short-term Assistance and Winter Heating Assistance) (Consequential Provision and Modifications) Order 2021 (SI 2021/886) inserted the following after para.85: **6.048**

"**86.** Any disability assistance given in accordance with regulations made section 31 of the Social Security (Scotland) Act 2018."

The first regulations made under s.31 of the 2018 Act were the Disability Assistance for Children and Young People (Scotland) Regulations 2021 (SSI 2021/174), also in effect from July 26, 2021, providing for the benefit known as a child disability payment. The regulations also authorise the payment of short-term assistance, to be disregarded under para.85. The Disability Assistance for Working Age People (Scotland) Regulations 2022 (SSI 2022/54), in effect from March 21, 2022, providing for the benefit known as adult disability payment, were also made under s.31, but the two potential elements (mobility component and daily living component) have been specifically covered by para.6 and para.9 from that date (see the entry for p.642). Short-term assistance under reg.62 of the 2022 Regulations is disregarded under para.85.

With effect from November 19, 2023, art.5(6) of the Carer's Assistance (Carer Support Payment) (Scotland) Regulations 2023 (Consequential Amendments) Order 2023 (SI 2023/1218) inserted the following after para.86:

"**87.** Any amount of carer support payment that is in excess of the amount the claimant would receive if they had an entitlement to carer's allowance under section 70 of the Contributions and Benefits Act."

Carer support payment (CSP) is newly defined in reg.2(1) by reference to the Scottish legislation (see the entry for p.229). Note that CSP in general counts as income and that the disregard is limited to any excess of the amount of the CSP over what the claimant would have been entitled to in carer's allowance under British legislation. That is in accordance with the Fiscal Framework Agreement governing the provision of devolved benefits in Scotland (see para.6.9 of the Explanatory Memorandum to SI 2023/1218). Initially, CSP is to be paid at the same rate as carer's allowance.

p.665, *annotations to the Income Support (General) Regulations 1987 (SI 1987/1967) Sch.9 paras 6 and 9 (Sums to be disregarded in the calculation of income other than earnings—mobility component and AA, care component and daily living component)*

6.049 Note the amendments to paras 6 and 9 on p.642 to take account of the introduction of Scottish adult disability payment (see Vol.IV of this series).

p.676, *annotation to the Income Support (General) Regulations 1987 (SI 1987/1967) Sch.9, para.31A (Sums to be disregarded in the calculation of income other than earnings—local welfare provision)*

6.050 No doubt, payments from the Household Support Fund, initially in operation from October 2021 to March 2022, and later extended in tranches to September 2024, constituted "local welfare provision", as with the schemes mentioned in the main volume. See para.18A of Sch.10 for the capital disregard. It was announced in the Autumn Budget 2024 that the Fund was to be extended into the 2025/26 financial year.

p.676, *annotation to the Income Support (General) Regulations 1987 (SI 1987/1967) Sch.9 para.34 (Sums to be disregarded in the calculation of income other than earnings—payments by trade unions during trade disputes)*

6.051 The relevant sum was increased to £50 with effect from April 8, 2024 (see the entries for pp.15 and 18).

p.677, *annotation to the Income Support (General) Regulations 1987 (SI 1987/1967) Sch.9 para.39 (Sums to be disregarded in the calculation of income other than earnings—payments from certain funds), and for the extensions from July 2023 to Post Office compensation payments and vaccine damage payments*

6.052 See the entries for pp.648 and 684 for the extension in a new sub-para. (1A) of the funds covered to child abuse compensation payments from certain schemes and to payments under the Windrush Compensation Scheme.

p.680, *annotation to the Income Support (General) Regulations 1987 (SI 1987/1967) Sch.9 para.84 (Sums to be disregarded in the calculation of income other than earnings—Scottish child payment)*

6.053 As at April 2024 the weekly amount of the Scottish child payment is £26.70.

p.680, *annotation to the Income Support (General) Regulations 1987 (SI 1987/1967) Sch.9 para.85 (Sums to be disregarded in the calculation of income other than earnings—Scottish short-term assistance)*

6.054 Provision for short-term assistance under s.36 of the Social Security (Scotland) Act 2018, thus falling within para.85, has been made by reg.42

of and Sch. to the Disability Assistance for Children and Young People (Scotland) Regulations 2021 (SSI 2021/174), with effect from July 26, 2021, and by reg.62 of and Sch. to the Disability Assistance for Working Age People (Scotland) Regulations 2022 (SSI 2022/54), with effect from March 21, 2022.

p.681, *amendment to the Income Support (General) Regulations 1987 (SI 1987/1967) Sch.10, para.7(1)(a) (Capital to be disregarded)*

With effect from July 26, 2021, art.11(3) of the Social Security (Scotland) Act 2018 (Disability Assistance, Young Carer Grants, Short-term Assistance and Winter Heating Assistance) (Consequential Provision and Modifications) Order 2021 (SI 2021/886) substituted "84, 85 or 86" for "84 or 85". See the entry for p.651 for the new para.86 of Sch.9. **6.055**

p.682, *amendment to the Income Support (General) Regulations 1987 (SI 1987/1967) Sch.10 para.7A (Capital to be disregarded—widowed parent's allowance)*

With effect from February 9, 2023, para.1(a) of the Schedule to the Bereavement Benefits (Remedial) Order 2023 (SI 2023/134) inserted the following after para.7 of Sch.10: **6.056**

"**7A.** Any payment of a widowed parent's allowance made pursuant to section 39A of the Contributions and Benefits Act (widowed parent's allowance)—

(a) to the survivor of a cohabiting partnership (within the meaning in section 39A(7) of the Contributions and Benefits Act) who is entitled to a widowed parent's allowance for a period before the Bereavement Benefits (Remedial) Order 2023 comes into force, and

(b) in respect of any period of time during the period ending with the day before the survivor makes the claim for a widowed parent's allowance,

but only for a period of 52 weeks from the date of receipt of the payment."

The legislation on widowed parent's allowance (WPA), abolished on April 5, 2017, and bereavement support payment (BSP) in operation for deaths after April 5, 2017, was declared incompatible with the ECHR by discriminating against children whose parents were cohabiting but not married to each other or in a civil partnership (see *Re McLaughlin's Application for Judicial Review* [2018] UKSC 48; [2018] 1 W.L.R. 4250 and *R(Jackson) v Secretary of State for Work and Pensions* [2020] EWHC 183 (Admin); [2020] 1 W.L.R. 1441 in Vol.I of this series). The Remedial Order allows retrospective claims to be made for those benefits from August 30, 2018 onwards and accordingly for arrears of benefit to be paid if the conditions of entitlement are met. The new para.7A, and the amended para.72 on BSP, deal with the consequences of such payments on income support entitlement, although with somewhat differing outcomes.

The Explanatory Memorandum misleadingly asserts in para.7.15 that the Remedial Order provides for payments of arrears under the Order to be treated as capital and disregarded for the purposes of income-related benefits, in line with assurances that had been given by the government to the Joint Committee on Human Rights and in its response to public consultation on a draft of the Order (see *Draft Bereavement Benefits (Remedial Order 2022: Second Report* (HC 834, HL Paper 108) (December 6, 2022), para.61). However, it is absolutely plain that the amendments made by the Order do nothing to deem any payment of arrears to be capital. The new provisions like para.7A merely provide for a disregard of the payment for 52 weeks in so far as it is properly to be regarded as capital. It has been firmly established at least since the decision in *R(SB) 4/89* (see para.2.245 of the 2021/22 main volume) that cumulative arrears of social security benefits that would have been income if paid on time retain their nature as income though paid as a lump sum. Then, as a result of regs 29 and 31 the periodical payments are to be treated for income support purposes as paid on the date on which they were due to be paid (i.e. in the past) for the payment period starting with that date. Thus, if a claimant receiving a sum of arrears of WPA had been in receipt of income support (or another "legacy" income-related benefit) for some part of the period to which the WPA is properly to be attributed as income (subject to the £10 per week disregard under Sch.9 para.16(h)) that would trigger the Secretary of State's power to revise the decision(s) awarding income support (Social Security and Child Support (Decisions and Appeals) Regulations 1999 (SI 1999/991) reg.3(7) and SSA 1998 s.9(3) in Vol.III of this series) and, if exercised, the creation of an overpayment that would be recoverable under the SSAA s.74, either by abatement of the amount payable by way of arrears of WPA or, if that was not exercised by recovery from the claimant.

That that is the legal position was effectively conceded by Viscount Younger, the Minister for Work and Pensions in the House of Lords, in a letter of February 2, 2023 to Baroness Sherlock (deposited in the Library of the House of Lords), in which he said this:

> "It is right that usual rules apply in these cases, to ensure that we don't treat cohabitee claimants differently to those claimants who were in a legal union with the deceased. WPA is taken into account as income when assessing entitlement to other means-tested benefits. Where a claimant was in receipt of a legacy income-related benefit during the period of entitlement for WPA, we will offset any overpayment of the relevant benefit from the retrospective lump sum of WPA and pay a net WPA award. Where a claimant was in receipt of Universal Credit during the period of WPA entitlement, the claimant may incur an overpayment of Universal Credit as a consequence of receiving a retrospective WPA award. We will make this clear to claimants, so that they are able to make an informed choice about making a claim."

The Explanatory Memorandum appears not so far to have been corrected and DMG Memo 2/23 makes no mention of this issue.

There remains something for the new para.7A to bite on. Because of the £10 weekly disregard, even if the abatement process is applied over the entire period to which the arrears of WPA are attributed, there will be some amount of arrears payable, which according to accepted principle would metamorphose from income into capital at the end of the period to which it is properly attributable as income (see *R(IS) 3/93* and paras 2.208 and 2.209 of the 2020/21 main volume). Such capital is to be disregarded for 52 weeks, as would capital deriving from weeks in the past in which no income-related benefit was in payment. If the abatement process had been available but did not take place, it is arguable that the arrears of income would only metamorphose into capital after deduction of the liability to recovery of the overpayment (*R(SB) 2/83* and *R(SB) 35/83*).

Note that the outcome for BSP (see the amendment to para.72) is different because BSP is disregarded entirely as income for income support purposes (Sch.9 para.80).

pp.684–685, *amendment to the Income Support (General) Regulations 1987 (SI 1987/1967) Sch.10 para.22 (Capital to be disregarded)*

With effect from January 1, 2022, reg.2(8)(a) of the Social Security (Income and Capital Disregards) (Amendment) Regulations 2021 (SI 2021/1405) amended sub-para.(1A) by inserting ", child abuse payment, Windrush payment" after "Grenfell Tower payment" and amended sub-paras (2) to (6) by inserting ", a child abuse payment or a Windrush payment" after "Grenfell Tower payment" in each place where those words occur. All of those payments are defined in reg.2(1). 6.057

There are some technical problems with the addition only with effect from January 1, 2022 of the disregards of payments from approved schemes providing compensation in respect of historic institutional child abuse in the UK (para.(1)(a)(vii)) and from the Windrush Compensation Scheme. All the schemes so far in existence provide payments in the nature of capital.

The Explanatory Memorandum to the amending regulations reveals that four child abuse compensation schemes had been approved by the Secretary of State as at January 1, 2022: under the Historical Institutional Abuse (Northern Ireland) Act 2019; under the Redress for Survivors (Historical Child Abuse in Care) (Scotland) Act 2021; the London Borough of Lambeth Redress Scheme and the London Borough of Islington's proposed support payment scheme. All provide one-off capital payments. The Memorandum also reveals that payments under the Northern Ireland and Lambeth schemes could have been made prior to January 1, 2022. The application of the disregards provided under SI 2021/1405 to such pre-January 2022 payments has been authorised by a ministerial direction from the Secretary of State, acting under "common law powers" (see the letters of December 3, 2021 between the Permanent Secretary and the Secretary of State, published on the internet). The Windrush Compensation Scheme has also been making payments for some time. The correspondence above states that extra-statutory arrangements agreed with HM Treasury provided for the disregard in practice of such payments in means-tested benefits from the outset. It might be thought that the delay in putting that outcome on a proper statutory basis is symptomatic of the way in which the victims of that scandal have been treated.

Those arrangements raise questions as to what a tribunal on appeal should do if it has evidence of receipt prior to January 1, 2022 of a payment that would have been disregarded under the amendments if it had been received on or after that date. The legislation that a tribunal is bound to apply would not allow a disregard of such a payment unless it fell within an existing "personal injury" disregard in para.12 or 12A (possible for some historic institutional child abuse payments, though not for payments to next of kin or those who had merely been in "harm's way" or for Windrush Compensation Scheme payments). However, if an express submission from the DWP recorded the practical result of the application of the disregard either on the basis of a ministerial direction or an extra-statutory arrangement, it would appear that the issue of the treatment of the payment would not arise on the appeal (see SSA 1998 s.12(8)(a)) and it is submitted that it would then be irrational for the tribunal to exercise its discretion to consider the issue nonetheless. If evidence of a payment that had not been taken into account as capital emerged in the course of an appeal, but there was no express DWP submission to explain that outcome, it is submitted that a tribunal with knowledge of the matters mentioned above could still legitimately conclude that the issue did not arise on the appeal and decline to exercise its discretion under s.12(8)(a). Memo DMG 15/21 on the effect of the amendment to Sch.10 says nothing about these questions, although it does name the currently approved historic institutional child abuse schemes and give the date of approval (December 10, 2021).

With effect from July 9, 2023, reg.2(8) of the Social Security (Income and Capital Disregards) (Amendment) Regulations 2023 (SI 2023/640) amended para.22(1A) by adding the following after "Windrush payment":

> ", Post Office compensation payment or vaccine damage payment"

Such payments are newly defined in reg.2(1), where there is now also an expanded definition of Grenfell Tower payments. With effect from the same date, the words substituted in sub-paras (2) to (6) have been further amended by substituting ", a Windrush payment, a Post Office compensation payment or a vaccine damage payment" for "or a Windrush payment".

The definition of "Post Office compensation payment" in reg.2(1) applies to any payments for compensation or support from the Post Office or the Secretary of State in connection with the failings of the Horizon computer accounting system (also defined in reg.2(1)) or the decision in the named test case on the Post Office's liability to the now famous group of 555 postmasters within the Group Litigation Order (GLO). The neutral citation number of the decision, as set out in a footnote to the amending regulation, is [2019] EWHC 606 (QB). Following on that and a consequent decision (the Horizon Issues judgment) a settlement was agreed, but the claimants actually received only a small proportion of the overall figure, the remainder being taken up by funding costs. Paragraph 7.3 of the Explanatory Memorandum describes the compensation schemes in being as at July 2023:

> "Government has announced funding to enable the Post Office to deliver compensation schemes and arrangements for various cohorts of postmasters, including the Historical Shortfall Scheme, compensation arrangements for postmasters whose convictions were overturned and a compensation scheme for postmasters who did not receive remuneration during a suspension period, to address issues expressly identified by the parties during the court proceedings or flowing from the Common Issues and Horizon Issues judgments. In March 2022, the Government agreed to provide funding to ensure that the claimants received compensation on a similar basis to other postmasters. A Department for Business and Trade scheme to deliver that outcome opened for applications in March 2023."

No doubt any compensation paid following the proposals announced in February 2024 for the automatic quashing of a much wider range of convictions than hitherto will fall within the condition of being "in connection with the failings of the Horizon system".

With effect from August 30, 2023, reg.2(1)(a) of the Social Security (Infected Blood Capital Disregard) (Amendment) Regulations 2023 (SI 2023/894) amended para.22 by inserting the following after sub-para.(5):

> "(5A) Any payment out of the estate of a person, which derives from a payment to meet the recommendation of the Infected Blood Inquiry in its interim report published on 29th July 2022 made under or by the Scottish Infected Blood Support Scheme or an approved blood scheme to the estate of the person, where the payment is made to the person's son, daughter, step-son or step-daughter."

Sir Brian Langstaff's interim report recommended that an interim payment of £100,000 should be made to all those infected from contaminated blood and blood products and all bereaved partners already registered on one of the four UK infected blood support schemes and those who registered before the inception of any future scheme. The Government committed that where the infected person or their bereaved partner died after registering for such a scheme but before the interim payment could be made, it would be paid to their estate. The amendment is intended to secure that a payment derived from an interim infected blood compensation payment from the estate will be disregarded as capital for income support purposes if it is made to a deceased person's son, daughter, step-son or step-daughter.

With effect from October 27, 2023, reg.3(3)(c) of the Social Security (Habitual Residence and Past Presence, and Capital Disregards) (Amendment) Regulations 2023 (SI 2023/1144) amended para.22(1) and (7) by inserting ", the Victims of Overseas Terrorism Compensation Scheme" after "the National Emergencies Trust" in both places. That scheme is newly defined in reg.2(1). It was set up under s.47 of the Crime and Security Act 2010 and is administered by the Criminal Injuries Compensation Authority. It enables compensation to be paid to persons injured and to partners or close family members of persons killed, where the injury or death is directly attributable to a designated incident. Payments for personal injury would be disregarded as capital under paras 12 and 12A (indefinitely only if held on trust, otherwise for 52 weeks), but will now if necessary be disregarded indefinitely under para.22, along with payments to family members (not previously covered). The amending regulations were made under urgency procedures following the UK's designation of some aspects of the violence in Israel from October 7, 2023 as incidents of terrorism, but many other incidents have been designated (as listed on the scheme's website). The official view, as set out in the note to para.16 of ADM Memo 17/23 is that capital retained from payments received before October 27, 2023 will be covered by the terms of the new provision as from that date:

> "While the classification of the Hamas attack on Israel on 7.10.23 has raised the need to disregard payments under the Victims of Overseas Terrorism Compensation scheme as capital, the regulations will cover any and all payments made under the scheme. There is no intention to differentiate between compensation payments made to victims of different terrorism attacks which are recognised under the compensation scheme."

The same view was expressed in a statement made to the Social Security Advisory Committee (see footnote 2 to para.1.6 of the minutes of the meeting of December 16, 2023).

With effect from October 10, 2024 reg.2(1)(a) of the Social Security (Infected Blood Capital Disregard) (Amendment) Regulations 2024 (SI 2024/964) amended para.22 by inserting the following after sub-para.(5A):

"(5B) Any payment out of the estate of a person, which derives from a payment made under or by the Scottish Infected Blood Support Scheme or an approved blood scheme to the estate of the person as a result of that person having been infected from contaminated blood products."

See the entry for p.472 of Vol.II in Pt.II of this Supplement for discussion of the terms of sub-para.(5B).

p.685, *amendment to the Income Support (General) Regulations 1987 (SI 1987/1967) Sch.10 para.29 (Capital to be disregarded—payments in kind)*

6.058 With effect from January 1, 2022, reg.2(8)(b) of the Social Security (Income and Capital Disregards) (Amendment) Regulations 2021 (SI 2021/1405) amended para.29 by inserting ", child abuse payment or Windrush payment" after "Grenfell Tower payment". All of those payments are defined in reg.2(1). See also the entry for pp.684–685.

p.689, *amendment to the Income Support (General) Regulations 1987 (SI 1987/1967) Sch.10 para.72 (Capital to be disregarded—bereavement support payment)*

6.059 With effect from February 9, 2023, para.1(b) of the Schedule to the Bereavement Benefits (Remedial) Order 2023 (SI 2023/134) amended para.72 by making the existing text sub-para.(1) and inserting the following:

"(2) Where bereavement support payment under section 30 of the Pensions Act 2014 is paid to the survivor of a cohabiting partnership (within the meaning in section 30(6B) of the Pensions Act 2014) in respect of a death occurring before the day the Bereavement Benefits (Remedial) Order 2023 comes into force, any amount of that payment which is—

(a) in respect of the rate set out in regulation 3(1) of the Bereavement Support Payment Regulations 2017, and

(b) paid as a lump sum for more than one monthly recurrence of the day of the month on which their cohabiting partner died,

but only for a period of 52 weeks from the date of receipt of the payment."

See the entry for p.682 for the general background. The operation of this amendment is much more straightforward than that of the new para.7A on widowed parent's allowance. Although a payment of arrears of bereavement support payment (BSP) is in its nature a payment of income and attributable to the past period in respect of which it is due, the payment could not affect any entitlement to income support in that past period because it would be disregarded entirely as income (Sch.9 para.80). The amount of the arrears would thus immediately metamorphose into capital, which would then be disregarded under para.72(2) subject to the 52 week limit.

p.695, *annotation to the Income Support (General) Regulations 1987 (SI 1987/1967) Sch.10 (Capital to be disregarded)*

In the list of categories of disregards of capital, insert the following between the entry for para.7 and the entry for para.8: 6.060

"*Para.7A* Arrears of widowed parent's allowance;"

p.697, *annotation to the Income Support (General) Regulations 1987 (SI 1987/1967) Sch.10 (Capital to be disregarded)*

With effect from June 28, 2022 "Cost of living payments" under the Social Security (Additional Payments) Act 2022 (see Part I of Vol.II of this series), both those to recipients of specified means-tested benefits and "disability" payments, are not to be taken into account for any income support purposes by virtue of s.8(b) of the Act. The same effect was achieved with effect from March 23, 2023 in relation to payments under the Social Security (Additional Payments) Act 2023 (s.8(b) of that Act). See Pt I of Vol.II for the text of both Acts. 6.061

p.707, *annotation to the Income Support (General) Regulations 1987 (SI 1987/1967) Sch.10 (Capital to be disregarded–arrears of certain benefits)*

With effect from October 18, 2021, the Social Security Benefits (Claims and Payments) (Amendment) Regulations 2021 (SI 2021/1065) have permitted the payment of arrears of many benefits to be made in instalments, where necessary to protect the interests of the beneficiary and the latter agrees. Once such payments become capital (see the main volume), presumably the 52-week limit on the para.7(1) disregard runs separately from the date of receipt of each instalment. The application of the conditions in para.7(2) for a longer disregard might be more problematic. 6.062

p.709, *annotation to the Income Support (General) Regulations 1987 (SI 1987/1967) Sch.10 para.7A (Capital to be disregarded—arrears of widowed parent's allowance)*

Insert the following before the note to para.8:

"*Paragraph 7A* 6.063

This new disregard as capital of arrears of widowed parent's allowance was introduced with effect from February 9, 2023. See the entry for p.682 for the text and discussion of its effect."

p.711, *annotation to the Income Support (General) Regulations 1987 (SI 1987/1967) Sch.10 para.12 (Capital to be disregarded—trusts derived from payments made in consequence of personal injury)*

Note that *R(IS) 15/96*, mentioned in para.2.819, holds that payments made under the Criminal Injuries Compensation Scheme are in consequence of personal injury. 6.064

In *DR v SSWP (UC)* [2024] UKUT 196 (AAC), the claimant received some £27,000 under an ACAS settlement of employment tribunal proceedings, comprising elements for loss of employment (£6,411.60), statutory redundancy pay (£6,945.90) and compensation for injury to feelings arising from alleged discrimination (£14,142.50). An immediate claim for universal credit was refused on the ground that she had capital exceeding £16,000 and a later claim, when her capital had reduced to £10,700, was allowed subject to the taking into account of an assumed yield from capital of £82.65 per assessment period. The tribunal had rejected the claimant's argument that the whole payment should have been disregarded as it was not taxable. On further appeal, Judge Wikeley held that it had been right to do so. Liability or otherwise to tax was not relevant. There was nothing in the universal credit legislation allowing a disregard as capital of the elements of the sum for loss of employment or for statutory redundancy. Nor could the element for injury to feelings be disregarded under reg.75, as compensation for injury to feelings is distinct from a payment "for actual injury to physical or mental health (by way of, for instance, psychiatric injury)". The same would follow under the income support legislation and paras 12 and 12A. It was therefore not necessary to decide whether the first decision was within the jurisdiction of the tribunal as well as the second.

The inclusion of the category of psychiatric injury has been further supported by the decision of the Court of Appeal in *Shehabi v Kingdom of Bahrain* [2024] EWCA Civ 1158, in the context of the application of a statutory exception to the principle of State immunity from legal action, holding that "personal injury" includes a standalone psychiatric injury.

p.714, *annotation to the Income Support (General) Regulations 1987 (SI 1987/1967) Sch.10 para.18A (Capital to be disregarded—local welfare provision)*

6.065 There has been no specific provision made under Sch.10 (or the equivalent old style ESA or JSA provisions) to disregard 2022 Energy Rebate Scheme payments as capital, as has been done for universal credit in the Universal Credit (Energy Rebate Scheme Disregard) Regulations 2022 (SI 2022/257) (see Pt II of Vol.II). That is because the payments to be administered by local authorities (the £150 council tax rebate for properties in bands A–D and under the discretionary scheme for the vulnerable) are considered already to be covered by para.18A.

p.717, *annotation to the Income Support (General) Regulations 1987 (SI 1987/1967) Sch.10, para.28 (Capital to be disregarded—premises intended to be occupied: essential repairs or alterations needed)*

6.066 In the second paragraph of this annotation in the main volume, the reference to the Housing Benefit Regulations should be to para.28 of Sch.6, not para.27 of Sch.5. Further, the works must be required to make the property fit for occupation by the claimant, not fit for human habitation as suggested in the first paragraph. There might sometimes be no difference in the practical effect, but sometimes there will be. In *SH v London Borough of Southwark (HB)* [2023] UKUT 198 (AAC), Judge Hemingway held in para.23, in the context of reg.7(4) of the Housing Benefit Regulations, that the evaluation of whether repairs were essential had to take account of the claimant's individual characteristics, including impairment or vulnerability in consequence of ill-health, as had also been decided by Commissioner Williams in *CH/393/2002*. "Essential" probably means something like "necessary" in the sense in which luxuries are differentiated from the necessaries of life, importing a test of substantial need (*R(SB) 10/81* on the supplementary benefit single payments scheme), but the ordinary word in para.28 should be applied rather than some attempted further explanation.

p.721, *annotation to the Income Support (General) Regulations 1987 (SI 1987/1967) Sch.10 para.72 (Capital to be disregarded—bereavement support payments)*

See the entry for p.689 for the text of the amendment with effect from February 9, 2023 extending this disregard to arrears of payments made under the Bereavement Benefits (Remedial) Order 2023 (SI 2023/134) and discussion of its effect. **6.067**

p.722, *annotation to the Income Support (General) Regulations 1987 (SI 1987/1967) Sch.10 para.77 (Capital to be disregarded—Scottish young carer grants)*

The amount of the annual young carer grant increased to £383.75 with effect from April 1, 2024. **6.068**

p.722, *annotation to the Income Support (General) Regulations 1987 (SI 1987/1967) Sch.10 para.78 (Capital to be disregarded—Scottish winter heating assistance)*

The amount of the annual child winter heating payment increased to £251.50 with effect from April 1, 2024. **6.069**

Further regulations (the Winter Heating Assistance (Low Income) (Scotland) Regulations 2023 (SSI 2023/16)) introduce, from January 25, 2023, one-off annual payments of (from April 1, 2024) £58.75 for certain recipients of income-related benefits (see Vol.IV of this series).

p.722, *annotation to the Income Support (Liable Relatives) Regulations 1990 (SI 1990/1777) reg.2 (Prescribed amounts for the purposes of section 24A of the Act)*

With effect from November 19, 2023, art.7 of the Carer's Assistance (Carer Support Payment) (Scotland) Regulations 2023 (Consequential Amendments) Order 2023 (SI 2023/1218) amended reg.2(1)(e) by inserting "or carer support payment under the Carer's Assistance (Carer Support Payment) (Scotland) Regulations 2023," after "carer's allowance". **6.070**

p.742, *amendment to the Fines (Deductions from Income Support) Regulations 1992 (SI 1992/2182) reg.4 (Deductions from offender's income support, universal credit, state pension credit or jobseeker's allowance)*

With effect from October 29, 2021, reg.2 of the Fines (Deductions from Income Support) (Miscellaneous Amendments) Regulations 2021 (SI 2021/1077) substitutes a new reg.4(1B): **6.071**

"(1B) The amount that may be deducted under paragraph (1A) is 5 per cent. of the appropriate universal credit standard allowance for the offender for the assessment period in question, as specified under regulation 36 of the UC Regulations."

This amendment follows the decision of Kerr J in *R. (Blundell) v SSWP* [2021] EWHC 608 (Admin); [2021] P.T.S.R. 1342, where the Secretary of State's policy on deductions was found to be unlawfully fettering her discretion about the amount to deduct under reg.4(1B). The new regulation removes that discretion, by limiting deductions to the smallest amount which could previously have been deducted.

p.773, *amendment to the Child Support Maintenance Calculation Regulations 2012 (SI 2012/2677) reg.44 (Flat rate)*

6.072 With effect from November 19, 2023, arts.1(2) and 22 of the Carer's Assistance (Carer Support Payment) (Scotland) Regulations 2023 (Consequential Amendments) Order 2023 (SI 2023/1218) deleted the "and" at the end of reg.44(1)(h), inserted "and" at the end of reg.44(1)(i) and inserted a new reg.44(1)(j) as follows:

(j) carer support payment under the Carer's Assistance (Carer Support Payment) (Scotland) Regulations 2023.

Part III

Old Style Jobseeker's Allowance Regulations

p.785, *amendments to list of regulations for the Jobseeker's Allowance Regulations 1996 (SI 1996/207)*

6.073 Insert the following entry between the entries for regs 136B and 137:

"136C. Treatment of loans for specific purposes"

p.787, *annotation to the Jobseeker's Allowance Regulations 1996 (SI 1996/207)*

6.074 Insert the following text at the end of the GENERAL NOTE as a new paragraph:

Note that after July 25, 2022, there are no longer any circumstances in which it is possible to make a new claim for old style JSA: see the entry for p.33.

p.787, *amendments to the Jobseeker's Allowance Regulations 1996 (SI 1996/207), reg.1 (Citation, commencement, interpretation and application)*

6.075 With effect from July 26, 2021, Sch.3 para.2 of the Social Security (Scotland) Act 2018 (Disability Assistance for Children and Young People) (Consequential Modifications) Order 2021 (SI 2021/786) inserts the following definitions:

- "child disability payment" has the meaning given in regulation 2 of the DACYP Regulations;
- "DACYP Regulations" means the Disability Assistance for Children and Young People (Scotland) Regulations 2021;

With effect from January 1, 2022, reg.3(2) of the Social Security (Income and Capital Disregards) (Amendment) Regulations 2021 (SI 2021/1405) inserts the following definitions:

- "child abuse payment" means a payment from a scheme established or approved by the Secretary of State for the purpose of providing compensation in respect of historic institutional child abuse in the United Kingdom;"
- "Windrush payment" means a payment made under the Windrush Compensation Scheme (Expenditure) Act 2020;"

With effect from January 1, 2022, reg.3(2) of the Social Security (Income and Capital Disregards) (Amendment) Regulations 2021 (SI 2021/1405) inserts ", a child abuse payment or a Windrush payment" into the definition of "qualifying person", after "Grenfell Tower payment".

With effect from March 21, 2022, art.5 of the Social Security (Disability Assistance for Working Age People) (Consequential Amendments) Order 2022 (SI 2022/177) inserts the following definition:

"adult disability payment" has the meaning given in regulation 2 of the Disability Assistance for Working Age People (Scotland) Regulations 2022;

With effect from July 9, 2023, reg.3 of the Social Security (Income and Capital Disregards) (Amendment) Regulations 2023 (SI 2023/640) amends reg.1 as follows:

- for the definition of "Grenfell Tower payment" substitute—""Grenfell Tower payment" means a payment made for the purpose of providing compensation or support in respect of the fire on 14th June 2017 at Grenfell Tower;";
- insert the following definitions:
  - "the Horizon system" means any version of the computer system used by the Post Office known as Horizon, Horizon Legacy, Horizon Online or HNG-X;
  - "the Post Office" means Post Office Limited (registered number 02154540);
  - "Post Office compensation payment" means a payment made by the Post Office or the Secretary of State for the purpose of providing compensation or support which is—
    (a) in connection with the failings of the Horizon system; or
    (b) otherwise payable following the judgment in Bates and Others v Post Office Ltd ((No. 3) "Common Issues") (10);
  - "vaccine damage payment" means a payment made under the Vaccine Damage Payments Act 1979(11);";
- in the definition of "qualifying person", for "or a Windrush payment" substitute ", a Windrush payment, a Post Office compensation payment or a vaccine damage payment".

With effect from October 27, 2023, reg.4 of the Social Security (Habitual Residence and Past Presence, and Capital Disregards) (Amendment) Regulations 2023 (SI 2023/1144) amends reg.1 as follows:

- in the definition of "qualifying person", after "the National Emergencies Trust" insert ", the Victims of Overseas Terrorism Compensation Scheme";
- insert the following definition:

  "the Victims of Overseas Terrorism Compensation Scheme" means the scheme of that name established by the Ministry of Justice in 2012 under section 47 of the Crime and Security Act 2010(20);

With effect from November 19, 2023, art.8 of the Carer's Assistance (Carer Support Payment) (Scotland) Regulations 2023 (Consequential Amendments) Order 2023 (SI 2023/1218) amends reg.1 as follows:
after the definition of "care home" insert—

> ""carer support payment" means carer's assistance given in accordance with the Carer's Assistance (Carer Support Payment) (Scotland) Regulations 2023;".

pp.851–852, *annotation to the Jobseeker's Allowance Regulations 1996 (SI 1996/207) reg.16 (Further circumstances in which a person is to be treated as available: permitted period)*

6.076 Note that there has been no amendment to reg.16, equivalent to that made for universal credit and new style JSA purposes by SI 2022/108 (see the notes to reg.97(4) and (5) of the Universal Credit Regulations 2013 in Pt II of Vol.II of this series and to reg.14(3) of the JSA Regulations 2013 in Vol.I of this series), to reduce the maximum length of a "permitted period" from 13 weeks to four.

pp.872–873, *annotation to the Jobseeker's Allowance Regulations 1996 (SI 1996/207) reg.20 (Further circumstances in which a person is to be treated as actively seeking employment: permitted period)*

6.077 Note that there has been no amendment to reg.20, equivalent to that made for universal credit and new style JSA purposes by SI 2022/108 (see the notes to reg.97(4) and (5) of the Universal Credit Regulations 2013 in Pt II of Vol.II of this series and to reg.14(3) of the JSA Regulations 2013 in Vol.I of this series), to reduce the maximum length of a "permitted period" from 13 weeks to four.

p.896, *amendments to the Jobseeker's Allowance Regulations 1996 (SI 1996/207) reg.46(1) (Waiting days)*

6.078 With effect from November 19, 2023, art.8(3) of the Carer's Assistance (Carer Support Payment) (Scotland) Regulations 2023 (Consequential Amendments) Order 2023 (SI 2023/1218) amended reg.46(1)(a) and (d) by substituting ", carer's allowance or carer support payment" for "carer's llowance" in both places. Carer support payment is newly defined in reg.1(3) by reference to the Scottish legislation (see the entry for p.787).

pp.902–903, *amendments to the Jobseeker's Allowance Regulations 1996 (SI 1996/207) reg.48(2) and (3) (Linking periods)*

With effect from November 19, 2023, art.8(4) of the Carer's Assistance (Carer Support Payment) (Scotland) Regulations 2023 (Consequential Amendments) Order 2023 (SI 2023/1218) amended reg.48(2)(a) and (3) by inserting "or carer support payment" after "Benefits Act" in para.(2)(a) and after "carer's allowance" in para.(3). Carer support payment is newly defined in reg.1(3) by reference to the Scottish legislation (see the entry for p.787). **6.079**

pp.910–912, *amendments to the Jobseeker's Allowance Regulations 1996 (SI 1996/207) reg.51 (Remunerative work)*

The text in the main volume at para.3.166 should be replaced with the following: **6.080**

"Remunerative work

51.—(1) For the purposes of the Act "remunerative work" means—
(a) in the case of [5 a claimant], work in which he is engaged or, where his hours of work fluctuate, is engaged on average, for not less than 16 hours per week; and
(b) in the case of any partner of the claimant, work in which he is engaged or, where his hours of work fluctuate, is engaged on average, for not less than 24 hours per week; [1 and
(c) in the case of a non-dependant, or of a child or young person to whom paragraph 18 of Schedule 6 refers, work in which he is engaged or, where his hours of work fluctuate, is engaged on average, for not less than 16 hours per week,]

and for those purposes, [3 "work" is work] for which payment is made or which is done in expectation of payment.

(2) For the purposes of paragraph (1), the number of hours in which [5 a claimant] or his partner is engaged in work shall be determined—
(a) where no recognisable cycle has been established in respect of a person's work, by reference to the number of hours or, where those hours are likely to fluctuate, the average of the hours, which he is expected to work in a week;
(b) where the number of hours for which he is engaged fluctuate, by reference to the average of hours worked over—
 (i) if there is a recognisable cycle of work, and sub-paragraph (c) does not apply, the period of one complete cycle (including, where the cycle involves periods in which the person does not work, those periods but disregarding any other absences);
 (ii) in any other case, the period of five weeks immediately before the date of claim or the date of [4 supersession], or such other length of time as may, in the particular case, enable the person's average hours of work to be determined more accurately;
(c) [7 . . .]

(3) In determining in accordance with this regulation the number of hours for which a person is engaged in remunerative work—

(a) that number shall include any time allowed to that person by his employer for a meal or for refreshments, but only where the person is, or expects to be, paid earnings in respect of that time;

(b) no account shall be taken of any hours in which the person is engaged in an employment or scheme to which any one of paragraphs (a) to (h) of regulation 53 (person treated as not engaged in remunerative work) applies;

(c) no account shall be taken of any hours in which the person is engaged otherwise than in an employment as an earner in caring for—

(i) a person who is in receipt of attendance allowance [1 . . .] [9 , the care component of disability living allowance at the highest or middle rate [11 the care component of child disability payment at the highest or middle rate in accordance with regulation 11(5) of the DACYP Regulations] [10 , armed forces independence payment] [12 . . .] the daily living component of personal independence payment at the standard or enhanced rate] [12 , or the daily living component of adult disability payment at the standard or enhanced rate]; or

(ii) a person who has claimed an attendance allowance [1 . . .] [9, disability living allowance [11 child disability payment] [10 , armed forces independence payment] [12 . . .] personal independence payment] [12 or adult disability payment], but only for the period beginning with the date of claim and ending on the date the claim is determined or, if earlier, on the expiration of the period of 26 weeks from the date of claim; or

(iii) another person [2 and] is in receipt of [6 carer's allowance] under Section 70 of the [1 Benefits Act [13 or carer support payment]; or

(iv) a person who has claimed either attendance allowance or disability living allowance and has an award of attendance allowance or the care component of disability living allowance at one of the two higher rates prescribed under section 72(4) of the Benefits Act for a period commencing after the date on which that claim was made] [9 ; or

[11 (iva) a person who has claimed child disability payment and has an award of the care component of child disability payment at the highest or middle rate in accordance with regulation 11(5) of the DACYP Regulations for a period commencing after the date on which the claim was made;] or

(v) a person who has claimed personal independence payment and has an award of the daily living component at the standard or enhanced rate under section 78 of the 2012 Act for a period commencing after the date on which that claim was made] [10 ; or

[12 (va) a person who has claimed adult disability payment and has an award of the daily living component at the standard or enhanced rate under regulation 5 of the Disability Assistance for Working Age People (Scotland) Regulations 2022 for a period commencing after the date on which that claim was made;] or

(vi) a person who has claimed and has an award of armed forces independence payment for a period commencing after the date on which that claim was made.]

[8 . . .]"

AMENDMENTS

1. Jobseeker's Allowance (Amendment) Regulations 1996 (SI 1996/15160) reg.9 (October 7, 1996).
2. Jobseeker's Allowance (Amendment) Regulations 1996 (SI 1996/1516) reg.20 and Sch. (October 7, 1996).
3. Social Security (Miscellaneous Amendments) Regulations 1997 (SI 1997/454) reg.2(5) (April 7, 1997).
4. Social Security Act 1998 (Commencement No. 11, and Savings and Consequential and Transitional Provisions) Order 1999 (SI 1999/2860 (C.75)) art.3(1) and (12) and Sch.12 para.5 (October 18, 1999)
5. Jobseeker's Allowance (Joint Claims) Regulations 2000 (SI 2000/1978) reg.2(5) and Sch.2 para.14 (March 19, 2001).
6. Social Security (Miscellaneous Amendments) Regulations 2003 (SI 2003/511) reg.3(4) and (5) (April 1, 2003).
7. Social Security (Miscellaneous Amendments) Regulations 2009 (SI 2009/583) reg.4(1) and (4) (April 6, 2009).
8. Social Security (Miscellaneous Amendments) (No. 3) Regulations 2011 (SI 2011/2425) reg.10(1) and (3) (October 31, 2011).
9. Personal Independence Payment (Supplementary Provisions and Consequential Amendments) Regulations 2013 (SI 2013/388) reg.8 and Sch. para.16(1) and (3) (April 8, 2013).
10. Armed Forces and Reserve Forces Compensation Scheme (Consequential Provisions: Subordinate Legislation) Order 2013 (SI 2013/591) art.7 and Sch. para.10(1) and (3) (April 8, 2013).
11. Social Security (Scotland) Act 2018 (Disability Assistance for Children and Young People) (Consequential Modifications) Order 2021 (SI 2021/786) Sch.3 para.3 (July 26, 2021).
12. Social Security (Disability Assistance for Working Age People) (Consequential Amendments) Order 2022 (SI 2022/177) art.5(3) (March 21, 2022).
13. Carer's Assistance (Carer Support Payment) (Scotland) Regulations 2023 (Consequential Amendments) Order 2023 (SI 2023/1218) art.8 (November 19, 2023).

DEFINITIONS

"the Act"—see reg.1(3).
"adult disability payment"—*ibid.*
"attendance allowance"—*ibid.*
"the Benefits Act"—see Jobseekers Act s.35(1).
"child"—*ibid.*
"child disability payment"—see reg.1(3).
"claimant"—see Jobseekers Act s.35(1).
"date of claim"—see reg.1(3).
"DACYP Regulations"—*ibid.*
"disability living allowance"—*ibid.*
"earnings"—*ibid.*
"employment"—see reg.3.
"partner"—see reg.1(3).
"payment"—*ibid.*
"personal independence payment"—*ibid.*
"week"—*ibid.*
"young person"—*ibid.*, reg.76.

For the General Note to reg.51, see Vol.V paras 3.167–3.169.

p.923, *amendment to the Jobseeker's Allowance Regulations 1996 (SI 1996/207) reg.55ZA(2)(a) (Extended period of sickness)*

6.081 With effect from July 1, 2022, reg.4(1) of the Social Security (Medical Evidence) and Statutory Sick Pay (Medical Evidence) (Amendment) (No. 2) Regulations 2022 (SI 2022/630) omitted the words "a doctor's" between "form of" and "statement".

p.970, *annotation to the Jobseeker's Allowance Regulations 1996 (SI 1996/207) reg.83 (Applicable amounts)*

6.082 On the lawfulness of not uplifting the amounts paid in IS, JSA and ESA by £20 per week (as was done with UC for 18 months during the coronavirus pandemic), see the annotation to the Income Support (General) Regulations 1987 (SI 1987/1967) reg.17 (Applicable amounts), above.

pp.974–977, *amendments to the Jobseeker's Allowance Regulations 1996 (SI 1996/207) reg.85A (Special cases: supplemental—persons from abroad)*

6.083 The text in the main volume at para.3.278 should be replaced with the following:

"**85A.**—(1) "Person from abroad" means, subject to the following provisions of this regulation, a claimant who is not habitually resident in the United Kingdom, the Channel Islands, the Isle of Man or the Republic of Ireland.

[10 (2) No claimant shall be treated as habitually resident in the United Kingdom, the Channel Islands, the Isle of Man or the Republic of Ireland unless—

(a) [12 subject to the exceptions in paragraph (2A),] the claimant has been living in any of those places for the past three months; and

(b) the claimant has a right to reside in any of those places, other than a right to reside which falls within paragraph (3) [13 or (3A)].]

[12 (2A) The exceptions are where the claimant has at any time during the period referred to in paragraph (2)(a)—

(a) paid either Class 1 or Class 2 contributions by virtue of regulation 114, 118, 146 or 147 of the Social Security (Contributions) Regulations 2001 or by virtue of an Order in Council having effect under section 179 of the Social Security Administration Act 1992; or

(b) been a Crown servant posted to perform overseas the duties of a Crown servant; or

(c) been a member of Her Majesty's forces posted to perform overseas the duties of a member of Her Majesty's forces.]

(3) A right to reside falls within this paragraph if it is one which exists by virtue of, or in accordance with, one or more of the following—

(a) regulation 13 of the [13 Immigration (European Economic Area) Regulations 2016]; [15 or]

[7[13(aa) regulation 16 of those Regulations, but only in a case where the right exists under that regulation because the claimant satisfies the criteria in paragraph (5) of that regulation;]]

(b) [15 . . .]

(c) [15 . . .]

[13 (3A) A right to reside falls within this paragraph if it exists by virtue of a claimant having been granted limited leave to enter, or remain in, the United Kingdom under the Immigration Act 1971 by virtue of—

(a) Appendix EU to the immigration rules made under section 3(2) of that Act; [16 . . .]

(b) being a person with a Zambrano right to reside as defined in Annex 1 of Appendix EU to the immigration rules made under section 3(2) of that Act.] [16; or

(c) having arrived in the United Kingdom with an entry clearance that was granted under Appendix EU (Family Permit) to the immigration rules made under section 3(2) of that Act.]

[14 (3B) Paragraph (3A)(a) does not apply to a person who—

(a) has a right to reside granted by virtue of being a family member of a relevant person of Northern Ireland; and

(b) would have a right to reside under the Immigration (European Economic Area) Regulations 2016 if the relevant person of Northern Ireland were an EEA national, provided that the right to reside does not fall within paragraph (3A).]

(4) A claimant is not a person from abroad if he is—

[16(zza) a person granted leave in accordance with the immigration rules made under section 3(2) of the Immigration Act 1971, where such leave is granted by virtue of—

(i) the Afghan Relocations and Assistance Policy; or

(ii) the previous scheme for locally-employed staff in Afghanistan (sometimes referred to as the ex-gratia scheme);

(zzb) a person in Great Britain not coming within sub-paragraph (zza) or [17 (h)] who left Afghanistan in connection with the collapse of the Afghan government that took place on 15th August 2021;]

[17(zzc) a person in Great Britain who was residing in Ukraine immediately before 1st January 2022, left Ukraine in connection with the Russian invasion which took place on 24th February 2022 and—

(i) has been granted leave in accordance with immigration rules made under section 3(2) of the Immigration Act 1971; [18 . . .]

(ii) has a right of abode in the United Kingdom within the meaning given in section 2 of that Act;] [18 or

(iii) does not require leave to enter or remain in the United Kingdom in accordance with section 3ZA of that Act;]

[19(zzd) a person who was residing in Sudan before 15th April 2023, left Sudan in connection with the violence which rapidly escalated on 15th April 2023 in Khartoum and across Sudan and—

(i) has been granted leave in accordance with immigration rules made under section 3(2) of the Immigration Act 1971(10);

(ii) has a right of abode in the United Kingdom within the meaning given in section 2 of that Act(11); or

(iii) does not require leave to enter or remain in the United Kingdom in accordance with section 3ZA of that Act;]

[20(zze) a person who was residing in Israel, the West Bank, the Gaza Strip, East Jerusalem, the Golan Heights or Lebanon immediately before 7th October 2023, who left Israel, the West Bank, the Gaza Strip, East Jerusalem, the Golan Heights or Lebanon in connection with the Hamas terrorist attack in Israel on 7th October 2023 or the violence which rapidly escalated in the region following the attack and—

(i) has been granted leave in accordance with immigration rules made under section 3(2) of the Immigration Act 1971;

(ii) has a right of abode in the United Kingdom within the meaning given in section 2 of that Act; or

(iii) does not require leave to enter or remain in the United Kingdom in accordance with section 3ZA of that Act;]

[[11](za) a qualified person for the purposes of regulation 6 of the [[13] Immigration (European Economic Area) Regulations 2016] as a worker or a self-employed person;

(zb) a family member of a person referred to in sub-paragraph (za) [[14] . . .];

(zc) a person who has a right to reside permanently in the United Kingdom by virtue of regulation 15(1)(c), (d) or I of those Regulations;]

[[14](zd) a family member of a relevant person of Northern Ireland, with a right to reside which falls within paragraph (3A)(a), provided that the relevant person of Northern Ireland falls within sub-paragraph (za), or would do so but for the fact that they are not an EEA national;]

[[15](ze) a frontier worker within the meaning of regulation 3 of the Citizens' Rights (Frontier Workers) (EU Exit) Regulations 2020;

(zf) a family member, of a person referred to in sub-paragraph (ze), who has been granted limited leave to enter, or remain in, the United Kingdom by virtue of Appendix EU to the immigration rules made under section 3(2) of the Immigration Act 1971;]

(g) a refugee within the definition in Article 1 of the Convention relating to the Status of Refugees done at Geneva on 28th July 1951, as extended by Article 1(2) of the Protocol relating to the Status of Refugees done at New York on 31st January 1967;

[[3][[9](h) a person who has been granted leave or who is deemed to have been granted leave outside the rules made under section 3(2) of the Immigration Act 1971 [[17] . . .]]

(hh) a person who has humanitarian protection granted under those rules;] [[9] or]

(i) a person who is not a person subject to immigration control within the meaning of section 115(9) of the Immigration and Asylum Act and who is in the United Kingdom as a result of his deportation, expulsion or other removal by compulsion of law from another country to the United Kingdom; [[5] . . .]

[[9] . . .]

[[14] (5) In this regulation—

"EEA national" has the meaning given in regulation 2(1) of the Immigration (European Economic Area) Regulations 2016;

"family member" has the meaning given in regulation 7(1)(a), (b) or (c) of the Immigration (European Economic Area) Regulations 2016 except that regulation 7(4) of those Regulations does not apply for the purposes of paragraphs (3B) and (4)(zd);

"relevant person of Northern Ireland" has the meaning given in Annex 1 of Appendix EU to the immigration rules made under section 3(2) of the Immigration Act 1971.]

[15 (6) In this regulation references to the Immigration (European Economic Area) Regulations 2016 are to be read with Schedule 4 to the Immigration and Social Security Co-ordination (EU Withdrawal) Act 2020 (Consequential, Saving, Transitional and Transitory Provisions) Regulations 2020.]"

AMENDMENTS

1. Social Security (Persons from Abroad) Amendment Regulations 2006 (SI 1026/2006) reg.7(3) (April 30, 2006).
2. Social Security (Lebanon) Amendment Regulations 2006 (SI 2006/1981) reg.3 (July 25, 2006). The amendment ceased to have effect from January 31, 2007.
3. Social Security (Persons from Abroad) Amendment (No. 2) Regulations 2006 (SI 2006/2528) reg.3 (October 9, 2006).
4. Social Security (Bulgaria and Romania) Amendment Regulations 2006 (SI 2006/3341) reg.3 (January 1, 2007).
5. Social Security (Habitual Residence) (Amendment) Regulations 2009 (SI 2009/362) reg.3 (March 18, 2009).
6. Social Security (Miscellaneous Amendments) (No. 3) Regulations 2011 (SI 2011/2425) reg.10(1) and (7) (October 31, 2011).
7. Social Security (Habitual Residence) (Amendment) Regulations 2012 (SI 2012/2587) reg.3 (November 8, 2012).
8. Social Security (Croatia) Amendment Regulations 2013 (SI 2013/1474) reg.3 (July 1, 2013).
9. Social Security (Miscellaneous Amendments) (No. 3) Regulations 2013 (SI 2013/2536) reg.6(1) and (8) (October 29,2013).
10. Jobseeker's Allowance (Habitual Residence) Amendment Regulations 2013 (SI 3196/2013) reg.2 (January 1, 2014).
11. Social Security (Habitual Residence) (Amendment) Regulations 2014 (SI 2014/902) reg.3 (May 31, 2014).
12. Jobseeker's Allowance (Habitual Residence) Amendment Regulations 2014 (SI 2014/2735) reg.3 (November 9, 2014).
13. Social Security (Income-related Benefits) (Updating and Amendment) (EU Exit) Regulations 2019 (SI 2019/872) reg.3 (May 7, 2019).
14. Social Security (Income-Related Benefits) (Persons of Northern Ireland—Family Members) (Amendment) Regulations 2020 (SI 2020/683) reg.3 (August 24, 2020).
15. Immigration and Social Security Co-ordination (EU Withdrawal) Act 2020 (Consequential, Saving, Transitional and Transitory Provisions) (EU Exit) Regulations 2020 (SI 2020/1309) reg.55 (December 31, 2020 at 11.00 pm).
16. Social Security (Habitual Residence and Past Presence) (Amendment) Regulations 2021 (SI 2021/1034), reg.2 (September 15, 2021).
17. Social Security (Habitual Residence and Past Presence) (Amendment) Regulations 2022 (SI 2022/344) reg.2 (March 22, 2022).
18. Social Security (Habitual Residence and Past Presence) (Amendment) (No. 2) Regulations 2022 (SI 2022/990) reg.2 (October 18, 2022).
19. Social Security (Habitual Residence and Past Presence) (Amendment) Regulations 2023 (SI 2023/532), reg.2 (May 15, 2023).
20. Social Security (Habitual Residence and Past Presence, and Capital Disregards) (Amendment) Regulations 2023, reg.2 (SI 2023/1144) (October 27, 2023).

p.1003, *amendments to the Jobseeker's Allowance Regulations 1996 (SI 1996/207) reg.102 (Deduction of tax and contributions for self-employed earners)*

With effect from April 6, 2024, reg.8(5)(a) of the Social Security (Class 6.084
2 National Insurance Contributions) (Consequential Amendments and

Savings) Regulations 2024 (SI 2024/377) amended reg.102 by omitting sub-para.(a) of both para.(3) and para.(4).

p.1014, *amendment to the Jobseeker's Allowance Regulations 1996 (SI 1996/207) reg.105(10A) (Notional income—exceptions)*

6.085 With effect from January 1, 2022, reg.3(3) of the Social Security (Income and Capital Disregards) (Amendment) Regulations 2021 (SI 2021/1405) amended para.(10A) by inserting the following after sub-para.(ab):

"(ac) a child abuse payment;
(ad) a Windrush payment;"

Those payments are defined in reg.1(3). See the entry for pp.684–685 for discussion of the nature of those payments.

With effect from July 9, 2023, reg.3(3) of the Social Security (Income and Capital Disregards) (Amendment) Regulations 2023 (SI 2023/640) amended reg.105(10A) by inserting the following after sub-para.(ad):

"(ae) a Post Office compensation payment;"

Such payments are newly defined in reg.1(3), where there is now also an expanded definition of Grenfell Tower payments (see sub-para.(ab)). See the entry for pp.684–685 for the background.

pp.1020–1021, *annotation to the Jobseeker's Allowance Regulations 1996 (SI 1996/207) reg.105(13) and (15) (Notional income)*

6.086 See the detailed discussion of *SSWP v NC (ESA)* [2024] UKUT 251 (AAC) in the entry above for pp.383–384 (income support), on the treatment of salary sacrifice arrangements involving the employer making occupational pension contributions of the amount of salary sacrificed by the employee. It is suggested there that that decision failed to consider the effect of reg.108(3) of the ESA Regulations 2008 (the equivalent of reg.105(13) and of reg.42(6) of the Income Support (General) Regulations 1987) on notional income where a claimant is paid less than the rate for comparable employment in the area. It is hard to see how reg.105(13) would not have applied in the circumstances. There would then be a potential problem in the application of para.(15).

p.1021, *annotation to the Jobseeker's Allowance Regulations 1996 (SI 1996/207) reg.107 (Capital limit)*

6.087 In the Institute for Government and the Social Security Advisory Committee's 2021 joint report *Jobs and benefits: The Covid-19 challenge* it was noted that if the capital limit of £16,000 had risen in line with prices since 2006 it would be close to £23,500 (or £25,000: different figures are given) and recommended that the limit should be increased to £25,000 and subsequently automatically indexed to maintain its real value (pp.22 and 31). That recommendation was summarily rejected in the Government's response of March 22, 2022.

p.1023, *amendment to the Jobseeker's Allowance Regulations 1996 (SI 1996/207) reg.110(10) (Income treated as capital—exceptions)*

With effect from January 1, 2022, reg.3(4) of the Social Security (Income and Capital Disregards) (Amendment) Regulations 2021 (SI 2021/1405) amended para.(10) by inserting the following after sub-para. (ab): **6.088**

"(ac) which is a child abuse payment;
(ad) which is a Windrush payment; or"

Those payments are defined in reg.1(3). See the entry for pp.684–685 for discussion of the nature of those payments. The "or" following sub-para. (ab), omitted in error in the main volume, has also been removed.

With effect from July 9, 2023, reg.3(4) of the Social Security (Income and Capital Disregards) (Amendment) Regulations 2023 (SI 2023/640) amended reg.110(10) by omitting "or" at the end of sub-para.(ad) and inserting the following:

"(ae) which is a Post Office compensation payment;"

Such payments are newly defined in reg.1(3), where there is now also an expanded definition of Grenfell Tower payments (see sub-para.(ab)). See the entry for pp.684–685 for the background.

With effect from October 27, 2023, reg.4(3)(a) of the Social Security (Habitual Residence and Past Presence, and Capital Disregards) (Amendment) Regulations 2023 (SI 2023/1144) amended reg.110(10)(c) by inserting ", the Victims of Overseas Terrorism Compensation Scheme" after "the National Emergencies Trust". That scheme is newly defined in reg.1(3). See the entry for pp.684–685 on income support for the background.

p.1027, *amendment to the Jobseeker's Allowance Regulations 1996 (SI 1996/207) reg.113(3B) (Notional capital—exceptions)*

With effect from January 1, 2022, reg.3(5) of the Social Security (Income and Capital Disregards) (Amendment) Regulations 2021 (SI 2021/1405) amended para.(3B) by substituting the following for "a payment of capital which is a Grenfell Tower payment": **6.089**

"any of the following payments of capital—

(a) a Grenfell Tower payment;
(b) a child abuse payment;
(c) a Windrush payment."

All of those payments are defined in reg.1(3). See the entry of pp.684–685 for discussion of the nature of child abuse and Windrush payments.

With effect from July 9, 2023, reg.3(5) of the Social Security (Income and Capital Disregards) (Amendment) Regulations 2023 (SI 2023/640) amended reg.113(3B) by inserting the following after sub-para.(c):

"(d) a Post Office compensation payment;
(e) a vaccine damage payment."

Such payments are newly defined in reg.1(3), where there is now also an expanded definition of Grenfell Tower payments (see sub-para.(a)). See the entry for pp.684–685 for the background.

With effect from October 27, 2023, reg.4(3)(b) of the Social Security (Habitual Residence and Past Presence, and Capital Disregards) (Amendment) Regulations 2023 (SI 2023/1144) amended reg.113(3A)(a) by inserting ", the Victims of Overseas Terrorism Compensation Scheme" after "the National Emergencies Trust". That scheme is newly defined in reg.1(3). See the entry for pp.684–685 on income support for the background.

pp.1029–1030, *annotation to the Jobseeker's Allowance Regulations 1996 (SI 1996/207) reg.113(1) (Notional capital—deprivation)*

6.090 *DB v DfC (JSA)* [2021] NICom 43 takes the same approach as set out in the main volume to the scope of the Northern Ireland equivalent (in identical terms) of reg.113(1). The claimant had been entitled to old style ESA. On November 25, 2016 the decision was given that she was not entitled from August 2015, apparently on the basis that, although she asserted that she had disposed of some £40,000 of capital that she said did not belong to her, it was her capital and she had not shown that she had disposed of it. She claimed old style JSA on September 14, 2017. On October 16, 2017 it was decided that she was not entitled, on the basis that her actual capital exceeded £16,000, despite her further assertions of having depleted bank accounts. A revision of that decision and submissions made on appeal were hopelessly confused as between actual and notional capital, but the decision of October 16, 2017 was never formally changed. The appeal tribunal found that the claimant had deprived herself of more than £40,000 in 2016 for the principal purpose of bringing her capital below the limits to obtain benefits including JSA, so that she was treated as having notional income over £16,000 after the application of the diminishing notional capital rule (reg.114). The Chief Commissioner held, as had been submitted by the DfC, that because reg.113(1) could only bite when the claimant's purpose was securing entitlement to or increasing the amount of old style JSA or income support, the appeal tribunal had failed to make the necessary findings of fact or show that it had applied the legally correct approach. It was inherently improbable that when depriving herself of capital while in receipt of ESA, more than a year before she claimed JSA, the claimant had possible entitlement to JSA in mind.

The decision also illustrates that on a new claim neither the decision-maker nor a tribunal on appeal is bound by the findings of fact on capital that have underpinned a decision of non-entitlement on capital grounds. The basis of the ESA decision, that the claimant as at that date still had actual capital of more than £40,000, did not have to be adopted on the JSA claim.

p.1054, *annotation to the Jobseeker's Allowance Regulations 1996 (SI 1996/207) reg.136(4) and (5) (Treatment of student loans and postgraduate loans)*

6.091 See the entry for p.539 on income support for details of the decision in *IB v Gravesham BC and SSWP (HB)* [2023] UKUT 193 (AAC); [2024]

P.T.S.R. 130 on when a claimant cannot acquire a loan by taking reasonable steps to do so.

p.1055, *amendment to the Jobseeker's Allowance Regulations 1996 (SI 1996/2077) reg.136C (Treatment of special support loans)*

With effect from April 1, 2024, reg.2 of the Social Security and Universal Credit (Migration of Tax Credit Claimants and Miscellaneous Amendments) Regulations 2024 (SI 2024/341) amended reg.136C by substituting the following for the existing text and heading: **6.092**

> **"Treatment of loans for specific purposes**
> **136C.** A loan under the Education (Student Support) Regulations 2011 or regulations made under section 73 of the Education (Scotland) Act 1980 that is intended to meet the cost of books, equipment, travel or childcare is to be disregarded as income."

The new form of reg.136C is intended to ensure that special support loans under a scheme to be introduced for full-time students by the Scottish government from the beginning of academic year 2024/25 are to be disregarded as income in same way as special support loans in England and Wales. Although the new form no longer refers to the definition of "special support loan" in reg.68 of the Education (Student Support) Regulations 2011, the restriction to loans intended (i.e., by necessary implication, intended by the awarding authority) to meet the cost of books, equipment, travel or childcare excludes loans under those regulations for other purposes. See reg.131 for the disregard of grants, as opposed to loans, for similar and other purposes.

pp.1059–1060, *amendments to the Jobseeker's Allowance Regulations 1996 (SI 1996/207) reg.140 (Hardship payments)*

With effect from July 26, 2021, Sch.3 para.4 of the Social Security (Scotland) Act 2018 (Disability Assistance for Children and Young People) (Consequential Modifications) Order 2021 (SI 2021/786) makes the following amendments to reg.140(1)(h): **6.093**

- in para.(i), after "Benefits Act", insert ", the care component of child disability payment at the highest or middle rate in accordance with regulation 11(5) of the DACYP Regulations";
- in para.(ii), after "disability living allowance", insert ", child disability payment";
- after para.(iii), insert "(iiia) has claimed child disability payment and has an award of the care component of child disability payment at the highest or middle rate in accordance with regulation 11(5) of the DACYP Regulations for a period commencing after the date on which the claim was made; or".

With effect from March 21, 2022, art.5 of the Social Security (Disability Assistance for Working Age People) (Consequential Amendments) Order 2022 (SI 2022/177) makes the following amendments to reg.140(1)(h):

- in para.(i):
  - after "DACYP Regulations" for "or" substitute ",";
  - after "the 2012 Act" insert ", the daily living component of adult disability payment at the standard or enhanced rate in accordance with regulation 5 of the Disability Assistance for Working Age People (Scotland) Regulations 2022";
- in para.(ii):
  - after "armed forces independence payment" for "or" substitute ",";
  - after "personal independence payment" insert "or adult disability payment";
- after para.(iv) insert "(iva) has claimed adult disability payment and has an award of the daily living component of adult disability payment at the standard or enhanced rate in accordance with regulation 5 of the Disability Assistance for Working Age People (Scotland) Regulations 2022 for a period commencing after the date on which that claim was made; or".

pp.1071–1072, *amendments to the Jobseeker's Allowance Regulations 1996 (SI 1996/207) reg.146A (Meaning of "couple in hardship")*

6.094 With effect from July 26, 2021, Sch.3 para.5 of the Social Security (Scotland) Act 2018 (Disability Assistance for Children and Young People) (Consequential Modifications) Order 2021 (SI 2021/786) makes the following amendments to reg.146A(1)(e):

- in para.(i), after "Benefits Act", insert ", the care component of child disability payment at the highest or middle rate in accordance with regulation 11(5) of the DACYP Regulations";
- in para.(ii), after "disability living allowance", insert ", child disability payment";
- after para.(iii), insert "(iiia) has claimed child disability payment and has an award of the care component of child disability payment at the highest or middle rate in accordance with regulation 11(5) of the DACYP Regulations for a period commencing after the date on which the claim was made; or".

With effect from March 21, 2022, art.5(5) of the Social Security (Disability Assistance for Working Age People) (Consequential Amendments) Order 2022 (SI 2022/177) makes the following amendments to reg.146A(1)(e):

- in para.(i):
  - after "armed forces independence payment", for "or" substitute ",";
  - after "the 2012 Act" insert ", or the daily living component of adult disability payment at the standard or enhanced rate in accordance with regulation 5 of the Disability Assistance for Working Age People (Scotland) Regulations 2022";
- in para.(ii):
  - after "armed forces independence payment", for "or" substitute ",";
  - after "personal independence payment" insert "or adult disability payment";

- after para.(iv) insert "(iva) has claimed adult disability payment and has an award of the daily living component at the standard or enhanced rate in accordance with regulation 5 of the Disability Assistance for Working Age People (Scotland) Regulations 2022 for a period commencing after the date on which that claim was made; or".

p.1080, *amendment to the Jobseeker's Allowance Regulations 1996 SI 1996/207), reg.150 (amount of a jobseeker's allowance payable)*

With effect from November 19, 2023, art.8 of the Carer's Assistance (Carer Support Payment) (Scotland) Regulations 2023 (Consequential Amendments) Order 2023 (SI 2023/1218) makes the following amendment to reg.150(2): 6.095

after "carer's allowance," insert "carer support payment,".

p.1081, *amendment to the Jobseeker's Allowance Regulations 1996 SI 1996/207), reg.153 (modification in the calculation of income),*

With effect from November 19, 2023, art.8 of the Carer's Assistance (Carer Support Payment) (Scotland) Regulations 2023 (Consequential Amendments) Order 2023 (SI 2023/1218) makes the following amendment to reg.153(c): 6.096

after "carer's allowance," insert "carer support payment,".

p.1086, *amendment to the Jobseeker's Allowance Regulations 1996 (SI 1996/207) reg.172 (Trade disputes: prescribed sum)*

With effect from April 8, 2024, art.27 of the Social Security Benefits Up-rating Order 2024 (SI 2024/242) substituted "£50.00" for "£47.00" (as had been in effect from April 10, 2023) in reg.172. 6.097

pp.1087–1088, *amendments to the Jobseeker's Allowance Regulations 1996 (SI 1996/207) Sch.A1 (Categories of members of a joint-claim couple who are not required to satisfy the conditions in section 1(2B)(b))*

With effect from July 26, 2021, Sch.3 para.6 of the Social Security (Scotland) Act 2018 (Disability Assistance for Children and Young People) (Consequential Modifications) Order 2021 (SI 2021/786) makes the following amendments to para.3(a) (member caring for another person): 6.098

- in para.(i), after "Benefits Act", insert ", the care component of child disability payment at the highest or middle rate in accordance with regulation 11(5) of the DACYP Regulations";
- in para.(iv), after "disability living allowance", insert ", child disability payment";
- after para.(v), insert "(va) the person being cared for ("P") has claimed entitlement to the care component of child disability payment in accordance with regulation 24 (when an application is to be treated as made and beginning of entitlement to assistance)

of the DACYP Regulations, an award at the highest or middle rate has been made in respect of P's claim, and where the period for which the award is payable has begun, P is in receipt of that payment;"

With effect from March 21, 2022, art.5(6) of the Social Security (Disability Assistance for Working Age People) (Consequential Amendments) Order 2022 (SI 2022/177) makes the following amendments to para.3(a) (member caring for another person):

- in para.3(a)(i) (member caring for another person):
  - after "armed forces independence payment" for "or" substitute ",";
  - after "the 2012 Act" insert "or the daily living component of adult disability payment at the standard or enhanced rate in accordance with regulation 5 of the Disability Assistance for Working Age People (Scotland) Regulations 2022";
- in para.3(a)(iv):
  - after "armed forces independence payment" for "or" substitute ",";
  - after "personal independence payment" insert "or adult disability payment";
- in para.3(a)(vi) omit "or" at the end; and
- after para.3(a)(vi) insert "(via) the person being cared for has claimed entitlement to the daily living component of adult disability payment in accordance with regulation 35 (when an application is to be treated as made and beginning of entitlement to assistance) of the Disability Assistance for Working Age People (Scotland) Regulations 2022, an award of the standard or enhanced rate of the daily living component has been made in respect of that claim and, where the period for which the award is payable has begun, that person is in receipt of that payment; or"

With effect from November 19, 2023, art.8 of the Carer's Assistance (Carer Support Payment) (Scotland) Regulations 2023 (Consequential Amendments) Order 2023 (SI 2023/1218) makes the following amendment to para.3(b):

after "carer's allowance," insert "or carer support payment".

p.1091, *amendments to the Jobseeker's Allowance Regulations 1996 (SI 1996/207) Sch.1 (Applicable amounts)*

6.099 Substitute the following for paras 3.479–3.508

Regulations 83 and 84(1)

"SCHEDULE 1

APPLICABLE AMOUNTS

[9 PART I

PERSONAL ALLOWANCES

1.—The weekly amounts specified in column (2) below in respect of each person or couple specified in column (1) shall be the weekly amounts specified for the purposes of regulations 83 [28 84(1), 86A and 86B] (applicable amounts and polygamous marriages). **3.479**

Column (1) *Person or Couple*	*Column (2)* *Amount*
(1) Single claimant aged— (a) except where head (b) or (c) of this sub-paragraph applies, less than 18; (b) less than 18 who falls within paragraph (2) of regulation 57 and who— (i) is a person to whom regulation 59, 60 or 61 applies [1 . . .]; or (ii) is the subject of a direction under section 16; (c) less than 18 who satisfies the condition in [33 paragraph 13(1)(a)] of Part 3; (d) not less than 18 but less than 25; (e) not less than 25.	1. (a) [56 £71.70]; (b) [56 £71.70]; (c) [56 £71.70]; (d) [56 £71.70]; (e) [56 £90.50];
(2) Lone parent aged— (a) except where head (b) or (c) of this sub-paragraph applies, less than 18; (b) less than 18 who falls within paragraph (2) of regulation 57 and who— (i) is a person to whom regulation 59, 60 or 61 applies [1 . . .]; or (ii) is the subject of a direction under section 16; (c) less than 18 who satisfies the condition in [33 paragraph 13(1)(a)] [2 of Part 3]; (d) not less than 18.	2. (a) [56 £71.70]; (b) [56 £71.70]; (c) [56 £71.70]; (d) [56 £90.50].
(3) Couple— (a) where both members are aged less than 18 and— (i) at least one of them is treated as responsible for a child; or (ii) had they not been members of a couple, each would have been a person to whom regulation 59, 60 or 61 (circumstances in which a person aged 16 or 17 is eligible for a jobseeker's allowance) applied or (iii) had they not been members of a couple, the claimant would have been a person to whom regulation 59, 60 or 61 (circumstances in which a person aged 16 or 17 is eligible for a	3. (a) [56 £108.30];

Column (1) *Person or Couple*	*Column (2)* *Amount*
jobseeker's allowance) applied and his partner satisfies the requirements for entitlement to income support [36 or an income-related employment and support allowance] other than the requirement to make a claim for it; or [1(iv) they are married [31 or civil partners]and one member a of the couple is person to whom regulation 59, 60 or 61 applies and the other member is registered in accordance with regulation 62; or (iva) they are married [31 or civil partners] and each member of the couple is a person to whom regulation 59, 60 or 61 applies; or] (v) there is a direction under section 16 (jobseeker's allowance in cases of severe hardship) in respect of each member; or (vi) there is a direction under section 16 in respect of one of them and the other is a person to whom regulation 59, 60 or 61 applies [1 . . .], or (vii) there is a direction under section 16 in respect of one of them and the other satisfies requirements for entitlement to income support [36 or an income-related employment and support allowance] other than the requirement to make a claim for it;	
(b) where both members are aged less than 18 and sub-paragraph (3)(a) does not apply but one member of the couple falls within paragraph (2) of regulation 57 and either— (i) is a person to whom regulation 59, 60 or 61 applies [1 . . .]; or (ii) is the subject of a direction under section 16 of the Act;	(b) [56 £71.70];
(c) where both members are aged less than 18 and neither head (a) nor (b) of sub-paragraph (3) applies but one member of the couple— (i) is a person to whom regulation 59, 60 or 61 applies [1 . . .]; or (ii) is the subject of a direction under section 16;	(c) [56 £71.70];
(d) where both members are aged less than 18 and none of heads (a), (b) or (c) of sub-paragraph (3) apply but one member of the couple is a person who satisfies the requirements of [33 paragraph 13(1)(a)];	(d) [56 £71.70];
[35 (e) where— (i) both members are aged not less than 18; or (ii) one member is aged not less than 18 and the other member is a person who is— (aa) under 18, and (bb) treated as responsible for a child;]	(e) [56 £142.75];
(f) where [35 paragraph (e) does not apply and] one member is aged not less than 18 and the other member is a person under 18 who— (i) is a person to whom regulation 59, 60 or 61 applies [1 . . .]; or (ii) is the subject of a direction under section 16; [38 or	(f) [56 £142.75];

Column (1) *Person or Couple*	*Column (2)* *Amount*
(iii) satisfies requirements for entitlement to income support or who would do so if he were not a member of a couple, other than the requirement to make a claim for it; or (iv) satisfies requirements for entitlement to an income-related employment and support allowance other than the requirement to make a claim for it;]	
(g) where one member is aged not less than 18 but less than 25 and the other member is a person under 18— (i) to whom none of the regulations 59 to 61 applies; or (ii) who is not the subject of a direction under section 16; and (iii) does not satisfy requirements for entitlement to income support [36 or an income-related employment and support allowance] disregarding the requirement to make a claim for it;	(g) [56 £71.70];
(h) where one member is aged not less than 25 and the other member is a person under 18— (i) to whom none of the regulations 59 to 61 applies; or (ii) is not the subject of a direction under section 16; and (iii) does not satisfy requirements for entitlement to income support [36 or an income-related employment and support allowance] disregarding the requirement to make a claim for it.	(h) [56 £90.50].
2.—[30 . . .]	
3.—[29 . . .]	

Part II

Family Premium

4.—[30 . . .] **3.480**

Part III

Premiums

5.—Except as provided in paragraph 6, the weekly premiums specified in Part IV of this Schedule shall for the purposes of regulations 83(e) and 84(1)(f), be applicable to a claimant who satisfies the condition specified in [4 15 paragraphs 9A] to 17 in respect of that premium. **3.481**

6.—Subject to paragraph 7, where a claimant satisfies the conditions in respect of more than one premium in this Part of this Schedule, only one premium shall be applicable to him and, if they are different amounts, the higher or highest amount shall apply.

[16 **7.**—(1) Subject to sub-paragraph (2), the following premiums, namely—

(a) a severe disability premium to which paragraph 15 applies;
(b) an enhanced disability premium to which paragraph 15A applies;
(c) [30 . . .]; and
(d) a carer premium in which paragraph 17 applies,

may be applicable in addition to any other premium which may apply under this Part of this Schedule.

(2) An enhanced disability premium in respect of a person shall not be applicable in addition to—

(a) a pensioner premium under paragraph 10 or 11; or

(b) a higher pensioner premium under paragraph 12.]

8.—(1) Subject to sub-paragraph (2) for the purposes of this Part of this Schedule, once a premium is applicable to a claimant under this Part, a person shall be treated as being in receipt of any benefit—

(a) in the case of a benefit to which the Social Security (Overlapping Benefits) Regulations 1979 applies, for any period during which, apart from the provisions of those Regulations, he would be in receipt of that benefit; [55 . . .]

[3(b) for any period spent by a claimant in undertaking a course of training or instruction provided or approved by the Secretary of State [35 . . .] under section 2 of the Employment and Training Act 1973, or by [37 Skills Development Scotland,] Scottish Enterprise or Highlands and Islands Enterprise under section 2 of the Enterprise and New Towns (Scotland) Act 1990 or for any period during which he is in receipt of a training allowance [55 . . . ; and

(c) in the case of carer support payment, for any period during which, apart from regulation 16 of the Carer's Assistance (Carer Support Payment) (Scotland) Regulations 2023, he would be in receipt of that benefit.]]

(2) For the purposes of the carer premium under paragraph 17, a person shall be treated as being in receipt of [24 carer's allowance] by virtue of sub-paragraph (1)(a) [55 or carer support payment by virtue of sub-paragraph (1)(c)] only if and for so long as the person in respect of whose care the allowance [48 or payment] has been claimed remains in receipt of attendance allowance, [46 the care component of disability living allowance at the highest or middle rate prescribed in accordance with section 72(3) of the Benefits Act [52 , the care component of child disability payment at the highest or middle rate prescribed in accordance with regulation 11(5) of the DACYP Regulations] [47 , armed forces independence payment] [53 ,] the daily living component of personal independence payment at the standard or enhanced rate prescribed in accordance with section 78(3) of the 2012 Act] [53 , or the daily living component of adult disability payment at the standard or enhanced rate prescribed in accordance with regulation 5 of the Disability Assistance for Working Age People (Scotland) Regulations 2022].

Lone Parent Premium

3.482 **9.**—[4 . . .]

[15 Bereavement Premium

3.483 **9A.**—[34 . . .]]

Pensioner premium for persons [40 over the qualifying age for state pension credit]

3.484 **10.**—The condition is that the claimant—

(a) is a single claimant or lone parent who has attained [40 the qualifying age for state pension credit]; or

(b) has attained [40 the qualifying age for state pension credit] and has a partner; or

(c) has a partner and the partner has attained [40 the qualifying age for state pension credit] but not the age of 75.

Pensioner premium where claimant's partner has attained the age of 75

3.485 **11.**—The condition is that the claimant has a partner who has attained the age of 75 but not the age of 80.

Higher Pensioner Premium

3.486 **12.**—(1) [33 Subject to sub-paragraph (5), the] condition is that—

(a) the claimant is a single claimant or lone parent who has attained [40 the qualifying age for state pension credit] and either—

(i) satisfies one of the additional conditions specified in paragraph 14(1)(a), (c), [51 (ca), (cb),] (e), (f) [51, (fa)] or (h); or

(ii) was entitled to either income support or income-based jobseeker's allowance [12, or was treated as being entitled to either of those benefits and the disability premium was or, as the case may be, would have been,] applicable to him in respect of a benefit week within 8 weeks of [40 the date he attained the qualifying age for state pension credit] and he has, subject to sub-paragraph (2), remained continuously entitled to one of those benefits since attaining that age; or

(b) the claimant has a partner and—
(i) the partner has attained the age of 80; or
(ii) the partner has attained [40 the qualifying age for state pension credit] but not the age of 80, and the additional conditions specified in paragraph 14 are satisfied in respect of him; or
(c) the claimant—
(i) has attained [40 the qualifying age for state pension credit];
[3(ii) satisfies the requirements of either sub-head (i) or (ii) of paragraph 12(1)(a); and]
(iii) has a partner.

(2) For the purposes of this paragraph and paragraph 14—
(a) once the higher pensioner premium is applicable to a claimant, if he then ceases, for a period of eight weeks or less, to be entitled to either income support or income-based jobseeker's allowance [12 or ceases to be treated as entitled to either of those benefits], he shall, on becoming re-entitled to either of those benefits, thereafter be treated as having been continuously entitled thereto;
(b) in so far as sub-paragraphs (1)(a)(ii) and (1)(c)(ii) are concerned, if a claimant ceases to be entitled to either income support or an income-based jobseeker's allowance [12 or ceases to be treated as entitled to either of those benefits] for a period not exceeding eight weeks which includes [40 the date he attained the qualifying age for state pension credit], he shall, on becoming re-entitled to either of those benefits, thereafter be treated as having been continuously entitled thereto.

[8(3) In this paragraph where a claimant's partner is a welfare to work beneficiary, sub-paragraphs (1)(a)(ii) and (2)(b) shall apply to him as if for the words "8 weeks" there were substituted the words "[32 104 weeks]".]

[12 (4) For the purposes of this paragraph, a claimant shall be treated as having been entitled to income support or to an income-based jobseeker's allowance throughout any period which comprises only days on which he was participating in an employment zone programme and was not entitled to—
(a) income support because, as a consequence of his participation in that programme, he was engaged in remunerative work or had income in excess of the claimant's applicable amount as prescribed in Part IV of the Income Support Regulations; or
(b) a jobseeker's allowance because, as a consequence of his participation in that programme, he was engaged in remunerative work or failed to satisfy the condition specified in section 2(1)(c) or in section 3(1)(a).]

[33 (5) The condition is not satisfied if—
(a) the claimant is a single claimant or a lone parent and (in either case) is a long-term patient;
(b) the claimant is a member of a couple or polygamous marriage and each member of the couple or polygamous marriage is a long-term patient; or
(c) the claimant is a member of a couple or a polygamous marriage and a member of that couple or polygamous marriage is—
(i) a long-term patient; and
(ii) the only member of the couple or polygamous marriage to whom sub-paragraph (1)(b) or (c) refers.]

Disability Premium

13. [33—(1) Subject to sub-paragraph (2), the] condition is that the claimant— 3.487
(a) is a single claimant or lone parent who has not attained [40 the qualifying age for state pension credit] and satisfies any one of the additional conditions specified in paragraph 14(1)(a), (c), [51 (ca), (cb),] (e), (f) [51, (fa)] or (h); or
(b) has not attained [40 the qualifying age for state pension credit], has a partner and the claimant satisfies any one of the additional conditions specified in paragraph 14(1)(a), (c), [51 (ca), (cb),] (e), (f) [51, (fa)] or (h); or
(c) has a partner and the partner has not attained [40 the qualifying age for state pension credit] and also satisfies any one of the additional conditions specified in paragraph 14.

[33 (2) The condition is not satisfied if—
(a) the claimant is a single claimant or a lone parent and (in either case) is a long-term patient;
(b) the claimant is a member of a couple or polygamous marriage and each member of the couple or polygamous marriage is a long-term patient; or

(c) the claimant is a member of a couple or polygamous marriage and a member of that couple or polygamous marriage—
(i) is a long-term patient; and
(ii) is the only member of the couple or polygamous marriage to whom the condition in sub-paragraph (1)(b) or (c) refers.]

Additional conditions for Higher Pensioner and Disability Premium

3.488 **14.**—(1) The additional conditions specified in this paragraph are that—
(a) the claimant or, as the case may be, his partner, is in receipt [25 the disability element or the severe disability element of working tax credit as specified in regulation 20(1)(b) and (f) of the Working Tax Credit (Entitlement and Maximum Rate) Regulations 2002] or mobility supplement;
(b) the claimant's partner is in receipt of severe disablement allowance;
(c) the claimant or, as the case may be, his partner, is in receipt of attendance allowance or disability living allowance or is a person whose disability living allowance is payable, in whole or in part, to another in accordance with regulation 44 of the Claims and Payments Regulations (payment of disability living allowance on behalf of third party);
[46 (ca) the claimant or, as the case may be, his partner, is in receipt of personal independence payment or is a person whose personal independence payment is payable, in whole or in part, to another in accordance with regulation 58(2) of the Universal Credit etc. Claims and Payments Regulations (payment to another person on the claimant's behalf);]
[53 (caa) the claimant or, as the case may be, the claimant's partner, is in receipt of adult disability payment or is a person whose adult disability payment is payable, in whole or in part, to another in accordance with regulation 33 of the Disability Assistance for Working Age People (Scotland) Regulations 2022 (making payments);]
[47 (cb) the claimant or, as the case may be, the claimant's partner, is in receipt of armed forces independence payment or is a person whose armed forces independence payment is payable, in whole or in part, to another in accordance with article 24D of the Armed Forces and Reserve Forces (Compensation Scheme) Order 2011;]
(d) the claimant's partner is in receipt of long-term incapacity benefit or is a person to whom section 30B(4) of the Benefits Act (long term rate of incapacity benefit payable to those who are terminally ill) applies;
(e) the claimant or, as the case may be, his partner, has an invalid carriage or other vehicle provided to him by the Secretary of State under section 5(2)(a) of and Schedule 2 to the National Health Service Act 1977 or under section 46 of the National Health Service (Scotland) Act 1978 or provided by the Department of Health and Social Services for Northern Ireland under article 30(1) of the Health and Personal Social Services (Northern Ireland) Order 1972, or receives payments by way of grant from the Secretary of State under paragraph 2 of Schedule 2 to the Act of 1977 (additional provisions as to vehicles) or, in Scotland, under section 46 of the Act of 1978;
(f) the claimant or, as the case may be, his partner, is a person who is entitled to the mobility component of disability living allowance but to whom the component is not payable in accordance with regulation 42 of the Claims and Payments Regulations (cases where disability living allowance not payable);
[46 (fa) the claimant or, as the case may be, his partner, is a person who is entitled to the mobility component of personal independence payment but to whom the component is not payable in accordance with regulation 61 of the Universal Credit etc. Claims and Payments Regulations (cases where mobility component of personal independence payment not payable);]
[53 (fb) the claimant or, as the case may be, the claimant's partner, is a person who is entitled to the mobility component of adult disability payment but to whom the component is not payable in accordance with regulation 34(6) of the Disability Assistance for Working Age People (Scotland) Regulations 2022 (amount and form of adult disability payment);]
(g) the claimant's partner was either—
(i) in receipt of long term incapacity benefit under section 30A(5) of the Benefits Act immediately before attaining pensionable age and he is still alive;
(ii) entitled to attendance allowance or disability living allowance but payment of that benefit was suspended in accordance with regulations under section 113(2) of the Benefits Act or otherwise abated as a consequence of [2 the partner] becoming a patient within the meaning of regulation 85(4) (special cases), [53 ; . . .]

(iii) entitled to personal independence payment but no amount is payable in accordance with regulations made under section 86(1) (hospital in-patients) of the 2012 Act] [53 ; or

(iv) entitled to adult disability payment but no amount is payable in accordance with regulation 28 (effect of admission to hospital on ongoing entitlement to Adult Disability Payment) of the Disability Assistance for Working Age People (Scotland) Regulations 2022;]

and [53 in any of the cases described in sub-paragraphs (i) to (iv),]the higher pensioner premium or disability premium had been applicable to the claimant or his partner;

[48 (h) the claimant or, as the case may be, his partner, is certified as severely sight impaired or blind by a consultant ophthalmologist.]

[48 (2) For the purposes of sub-paragraph (1)(h), a person who has ceased to be certified as severely sight impaired or blind on regaining his eyesight shall nevertheless be treated as severely sight impaired or blind, as the case may be, and as satisfying the additional condition set out in that sub-paragraph for a period of 28 weeks following the date on which he ceased to be so certified.]

Severe Disability Premium

15.—(1) In the case of a single claimant, a lone parent or a claimant who is treated as having no partner in consequence of sub-paragraph (3), the condition is that— **3.489**

(a) he is in receipt of attendance allowance [46 , the care component of disability living allowance at the highest or middle rate prescribed in accordance with section 72(3) of the Benefits Act [47 , armed forces independence payment] [53 ,] the daily living component of personal independence payment at the standard or enhanced rate in accordance with section 78(3) of the 2012 Act] [53 , or the daily living component of adult disability payment at the standard or enhanced rate in accordance with regulation 5 of the Disability Assistance for Working Age People (Scotland) Regulations 2022]; and

(b) subject to sub-paragraph (4), there are no non-dependants aged 18 or over normally residing with him or with whom he is normally residing; and

[11(c) no person is entitled to, and in receipt of, [24 a carer's allowance] under section 70 of the Benefits Act [55 or has an award of universal credit which includes the carer element] in respect of caring for him;]

(2) Where the claimant has a partner, the condition is that—

(a) the claimant is in receipt of attendance allowance [46 , the care component of disability living allowance at the highest or middle rate prescribed in accordance with section 72(3) of the Benefits Act [47 , armed forces independence payment] [53 ,] the daily living component of personal independence payment at the standard or enhanced rate in accordance with section 78(3) of the 2012 Act] [53 , or the daily living component of adult disability payment at the standard or enhanced rate in accordance with regulation 5 of the Disability Assistance for Working Age People (Scotland) Regulations 2022]; and

(b) the partner is also in receipt of a qualifying benefit, or if he is a member of a polygamous marriage, all the partners of that marriage are in receipt of a qualifying benefit; and

(c) subject to sub-paragraph (4), there is no non-dependant aged 18 or over normally residing with him or with whom he is normally residing; and

(d) either—

(i) [11 no person is entitled to, and in receipt of, [24 a carer's allowance] under section 70 of the Benefits Act [55 or has an award of universal credit which includes the carer element] in respect of] caring for either member of the couple or all the members of the polygamous marriage; or

(ii) a person is engaged in caring for one member (but not both members) of the couple, or one or more but not all members of the polygamous marriage, and in consequence is [11 entitled to] [24 a carer's allowance] under section 70 of the Benefits Act [55 or carer support payment] [50 or has an award of universal credit which includes the carer element].

(3) Where the claimant has a partner who does not satisfy the condition in sub-paragraph (2)(b), and that partner is [48 severely sight impaired or blind or treated as severely sight impaired or blind] within the meaning of paragraph 14(1)(h) and (2), that partner shall be treated for the purposes of sub-paragraph (2) as if he were not a partner of the claimant.

(4) The following persons shall not be regarded as a non-dependant for the purposes of sub-paragraphs (1)(b) and (2)(c)—

(a) a person in receipt of attendance allowance [46 , the care component of disability living allowance at the highest or middle rate prescribed in accordance with section 72(3) of the Benefits Act [47 , armed forces independence payment] [53 ,] the daily living component of personal independence payment at the standard or enhanced rate in accordance with section 78(3) of the 2012 Act] [53 , or the daily living component of adult disability payment at the standard or enhanced rate in accordance with regulation 5 of the Disability Assistance for Working Age People (Scotland) Regulations 2022];

(b) subject to sub-paragraph (6), a person who joins the claimant's household for the first time in order to care for the claimant or his partner and immediately before so joining the claimant or his partner satisfied the condition in sub-paragraph (1) or, as the case may be, (2);

(c) a person who is [48 severely sight impaired or blind or treated as severely sight impaired or blind] within the meaning of paragraph 14(1)(h) and (2).

(5) For the purposes of sub-paragraph (2), a person shall be treated [11 . . .] (a) [11 as being in receipt of] attendance allowance, or the care component of disability living allowance at the highest or middle rate prescribed in accordance with section 72(3) of the Benefits Act if he would, but for his being a patient for a period exceeding 28 days, be so in receipt;

[46 (aa) as being in receipt of the daily living component of personal independence payment at the standard or enhanced rate in accordance with section 78 of the 2012 Act if he would, but for regulations made under section 86(1) (hospital in-patients) of the 2012 Act, be so in receipt;]

[53 (ab) as being in receipt of the daily living component of adult disability payment at the standard or enhanced rate in accordance with regulation 5 of the Disability Assistance for Working Age People (Scotland) Regulations 2022 if they would, but for regulation 28 (effect of admission to hospital on ongoing entitlement to Adult Disability Payment) of those Regulations be so in receipt;]

[11(b) as being entitled to and in receipt of [24 a carer's allowance] [55 or carer support payment] [50 or having an award of universal credit which includes the carer element] if he would, but for the person for whom he was caring being a patient in hospital for a period exceeding 28 days, be so entitled and in receipt [50 of carer's allowance or have such an award of universal credit].]

(6) Sub-paragraph (4)(b) shall apply only for the first 12 weeks following the date on which the person to whom that provision applies first joins the claimant's household.

(7) For the purposes of sub-paragraph (1)(c) and (2)(d), no account shall be taken of an award of [24 carer's allowance] [55 carer support payment] [50 or universal credit which includes the carer element] to the extent that payment of such an award is backdated for a period before [34 the date on which the award is first paid].

(8) A person shall be treated as satisfying this condition if he would have satisfied the condition specified for a severe disability premium in income support in paragraph 13 of Schedule 2 to the Income Support Regulations by virtue only of regulations 4 to 6 of the Income Support (General) Amendment (No. 6) Regulations 1991 (savings provisions in relation to severe disability premium) and for the purposes of determining whether in the particular case regulation 4 of those Regulations had ceased to apply in accordance with regulation 5(2)(a) of those Regulations, a person who is entitled to an income-based jobseeker's allowance shall be treated as entitled to income support.

[20 (9) In sub-paragraphs (1)(c) and (2)(d), references to a person being in receipt of [24 a carer's allowance] [50 or as having an award of universal credit which includes the carer element] shall include references to a person who would have been in receipt of that allowance [50 or had such an award] but for the application of a restriction under section [39 6B or] 7 of the Social Security Fraud Act 2001 (loss of benefit provisions).]

[50 (10) For the purposes of this paragraph, a person has an award of universal credit which includes the carer element if the person has an award of universal credit which includes an amount which is the carer element under regulation 29 of the Universal Credit Regulations 2013.]

[16 Enhanced disability premium

3.490 **15A.**—[46 (1) Subject to sub-paragraph (2), the condition is that—

(a) the claimant; or

(b) the claimant's partner (if any), is a person who has not attained the qualifying age for state pension credit and is a person to whom sub-paragraph (1ZA) applies.

(1ZA) This sub-paragraph applies to the person mentioned in sub-paragraph (1) where—

(a) the care component of disability living allowance is, or would, but for a suspension of benefit in accordance with regulations under section 113(2) of the Benefits Act or but for an abatement as a consequence of hospitalisation, be payable to that person at the highest rate prescribed under section 72(3) of the Benefits Act; or

[52 (aa) the care component of child disability payment is payable to that person at the highest rate in accordance with regulation 11(5) of the DACYP Regulations; or]
(b) the daily living component of personal independence payment is, or would, but for a suspension of benefits in accordance with regulations under section 86(1) (hospital in-patients) of the 2012 Act, be payable to that person at the enhanced rate in accordance with section 78(2) of the 2012 Act] [47 ; or
[53 (ba) the daily living component of adult disability payment is, or would, but regulation 28 (effect of admission to hospital on ongoing entitlement to Adult Disability Payment) of the Disability Assistance for Working Age People (Scotland) Regulations 2022, be payable to that person at the enhanced rate in accordance with regulation 5 of those Regulations]
(c) armed forces independence payment is payable to that person.]

[42 (1A) Where the condition in sub-paragraph (1) ceases to be satisfied because of the death of a child or young person, the condition is that the claimant is entitled to child benefit in respect of that person under section 145A of the Benefits Act (entitlement after death of child or qualifying young person).]

[33 (2) The condition is not satisfied where the person to whom sub-paragraph (1) refers is—
(a) a child or young person—
(i) whose capital if calculated in accordance with Part 8 of these Regulations in like manner as for the claimant, except as provided in regulation 106(1), would exceed £3,000; or
(ii) who is a long-term patient;
(b) a single claimant or a lone parent and (in either case) is a long-term patient;
(c) a member of a couple or polygamous marriage and each member of the couple or polygamous marriage is a long-term patient; or
(d) a member of a couple or polygamous marriage who is—
(i) a long-term patient; and
(ii) the only member of the couple or polygamous marriage to whom sub-paragraph (1) refers.]]

Disabled Child Premium

16.—[30 . . . 33] 3.491

Carer Premium

17.—(1) Subject to sub-paragraphs (3) and (4), the condition is that the claimant or his partner is, or both of them are, [11 entitled to] [24 a carer's allowance] under section 70 of the Benefits Act [55 or carer support payment]. 3.492

(2) [28 . . .]

[23 (3) Where a carer premium is awarded but—
(a) the person in respect of whose care the [24 carer's allowance] [55 or carer support payment] has been awarded dies; or
(b) in any other case the person in respect of whom a carer premium has been awarded ceases to be entitled [28 . . .] to [24 a carer's allowance] [55 or carer support payment], the condition for the award of the premium shall be treated as satisfied for a period of eight weeks from the relevant date specified in sub-paragraph (3A) below.

(3A) The relevant date for the purposes of sub-paragraph (3) above shall be—
(a) [28 where sub-paragraph (3)(a) applies,] the Sunday following the death of the person in respect of whose care [24 a carer's allowance] [55 or carer support payment] has been awarded or the date of death if the death occurred on a Sunday;
(b) [28 . . .]
(c) in any other case, the date of which the person who has been entitled to [24 a carer's allowance] [55 or carer support payment] ceases to be entitled to that allowance [55 or payment].]

(4) Where a person who has been entitled to [24 a carer's allowance] [55 or carer support payment] ceases to be entitled to that allowance [55 or payment] and makes a claim for a jobseeker's allowance, the condition for the award of the carer premium shall be treated as satisfied for a period of eight weeks from the date on which—
[23(a) the person in respect of whose care the [24 carer's allowance] [55 or carer support payment] has been awarded dies;
(b) [28 . . .]
[28 (c) in any other case, the person who has been entitled to a carer's allowance [55 or carer support payment] ceased to be entitled to that allowance [55 or payment].]]

Persons in receipt of concessionary payments

3.493 **18.**—For the purpose of determining whether a premium is applicable to a person under paragraphs 14 to 17, any concessionary payment made to compensate that person for the non-payment of any benefit mentioned in those paragraphs shall be treated as if it were a payment of that benefit.

Person in receipt of benefit

3.494 **19.**—For the purposes of this Part of this Schedule, a person shall be regarded as being in receipt of any benefit if, and only if, it is paid in respect of him and shall be so regarded only for any period in respect of which that benefit is paid.

PART IV

WEEKLY AMOUNTS OF PREMIUMS SPECIFIED IN PART III

Premium	*Amount*
20.—(1) [4 . . .]	(1) [4 . . .]
(1A) [34 . . .];	(1A) [34 . . .];
(2) Pensioner premium for persons [40 who have attained the qualifying age for state pension credit]— (a) where the claimant satisfies the condition in paragraph 10(a); (b) where the claimant satisfies the condition in paragraph 10(b). (c) where the claimant satisfies the condition in paragraph 10(c).	(2) (a) [57 £127.65]; (b) [57 £190.70]; (c) [57 £190.70];
(3) Pensioner premium for claimants whose partner has attained the age of 75 where the claimant satisfies the condition in paragraph 11;	(3) [57 £190.70];
(4) Higher Pensioner Premium— (a) where the claimant satisfies the condition in paragraph 12(1)(a); (b) where the claimant satisfies the condition in paragraph 12(1)(b) or (c).	(4) (a) [57 £127.65]; (b) [57 £190.70];
(5) Disability Premium— (a) where the claimant satisfies the condition in [33 paragraph 13(1)(a)]; (b) where the claimant satisfies the condition in [33 paragraph 13(1)(b) or (c)].	(5) (a) [57 £42.50]; (b) [57 £60.60].
(6) Severe Disability Premium— (a) where the claimant satisfies the condition in paragraph 15(1); (b) where the claimant satisfies the condition in paragraph 15(2)— (i) if there is someone in receipt of [24 a carer's allowance] or [2 if any partner of the claimant] satisfies that condition by virtue of paragraph 15(5); (ii) if no-one is in receipt of such an allowance.	(6) (a) [57 £81.50]; (b) (i) [57 £81.50] (ii) [57 £163.00]
(7) [30 . . .]	(7) [30 . . .]
(8) Carer Premium.	(8) [57 £45.60] in respect of each person who satisfied the condition specified in paragraph 17.

Premium	*Amount*
[16 (9) Enhanced disability premium where the conditions in paragraph 15A are satisfied.]	[16 (9) (a) [30 . . .] (b) [57 £20.85] in respect of each person who is neither— (i) a child or young person; nor (ii) a member of a couple or a polygamous marriage, respect of whom the in conditions specified in paragraph 15A are satisfied; (c) [57 £29.75] where the claimant is a member of a couple or a polygamous marriage and the conditions specified in paragraph 15A are satisfied in respect of a member of that couple or polygamous marriage.]

[14 Part IVA

Premiums for Joint-claim Couples

20A.—Except as provided in paragraph 20B, the weekly premium specified in Part IVB of this Schedule shall, for the purposes of regulations 86A(c) and 86B(d), be applicable to a joint-claim couple where either or both members of a joint-claim couple satisfy the condition specified in paragraphs 20E to 20J in respect of that premium. 3.497

20B.—Subject to paragraph 20C, where a member of a joint-claim couple satisfies the conditions in respect of more than one premium in this Part of this Schedule, only one premium shall be applicable to the joint-claim couple in respect of that member and, if they are different amounts, the higher or highest amount shall apply.

[16 **20C.**—(1) Subject to sub-paragraph (2), the following premiums, namely—

(a) a severe disability premium to which paragraph 20I applies;
(b) an enhanced disability premium to which paragraph 20IA applies; and
(c) a carer premium to which paragraph 20J applies,

may be applicable in addition to any other premium which may apply under this Part of this Schedule.

(2) An enhanced disability premium in respect of a person shall not be applicable in addition to—

(a) a pensioner premium under paragraph 20E; or
(b) a higher pensioner premium under paragraph 20F.]

20D.—(1) Subject to sub-paragraph (2) for the purposes of this Part of this Schedule, once a premium is applicable to a joint-claim couple under this Part, a person shall be treated as being in receipt of any benefit—

(a) in the case of a benefit to which the Social Security (Overlapping Benefits) Regulations 1979 applies, for any period during which, apart from the provisions of those Regulations, he would be in receipt of that benefit; [55 . . .]
(b) for any period spent by a person in undertaking a course of training or instruction provided or approved by the Secretary of State under section 2 of the Employment and Training Act 1973, or by [37 Skills Development Scotland,] Scottish Enterprise or Highlands and Islands Enterprise under section 2 of the Enterprise and New Towns (Scotland) Act 1990, or for any period during which he is in receipt of a training allowance [55 ; and
(c) in the case of carer support payment, for any period during which, apart from regulation 16 of the Carer's Assistance (Carer Support Payment) (Scotland) Regulations 2023, he would be in receipt of that benefit.]

(2) For the purposes of the carer premium under paragraph 20J, a person shall be treated as being in receipt of [24 carer's allowance] by virtue of sub-paragraph (1)(a) [55 or carer support payment by virtue of sub-paragraph (1)(c)] only if and for so long as the person in respect of

whose care the allowance [55 or payment] has been claimed remains in receipt of attendance allowance, [46 the care component of disability living allowance at the highest or middle rate prescribed in accordance with section 72(3) of the Benefits Act [52 or the care component of child disability payment at the highest or middle rate in accordance with regulation 11(5) of the DACYP Regulations]or the daily living component of personal independence payment at the standard or enhanced rate in accordance with section 78(3) of the 2012 Act [53 , the daily living component of adult disability payment at the standard or enhanced rate in accordance with regulation 5 of the [54 Disability Assistance for Working Age People (Scotland) Regulations 2022] [47 or armed forces independence payment]].

Pensioner premium where one member of a joint-claim couple has attained [40 the qualifying age for state pension credit]

3.498 **20E.**—The condition is that one member of a joint-claim couple has attained [40 the qualifying age for state pension credit] but not the age of 75.

Higher Pensioner Premium

3.499 **20F.**—(1) [33 Subject to sub-paragraph (5), the] condition is that one member of a joint claim couple—

(a) has attained [40 the qualifying age for state pension credit] but not the age of 80, and either the additional conditions specified in paragraph 20H are satisfied in respect of him; or

(b) has attained [40 the qualifying age for state pension credit] and—

(i) was entitled to or was treated as entitled to either income support or an income-based jobseeker's allowance and the disability premium was or, as the case may be, would have been applicable to him in respect of a benefit week within 8 weeks of [40 the date he attained the qualifying age for state pension credit] and he has, subject to sub-paragraph (2), remained continuously entitled to one of those benefits since attaining that age; or

(ii) was a member of a joint-claim couple who had been entitled to, or who had been treated as entitled to, a joint-claim jobseeker's allowance and the disability premium was or, as the case may be, would have been applicable to that couple in respect of a benefit week within 8 weeks of [40 the date either member of that couple attained the qualifying age for state pension credit] and the couple have, subject to that sub-paragraph (2), remained continuously entitled to a joint claim jobseeker's allowance since that member attained that age.

(2) For the purpose of this paragraph and paragraph 20H—

(a) once the higher pensioner premium is applicable to a joint-claim couple, if that member then ceases, for a period of 8 weeks or less, to be entitled or treated as entitled to either income support or income-based jobseeker's allowance or that couple cease to be entitled to or treated as entitled to a joint-claim jobseeker's allowance, he shall or, as the case may be, that couple shall, on becoming re-entitled to any of those benefits, thereafter be treated as having been continuously entitled thereto;

(b) in so far as sub-paragraph (1)(b)(i) or (ii) is concerned, if a member of a joint-claim couple ceases to be entitled or treated as entitled to either income support or an income-based jobseeker's allowance or that couple cease to be entitled to or treated as entitled to a joint-claim jobseeker's allowance for a period not exceeding 8 weeks which includes [40 the date either member of that couple attained the qualifying age for state pension credit], he shall or, as the case may be, the couple shall, on becoming re-entitled to either of those benefits, thereafter be treated as having been continuously entitled thereto.

(3) In this paragraph, where a member of a joint-claim couple is a welfare to work beneficiary, sub-paragraphs (1)(b)(i) and (2)(b) shall apply to him as if for the words "8 weeks" there were substituted the words "[32104 weeks]".

(4) For the purposes of this paragraph, a member of a joint-claim couple shall be treated as having been entitled to income support or to an income-based jobseeker's allowance or the couple of which he is a member shall be treated as having been entitled to a joint-claim jobseeker's allowance throughout any period which comprises only days on which a member was participating in an employment zone scheme and was not entitled to—

(a) income support because, as a consequence of his participation in that scheme, he was engaged in remunerative work or had income in excess of the claimant's applicable amount as prescribed in Part IV of the Income Support Regulations; or

(b) a jobseeker's allowance because, as a consequence of his participation in that scheme, he was engaged in remunerative work or failed to satisfy the condition specified in section 2(1)(c) or the couple of which he was a member failed to satisfy the condition in section 3A(1)(a).

[33 (5) The condition is not satisfied if the member of the joint-claim couple to whom sub-paragraph (1) refers is a long-term patient.]

[33 Disability Premium

20G.—(1) Subject to sub-paragraph (2), the condition is that a member of a joint-claim couple has not attained [40 the qualifying age for state pension credit] and satisfies any one of the additional conditions specified in paragraph 20H. **3.500**

(2) The condition is not satisfied if—

(a) paragraph (1) only refers to one member of a joint-claim couple and that member is a long-term patient; or

(b) paragraph (1) refers to both members of a joint-claim couple and both members of the couple are long-term patients.]

Additional conditions for Higher Pensioner and Disability Premium

20H.—(1) The additional conditions specified in this paragraph are that a member of a joint-claim couple— **3.501**

(a) is in receipt of [26 the disability element or the severe disability element of working tax credit as specified in regulation 20(1)(b) and (f) of the Working Tax Credit (Entitlement and Maximum Rate) Regulations 2002] or mobility supplement;

(b) is in receipt of severe disablement allowance;

(c) is in receipt of attendance allowance or disability living allowance or is a person whose disability living allowance is payable, in whole or in part, to another in accordance with regulation 44 of the Claims and Payments Regulations (payment of disability living allowance on behalf of third party);

[46 (ca) is in receipt of personal independence payment or is a person whose personal independence payment is payable, in whole or in part, to another in accordance with regulation 58(2) of the Universal Credit etc. Claims and Payments Regulations (payment to another person on the claimant's behalf);]

[53 (caa) is in receipt of adult disability payment or is a person whose adult disability payment is payable, in whole or in part, to another in accordance with regulation 33 of the Disability Assistance for Working Age People (Scotland) Regulations 2022 (making payments);]

[47 (cb) is in receipt of armed forces independence payment or is a person whose armed forces independence payment is payable, in whole or in part, to another in accordance with article 24D of the Armed Forces and Reserve Forces (Compensation Scheme) Order 2011;]

(d) is in receipt of long-term incapacity benefit or is a person to whom section 30B(4) of the Benefits Act (long-term rate of incapacity benefit payable to those who are terminally ill) applies;

(e) has been entitled to statutory sick pay, has been incapable of work or has been treated as incapable of work for a continuous period of not less than—

(i) 196 days in the case of a member of a joint-claim couple who is terminally ill within the meaning of section 30B(4) of the Benefits Act; or

(ii) 364 days in any other case,

and for these purposes, any two or more periods of entitlement or incapacity separated by a break of not more than 56 days shall be treated as one continuous period;

[36 (ee) has had limited capability for work or has been treated as having limited capability for work for a continuous period of not less than—

(i) 196 days in the case of a member of a joint-claim couple who is terminally ill within the meaning of regulation 2(1) of the Employment and Support Allowance Regulations; or

(ii) 364 days in any other case,

and for these purposes any two or more periods of limited capability for work separated by a break of not more than 12 weeks is to be treated as one continuous period;]

(f) has an invalid carriage or other vehicle provided to him by the Secretary of State under section 5(2)(a) of, and Schedule 2 to, the National Health Service Act 1977 or under section 46 of the National Health Service (Scotland) Act 1978 or provided by the Department of Health and Social Services for Northern Ireland under article 30(1) of the Health and Personal Social Services (Northern Ireland) Order 1972, or receives payments by way of grant from the Secretary of State under paragraph 2 of Schedule 2 to the Act of 1977 (additional provisions as to vehicles) or, in Scotland, under section 46 of the Act of 1978;

(g) is a person who is entitled to the mobility component of disability living allowance but to whom the component is not payable in accordance with regulation 42 of the Claims and Payments Regulations (cases where disability living allowance not payable);

[46 (ga) is a person who is entitled to the mobility component of personal independence payment but to whom the component is not payable in accordance with regulation 61 of the Universal Credit etc. Claims and Payments Regulations (cases where mobility component of personal independence payment not payable);]

[53 (gb) is a person who is entitled to the mobility component of adult disability payment but to whom the component is not payable in accordance with regulation 34(6) of the Disability Assistance for Working Age People (Scotland) Regulations 2022 (amount and form of adult disability payment);]

(h) was either—

(i) in receipt of long-term incapacity benefit under section 30A(5) of the Benefits Act immediately before attaining pensionable age and he is still alive; or

(ii) entitled to attendance allowance or disability living allowance but payment of that benefit was suspended in accordance with regulations under section 113(2) of the Benefits Act or otherwise abated as a consequence of either member of the joint-claim couple becoming a patient within the meaning of regulation 85(4) (special cases), [46 [53 . . .]

(iii) entitled to personal independence payment but no amount is payable in accordance with regulations under section 86(1) (hospital in-patients) of the 2012 Act,] [53 or

(iv) entitled to adult disability payment but no amount is payable in accordance with regulation 28 (effect of admission to hospital on ongoing entitlement to Adult [54 Disability Payment) of the Disability Assistance for Working Age People (Scotland) Regulations 2022,]

and [53 in any of the cases described in paragraphs (i) to (iv)], the higher pensioner premium or disability premium had been applicable to the joint-claim couple; or

[48 (l) is certified as severely sight impaired or blind by a consultant ophthalmologist.]

(2) [41 . . . [32 . . .]]

[48 (3) For the purposes of sub-paragraph (1)(i), a person who has ceased to be certified as severely sight impaired or blind on regaining his eyesight shall nevertheless be treated as severely sight impaired or blind, as the case may be, and as satisfying the additional condition set out in that sub-paragraph for a period of 28 weeks following the date on which he ceased to be so certified.]

Severe Disability Premium

3.502 **20I.**—(1) The condition is that—

(a) a member of a joint-claim couple is in receipt of attendance allowance [46 , the care component of disability living allowance at the highest or middle rate prescribed in accordance with section 72(3) of the Benefits Act [47 , armed forces independence payment] [53 ,] the daily living component of personal independence payment at the standard or enhanced rate in accordance with section 78(3) of the 2012 Act] [53 , or the daily living component of adult disability payment at the standard or enhanced rate in accordance with regulation 5 of the Disability Assistance for Working Age People (Scotland) Regulations 2022]; and

(b) the other member is also in receipt of such an allowance, or if he is a member of a polygamous marriage, all the partners of that marriage are in receipt of a qualifying benefit; and

(c) subject to sub-paragraph (3), there is no non-dependant aged 18 or over normally residing with the joint-claim couple or with whom they are normally residing; and

(d) either—

(i) no person is entitled to, and in receipt of, [24 a carer's allowance] [55 or carer support payment] under section 70 of the Benefits Act [50 or has an award of universal credit which includes the carer element] in respect of caring for either member or the couple or all the members of the polygamous marriage; or

(ii) a person is engaged in caring for one member (but not both members) of the couple, or one or more but not all members of the polygamous marriage, and in consequence is entitled to [24 a carer's allowance] under section 70 of the Benefits Act [55 or carer support payment] [50 or has an award of universal credit which includes the carer element].

(2) Where the other member does not satisfy the condition in sub-paragraph (1)(b), and that member is [48 severely sight impaired or blind or treated as severely sight impaired or blind] within the meaning of paragraph 20H(1)(i) and (2), that member shall be treated for the purposes of sub-paragraph (1) as if he were not a member of the couple.

(3) The following persons shall not be regarded as non-dependant for the purposes of sub-paragraph (1)(c)—

(a) a person in receipt of attendance allowance [46 , the care component of disability living allowance at the highest or middle rate prescribed in accordance with section 72(3) of the Benefits Act [47 , armed forces independence payment] [53 ,] the daily living component of personal independence payment at the standard or enhanced rate in accordance with section 78(3) of the 2012 Act] [53 , or the daily living component of adult disability payment at the standard or enhanced rate in accordance with regulation 5 of the Disability Assistance for Working Age People (Scotland) Regulations 2022];

(b) subject to sub-paragraph (5), a person who joins the joint-claim couple's household for the first time in order to care for a member of a joint claim couple and immediately before so joining, that member satisfied the condition in sub-paragraph (1);

(c) a person who is [48 severely sight impaired or blind or treated as severely sight impaired or blind] within the meaning of paragraph 20H(1)(i) and (2).

(4) For the purposes of sub-paragraph (1), a member of a joint-claim couple shall be treated—

(a) as being in receipt of attendance allowance, or the care component of disability living allowance at the highest or middle rate prescribed in accordance with section 72(3) of the Benefits Act if he would, but for his being a patient for a period exceeding 28 days, be so in receipt;

(b) as being entitled to and in receipt of [24 a carer's allowance] [55 or carer support payment] [50 or having an award of universal credit which includes the carer element] if he would, but for the person for whom he was caring being a patient in hospital for a period exceeding 28 days, be so entitled and in receipt [50 of carer's allowance [55 or carer support payment] or have such an award of universal credit].

[46 (c) as being in receipt of the daily living component of personal independence payment at the standard or enhanced rate in accordance with section 78 of the 2012 Act if he would, but for regulations made under section 86(1) (hospital in-patients) of the 2012 Act, be so in receipt.]

[53 (d) as being in receipt of the daily living component of adult disability payment at the standard or enhanced rate in accordance with regulation 5 of the [54 Disability Assistance for Working Age People (Scotland) Regulations 2022], if he would, but for regulation 28 (effect of admission to hospital on ongoing entitlement to Adult Disability Payment) of those Regulations, be so in receipt]

(5) Sub-paragraph (3)(b) shall apply only for the first 12 weeks following the date on which the person to whom that provision applies first joins the joint-claim couple's household.

(6) For the purposes of sub-paragraph (1)(d), no account shall be taken of an award of [24 carer's allowance] [55 or carer support payment] [50 or universal credit which includes the carer element] to the extent that payment of such an award is back-dated for a period before [34 the date on which the award is first paid].

[20 (7) In sub-paragraph (1)(d), the reference to a person being in receipt of [24 a carer's allowance] [55 or carer support payment] [50 or as having an award of universal credit which includes the carer element] shall include a reference to a person who would have been in receipt of that allowance [58 or payment] [50 or had such an award] but for the application of a restriction under section [39 6B or] 7 of the Social Security Fraud Act 2001 (loss of benefit provisions).]

[50 (8) For the purposes of this paragraph, a person has an award of universal credit which includes the carer element if the person has an award of universal credit which includes an amount which is the carer element under regulation 29 of the Universal Credit Regulations 2013.]

[16 Enhanced disability premium

20IA.—[46 (1) Subject to sub-paragraph (2), the condition is that in respect of a member of a joint-claim couple who has not attained the qualifying age for state pension credit— **3.503**

(a) the care component of disability living allowance is, or would, but for a suspension of benefit in accordance with regulations under section 113(2) of the Benefits Act or but for an abatement as a consequence of hospitalisation, be payable at the highest rate prescribed under section 72(3) of the Benefits Act; or

(b) the daily living component of personal independence payment is, or would, but for regulations made under section 86(1) (hospital in-patients) of the 2012 Act, be payable at the enhanced rate in accordance with section 78(2) of the 2012 Act [53 , the daily living component of adult disability payment is, or would, but for regulation 28 (effect of admission to hospital on ongoing entitlement to Adult Disability Payment) of the [54 Disability Assistance for Working Age People (Scotland) Regulations 2022], be payable at the enhanced rate under those Regulations,] [47 or armed forces independence payment is payable].]

[33 (2) The condition is not satisfied if—

(a) paragraph (1) only refers to one member of a joint-claim couple and that member is a long-term patient; or

(b) paragraph (1) refers to both members of a joint-claim couple and both members of the couple are long-term patients.]]

Carer Premium

3.504 **20J.**—(1) Subject to sub-paragraphs (3) and (4), the condition is that either or both members of a joint-claim couple are entitled to [28 . . .] [24 a carer's allowance] under section 70 of the Benefits Act [55 or carer support payment].

(2) [28 . . .]

[23 (3) Where a carer premium is awarded but—

(a) the person in respect of whose care the [24 carer's allowance] [55 or carer support payment] has been awarded dies: or

(b) in any other case the member of the joint-claim couple in respect of whom a carer premium has been awarded ceases to be entitled [28 . . .] to [24 a carer's allowance] [55 or carer support payment],

the condition for the award of the premium shall be treated as satisfied for a period of eight weeks from the relevant date specified in sub-paragraph (3A) below.

(3A) The relevant date for the purposes of sub-paragraph (3) above shall be—

(a) [28 where sub-paragraph (3)(a) applies,] the Sunday following the death of the person in respect of whose care [24 a carer's allowance] [55 or carer support payment] has been awarded or beginning with the date of death if the death occurred on a Sunday;

(b) [28 . . .]

(c) in any other case, the date on which that member ceased to be entitled to [24 a carer's allowance] [55 or carer support payment].]

(4) Where a member of a joint-claim couple who has been entitled to [24 a carer's allowance] [58 or carer support payment] ceases to be entitled to that allowance [55 or payment] and makes a claim for a jobseeker's allowance jointly with the other member of that couple, the condition for the award of the carer premium shall be treated as satisfied for a period of eight weeks from the date on which—

[23(a) the person in respect of whose care the [24 a carer's allowance] [55 or carer support payment] has been awarded dies;

(b) [28 . . .]

(c) [28 in any other case, the person who has been entitled to a carer's allowance [55 or carer support payment] ceased to be entitled to that allowance [55 or payment].]]

Member of a joint-claim couple in receipt of concessionary payments

3.505 **20K.**—For the purpose of determining whether a premium is applicable to a joint-claim couple under paragraphs 20H to 20J, any concessionary payment made to compensate a person for the non-payment of any benefit mentioned in those paragraphs shall be treated as if it were a payment of that benefit.

Person in receipt of benefit

3.506 **20L.**—For the purposes of this Part of this Schedule, a member of a joint-claim couple shall be regarded as being in receipt of any benefit if, and only if, it is paid in respect of him and shall be so regarded only for any period in respect of which that benefit is paid.

PART IVB

Premium	*Amount*
20M.—	
(1) Pensioner premium where one member of a joint-claim couple [40 has attained the qualifying age for state pension credit] and the condition in paragraph 20E is satisfied.	(1) [58 £190.70].
(2) Higher Pensioner Premium where one member of a joint-claim couple satisfies the condition in paragraph 20F.	(2) [58 £190.70].
(3) Disability Premium where one member of a joint-claim couple satisfies the condition in paragraph [33 20G(1)].	(3) [58 £60.60].
(4) Severe Disability Premium where one member of a joint-claim couple satisfies the condition in paragraph 20I(1)— (i) if there is someone in receipt of [24 a carer's allowance] or if either member satisfies that condition only by virtue of paragraph [16 20I(4)]; (ii) if no-one is in receipt of such an allowance.	(4) (i) [58 £81.50]; (ii) [58 £163.00].
(5) Carer Premium.	(5) [58 £45.60] in respect of each person who satisfied the condition specified in paragraph 20J.]
[16 (6) Enhanced disability premium where the conditions specified in paragraph 20IA are satisfied.	(6) [58 £29.75] where the conditions in paragraph 20IA are satisfied in respect of a member of a joint-claim couple.]

PART V

ROUNDING OF FRACTIONS

21.—Where an income-based jobseeker's allowance is awarded for a period which is not a complete benefit week and the applicable amount in respect of that period results in an amount which includes a fraction of one penny that fraction shall be treated as one penny." **3.508**

AMENDMENTS

1. Jobseeker's Allowance (Amendment) Regulations 1996 (SI 1996/1516) reg.18 (October 7, 1996).
2. Jobseeker's Allowance (Amendment) Regulations 1996 (SI 1996/1516) reg.20 and Sch. (October 7, 1996).
3. Social Security and Child Support (Jobseeker's Allowance) (Miscellaneous Amendments) Regulations 1996 (SI 1996/2538) reg.2(11) (October 28, 1996).
4. Child Benefit, Child Support and Social Security (Miscellaneous Amendments) Regulations 1996 (SI 1996/1803) reg.44 (April 7, 1997).
5. Income-related Benefits and Jobseeker's Allowance (Personal Allowances for Children and Young Persons) (Amendment) Regulations 1996 (SI 1996/2545) reg.2 (April 7, 1997).

6. Income-related Benefits and Jobseeker's Allowance (Amendment) (No. 2) Regulations 1997 (SI 1997/2197) reg.7(5) and (6)(b) (October 6, 1997).

7. Social Security Amendment (Lone Parents) Regulations 1998 (SI 1998/766) reg.14 (April 6, 1998).

8. Social Security (Welfare to Work) Regulations 1998 (SI 1998/2231) reg.14(3) (October 5, 1998).

9. Social Security Amendment (Personal Allowances for Children and Young Persons) Regulations 1999 (SI 1999/2555) reg.2(1)(b) and (2) (April 10, 2000).

10. Social Security and Child Support (Tax Credits) Consequential Amendments Regulations 1999 (SI 1999/2566) reg.2(2) and Sch.2 Pt III (October 5, 1999).

11. Social Security (Miscellaneous Amendments) Regulations 2000 (SI 2000/681) reg.4(3) (April 3, 2000).

12. Social Security Amendment (Employment Zones) Regulations 2000 (SI 2000/724) reg.4 (April 3, 2000).

13. Social Security Amendment (Personal Allowances for Children) Regulations 2000 (SI 2000/1993) reg.2 (October 23, 2000).

14. Jobseeker's Allowance (Joint Claims) Regulations 2000 (SI 2000/1978) reg.2(5) and Sch.2 para.53 (March 19, 2001).

15. Social Security Amendment (Bereavement Benefits) Regulations 2000 (SI 2000/2239) reg.3(2) (April 9, 2001).

16. Social Security Amendment (Enhanced Disability Premium) Regulations 2000 (SI 2629) reg.5(c) (April 9, 2001).

17. Social Security Amendment (Joint Claims) Regulations 2001 (SI 2001/518) reg.2(7) (March 19, 2001).

18. Social Security Amendment (Bereavement Benefits) Regulations 2000 (SI 2000/2239) reg.3(2)(c) (April 9, 2001).

19. Social Security Amendment (Residential Care and Nursing Homes) Regulations 2001 (SI 2001/3767) reg.2 and Sch. Pt II para.18 (April 8, 2002).

20. Social Security (Loss of Benefit) (Consequential Amendments) Regulations 2002 (SI 2002/490) reg.2 (April 1, 2002).

21. Social Security Amendment (Residential Care and Nursing Homes) Regulations 2001 (SI 2001/3767) reg.2 and Sch. Pt II para.18 (as amended by Social Security Amendment (Residential Care and Nursing Homes) Regulations 2002 (SI 2002/398) reg.4(3)) (April 8, 2002).

22. Social Security Amendment (Personal Allowances for Children and Young Persons) Regulations 2002 (SI 2002/2019) reg.2 (October 14, 2002).

23. Social Security Amendment (Carer Premium) Regulations 2002 (SI 2002/2020) reg.3 (October 28, 2002).

24. Social Security (Miscellaneous Amendments) Regulations 2003 (SI 2003/511) reg.3(4) and (5) (April 1, 2003).

25. Social Security (Working Tax Credit and Child Tax Credit) (Consequential Amendments) Regulations 2003 (SI 2003/455) regs 1(9), 3 and Sch.2 para.20(b) (April 7, 2003).

26. Social Security (Working Tax Credit and Child Tax Credit) (Consequential Amendments) Regulations 2003 (SI 2003/455) regs 1(9), 3 and Sch.2 para.20(e) (April 7, 2003).

27. Social Security (Hospital In-Patients and Miscellaneous Amendments) Regulations 2003 (SI 2003/1195) reg.6 (May 21, 2003).

28. Social Security (Miscellaneous Amendments) (No. 2) Regulations 2003 (SI 2003/2279) reg.3(3) (October 1, 2003).

29. Social Security (Removal of Residential Allowance and Miscellaneous Amendments) Regulations 2003 (SI 2003/1121) reg.4 and Sch.2 para.9 (October 6, 2003).

30. Social Security (Working Tax Credit and Child Tax Credit) (Consequential Amendments) Regulations 2003 (SI 2003/455) reg.3 and Sch.2 para.20 (April 6, 2004, except in "transitional cases" and see further the note to regs 83 and to 17 of the Income Support Regulations).

31. Civil Partnership (Pensions, Social Security and Child Support) (Consequential, etc. Provisions) Order 2005 (SI 2005/2877) art.2(3) and Sch.3 para.26(11) (December 5, 2005).

32. Social Security (Miscellaneous Amendments) (No. 4) Regulations 2006 (SI 2006/2378) reg.13(10) (October 1, 2006).

33. Social Security (Miscellaneous Amendments) Regulations 2007 (SI 2007/719) reg.3(8) (April 9, 2007). As it relates to paras 15(2)(a) and 16, the amendment only affects "transitional cases". See further the note to reg.17 of the Income Support Regulations and the commentary below.

34. Social Security (Miscellaneous Amendments) (No. 5) Regulations 2007 (SI 2007/2618) reg.2 and Sch. (October 1, 2007).

35. Social Security (Miscellaneous Amendments) Regulations 2008 (SI 2008/698) reg.4(14) (April 14, 2008).

36. Employment and Support Allowance (Consequential Provisions) (No. 2) Regulations 2008 (SI 2008/1554) reg.3(1) and (24) (October 27, 2008).

37. Social Security (Miscellaneous Amendments) Regulations 2009 (SI 2009/583) reg.4(1) and (3) (April 6, 2009).

38. Social Security (Students and Miscellaneous Amendments) Regulations 2009 (SI 2009/1575) reg.3 (August 1, 2009).

39. Social Security (Loss of Benefit) Amendment Regulations 2010 (SI 2010/1160) reg.11(1) and (3) (April 1, 2010).

40. Social Security (Equalisation of State Pension Age) Regulations 2009 (SI 2009/1488) reg.13 (April 6, 2010).

41. Employment and Support Allowance (Transitional Provisions, Housing Benefit and Council Tax Benefit) (Existing Awards) (No. 2) Regulations 2010 (SI 2010/1907) reg.26(1) and Sch.4 para.1A(3) (as amended by the Employment and Support Allowance (Transitional Provisions, Housing Benefit and Council Tax Benefit) (Existing Awards) (No. 2) (Amendment) Regulations 2010 (SI 2010/2430) reg.15) (November 1, 2010).

42. Social Security (Miscellaneous Amendments) Regulations 2011 (SI 2011/674) reg.7(7) (April 11, 2011).

43. Social Security Benefits Up-rating Order 2012 (SI 2012/780) art.25(3) and Sch.13 (April 9, 2012).

44. Social Security Benefits Up-rating Order 2012 (SI 2012/780) art.25(5) and Sch.14 (April 9, 2012).

45. Social Security Benefits Up-rating Order 2012 (SI 2012/780) art.25(6) and Sch.15 (April 9, 2012).

46. Personal Independence Payment (Supplementary Provisions and Consequential Amendments) Regulations 2013 (SI 2013/388) reg.8 and Sch. para.16(1) and (7) (April 8, 2013).

47. Armed Forces and Reserve Forces Compensation Scheme (Consequential Provisions: Subordinate Legislation) Order 2013 (SI 2013/591) art.7 and Sch. para.10(1) and (7) (April 8, 2013).

48. Universal Credit and Miscellaneous Amendments (No. 2) Regulations 2014 (SI 2014/2888) reg.3(3) (November 26, 2014).

49. Welfare Benefits Up-rating Order 2015 (SI 2015/30) art.9 and Sch.3 (April 6, 2015).

50. Universal Credit and Miscellaneous Amendments Regulations 2015 (SI 2015/1754) reg.15 (October 28, 2015).

51. Universal Credit and Jobseeker's Allowance (Miscellaneous Amendments) Regulations 2018 (SI 2018/1129) reg.2 (November 28, 2018).

52. Social Security (Scotland) Act 2018 (Disability Assistance for Children and Young People) (Consequential Modifications) Order 2021 (SI 2021/786) Sch.3 paras 7–8 (July 26, 2021).

53. Social Security (Disability Assistance for Working Age People) (Consequential Amendments) Order 2022 (SI 2022/177) art.7 (March 21, 2022).

54. Social Security (Disability Assistance for Working Age People) (Consequential Amendments) (No. 2) Order 2022 (SI 2022/530) art.3(2) (June 6, 2022).

55. Carers Assistance (Carer Support Payment) (Scotland) Regulations 2023 (Consequential Amendments) Order 2023 (SI 2023/1218) art.8 (November 19, 2023).
56. Social Security Benefits Up-rating Order 2024 (SI 2024/242) art.26(3) and Sch.8 (April 8, 2024).
57. Social Security Benefits Up-rating Order 2024 (SI 2024/242) art.26(5) and (Sch.9 (April 8, 2024).
58. Social Security Benefits Up-rating Order 2024 (SI 2024/242) art.26(6) and Sch.10 (April 8, 2024).

DEFINITIONS

"adult disability payment"—see reg.1(3).
"attendance allowance"—*ibid.*
"the Benefits Act"—see Jobseekers Act s.35(1).
"child"—*ibid.*
"child disability payment"—*ibid.*
"claimant"—*ibid.*
"couple"—see reg.1(3).
"DACYP Regulations"—*ibid.*
"disability living allowance"—*ibid.*
"family"—see Jobseekers Act s.35(1).
"invalid carriage or other vehicle"—see reg.1(3).
"lone parent"—*ibid.*
"mobility supplement"—*ibid.*
"non-dependent"—see reg.2.
"partner"—see reg.1(3).
"personal independence payment"—*ibid.*
"polygamous marriage"—*ibid.*
"preserved right"—*ibid.*
"single claimant"—*ibid.*
"welfare to work beneficiary"—*ibid.*
"young person"—see reg.76.

For the General Note to Sch.1, see Vol.V paras 3.509–3.518.

p.1120, *amendments to the Jobseeker's Allowance Regulations 1996 (SI 1996/207) Sch.2 para.17 (Non-dependant deductions)*

6.100 With effect from April 8, 2024, art.26(7) of the Social Security Benefits Up-rating Order 2024 (SI 2024/242) makes the following amendments:

- in sub-paragraph (1)(a) for "£116.75" substitute "£124.55";
- in sub-paragraph (1)(b) for "£18.10" substitute "£19.30";
- in sub-paragraph (2)(a) for "£162.00" substitute "£176.00";
- in sub-paragraph (2)(b)—
  (i) for "£41.60" substitute "£44.40";
  (ii) for "£162.00" substitute "£176.00"; and
  (iii) for "£236.00" substitute "£256.00";
- in sub-paragraph (2)(c)—
  (i) for "£57.10" substitute "£60.95";
  (ii) for "£236.00" substitute "£256.00"; and
  (iii) for "£308.00" substitute "£334.00";
- in sub-paragraph (2)(d)—
  (i) for "£93.40" substitute "£99.65";
  (ii) for "£308.00" substitute "£334.00"; and
  (iii) for "£410.00" substitute "£445.00"; and

- in sub-paragraph (2)(e)—
  (i) for "£106.35" substitute "£113.50";
  (ii) for "£410.00" substitute "£445.00"; and
  (iii) for "£511.00" substitute "£554.00".

pp.1120–1122, *amendments to the Jobseeker's Allowance Regulations 1996 (SI 1996/207) Sch.2 para.17 (Housing costs—non-dependant deductions)*

With effect from July 26, 2021, Sch.3 para.9 of the Social Security (Scotland) Act 2018 (Disability Assistance for Children and Young People) (Consequential Modifications) Order 2021 (SI 2021/786) makes the following amendments to Sch.2 para.17: 6.101

- in sub-para.(6)(b), at the end of para.(ii), insert "or (iia) the care component of child disability payment;"
- in sub-para.(8)(a), after "disability living allowance", insert ", child disability payment".

With effect from January 1, 2022, reg.3(6) of the Social Security (Income and Capital Disregards) (Amendment) Regulations 2021 (SI 2021/1405) inserts into para.17(8)(b), after "Grenfell Tower payment", ", child abuse payment or Windrush payment".

With effect from March 21, 2022, art.5(8) of the Social Security (Disability Assistance for Working Age People) (Consequential Amendments) Order 2022 (SI 2022/177) makes the following amendments to Sch.2 para.17:

- after para.17(6)(b)(iii) (non-dependant deductions), insert "(iiia) the daily living component of adult disability payment;";
- in para.17(8)(a):
  - after "armed forces independence payment" for "or" substitute ",";
  - after "personal independence payment" insert "or adult disability payment".

With effect from July 9, 2023, reg.3 of the Social Security (Income and Capital Disregards) (Amendment) Regulations 2023 (SI 2023/640) amends para.17 as follows:

- in paragraph 17(8)(b) (non-dependant deductions), for "or Windrush payment" insert ", Windrush payment or Post Office compensation payment".

p.1138, *amendment to the Jobseeker's Allowance Regulations 1996 (SI 1996/207) Sch.6 para.7(1) (Sums to be disregarded in the calculation of earnings)*

With effect from November 19, 2023, art.8(10) of the Carer's Assistance (Carer Support Payment) (Scotland) Regulations 2023 (Consequential Amendments) Order 2023 (SI 2023/1218) amended para.7(1) by inserting "or carer support payment" after "carer's allowance" in the first place where that occurs. Carer support payment is newly defined in reg.1(3) by reference to the Scottish legislation (see the entry for p.787). 6.102

p.1144, *amendment to the Jobseeker's Allowance Regulations 1996 (SI 1996/207) Sch.6A para.2(1) (Sums to be disregarded in the calculation of earnings of members of joint-claim couples)*

6.103 With effect from November 19, 2023, art.8(11) of the Carer's Assistance (Carer Support Payment) (Scotland) Regulations 2023 (Consequential Amendments) Order 2023 (SI 2023/1218) amended para.2(1) by inserting "or carer support payment" after "carer's allowance" in the first place where that occurs. Carer support payment is newly defined in reg.1(3) by reference to the Scottish legislation (see the entry for p.787).

p.1146, *amendment to the Jobseeker's Allowance Regulations 1996 (SI 1996/207) Sch.7 para.7 (Sums to be disregarded in the calculation of income other than earnings—mobility component)*

6.104 With effect from March 21, 2022, art.5(9)(a) of the Social Security (Disability Assistance for Working Age People) (Consequential Amendments) Order 2022 (SI 2022/177) amended para.7 to read as follows (square brackets indicate only the present amendment, those indicating previous amendments having been omitted):

> "**7.**—The mobility component of disability living allowance[,] the mobility component of personal independence payment [or the mobility component of adult disability payment]."

"Adult disability payment" is defined in reg.1(3) by reference to reg.2 of the Disability Assistance for Working Age People (Scotland) Regulations 2022 (SSI 2022/54) (see Vol.IV of this series).

p.1147, *amendment to the Jobseeker's Allowance Regulations 1996 (SI 1996/207) Sch.7 para.10 (Sums to be disregarded in the calculation of income other than earnings—attendance allowance, care component of DLA or daily living component)*

6.105 With effect from March 21, 2022, art.5(9)(b) of the Social Security (Disability Assistance for Working Age People) (Consequential Amendments) Order 2022 (SI 2022/177) amended para.10 to read as follows (square brackets indicate only the present amendment, those indicating previous amendments having been omitted):

> "**10.**—Any attendance allowance, the care component of disability living allowance[,] the daily living component of personal independence payment [or the daily living component of adult disability payment]."

"Adult disability payment" is defined in reg.1(3) by reference to reg.2 of the Disability Assistance for Working Age People (Scotland) Regulations 2022 (SSI 2022/54) (see Vol.IV of this series).

p.1149, *amendment to the Jobseeker's Allowance Regulations 1996 (SI 1996/207) Sch.7 para.22(2) (Sums to be disregarded in the calculation of income other than earnings—income in kind)*

6.106 With effect from January 1, 2022, reg.3(7)(a) of the Social Security (Income and Capital Disregards) (Amendment) Regulations 2021 (SI

2021/1405) amended sub-para.(2) by inserting ", a child abuse payment or a Windrush payment" after "Grenfell Tower payment". All of those payments are defined in reg.1(3). See the entry for pp.684–685 for discussion of the nature of child abuse and Windrush payments.

p.1151, *amendment to the Jobseeker's Allowance Regulations 1996 (SI 1996/207) Sch.7 para.28 (Sums to be disregarded in the calculation of income other than earnings—payments for persons temporarily in care of claimant)*

With effect from July 1, 2022, reg.10 of the Health and Care Act 2022 (Consequential and Related Amendments and Transitional Provisions) Regulations 2022 (SI 2022/634) amended para.28 by substituting the following for sub-para.(da): **6.107**

"(da) an integrated care board established under Chapter A3 of Part 2 of the National Health Service Act 2006;"

Note that sub-para.(dzb) seems to be out of the proper order in the 2021/22 main volume.

With effect from November 6, 2023, reg.4 of the Health and Care Act 2022 (Further Consequential Amendments) (No.2) Regulations 2023 (SI 2023/1071) amended para.28(db) by substituting "NHS England" for "the National Health Service Commissioning Board".

p.1153, *amendments to the Jobseeker's Allowance Regulations 1996 (SI 1996/207) Sch.7 para.41 (Sums to be disregarded in the calculation of income other than earnings)*

With effect from January 1, 2022, reg.3(7)(b) of the Social Security (Income and Capital Disregards) (Amendment) Regulations 2021 (SI 2021/1405) amended para.41 by substituting the following for sub-para.(1A): **6.108**

"(1A) Any—
(a) Grenfell Tower payment;
(b) child abuse payment;
(c) Windrush payment."

In addition, reg.3(7)(c) amended sub-paras (2) to (6) by inserting ", a child abuse payment or a Windrush payment" after "Grenfell Tower payment" in each place where those words occur. All of those payments are defined in reg.1(3).

See the entry for p.684–685 (Income Support Regulations, Sch.10 (capital to be disregarded) para.22) for some technical problems arising from the date of effect of these amendments. Because all the payments so far made from the approved historic institutional child abuse compensation schemes and from the Windrush Compensation Scheme have been in the nature of capital, the question of disregarding income has not yet arisen.

With effect from July 9, 2023, reg.3(7) of the Social Security (Income and Capital Disregards) (Amendment) Regulations 2023 (SI 2023/640) amended para.41(1A) by adding the following after head (c):

"(d) Post Office compensation payment."

Such payments are newly defined in reg.1(3), where there is now also an expanded definition of Grenfell Tower payments (see head (a)). With effect from the same date, the words substituted in sub-paras (2) to (6) have been further amended by substituting ", a Windrush payment, a Post Office compensation payment or a vaccine damage payment" for "or a Windrush payment". "Vaccine damage payment" is also newly defined in reg.1(3). See the entry for pp.684–685 for the background.

p.1156, *amendments to the Jobseeker's Allowance Regulations 1996 (SI 1996/207) Sch.7 (Sums to be disregarded in the calculation of income other than earnings)*

6.109 With effect from July 26, 2021, art.12(2) of the Social Security (Scotland) Act 2018 (Disability Assistance, Young Carer Grants, Shortterm Assistance and Winter Heating Assistance) (Consequential Provision and Modifications) Order 2021 (SI 2021/886) inserted the following after para.81:

> "**82.** Any disability assistance given in accordance with regulations made section 31 of the Social Security (Scotland) Act 2018."

The first regulations made under s.31 of the 2018 Act were the Disability Assistance for Children and Young People (Scotland) Regulations 2021 (SSI 2021/174), also in effect from July 26, 2021, providing for the benefit known as a child disability payment. The regulations also authorise the payment of short-term assistance, to be disregarded under para.81. The Disability Assistance for Working Age People (Scotland) Regulations 2022 (SSI 2022/54), in effect from March 21, 2022, providing for the benefit known as adult disability payment, were also made under s.31, but the two potential elements (mobility component and daily living component) have been specifically covered by para.7 and para.10 from that date (see the entries for pp.1146 and 1147). Shortterm assistance under reg.62 of the 2022 Regulations is disregarded under para.81.

With effect from November 19, 2023, art.8(12) of the Carer's Assistance (Carer Support Payment) (Scotland) Regulations 2023 (Consequential Amendments) Order 2023 (SI 2023/1218) inserted the following after para.82:

> "**83.** Any amount of carer support payment that is in excess of the amount the claimant would receive if they had an entitlement to carer's allowance under section 70 of the Benefits Act."

Carer support payment (CSP) is newly defined in reg.1(3) by reference to the Scottish legislation (see the entry for p.787). Note that CSP in general counts as income and that the disregard is limited to any excess of the amount of the CSP over what the claimant would have been entitled to in carer's allowance under British legislation. That is in accordance with the Fiscal Framework Agreement governing the provision of devolved benefits in Scotland (see para.6.9 of the Explanatory Memorandum to SI 2023/1218). Initially, CSP is to be paid at the same rate as carer's allowance.

p.1165, *amendment to the Jobseeker's Allowance Regulations 1996 (SI 1996/207) Sch.8 para.12(1)(a) (Capital to be disregarded)*

6.110 With effect from July 26, 2021, art.12(3) of the Social Security (Scotland) Act 2018 (Disability Assistance, Young Carer Grants, Shortterm

Assistance and Winter Heating Assistance) (Consequential Provision and Modifications) Order 2021 (SI 2021/886) substituted "80, 81 or 82" for "80 or 81". See the entry for p.1156 for the new para.82 of Sch.7.

p.1166, *amendment to the Jobseeker's Allowance Regulations 1996 (SI 1996/207) Sch.8 para.12A (Capital to be disregarded—widowed parent's allowance)*

With effect from February 9, 2023, para.3(a) of the Schedule to the Bereavement Benefits (Remedial) Order 2023 (SI 2023/134) inserted the following after para.12: 6.111

> "**12A.** Any payment of a widowed parent's allowance made pursuant to section 39A of the Contributions and Benefits Act (widowed parent's allowance)—
> (a) to the survivor of a cohabiting partnership (within the meaning in section 39A(7) of the Contributions and Benefits Act) who is entitled to a widowed parent's allowance for a period before the Bereavement Benefits (Remedial) Order 2023 comes into force, and
> (b) in respect of any period of time during the period ending with the day before the survivor makes the claim for a widowed parent's allowance,
> but only for a period of 52 weeks from the date of receipt of the payment."

The legislation on widowed parent's allowance (WPA), abolished on April 5, 2017, and bereavement support payment (BSP) in operation for deaths after April 5, 2017, was declared incompatible with the ECHR by discriminating against children whose parents were cohabiting but not married to each other or in a civil partnership (see *Re McLaughlin's Application for Judicial Review* [2018] UKSC 48; [2018] 1 W.L.R. 4250 and *R(Jackson) v Secretary of State for Work and Pensions* [2020] EWHC 183 (Admin); [2020] 1 W.L.R. 1441 in Vol.I of this series). The Remedial Order allows retrospective claims to be made for those benefits from August 30, 2018 onwards and accordingly for arrears of benefit to be paid if the conditions of entitlement are met. The new para.12A, and the amended para.65 on BSP, deal with the consequences of such payments on old style JSA entitlement, by providing for them to be disregarded as capital for 52 weeks from receipt. See the entry for p.682 on income support for the effect of the payment of arrears of WPA being in its nature a payment of income to be taken into account (subject to a £10 per week disregard under para.17(i) of Sch.7 to the JSA Regulations 1996) against entitlement in past periods (allowing revision and the creation of an overpayment) and the misleading state of para.7.15 of the Explanatory Memorandum to the Order.

pp.1167–1168, *amendments to the Jobseeker's Allowance Regulations 1996 (SI 1996/207) Sch.8 para.27 (Capital to be disregarded)*

With effect from January 1, 2022, reg.3(8)(a) of the Social Security (Income and Capital Disregards) (Amendment) Regulations 2021 (SI 2021/1405) amended sub-para.(1A) by inserting ", child abuse payment, Windrush payment" after "Grenfell Tower payment" and amended sub-paras (2) to (6) by inserting ", a child abuse payment or a Windrush payment" after "Grenfell Tower payment" in each place where those words occur. All of those payments are defined in reg.1(3). 6.112

See the entry for pp.684–685 (Income Support Regulations Sch.10 (Capital to be disregarded) para.22) for some technical problems with the addition only with effect from January 1, 2022 of the disregards of payments from approved schemes providing compensation in respect of historic institutional child abuse in the UK and from the Windrush Compensation Scheme. All the schemes so far in existence provide payments in the nature of capital. That entry also contains information about the nature of the schemes involved, including the child abuse compensation schemes so far approved.

With effect from July 9, 2023, reg.3(8) of the Social Security (Income and Capital Disregards) (Amendment) Regulations 2023 (SI 2023/640) amended para.27(1A) by adding the following after "Windrush payment":

> ", Post Office compensation payment or vaccine damage payment."

Such payments are newly defined in reg.1(3), where there is now also an expanded definition of Grenfell Tower payments. With effect from the same date, the words substituted in sub-paras (2) to (6) have been further amended by substituting ", a Windrush payment, a Post Office compensation payment or a vaccine damage payment" for "or a Windrush payment". See the entry for pp.684–685 on income support in this Supplement.

With effect from August 30, 2023, reg.2(1)(b) of the Social Security (Infected Blood Capital Disregard) (Amendment) Regulations 2023 (SI 2023/894) amended para.27 by inserting the following after sub-para.(5):

> "(5A) Any payment out of the estate of a person, which derives from a payment to meet the recommendation of the Infected Blood Inquiry in its interim report published on 29th July 2022 made under or by the Scottish Infected Blood Support Scheme or an approved blood scheme to the estate of the person, where the payment is made to the person's son, daughter, step-son or step-daughter."

See the entry for pp.684–685 on income support for the background.

With effect from October 27, 2023, reg.4(3)(c) of the Social Security (Habitual Residence and Past Presence, and Capital Disregards) (Amendment) Regulations 2023 (SI 2023/1144) amended para.27(1) by inserting ", the Victims of Overseas Terrorism Compensation Scheme" after "the National Emergencies Trust". That scheme is newly defined in reg.1(3).

See the entry for pp.684–685 on income support for the background.

With effect from October 10, 2024 reg.2(1)(b) of the Social Security (Infected Blood Capital Disregard) (Amendment) Regulations 2024 (SI 2024/964) amended para.27 by inserting the following after sub-para.(5A):

> "(5B) Any payment out of the estate of a person, which derives from a payment made under or by the Scottish Infected Blood Support Scheme or an approved blood scheme to the estate of the person as a result of that person having been infected from contaminated blood products."

See the entry for p.472 of Vol.II in Pt III of this Supplement for discussion of the terms of sub-para.(5B).

p.1168, *amendment to the Jobseeker's Allowance Regulations 1996 (SI 1996/207) Sch.8 para.31 (Capital to be disregarded—payments in kind)*

6.113 With effect from January 1, 2022, reg.3(8)(b) of the Social Security (Income and Capital Disregards) (Amendment) Regulations 2021 (SI

2021/1405) amended para.31 by inserting ", a child abuse payment or a Windrush payment" after "Grenfell Tower payment". All of those payments are defined in reg.1(3). See also the entry for pp.684–685.

p.1172, *amendment to the Jobseeker's Allowance Regulations 1996 (SI 1996/207) Sch.8 para.65 (Capital to be disregarded—bereavement support payment)*

With effect from February 9, 2023, para.3(b) of the Schedule to the Bereavement Benefits (Remedial) Order 2023 (SI 2023/134) amended para.65 by making the existing text sub-para.(1) and inserting the following: 6.114

"(2) Where bereavement support payment under section 30 of the Pensions Act 2014 is paid to the survivor of a cohabiting partnership (within the meaning in section 30(6B) of the Pensions Act 2014) in respect of a death occurring before the day the Bereavement Benefits (Remedial) Order 2023 comes into force, any amount of that payment which is—

(a) in respect of the rate set out in regulation 3(1) of the Bereavement Support Payment Regulations 2017, and

(b) paid as a lump sum for more than one monthly recurrence of the day of the month on which their cohabiting partner died,

but only for a period of 52 weeks from the date of receipt of the payment."

See the entry for p.682 on income support for the general background. The operation of this amendment is much more straightforward than that of the new para.12A on widowed parent's allowance. Although a payment of arrears of bereavement support payment (BSP) is in its nature a payment of income and attributable to the past period in respect of which it is due, the payment could not affect any entitlement to old style JSA in that past period because it would be disregarded entirely as income (Sch.7 para.76). The amount of the arrears would thus immediately metamorphose into capital, which would then be disregarded under para.65(2) subject to the 52 week limit.

p.1177, *annotation to the Jobseeker's Allowance Regulations 1996 (SI 1996/207) Sch.8 (Capital to be disregarded)*

With effect from June 28, 2022 "Cost of living payments" under the Social Security (Additional Payments) Act 2022, both those to recipients of specified means-tested benefits and "disability" payments are not to be taken into account for any old style JSA purposes by virtue of s.8(b) of the Act. The same effect was achieved with effect from March 23, 2023 in relation to payments under the Social Security (Additional Payments) Act 2023 (s.8(b) of that Act). See Pt I of Vol.II for the text of both Acts. 6.115

p.1184, *annotation to the Jobseeker's Allowance (Schemes for Assisting Persons to Obtain Employment) Regulations 2013 (SI 2013/276)*

Note the doubts expressed in the note to reg.3 in the 2021/22 main volume about the validity of the prescription of the Work and Health Programme in reg.3(8C) and in the entry below for p.1187 about the validity of the prescription of the Restart Scheme in reg.3(8D). 6.116

p.1187, *amendment to the Jobseeker's Allowance (Schemes for Assisting Persons to Obtain Employment) Regulations 2013 (SI 2013/276) reg.3 (Schemes for assisting persons to obtain employment)*

6.117 With effect from March 14, 2022, reg.2(3) of the Jobseeker's Allowance (Schemes for Assisting Persons to Obtain Employment) (Amendment) Regulations 2022 (SI 2022/154) amended reg.3 by omitting para.(8) and by inserting the following after para.(8C):

> "(8D) The Restart Scheme is a scheme which provides support for a period of up to 12 months for claimants who have been unemployed for 9 months or more and reside in England and Wales."

The Explanatory Memorandum to SI 2022/154 (note that a revised Memorandum, not labelled as such in its heading but with an additional "001" in the version online, was issued on April 13, 2022) explains that the Work Programme no longer exists. There is therefore no controversy about the removal of para.(8), which described that scheme.

However, the introduction of the new para.(8D) is of very doubtful validity. That is because s.17A(1) of the old style Jobseekers Act 1995 only allows claimants to be required to participate in schemes designed to assist them to obtain employment that are of a "prescribed description". The Supreme Court in *R. (Reilly and Wilson) v Secretary of State for Work and Pensions* [2013] UKSC 68; [2014] 1 A.C. 453 held that the Jobseeker's Allowance (Employment, Skills and Enterprise Scheme) Regulations 2011 (SI 2011/917) reg.2 did not satisfy that test because it did not add anything to the description of the schemes in the Act itself, which was necessary for the requirement for a prescribed description to have any point. Regulation 2 had provided that the Employment, Skills and Enterprise Scheme (ESES) meant a scheme of that name within s.17A and provided pursuant to arrangements by the Secretary of State that was designed to assist claimants to obtain employment or self-employment and which might include for any individual work-related activity, including work experience or job search. The Supreme Court must therefore have regarded the reference to the possible inclusion of work-related activity as too vague to constitute any kind of description of what the scheme involved. The Court agreed that it was not necessary in the case of the ESES to explore how much detail needed to be included in the regulations to comply with s.17A(1), as no description at all was given.

The amendment contained in SI 2022/154 may therefore not be on all fours with the ESES Regulations reg.2, because the new para.(8D) could be said to contain *some* description of the Restart Scheme, in identifying the categories of claimants who could be directed to the Restart Scheme, the maximum length of the scheme and that it would provide support (although arguably that word, in conjunction with the other specified elements, is also so vague as not to constitute any meaningful description at all). If it is accepted that there is *some* description, the question then, as in *R. (Smith) v Secretary of State for Work and Pensions* [2015] EWCA Civ 229 on the Jobseeker's Allowance (Mandatory Work Activity Scheme) Regulations 2011 (SI 2021/688), would be whether there is sufficient description for the purposes of s.17A(1). In *Smith*, Underhill LJ suggested at para.25 that the natural reading of "prescribed description" connoted "no more than an indication of the character of the scheme provided for, such as a scheme in which the claimant was required to undergo training or education or to work with a mentor, or—as here—to do work or work-related activity". So the CA held that the mention of work or work-related activity, with the specification of maximum weekly hours and length of participation, was enough for the MWAS Regulations to be valid. Although the present amendment specifies which claimants fall into the scope of the Restart Scheme and the maximum length, it says nothing worthwhile about the nature of the scheme. All it says is that it "provides support", nothing about what kind of support or who it will be provided by. Equally, if not more, important, it says nothing about what a claimant is to be expected to do by way of participation. What does it mean to have "support" thrust on a claimant? The argument that the new para.(8D) provides an insufficient description seems very strong. It might be thought that the Explanatory Memorandum betrays the faulty approach in paras 7.8 and 7.9, where it is said that the current legislation "lists" the employment schemes claimants can be required to participate in and that the amendment adds the Restart Scheme to the list. To be valid, and to carry the requirement to participate backed by sanctions, a regulation must not merely "list" a scheme, but must describe it.

The Explanatory Memorandum records that the Restart Scheme was already in existence through 12 providers in England and Wales, initially for universal credit claimants who had spent 12 to 18 months uninterrupted time in the Intensive Work Search Regime (i.e. subject to all work-related requirements), but now with the time reduced to nine months. Because of improved labour market conditions the opportunity arose to widen the eligibility criteria to provide intensive employment support for old style JSA claimants that had previously only been available to limited groups. The Scheme is still only available in England and Wales. The emphasis is said to be on positive engagement with the claimant to encourage participation, with the requirement to participate being "used as a backstop where reasonable attempts at engagement fail without good reason" (para.6.7). However, it is stated that claimants who fail to comply with the requirement to participate in compulsory activities may be issued with a low-level sanction (para.6.6). It is far from clear that "compulsory activities" are adequately described by the term "support" in para.(8D).

The policy paper *How the Restart Scheme will work* (January 18, 2022, updated April 26, 2022, available on the gov.uk website, although withdrawn on August 21, 2024 as out of date) states:

> "Through regular contact with all participants, providers will develop a strong understanding of individuals' employment history, skills, aspirations and support needs to develop the right package of support to help each participant succeed.
>
> For some this might be bespoke training to take advantage of opportunities in a growth sector or to succeed in a major recruitment exercise, for others it might be support to get the right certificate to take up a job in a different industry such as construction or transport or to update skills such as IT."

That document thus gets to a description of the scheme, but as there is no reference to it in para.(8D) there can be no reliance on its description merely by use of the label "Restart Scheme".

Providers will be given letters of empowerment under reg.17 authorising them to exercise the functions of the Secretary of State to issue notices requiring participation (reg.5) or that that requirement has ceased (reg.6(3) (a)) (Explanatory Memorandum, para.6.3). It is understood that providers and employees will not be designated as "employment officers" under s.35 of the old style Jobseekers Act 1995, so that they will have no power to issue jobseeker's directions under s.19A(2)(c).

p.1188, *annotation to the Jobseeker's Allowance (Schemes for Assisting Persons to Obtain Employment) Regulations 2013 (SI 2013/276) reg.3 (Schemes for assisting persons to obtain employment)*

6.118 Note, in addition to the points made in the entry for p.1187, that in the last paragraph of the existing note the reference to s.19(2)(c) should be to s.19A(2)(c).

Part IV

Old Style Employment and Support Allowance Regulations

p.1205 *amendments to list of regulations for the Employment and Support Allowance Regulations 2008 (SI 2008/794)*

6.119 Substitute the following for the text of the entry for reg.139A:

"139A. Treatment of loans for specific purposes"

pp.1209, 1214, 1218, 1219 and 1221 *amendments to the Employment and Support Allowance Regulations 2008 (SI 2008/794) reg.2 (Interpretation)*

6.120 With effect from July 26, 2021, Sch.9 para.2 of the Social Security (Scotland) Act 2018 (Disability Assistance for Children and Young People) (Consequential Modifications) Order 2021 (SI 2021/786) adds the following definitions:

"child disability payment" has the meaning given in regulation 2 of the DACYP Regulations;

"the DACYP Regulations" means the Disability Assistance for Children and Young People (Scotland) Regulations 2021;

With effect from January 1, 2022, reg.7(2) of the Social Security (Income and Capital Disregards) (Amendment) Regulations 2021 (SI 2021/1405) inserts the following definitions:

"child abuse payment" means a payment from a scheme established or approved by the Secretary of State for the purpose of providing compensation in respect of historic institutional child abuse in the United Kingdom;"

"Windrush payment" means a payment made under the Windrush Compensation Scheme (Expenditure) Act 2020;"

With effect from January 1, 2022, reg.7(2) of the Social Security (Income and Capital Disregards) (Amendment) Regulations 2021 (SI 2021/1405) inserts ", a child abuse payment or a Windrush payment" into the definition of "qualifying person", after "Grenfell Tower payment".

With effect from March 21, 2022, art.11 of the Social Security (Disability Assistance for Working Age People) (Consequential Amendments) Order 2022 (SI 2022/177) adds the following definition:

"adult disability payment" has the meaning given in regulation 2 of the Disability Assistance for Working Age People (Scotland) Regulations 2022;

With effect from April 4, 2022, reg.2(1) of the Universal Credit and Employment and Support Allowance (Terminal Illness) (Amendment) Regulations 2022 (SI 2022/260) amends the definition of "terminally ill" by substituting for "6 months", "12 months".

With effect from July 9, 2023, reg.7(2)(a) of the Social Security (Income and Capital Disregards) (Amendment) Regulations 2023 (SI 2023/640) substituted for the definition of "Grenfell Tower payment" the following new definition: 6.121

""Grenfell Tower payment" means a payment made for the purpose of providing compensation or support in respect of the fire on 14th June 2017 at Grenfell Tower;".

With effect from July 9, 2023, reg.7(2)(b) of the Social Security (Income and Capital Disregards) (Amendment) Regulations 2023 (SI 2023/640) inserted at the appropriate places the following new definitions: 6.122

- ""the Horizon system" means any version of the computer system used by the Post Office known as Horizon, Horizon Legacy, Horizon Online or HNG-X;";"
- ""the Post Office" means Post Office Limited (registered number 02154540);";"
- ""Post Office compensation payment" means a payment made by the Post Office or the Secretary of State for the purpose of providing compensation or support which is—
  (a) in connection with the failings of the Horizon system; or
  (b) otherwise payable following the judgment in *Bates and Others v Post Office Ltd* ((No. 3) "Common Issues");";"
- ""vaccine damage payment" means a payment made under the Vaccine Damage Payments Act 1979;".

With effect from October 27, 2023, reg.8(2) of the Social Security (Habitual Residence and Past Presence, and Capital Disregards) (Amendment) Regulations 2023 (SI 2023/1144) inserts the following definitions:

- in the definition of "qualifying person" after "the National Emergencies Trust" insert ", the Victims of Overseas Terrorism Compensation Scheme";
- after the definition of "vaccine damage payment" insert— "'the Victims of Overseas Terrorism Compensation Scheme' means the scheme of that name established by the Ministry of Justice in 2012 under section 47 of the Crime and Security Act 2010;";

With effect from November 19, 2023, art.19(2) of the Carer's Assistance (Carer Support Payment) (Scotland) Regulations 2023 (Consequential Amendments) Order 2023 (SI 2023/1218) inserts the following definition after the definition of "carer's allowance":

"'carer support payment' means carer's assistance given in accordance with the Carer's Assistance (Carer Support Payment) (Scotland) Regulations 2023;".

6.123 With effect from July 9, 2023, reg.7(2)(c) of the Social Security (Income and Capital Disregards) (Amendment) Regulations 2023 (SI 2023/640) substituted ", a Windrush payment, a Post Office compensation payment or a vaccine damage payment" for "or a Windrush payment" in the definition of "qualifying person".

p.1230, *revocation of the Employment and Support Allowance Regulations 2008 (SI 2008/794) reg.6 (The assessment phase—a claimants appealing against a decision)*

6.124 Strictly speaking, reg.6 was *revoked* by reg.9(5) of the Social Security (Miscellaneous Amendments) (No. 3) Regulations 2010/840 (rather than *omitted* by the annotator).

pp.1238–1239, *amendment of the Employment and Support Allowance Regulations 2008 (SI 2008/794) reg.18 (Circumstances in which the condition that the claimant is not receiving education does not apply)*

6.125 Regulation 18 now reads, as amended, as follows:

"Paragraph 6(1)(g) of Schedule 1 to the Act does not apply where the claimant is entitled to a disability living allowance [3, child disability payment] [2, armed forces independence payment] [4,] [1 personal independence payment] [4 or adult disability payment]."

In addition, the following notes should be added to the list of

AMENDMENTS:

3. Social Security (Scotland) Act 2018 (Disability Assistance for Children and Young People) (Consequential Modifications) Order 2021 (SI 2021/786) Sch.9 para.3 (July 26, 2021).
4. Social Security (Disability Assistance for Working Age People) (Consequential Amendments) Order 2022 (SI 2022/177) art.11(3) (March 21, 2022).

p.1250, *amendment to the Employment and Support Allowance Regulations 2008 (SI 2008/794) reg.21 (Information required for determining capability for work)*

6.126 With effect from July 1, 2022, reg.4(2) of the Social Security (Medical Evidence) and Statutory Sick Pay (Medical Evidence) (Amendment) (No. 2) Regulations 2022 (SI 2022/630) omitted the words "a doctor's" between "form of" and "statement".

p.1260, *annotation to the Employment and Support Allowance Regulations 2008 (SI 2008/794) reg.24 (Matters to be taken into account in determining good cause in relation to regs 22 or 23)*

6.127 See, however, the successful application for a new inquest in *Dove v HM Assistant Coroner for Teesside and Hartlepool, Rahman and SSWP* [2023] EWCA Civ 289. Mrs Dove's daughter, Jodey, had died of an overdose shortly after her ESA award had been stopped. Jodey, who had been in receipt of ESA for several years, had a history of mental health problems, suicidal ideation and overdoses, as well as physical ill-health. In 2016, on a periodic review, she asked the DWP for a home visit. The DWP neglected to deal with that request and required her to attend an HCP assessment, which she failed to do. The DWP decided that Jodey had shown neither good cause for the failure to attend nor that she had limited capability for work. Jodey's ESA was duly stopped on February 7, 2017, and she died a fortnight later. Mrs Dove believed that the withdrawal of benefit had created extra stress and contributed to her daughter's death. The coroner ruled that questioning the DWP's decisions was beyond her remit under the Coroners and Justice Act 2009.

Mrs Dove applied to the High Court under the Coroners Act 1988 s.13, seeking two remedies: (a) to quash the coroner's suicide verdict; and (b) to order a new inquest covering the circumstances surrounding her daughter's death. Mrs Dove submitted that (1) the coroner's inquiry was insufficient in scope and should have covered the DWP's failings; (2) those failings meant that the state was in breach of ECHR art.2, so requiring a wider inquiry; (3) fresh evidence (in the form of an expert psychiatrist's report, obtained after the inquest, which concluded it was likely that Jodey's mental state would have been substantially affected by the decision to stop her benefits and an ICE report on a complaint about the DWP's handling of Jodey's claim) showed that a new inquest was necessary. At first instance the Divisional Court ([2021] EWHC 2511 (Admin); Warbey LJ, Farbey J and HH Judge Teague QC) dismissed the application on all three grounds.

However, the Court of Appeal allowed Mrs Dove's appeal and directed a fresh inquest ([2023] EWCA Civ 289: Lewis LJ, William Davis LJ and Whipple LJ). The Court ruled that the psychiatrist's report (but not the ICE report) was fresh evidence making it desirable in the interests of justice to hold a fresh inquest (*R v HM Coroner for North Humberside and Scunthorpe Ex p. Jamieson* [1995] Q.B. 1). Thus, "it is in the interests of justice that Mrs Dove and her family should have the opportunity to invite a coroner, at a fresh inquest, to make a finding of fact that the Department's actions contributed to Jodey's deteriorating mental health and, if that finding is made, to invite the coroner to include reference to that finding in the conclusion on how Jodey came by her death" (per Whipple LJ at [72]). One of the reasons for the Court reaching this conclusion was that "there is a public interest in a coroner considering the wider issue of causation raised on this appeal. If Jodey's death was connected with the abrupt cessation of benefits by the Department, the public has a legitimate interest in knowing that. After all, the Department deals with very many people who are vulnerable and dependent on benefits to survive, and the consequences of terminating benefit payments to such people should be examined in public, where it can be followed and reported on by others who might be interested in it."

p.1302, *annotation to the Employment and Support Allowance Regulations 2008 (SI 2008/794) reg.35 (Certain claimants to be treated as having limited capability for work-related activity)*

For further examples of the need for sufficient fact-finding and adequate reasons in appeals where reg.35 is in issue, see *MH v SSWP (ESA)* [2021] UKUT 90 (AAC) and *CT v SSWP (ESA)* [2021] UKUT 131 (AAC). On the importance of tribunals in universal credit appeals (that turn on the equivalent provision to reg.35 in Sch.9 para.4) ensuring they have been 6.128

provided with an accurate list of work-related activities, see *KS v SSWP (UC)* [2021] UKUT 132 (AAC). Secretary of State appeal responses on such appeals may not have included accurate lists of work-related activities until after July 2020.

pp.1334–1335, *amendment of the Employment and Support Allowance Regulations 2008 (SI 2008/794) reg.64D (The amount of a hardship payment)*

6.129 The text in the main volume at para.4.174 should be replaced with the following:

"[1 The amount of a hardship payment

64D.—[2 (1) A hardship payment is either—

(a) 80% of the prescribed amount for a single claimant as set out in paragraph (1)(a) of Part 1 of Schedule 4 where—

(i) the claimant has an award of employment and support allowance which does not include entitlement to a work-related activity component under section 4(2)(b) of the Welfare Reform Act 2007 as in force immediately before 3rd April 2017; and

(ii) the claimant or any other member of their family is either pregnant or seriously ill; or

(b) 60% of the prescribed amount for a single claimant as set out in paragraph (1)(a) of Part 1 of Schedule 4 in any other case.]

(2) A payment calculated in accordance with paragraph (1) shall, if it is not a multiple of 5p, be rounded to the nearest such multiple or, if it is a multiple of 2.5p but not of 5p, to the next lower multiple of 5p.]"

AMENDMENTS

1. Employment and Support Allowance (Sanctions) (Amendment) Regulations 2012 (SI 2012/2756) reg.6 (December 3, 2012).

2. Employment and Support Allowance (Exempt Work Hardship Amounts) (Amendment) Regulations 2017 (SI 2017/205) reg.5 (April 3, 2017).

p.1336, *annotation to the Employment and Support Allowance Regulations 2008 (SI 2008/794) reg.67 (Prescribed amounts)*

6.130 On the lawfulness of not uplifting the amounts paid in IS, JSA and ESA by £20 per week (as was done with UC for 18 months during the coronavirus pandemic), see the annotation to the Income Support (General) Regulations 1987 (SI 1987/1967) reg.17 (Applicable amounts), above.

p.1340, *annotation to the Employment and Support Allowance Regulations 2008 (SI 2008/794) reg.69 (Special cases)*

6.131 Concerning the definition of 'prisoner', in *JC v Secretary of State for Work and Pensions* [2024] UKUT 13 (AAC), §30 Upper Tribunal Judge Jones holds that reg.69(2) 'should be interpreted as providing a restricted definition of a prisoner as being one detained or sentenced for a criminal offence or detained or sentenced to imprisonment by a criminal court rather than including a finding of guilt and sentence by a civil court in respect of a civil contempt of court'. The reasoning for this is to achieve parity with past judicial interpretation of primary legislation depriving prisoners of benefit—see currently s.113(1)(b) SSCBA 1992. That provision states that benefits under Parts II to V of the Act shall not be received by or payable in respect of any person for any period during which the person 'is undergoing imprisonment or detention in legal custody'. In *R(S) 8/79*, §8 the Commissioner found imprisonment in this sense 'means only imprisonment imposed by a court exercising criminal jurisdiction'.

pp.1341–1342, *amendment to the Employment and Support Allowance Regulations 2008 (SI 2008/794) reg.70 (Special cases: supplemental—persons from abroad)*

The text in the main volume at para.4.187 should be replaced with the following: **6.132**

"Special cases: supplemental—persons from abroad

70.—(1) "Person from abroad" means, subject to the following provisions of this regulation, a claimant who is not habitually resident in the United Kingdom, the Channel Islands, the Isle of Man or the Republic of Ireland.

(2) A claimant must not be treated as habitually resident in the United Kingdom, the Channel Islands, the Isle of Man or the Republic of Ireland unless the claimant has a right to reside in (as the case may be) the United Kingdom, the Channel Islands, the Isle of Man or the Republic of Ireland other than a right to reside which falls within paragraph (3) [8 or (3A)].

(3) A right to reside falls within this paragraph if it is one which exists by virtue of, or in accordance with, one or more of the following—

(a) regulation 13 of the [8 Immigration (European Economic Area) Regulations 2016];

(b) regulation 14 of those Regulations, but only in a case where the right exists under that regulation because the claimant is—

(i) a jobseeker for the purpose of the definition of "qualified person" in regulation 6(1) of those Regulations; or

(ii) a family member (within the meaning of regulation 7 of those Regulations) of such a jobseeker; [10 or]

[4[8(bb) regulation 16 of those Regulations, but only in a case where the right exists under that regulation because the claimant satisfies the criteria in paragraph (5) of that regulation;]]

(c) [10 . . .]

(d) [10 . . .]

(e) [10 . . .]

[8 (3A) A right to reside falls within this paragraph if it exists by virtue of a claimant having been granted limited leave to enter, or remain in, the United Kingdom under the Immigration Act 1971 by virtue of—

(a) Appendix EU to the immigration rules made under section 3(2) of that Act; [11 . . .];

(b) being a person with a Zambrano right to reside as defined in Annex 1 of Appendix EU to the immigration rules made under section 3(2) of that Act.] [11; or

(c) having arrived in the United Kingdom with an entry clearance that was granted under Appendix EU (Family Permit) to the immigration rules made under section 3(2) of that Act.]

[9 (3B) Paragraph (3A)(a) does not apply to a person who—

(a) has a right to reside granted by virtue of being a family member of a relevant person of Northern Ireland; and

(b) would have a right to reside under the Immigration (European Economic Area) Regulations 2016 if the relevant person of Northern Ireland were an EEA national, provided that the right to reside does not fall within paragraph (3).]

(4) A claimant is not a person from abroad if the claimant is—

[12(zza) a person granted leave in accordance with the immigration rules made under section 3(2) of the Immigration Act 1971, where such leave is granted by virtue of—

(i) the Afghan Relocations and Assistance Policy; or

(ii) the previous scheme for locally-employed staff in Afghanistan (sometimes referred to as the ex-gratia scheme);

(zzb) a person in Great Britain not coming within sub-paragraph (zza) or [13 (h)] who left Afghanistan in connection with the collapse of the Afghan government that took place on 15th August 2021;]

[13(zzc) a person in Great Britain who was residing in Ukraine immediately before 1st January 2022, left Ukraine in connection with the Russian invasion which took place on 24th February 2022 and—

(i) has been granted leave in accordance with immigration rules made under section 3(2) of the Immigration Act 1971; [14 . . .]

(ii) has a right of abode in the United Kingdom within the meaning given in section 2 of that Act;] [14 or

(iii) does not require leave to enter or remain in the United Kingdom in accordance with section 3ZA of that Act;]

[15(zzd) a person who was residing in Sudan before 15th April 2023, left Sudan in connection with the violence which rapidly escalated on 15th April 2023 in Khartoum and across Sudan and—

(i) has been granted leave in accordance with immigration rules made under section 3(2) of the Immigration Act 1971;

(ii) has a right of abode in the United Kingdom within the meaning given in section 2 of that Act; or

(iii) does not require leave to enter or remain in the United Kingdom in accordance with section 3ZA of that Act;]

[16(zze) a person who was residing in Israel, the West Bank, the Gaza Strip, East Jerusalem, the Golan Heights or Lebanon immediately before 7th October 2023, who left Israel, the West Bank, the Gaza Strip, East Jerusalem, the Golan Heights or Lebanon in connection with the Hamas terrorist attack in Israel on 7th October 2023 or the violence which rapidly escalated in the region following the attack and—

(i) has been granted leave in accordance with immigration rules made under section 3(2) of the Immigration Act 1971;

(ii) has a right of abode in the United Kingdom within the meaning given in section 2 of that Act; or

(iii) does not require leave to enter or remain in the United Kingdom in accordance with section 3ZA of that Act;]

[7(za) a qualified person for the purposes of regulation 6 of the [8 Immigration (European Economic Area) Regulations 2016] as a worker or a self-employed person;

(zb) a family member of a person referred to in sub-paragraph (za) [9 . . .];

(zc) a person who has a right to reside permanently in the United Kingdom by virtue of regulation 15(1)(c), (d) or (e) of those Regulations;]

[9(zd) a family member of a relevant person of Northern Ireland, with a right to reside which falls within paragraph (3A)(a), provided that the relevant person of Northern Ireland falls within sub-paragraph (za), or would do so but for the fact that they are not an EEA national;]

[10(ze) a frontier worker within the meaning of regulation 3 of the Citizens' Rights (Frontier Workers) (EU Exit) Regulations 2020;

(zf) a family member of a person referred to in sub-paragraph (ze), who has been granted limited leave to enter, or remain in, the United Kingdom by virtue of Appendix EU to the immigration rules made under section 3(2) of the Immigration Act 1971;]

(g) a refugee within the definition in Article 1 of the Convention relating to the Status of Refugees done at Geneva on 28th July 1951, as extended by Article 1(2) of the Protocol relating to the Status of Refugees done at New York on 31st January 1967;

[6(h) a person who has been granted leave or who is deemed to have been granted leave outside the rules made under section 3(2) of the Immigration Act 1971 [13 . . .]

(i) a person who has humanitarian protection granted under those rules; [6 or]

(j) a person who is not a person subject to immigration control within the meaning of section 115(9) of the Immigration and Asylum Act and who is in the United Kingdom as a result of deportation, expulsion or other removal by compulsion of law from another country to the United Kingdom; [1 . . .]

(k) [6 . . .]

(l) [1 [6 . . .]]]

[9 (5) In this regulation—

"EEA national" has the meaning given in regulation 2(1) of the Immigration (European Economic Area) Regulations 2016;

"family member" has the meaning given in regulation 7(1)(a), (b) or (c) of the Immigration (European Economic Area) Regulations 2016 except that regulation 7(4) of those Regulations does not apply for the purposes of paragraphs (3B) and (4)(zd);

"relevant person of Northern Ireland" has the meaning given in Annex 1 of Appendix EU to the immigration rules made under section 3(2) of the Immigration Act 1971.]

[10 (6) References in this regulation to the Immigration (European Economic Area) Regulations 2016 are to be read with Schedule 4 to the Immigration and Social Security Co-ordination (EU Withdrawal) Act 2020(Consequential, Saving, Transitional and Transitory Provisions) Regulations 2020.]"

AMENDMENTS

1. Social Security (Habitual Residence) (Amendment) Regulations 2009 (SI 2009/362) reg.9 (March 18, 2009).
2. Social Security (Miscellaneous Amendments) (No. 3) Regulations 2011 (SI 2011/2425) reg.23(1) and (7) (October 31, 2011).
3. Treaty of Lisbon (Changes in Terminology or Numbering) Order 2012 (SI 2012/1809) art.3(1) and Sch.1 Pt.2 (August 1, 2012).
4. Social Security (Habitual Residence) (Amendment) Regulations 2012 (SI 2012/2587) reg.2 (November 8, 2012).
5. Social Security (Croatia) Amendment Regulations 2013 (SI 2013/1474) reg.7 (July 1, 2013).
6. Social Security (Miscellaneous Amendments) (No. 3) Regulations 2013 (SI 2013/2536) reg.13(1) and (24) (October 29, 2013).
7. Social Security (Habitual Residence) (Amendment) Regulations 2014 (SI 2014/902) reg.7 (May 31, 2014).
8. Social Security (Income-related Benefits) (Updating and Amendment) (EU Exit) Regulations 2019 (SI 2019/872) reg.7 (May 7, 2019).
9. Social Security (Income-Related Benefits) (Persons of Northern Ireland – Family Members) (Amendment) Regulations 2020 (SI 2020/638) reg.7 (August 24, 2020).
10. Immigration and Social Security Co-ordination (EU Withdrawal) Act 2020 (Consequential, Saving, Transitional and Transitory Provisions) (EU Exit) Regulations 2020 (SI 2020/1309) reg 73 (December 31, 2020 at 11.00 pm).
11. Immigration (Citizens' Rights etc.) (EU Exit) Regulations 2020 (SI 2020/1372) reg.23 (December 31, 2020 at 11.00 pm).
12. Social Security (Habitual Residence and Past Presence) (Amendment) Regulations 2021 (SI 2021/1034) reg.2 (September 15, 2021).
13. Social Security (Habitual Residence and Past Presence) (Amendment) Regulations 2022 (SI 2022/344) reg.2 (March 22, 2022).
14. Social Security (Habitual Residence and Past Presence) (Amendment) (No. 2) Regulations 2022 (SI 2022/990) reg.2 (October 18, 2022).
15. Social Security (Habitual Residence and Past Presence) (Amendment) Regulations 2023 (SI 2023/532) reg.2(1) and 2(2)(f) (May 15, 2023).
16. Social Security (Habitual Residence and Past Presence, and Capital Disregards) (Amendment) Regulations 2023, reg.2 (SI 2023/1144) (October 27, 2023).

MODIFICATION

Regulation 70 is modified by Sch.1 para.10A of the Employment and Support Allowance (Transitional Provisions, Housing Benefit and Council Tax Benefit) (Existing Awards) (No. 2) Regulations 2010 (SI 2010/1907) as amended for the purposes specified in reg.6(1) of those Regulations. For the details of the modification, pp.1410–1452 of Vol.I of the 2020/21 edition.

DEFINITION

"Immigration and Asylum Act"—reg.2(1).

pp.1358–1359, *annotation to the Employment Support Allowance Regulations 2008 (SI 2008/794) regs 95 and 96 (Earnings of employed earners and calculation of net earnings of employed earners)*

6.133 See the detailed discussion of *SSWP v NC (ESA)* [2024] UKUT 251 (AAC) in the entry above for pp.383–384 (income support), on the treatment of salary sacrifice arrangements involving the employer making occupational pension contributions of the amount of salary sacrificed by the employee. It is suggested there that that decision failed to consider the effect of reg.108(3) of the ESA Regulations 2008 (the equivalent of reg.42(6) of the Income Support (General) Regulations 1987) on notional income where a claimant is paid less than the rate for comparable employment in the area.

pp.1362–1363, *amendment to the Employment and Support Allowance Regulations 2008 (SI 2008/794) reg.99(3) (Deduction of tax and contributions for self-employed earners)*

With effect from April 6, 2024, reg.8(15) of the Social Security (Class 2 National Insurance Contributions) (Consequential Amendments and Savings) Regulations 2024 (SI 2024/377) amended reg.99(3) by omitting sub-para.(a). **6.134**

p.1373, *amendment to the Employment and Support Allowance Regulations 2008 (SI 2008/794) reg.107(5A) (Notional income—exceptions)*

With effect from January 1, 2022, reg.7(3) of the Social Security (Income and Capital Disregards) (Amendment) Regulations 2021 (SI 2021/1405) amended para.(5A) by substituting the following for "a payment of income which is a Grenfell Tower payment": **6.135**

"any of the following payments of income—
(a) a Grenfell Tower payment;
(b) a child abuse payment;
(c) a Windrush payment."

All of those payments are defined in reg.2(1). See the entry for p.684 for discussion of the nature of child abuse and Windrush payments.

With effect from July 9, 2023, reg.7(3) of the Social Security (Income and Capital Disregards) (Amendment) Regulations 2023 (SI 2023/640) amended reg.107(5A) by inserting the following after sub-para.(c):

"(d) a Post Office compensation payment."

Such payments are newly defined in reg.2(1), where there is now also an expanded definition of Grenfell Tower payments (see sub-para.(a). See the entry for pp.684–685 of Vol.II in this Supplement.

pp.1376–1377, *annotation to the Employment Support Allowance Regulations 2008 (SI 2008/794) regs 108(3) (Notional income—other income) and 109(2)(d) (Notional income—calculation and interpretation)*

See the detailed discussion of *SSWP v NC (ESA)* [2024] UKUT 251 (AAC) in the entry above for pp.383–384 (income support), on the treatment of salary sacrifice arrangements involving the employer making occupational pension contributions of the amount of salary sacrificed by the employee. It is suggested there that that decision failed to consider the effect of reg.108(3) (the equivalent of reg.42(6) of the Income Support (General) Regulations 1987) on notional income where a claimant is paid less than the rate for comparable employment in the area. It is hard to see how reg.108(3) would not have applied in the circumstances. There would then be a potential problem in the application of reg.109(2)(d) (the equivalent of reg.42(8)(c)). **6.136**

p.1377, *annotation to the Employment and Support Allowance Regulations 2008 (SI 2008/794) reg.110 (Capital limit)*

6.137 In the Institute for Government and the Social Security Advisory Committee's 2021 joint report *Jobs and benefits: The Covid-19 challenge* it was noted that if the capital limit of £16,000 had risen in line with prices since 2006 it would be close to £23,500 (or £25,000: different figures are given) and recommended that the limit should be increased to £25,000 and subsequently automatically indexed to maintain its real value (pp.22 and 31). That recommendation was summarily rejected in the Government's response of March 22, 2022.

p.1378, *amendment to the Employment and Support Allowance Regulations 2008 (SI 2008/794) reg.112(8) (Income treated as capital—exceptions)*

6.138 With effect from January 1, 2022, reg.7(4) of the Social Security (Income and Capital Disregards) (Amendment) Regulations 2021 (SI 2021/1405) amended para.(8) by substituting the following for sub-para.(b):

"any—
(a) Grenfell Tower payment;
(b) child abuse payment;
(c) Windrush payment."

All of those payments are defined in reg.2(1). See the entry for p.684 for discussion of the nature of child abuse and Windrush payments.

With effect from July 9, 2023, reg.7(4) of the Social Security (Income and Capital Disregards) (Amendment) Regulations 2023 (SI 2023/640) amended reg.112(8)(b) by inserting the following after head (iii):

"(iv) Post Office compensation payment."

Such payments are newly defined in reg.2(1), where there is now also an expanded definition of Grenfell Tower payments (see head (a)). See the entry for pp.684–685 on income support for the background.

With effect from October 27, 2023, reg.8(3)(a) of the Social Security (Habitual Residence and Past Presence, and Capital Disregards) (Amendment) Regulations 2023 (SI 2023/1144) amended reg.112(8)(a) by inserting ", the Victims of Overseas Terrorism Compensation Scheme" after "the National Emergencies Trust". That scheme is newly defined in reg.2(1). See the entry for pp.684–685 on income support for the background.

p.1382, *amendment to the Employment and Support Allowance Regulations 2008 (SI 2008/794) reg.115(5) and (5A) (Notional capital—exceptions)*

6.139 With effect from January 1, 2022, reg.7(5) of the Social Security (Income and Capital Disregards) (Amendment) Regulations 2021 (SI 2021/1405) amended para.(5A) by substituting the following for "a payment of capital which is a Grenfell Tower payment":

"any of the following payments of capital—
(a) a Grenfell Tower payment;
(b) a child abuse payment;
(c) a Windrush payment."

All of those payments are defined in reg.2(1). See the entry for p.684 for discussion of the nature of child abuse and Windrush payments.

With effect from July 9, 2023, reg.7(5) of the Social Security (Income and Capital Disregards) (Amendment) Regulations 2023 (SI 2023/640) amended reg.115(5A) by inserting the following after sub-para.(c):

"(d) a Post Office compensation payment;
(e) a vaccine damage payment."

Such payments are newly defined in reg.2(1), where there is now also an expanded definition of Grenfell Tower payments (see sub-para.(a)). See the entry for pp.684–685 on income support in this Supplement.

With effect from October 27, 2023, reg.8(3)(b) of the Social Security (Habitual Residence and Past Presence, and Capital Disregards) (Amendment) Regulations 2023 (SI 2023/1144) amended reg.115(5)(a) by inserting ", the Victims of Overseas Terrorism Compensation Scheme" after "the National Emergencies Trust". That scheme is newly defined in reg.2(1). See the entry for pp.684–685 on income support for the background.

pp.1406–1407, *annotation to the Employment and Support Allowance Regulations 2008 (SI 2008/794) reg.137(4) and (5) (Treatment of student loans and postgraduate loans)*

See the entry for p.539 on income support for details of the decision in *IB v Gravesham BC and SSWP (HB)* [2023] UKUT 193 (AAC); [2024] P.T.S.R. 130 on when a claimant cannot acquire a loan by taking reasonable steps to do so. 6.140

p.1409, *amendment to the Employment and Support Allowance Regulations 2008 (SI 2008/794) reg.139A (Treatment of special support loans)*

With effect from April 1, 2024, reg.5 of the Social Security and Universal Credit (Migration of Tax Credit Claimants and Miscellaneous Amendments) Regulations 2024 (SI 2024/341) amended reg.139A by substituting the following for the existing text and heading: 6.141

> **"Treatment of loans for specific purposes**
> **139A.** A loan under the Education (Student Support) Regulations 2011 or regulations made under section 73 of the Education (Scotland) Act 1980 that is intended to meet the cost of books, equipment, travel or childcare is to be disregarded as income."

The new form of reg.139A is intended to ensure that special support loans under a scheme to be introduced for full-time students by the Scottish government from the beginning of academic year 2024/25 are to be disregarded as income in same way as special support loans in England and Wales. Although the new form no longer refers to the definition of "special support loan" in reg.68 of the Education (Student Support) Regulations 2011, the restriction to loans intended (i.e., by necessary implication, intended by the awarding authority) to meet the cost of books, equipment, travel or childcare excludes loans under those regulations for other purposes. See reg.132 for the disregard of grants, as opposed to loans, for similar and other purposes.

p.1411, *amendment to the Employment and Support Allowance Regulations 2008 (SI 2008/794) reg.144 (Waiting days)*

6.142 With effect from November 19, 2023, art.19(4) of the Carer's Assistance (Carer Support Payment) (Scotland) Regulations 2023 (Consequential Amendments) Order 2023 (SI 2023/1218) amended reg.144(2)(a) by inserting ", carer support payment" after "carer's allowance".

p.1413, *annotation to the Employment and Support Allowance Regulations 2008 (SI 2008/794) reg.145 (Linking rules)*

6.143 For more detailed analysis see the commentary on SSCBA 1992 s.30C(1)(c) in Vol.I of the 2011/12 edition of this work (at paras 1.67–1.77).

p.1423, *annotation to the Employment and Support Allowance Regulations 2008 (SI 2008/794) reg.153 (Absence to receive medical treatment)*

6.144 Regulation 153 is considered in *SSWP v NJ* [2024] UKUT 194 (AAC). The Upper Tribunal finds that the FTT did not err where it decided a person whose mental illness was improved by sunshine was "undergoing treatment" when she spent time at her holiday home in Spain (there being some medical support for the proposition that the sunshine improved her mental health); that it was "solely" for the purpose of that treatment ("solely" relating to the overall purpose of the visit, not the question of whether the claimant did anything else while there, given that almost no treatment regime would last 24 hours per day); and that it was being "supervised" by her "appropriately qualified" husband, a retired doctor.

pp.1431–1432, *amendments to the Employment and Support Allowance Regulations 2008 (SI 2008/794) reg.158 (Meaning of "person in hardship")*

6.145 With effect from July 26, 2021, Sch.9 para.4 of the Social Security (Scotland) Act 2018 (Disability Assistance for Children and Young People) (Consequential Modifications) Order 2021 (SI 2021/786) makes the following amendments to reg.158:

- In para.(3):
  - in sub-para.(c), after "disability living allowance", insert ", child disability payment";
  - in sub-para.(d)(ii), after "disability living allowance", insert ", child disability payment".
- For para.(7), substitute:

"(7) In this regulation, "care component" means—

(a) the care component of disability living allowance at the highest or middle rate prescribed under section 72(3) of the Contributions and Benefits Act; or

(b) the care component of child disability payment at the highest or middle rate provided for in regulation 11(5) of the DACYP Regulations.".

With effect from March 21, 2022, art.11(4) of the Social Security (Disability Assistance for Working Age People) (Consequential

Amendments) Order 2022 (SI 2022/177) makes the following amendments to reg.158(3):

- in sub-para.(b):
  - after "armed forces independence payment" for "or" substitute ",";
  - after "daily living component" insert "or the daily living component of adult disability payment";
- in sub-para.(c):
  - after "armed forces independence payment" for "or" substitute ",";
  - after "personal independence payment", insert "or adult disability payment";
- in sub-para.(d):
  - in para.(i):
    - after "armed forces independence payment" for "or" substitute ",";
    - after "daily living component" insert "or the daily living component of adult disability payment";
  - in para.(ii):
    - after "armed forces independence payment" for "or" substitute ",";
    - after "personal independence payment", insert "or adult disability payment".

p.1437, *amendment to the Employment and Support Allowance Regulations 2008 (SI 2008/794) reg.165 (entitlement for less than a week—amount of an employment and support allowance payable)*

With effect from November 19, 2023, art.19 of the Carer's Assistance (Carer Support Payment) (Scotland) Regulations 2023 (Consequential Amendments) Order 2023 (SI 2023/1218) amends reg.165(3) as follows: **6.146**

after "carer's allowance" insert ", carer support payment".

p.1438, *amendment to the Employment and Support Allowance Regulations 2008 (SI 2008/794) reg.167 (modification in the calculation of income)*

With effect from November 19, 2023, art.19 of the Carer's Assistance (Carer Support Payment) (Scotland) Regulations 2023 (Consequential Amendments) Order 2023 (SI 2023/1218) amends reg.167(d) as follows: **6.147**

after "carer's allowance" insert ", carer support payment".

pp.1494–1496, *annotation to the Employment and Support Allowance Regulations 2008 (SI 2008/794) Sch.2 Activity 17 (Appropriateness of behaviour with other people, due to cognitive impairment or mental disorder)*

Consideration of Activity 17 may require the disclosure of Unacceptable Customer Behaviour (UCB) forms as provided in confidence by the DWP to HMCTS: *MH v SSWP (ESA)* [2021] UKUT 90 (AAC). **6.148**

pp.1507–1514, *amendments to the Employment and Support Allowance Regulations 2008 (SI 2008/794) Sch.4 (Amounts)*

Substitute the following for paras 4.420–4.429 **6.149**

Regulations 67(1)(a) and (2) and 68(1)(a) and (b)

"SCHEDULE 4

AMOUNTS

PART 1

PRESCRIBED AMOUNTS

4.420 **1.** The weekly amounts specified in column (2) in respect of each person or couple specified in column (1) are the weekly amounts specified for the purposes of regulations 67(1) and 68 (prescribed amounts and polygamous marriages).

(1) *Person or Couple*	*(2)* *Amount*
(1) *Single claimant*— (a) who satisfies the conditions set out in section 2(2) [[12] . . .] or 4(4) [[12] . . .] of the Act [[13] or who is a member of the work-related activity group]; (b) aged not less than 25 (c) aged less than 25.	(1) (a) [[16] £90.50]; (b) [[16] £90.50]; (c) [[16] £71.70];
(2) Lone parent [[6] or a person who has no partner and who is responsible for and a member of the same household as a young person]— (a) who satisfies the conditions set out in section 4(4) [[12] ...] of the Act[[13] or who is a member of the work-related activity group and satisfies the conditions set out in Part 2 of Schedule 1 to the Act]; (b) aged not less than 18; (c) aged less than 18.	(2) (a) [[16] £90.50]; (b) [[16] £90.50]; (c) [[16] £71.70];
(3) Couple— (a) where both members are aged not less than 18; (b) where one member is aged not less than 18 and the other member is a person under 18 who— (i) [[3] if that other member had not been a member] of a couple, would satisfy the requirements for entitlement to income support other than the requirement to make a claim for it; or (ii) [[3] if that other member had not been a member] of a couple, would satisfy the requirements for entitlement to an income-related allowance; or (iii) satisfies the requirements of section 3(1)(f)(iii) of the Jobseekers Act (prescribed circumstances for persons aged 16 but less than 18); or (iv) is the subject of a direction under section 16 of that Act (persons under 18: severe hardship); (c) where the claimant satisfies the conditions set out in section 4(4) [[12] . . .] of the Act [[13] or the claimant is a member of the work-related activity group and satisfies the conditions set out in Part 2 of Schedule 1 to the Act] and both members are aged less than 18 and— (i) at least one of them is treated as responsible for a child; or	(3) (a) [[16] £192.25]; (b) [[16] £192.25]; (c) [[16] £192.25];

(1) *Person or Couple*	*(2)* *Amount*
(ii) had they not been members of a couple, each would have qualified for an income-related allowance; or (iii) had they not been members of a couple the claimant's partner would satisfy the requirements for entitlement to income support other than the requirement to make a claim for it; or (iv) the claimant's partner satisfies the requirements of section 3(1)(f)(iii) of the Jobseekers Act (prescribed circumstances for persons aged 16 but less than 18); or (v) there is in force in respect of the claimant's partner a direction under section 16 of that Act (persons under 18: severe hardship);	
(d) where both members are aged less than 18 and— (i) at least one of them is treated as responsible for a child; or (ii) had they not been members of a couple, each would have qualified for an income-related allowance; or (iii) had they not been members of a couple the claimant's partner satisfies the requirements for entitlement to income support other than a requirement to make a claim for it; or (iv) the claimant's partner satisfies the requirements of section 3(1)(f)(iii) of the Jobseekers Act (prescribed circumstances for persons aged 16 but less than 18); or (v) there is in force in respect of the claimant's partner a direction under section 16 of that Act (persons under 18: severe hardship);	(d) [15 £101.50];
(e) where the claimant is aged not less than 25 and the claimant's partner is a person under 18 who— (i) would not qualify for an income-related allowance if the person were not a member of a couple; (ii) would not qualify for income support if the person were not a member of a couple; (iii) does not satisfy the requirements of section 3(1)(f)(iii) of the Jobseekers Act (prescribed circumstances for persons aged 16 but less than 18); and (iv) is not the subject of a direction under section 16 of that Act (persons under 18: severe hardship);	(e) [16 £90.50];
(f) where the claimant satisfies the conditions set out in section 4(4) [12 . . .] of the Act [13 or the claimant is a member of the work-related activity group and satisfies the conditions set out in Part 2 of Schedule 1 to the Act] and the claimant's partner is a person under 18 who— (i) would not qualify for an income-related allowance if the person were not a member of a couple; (ii) would not qualify for income support if the person [1 were] not a member of a couple;	(f) [16 £90.50];

(1) Person or Couple	(2) Amount
(iii) does not satisfy the requirements of section 3(1)(f)(iii) of the Jobseekers Act (prescribed circumstances for persons aged 16 but less than 18); and	
(iv) is not the subject of a direction under section 16 of that Act (persons under 18: severe hardship);	
(g) where the claimant satisfies the conditions set out in section 4(4) [12 . . .] of the Act [13 or the claimant is a member of the work-related activity group and satisfies the conditions set out in Part 2 of Schedule 1 to the Act] and both members are aged less than 18 and paragraph (c) does not apply;	(g) [16 £90.50];
(h) where the claimant is aged not less than 18 but less than 25 and the claimant's partner is a person under 18 who—	(h) [16 £71.70];
(i) would not qualify for an income-related allowance if the person were not a member of a couple;	
(ii) would not qualify for income support if the person were not a member of a couple;	
(iii) does not satisfy the requirements of section 3(1)(f)(iii) of the Jobseekers Act (prescribed circumstances for persons aged 16 but less than 18); and	
(iv) is not the subject of a direction under section 16 of that Act (persons under 18: severe hardship);	
(i) where both members are aged less than 18 and paragraph (d) does not apply.	(i) [16 £71.70].

Regulations 67(1)(b) and 68(1)(c)

PART 2

PREMIUMS

4.421 **2.** Except as provided in paragraph 4, the weekly premiums specified in Part 3 of this Schedule are, for the purposes of regulation 67(1)(b) and 68(1)(c), to be applicable to a claimant who satisfies the condition specified in paragraphs 5 to 8 in respect of that premium.

3. An enhanced disability premium in respect of a person is not applicable in addition to a pensioner premium.

4.—(1) For the purposes of this Part of this Schedule, once a premium is applicable to a claimant under this Part, a person is to be treated as being in receipt of any benefit—

(a) in the case of a benefit to which the Social Security (Overlapping Benefits) Regulations 1979 applies, for any period during which, apart from the provisions of those Regulations, the person would be in receipt of that benefit; and

(b) for any period spent by a person in undertaking a course of training or instruction provided or approved by the Secretary of State under section 2 of the Employment and Training Act 1973, or by [3 Skills Development Scotland] or Highlands and Islands Enterprise under section 2 of the Enterprise and New Towns (Scotland) Act 1990, or for any period during which the person is in receipt of a training allowance]. [15 ; and

(c) in the case of carer support payment, for any period during which, apart from regulation 16 of the Carer's Assistance (Carer Support Payment) (Scotland) Regulations 2023, he would be in receipt of that benefit.]

[7 (2) For the purposes of the carer premium under paragraph 8, a person is to be treated as being in receipt of a carer's allowance by virtue of sub-paragraph (1)(a) [15 or carer support payment by virtue of sub-paragraph (1)(c)] only if and for so long as the person in respect of whose care the allowance [15 or payment] has been claimed

(a) attendance allowance;

(b) the care component of disability living allowance at the highest or middle rate prescribed in accordance with section 72(3) of the Contributions and Benefits Act; [8 . . .]

(c) the daily living component of personal independence payment at the standard or enhanced rate in accordance with section 78(3) of the 2012 Act [8 [14 . . .

(ca) the daily living component of adult disability payment at the standard or enhanced rate in accordance with regulation 5 of the Disability Assistance for Working Age People (Scotland) Regulations 2022; or]

(d) armed forces independence payment.]]

Pensioner premium

5. The condition is that the claimant or the claimant's partner has attained the qualifying age for state pension credit. **4.422**

Severe disability premium

6.—(1) The condition is that the claimant is a severely disabled person. **4.423**

(2) For the purposes of sub-paragraph (1), a claimant is to be treated as being a severely disabled person if, and only if—

(a) in the case of a single claimant, a lone parent [6 , a person who has no partner and who is responsible for and a member of the same household as a young person] or a claimant who is treated as having no partner in consequence of subparagraph (3)—

(i) the claimant is in receipt of the care component [7 , the daily living component] [14 , the daily living component of adult disability payment] [8 , armed forces independence payment] [5 or attendance allowance];

(ii) subject to sub-paragraph (4), the claimant has no non-dependants aged 18 or over normally residing with the claimant or with whom the claimant is normally residing; and

(iii) no person is entitled to, and in receipt of, [11 a carer's allowance [15 or carer support payment] or has an award of universal credit which includes the carer element] in respect of caring for the claimant;

(b) in the case of a claimant who has a partner—

(i) the claimant is in receipt of the care component [7 , the daily living component] [14 , the daily living component of adult disability payment] [8 , armed forces independence payment] [5 or attendance allowance];

(ii) the claimant's partner is also in receipt of the care component [7 , the daily living component] [14 , the daily living component of adult disability payment] [8 , armed forces independence payment] or attendance allowance or, if the claimant is a member of a polygamous marriage, all the partners of that marriage are in receipt of the care component [7 , the daily living component] [14 , the daily living component of adult disability payment] [8 , armed forces independence payment] or attendance allowance; and

(iii) subject to sub-paragraph (4), the claimant has no non-dependants aged 18 or over normally residing with the claimant or with whom the claimant is normally residing,

and, either a person is entitled to, and in receipt of, a carer's allowance [15 or carer support payment] [11 or has an award of universal credit which includes the carer element] in respect of caring for only one of the couple or, in the case of a polygamous marriage, for one or more but not all the partners of the marriage or, as the case may be, no person is entitled to, and in receipt of, such an allowance [15 or payment] [11 or has such an award of universal credit] in respect of caring for either member of the couple or any partner of the polygamous marriage.

(3) Where a claimant has a partner who does not satisfy the condition in sub-paragraph (2)(b)(ii) and that partner is blind or severely sight impaired or is treated as blind or severely sight impaired that partner is to be treated for the purposes of sub-paragraph (2) as if the partner were not a partner of the claimant.

(4) For the purposes of sub-paragraph (2)(a)(ii) and (b)(iii) no account is to be taken of—

(a) a person receiving attendance allowance, [7 the daily living component] [14 , the daily living component of adult disability payment] [8 , armed forces independence payment] or the care component;

(b) subject to sub-paragraph (7), a person who joins the claimant's household for the first time in order to care for the claimant or the claimant's partner and immediately before so joining the claimant or the claimant's partner was treated as a severely disabled person; or

(c) a person who is blind or severely sight impaired or is treated as blind or severely sight impaired.

(5) For the purposes of sub-paragraph (2)(b) a person is to be treated—

(a) as being in receipt of attendance allowance or the care component if the person would, but for the person being a patient for a period exceeding 28 days, be so in receipt;

(b) as being entitled to, and in receipt of, a carer's allowance [15 or carer support payment] [11 or having an award of universal credit which includes the carer element] if the person would, but for the person for whom the person was caring being a patient in hospital for a period exceeding 28 days, be so entitled and in receipt [11 of carer's allowance or have such an award of universal credit].

[7(c) as being in entitled to, and in receipt of, the daily living component if the person would, but for regulations under section 86(1) (hospital in-patients) of the 2012 Act, be so entitled and in receipt.]

[14 (d) as being in entitled to, and in receipt of, the daily living component of adult disability payment if the person would, but for regulation 28 (effect of admission to hospital on ongoing entitlement to Adult Disability Payment) of the Disability Assistance for Working Age People (Scotland) Regulations 2022, be so in receipt.]

(6) For the purposes of sub-paragraph (2)(a)(iii) and (b), no account is to be taken of an award of carer's allowance [15 or carer support payment] [11 or universal credit which includes the carer element] to the extent that payment of such an award is backdated for a period before the date on which the award is first paid.

(7) Sub-paragraph (4)(b) is to apply only for the first 12 weeks following the date on which the person to whom that provision applies first joins the claimant's household.

(8) In sub-paragraph (2)(a)(iii) and (b), references to a person being in receipt of a carer's allowance [11 or as having an award of universal credit which includes the carer element] are to include references to a person who would have been in receipt of that allowance [11 or had such an award] but for the application of a restriction under section [4 6B or] 7 of the Social Security Fraud Act 2001 (loss of benefit provisions).

(9) [11 (a)] In this paragraph—

[9 "blind or severely sight impaired" means certified as blind or severely sight impaired by a consultant ophthalmologist and a person who has ceased to be certified as blind or severely sight impaired where that person's eyesight has been regained is, nevertheless, to be treated as blind or severely sight impaired for a period of 28 weeks following the date on which the person ceased to be so certified;]

"the care component" means the care component of disability living allowance at the highest or middle rate prescribed in accordance with section 72(3) of the Contributions and Benefits Act.

[11 (b) A person has an award of universal credit which includes the carer element if the person has an award of universal credit which includes an amount which is the carer element under regulation 29 of the Universal Credit Regulations 2013.]

Enhanced disability premium

4.424 7.—(1) Subject to sub-paragraph (2), the condition is that—

(a) the claimant's applicable amount includes the support component; [7 . . .]

(b) the care component of disability living allowance is, or would, but for a suspension of benefit in accordance with regulations under section 113(2) of the Contributions and Benefits Act or, but for an abatement as a consequence of hospitalisation, be payable at the highest rate prescribed under section 72(3) of that Act in respect of—

(i) the claimant; or

(ii) the claimant's partner (if any) who is aged less than the qualifying age for state pension credit [7 ; [8 . . .]

(c) the daily living component is, or would, but for regulations made under section 86(1) (hospital in-patients) of the 2012 Act, be payable at the enhanced rate under section 78(2) of that Act in respect of—

(i) the claimant; or

(ii) the claimant's partner (if any) who is aged less than the qualifying age for state pension credit"]; [14 . . .

(ca) the daily living component of adult disability payment is, or would, but for regulation 28 (effect of admission to hospital on ongoing entitlement to Adult Disability Payment) of the Disability Assistance for Working Age People (Scotland) Regulations 2022, be payable at the enhanced rate under section 78(2) of those Regulations in respect of—
(i) the claimant; or
(ii) the claimant's partner (if any) who is aged less than the qualifying age for state pension credit; or]
(d) armed forces independence payment is payable in respect of—
(i) the claimant; or
(ii) the claimant's partner (if any) who is aged less than the qualifying age for state pension credit.]

(2) An enhanced disability premium is not applicable in respect of—
(a) a claimant who—
(i) is not a member of a couple or a polygamous marriage; and
(ii) is a patient within the meaning of regulation 69(2) and has been for a period of more than 52 weeks; or
(b) a member of a couple or a polygamous marriage where each member is a patient within the meaning of regulation 69(2) and has been for a period of more than 52 weeks.

Carer premium

8.—(1) Subject to sub-paragraphs (2) and (4), the condition is that the claimant or the claimant's partner is, or both of them are, entitled to a carer's allowance under section 70 of the Contributions and Benefits Act [[15] or carer support payment]. 4.425

(2) Where a carer premium is awarded but—
(a) the person in respect of whose care the carer's allowance [[15] or carer support payment] has been awarded dies; or
(b) in any other case the person in respect of whom a carer premium has been awarded ceases to be entitled to a carer's allowance [[15] or carer support payment], the condition for the award of the premium is to be treated as satisfied for a period of 8 weeks from the relevant date specified in sub-paragraph (3).

(3) The relevant date for the purposes of sub-paragraph (2) is—
(a) where sub-paragraph (2)(a) applies, the Sunday following the death of the person in respect of whose care a carer's allowance [[15] or carer support payment] has been awarded or the date of death if the death occurred on a Sunday; or
(b) in any other case, the date on which the person who has been entitled to a carer's allowance [[15] or carer support payment] ceases to be entitled to that allowance [[15] or payment].

(4) Where a person who has been entitled to a carer's allowance [[15] or carer support payment] ceases to be entitled to that allowance [[15] or payment] and makes a claim for an income-related allowance, the condition for the award of the carer premium is to be treated as satisfied for a period of 8 weeks from the date on which—
(a) the person in respect of whose care the carer's allowance [[15] or carer support payment] has been awarded dies; or
(b) in any other case, the person who has been entitled to a carer's allowance [[15] or carer support payment] ceased to be entitled to that allowance [[15] or payment].

Persons in receipt of concessionary payments

9. For the purpose of determining whether a premium is applicable to a person under paragraphs 6, 7 and 8, any concessionary payment made to compensate that person for the non-payment of any benefit mentioned in those paragraphs is to be treated as if it were a payment of that benefit. 4.426

Persons in receipt of benefit

10. For the purposes of this Part of this Schedule, a person is to be regarded as being in receipt of any benefit if, and only if, it is paid in respect of the person and is to be so regarded only for any period in respect of which that benefit is paid. 4.427

PART 3

WEEKLY AMOUNT OF PREMIUMS SPECIFIED IN PART 2

4.428 **11.**—

Premium	*Amount*
(1) Pension premium for a person to whom paragraph 5 applies who— (a) is a single claimant and— (i) [12 . . .]; (ii) is entitled to the support component; or [12(iii) is not entitled to the support component;] (b) is a member of a couple and— (i) [12 . . .] (ii) is entitled to the support component; or [12 (iii) is not entitled to the support component;]	(1) (a) (i) [12 . . .]; (ii) [17 £79.95]; (iii) [17 £127.65]; (b) (i) [12]; (ii) [17 £143.00]; (iii) [17 £190.70];
(2) Severe disability premium— (a) where the claimant satisfies the condition in paragraph 6(2)(a); (b) where the claimant satisfies the condition in paragraph 6(2)(b)— (i) if there is someone in receipt of a carer's allowance or if the person or any partner satisfies that condition only by virtue of paragraph 6(5); (ii) if no-one is in receipt of such an allowance.	(2) (a) [17 £181.50]; (b) (i) [17 £81.50]; (ii) [17 £163.00].
(3) Carer premium.	(3) [17 £45.60]; in respect of each person who satisfies the condition specified in [1 paragraph 8(1)].
(4) Enhanced disability premium where the conditions in paragraph 7 are satisfied.	(4)(a) [17 £20.85]; in respect of each person who is neither— (i) a child or young person; nor (ii) a member of a couple or a polygamous marriage, in respect of whom the conditions specified in paragraph 7 are satisfied; (b) [17 £29.75]; where the claimant is a member of a couple or a polygamous marriage and the conditions specified in [1 paragraph 7] are satisfied in respect of a member of that couple or polygamous marriage.

Regulation 67(3)

PART 4

[12 THE COMPONENT]

12. [12 . . .]. 4.429

13. The amount of the support component is [17 £44.70]."

AMENDMENTS

1. Employment and Support Allowance (Miscellaneous Amendments) Regulations 2008 (SI 2008/2428) reg.14 (October 27, 2008).
2. Social Security (Miscellaneous Amendments) Regulations 2009 (SI 2009/583) reg.10(2) (April 6, 2009).
3. Social Security (Miscellaneous Amendments) (No. 4) Regulations 2009 (SI 2009/2655) reg.11(1) and (16) (October 26, 2009).
4. Social Security (Loss of Benefit) Amendment Regulations 2010 (SI 2010/1160) reg.12(1) and (3) (April 1, 2010).
5. Social Security (Miscellaneous Amendments) (No. 3) Regulations 2011 (SI 2011/2425) reg.23(14) (October 30, 2011).
6. Social Security (Work-focused Interviews for Lone Parents and Partners) (Amendment) Regulations 2011 (SI 2011/2428) reg.5(5) (October 30, 2011).
7. Personal Independence Payment (Supplementary Provisions and Consequential Amendments) Regulations 2013 (SI 2013/388) reg.8 and Sch. para.40(1) and (5) (April 8, 2013).
8. Armed Forces and Reserve Forces Compensation Scheme (Consequential Provisions: Subordinate Legislation) Order 2013 (SI 2013/591) art.7 and Sch. para.37(1) and (5) (April 8, 2013).
9. Universal Credit and Miscellaneous Amendments (No. 2) Regulations 2014 (SI 2014/2888) reg.3(7)(a) (November 26, 2014).
10. Welfare Benefits Up-rating Order 2015 (SI 2015/30) art.11(1) and Sch.4 (April 6, 2015).
11. Universal Credit and Miscellaneous Amendments Regulations 2015 (SI 2015/1754) reg.19 (November 4, 2015).
12. Employment and Support Allowance and Universal Credit (Miscellaneous Amendments and Transitional and Savings Provisions) Regulations 2017 (SI 2017/204) reg.2(1) and (4) (April 3, 2017).
13. Employment and Support Allowance (Miscellaneous Amendments and Transitional and Savings Provision) Regulations 2017 (SI 2017/581) reg.7(1) and (4) (June 23, 2017, subject to the transitional and savings provision in reg.10).
14. Social Security (Disability Assistance for Working Age People) (Consequential Amendments) Order 2022 (SI 2022/177) art.11(5) (March 21 2022).
15. Carers Assistance (Carer Support Payment) (Scotland) Regulations 2023 (Consequential Amendments) Order 2023 (SI 2023/1218) art.19 (November 19, 2023).
16. Social Security Benefits Up-rating Order 2024 (SI 2024/242) art.30(2) and Sch.11 (April 8, 2024).
17. Social Security Benefits Up-rating Order 2024 (SI 2024/242) art.30(4) and Sch.12 (April 8, 2024).
18. Social Security Benefits Up-rating Order 2024 (SI 2024/242) art.30(7) (April 8, 2024).

For the General Note to Sch.4, see Vol.V para.4.430.

pp.1525–1532, *amendments to the Employment and Support Allowance Regulations 2008 (SI 2008/794) Sch.6 (Housing costs)*

6.150 With effect from July 26, 2021, Sch.9 para.5 of the Social Security (Scotland) Act 2018 (Disability Assistance for Children and Young People) (Consequential Modifications) Order 2021 (SI 2021/786) makes the following amendments to Sch.6:

- In para.15(11)(b) (linking rule), after "disability living allowance", insert ", child disability payment".
- In para.19(6)(b) (non-dependent deductions), after sub-para.(ii), insert "(iia) the care component of child disability payment;".

With effect from January 1, 2022, reg.7(6) of the Social Security (Income and Capital Disregards) (Amendment) Regulations 2021 (SI 2021/1405) inserts into para.19(8)(b), after "Grenfell Tower payment", ", child abuse payment or Windrush payment".

With effect from March 21, 2022, art.11(5) of the Social Security (Disability Assistance for Working Age People) (Consequential Amendments) Order 2022 (SI 2022/177) makes the following amendments to Sch.6:

- in para.15(11)(b) (linking rule):
  - after "armed forces independence payment" for "or" substitute ",";
  - after "personal independence payment", insert "or adult disability payment";
- in para.19(8)(a) (non-dependent deductions):
  - after "armed forces independence payment" for "or" substitute ",";
  - after "personal independence payment", insert "or adult disability payment";
- at the end of para.19(6)(b)(iii) omit "or";
- after para.19(6)(b)(iii) insert "(iiia) the daily living component of adult disability payment; or".

With effect from April 8, 2024, art.30(7) of the Social Security Benefits Up-rating Order 2024 (SI 2024/242) makes the following amendments:

- in sub-paragraph (1)(a) for "£116.75" substitute "£124.55";
- in sub-paragraph (1)(b) for "£18.10" substitute "£19.30";
- in sub-paragraph (2)(a) for "£162.00" substitute "£176.00";
- in sub-paragraph (2)(b)—
  (i) for "£41.60" substitute "£44.40";
  (ii) for "£162.00" substitute "£176.00"; and
  (iii) for "£236.00" substitute "£256.00";
- in sub-paragraph (2)(c)—
  (i) for "£57.10" substitute "£60.95";
  (ii) for "£236.00" substitute "£256.00"; and
  (iii) for "£308.00" substitute "£334.00";
- in sub-paragraph (2)(d)—
  (i) for "£93.40" substitute "£99.65";
  (ii) for "£308.00" substitute "£334.00"; and
  (iii) for "£410.00" substitute "£445.00"; and

- in sub-paragraph (2)(e)—
  (i) for "£106.35" substitute "£113.50";
  (ii) for "£410.00" substitute "£445.00"; and
  (iii) for "£511.00" substitute "£554.00".

With effect from July 9, 2023, reg.7 of the Social Security (Income and Capital Disregards) (Amendment) Regulations 2023 (SI 2023/640) amends para.19 as follows:

- in paragraph 19(8)(b) (non-dependant deductions), for "or Windrush payment" insert ", Windrush payment or Post Office compensation payment".

p.1540, *amendments to the Employment and Support Allowance Regulations 2008 (SI 2008/794) Sch.8 paras 8 and 11 (Sums to be disregarded in the calculation of income other than earnings—mobility component and AA, care component and daily living component)*

With effect from March 21, 2022, art.11(7)(a) of the Social Security (Disability Assistance for Working Age People) (Consequential Amendments) Order 2022 (SI 2022/177) amended para.8 to read as follows (square brackets indicate only the present amendment, those indicating previous amendments having been omitted): 6.151

"**8.**—The mobility component of disability living allowance [, the mobility component of adult disability payment] or the mobility component of personal independence payment.]."

With effect from March 21, 2022, art.11(7)(b) of the same Order amended para.11 to read as follows (square brackets indicate only the present amendment, those indicating previous amendments having been omitted):

"**11.**—Any attendance allowance, the care component of disability living allowance[,] the daily living component [or the daily living component of adult disability payment]."

"Adult disability payment" is defined in reg.2(1) by reference to reg.2 of the Disability Assistance for Working Age People (Scotland) Regulations 2022 (SSI 2022/54) (see Vol.IV of this series).

p.1542, *amendment to the Employment and Support Allowance Regulations 2008 (SI 2008/794) Sch.8 para.22(2) (Sums to be disregarded in the calculation of income other than earnings—income in kind)*

With effect from January 1, 2022, reg.7(7)(a) of the Social Security (Income and Capital Disregards) (Amendment) Regulations 2021 (SI 2021/1405) amended sub-para.(2) by inserting ", a child abuse payment or a Windrush payment" after "Grenfell Tower payment". All of those payments are defined in reg.2(1). See the entry for pp.684–685 for discussion of the nature of child abuse and Windrush payments. 6.152

p.1544, *amendment to the Employment and Support Allowance Regulations 2008 (SI 2008/794) Sch.8 para.29 (Sums to be disregarded in the calculation of income other than earnings—payments for persons temporarily in care of claimant)*

6.153 With effect from July 1, 2022, reg.99 of and Sch. to the Health and Care Act 2022 (Consequential and Related Amendments and Transitional Provisions) Regulations 2022 (SI 2022/634) amended para.29(da) by substituting the following for the text after "(da)":

"an integrated care board established under Chapter A3 of Part 2 of the National Health Service Act 2006;"

With effect from November 6, 2023, reg.28 of the Health and Care Act 2022 (Further Consequential Amendments) (No.2) Regulations 2023 (SI 2023/1071) amended para.29(db) by substituting "NHS England" for "the National Health Service Commissioning Board".

p.1546, *amendments to the Employment and Support Allowance Regulations 2008 (SI 2008/794) Sch.8 para.41 (Sums to be disregarded in the calculation of income other than earnings)*

6.154 With effect from January 1, 2022, reg.7(7)(b) of the Social Security (Income and Capital Disregards) (Amendment) Regulations 2021 (SI 2021/1405) amended para.41 by substituting the following for sub-para.(1A):

"(1A) Any—
(a) Grenfell Tower payment;
(b) child abuse payment;
(c) Windrush payment."

In addition, reg.7(7)(c) amended sub-paras (2) to (6) by inserting ", a child abuse payment or a Windrush payment" after "Grenfell Tower payment" in each place where those words occur. All of those payments are defined in reg.2(1).

See the entry for pp.684–685 (Income Support Regulations Sch.10 (capital to be disregarded) para.22) for some technical problems arising from the date of effect of these amendments. Because all the payments so far made from the approved historic institutional child abuse compensation schemes and from the Windrush Compensation Scheme have been in the nature of capital, the question of disregarding income has not yet arisen.

With effect from July 9, 2023, reg.3(7) of the Social Security (Income and Capital Disregards) (Amendment) Regulations 2023 (SI 2023/640) amended para.41(1A) by adding the following after head (c):

"(d) Post Office compensation payment."

Such payments are newly defined in reg.2(1), where there is now also an expanded definition of Grenfell Tower payments (see head (a)). With effect from the same date, the words substituted in sub-paras (2) to (6) have been further amended by substituting ", a Windrush payment, a Post Office compensation payment or a vaccine damage payment" for "or a Windrush payment". "Vaccine damage payment" is also newly defined in reg.2(1). See the entry for pp.684–685 on income support in this Supplement.

p.1549, *amendments to the Employment and Support Allowance Regulations 2008 (SI 2008/794) Sch.8 (Sums to be disregarded in the calculation of income other than earnings)*

With effect from July 26, 2021, art.16(2) of the Social Security (Scotland) Act 2018 (Disability Assistance, Young Carer Grants, Short-term Assistance and Winter Heating Assistance) (Consequential Provision and Modifications) Order 2021 (SI 2021/886) inserted the following after para.73: 6.155

"**74.** Any disability assistance given in accordance with regulations made section 31 of the Social Security (Scotland) Act 2018."

The first regulations made under s.31 of the 2018 Act were the Disability Assistance for Children and Young People (Scotland) Regulations 2021 (SSI 2021/174), also in effect from July 26, 2021, providing for the benefit known as a child disability payment. The regulations also authorise the payment of short-term assistance, to be disregarded under para.73. The Disability Assistance for Working Age People (Scotland) Regulations 2022 (SSI 2022/54), in effect from March 21, 2022, providing for the benefit known as adult disability payment, were also made under s.31, but the two potential elements (mobility component and daily living component) have been specifically covered by para.8 and para.11 from that date (see the entry for p.1540). Short-term assistance under reg.62 of the 2022 Regulations is disregarded under para.73.

With effect from November 19, 2023, art.19(8) of the Carer's Assistance (Carer Support Payment) (Scotland) Regulations 2023 (Consequential Amendments) Order 2023 (SI 2023/1218) inserted the following after para.74:

"**75.** Any amount of carer support payment that is in excess of the amount the claimant would receive if they had an entitlement to carer's allowance under section 70 of the Contributions and Benefits Act."

Carer support payment (CSP) is newly defined in reg.2(1) by reference to the Scottish legislation (see the entry for p.1211). Note that CSP in general counts as income and that the disregard is limited to any excess of the amount of the CSP over what the claimant would have been entitled to in carer's allowance under British legislation. That is in accordance with the Fiscal Framework Agreement governing the provision of devolved benefits in Scotland (see para.6.9 of the Explanatory Memorandum to SI 2023/1218). Initially, CSP is to be paid at the same rate as carer's allowance.

p.1554, *annotation to the Employment and Support Allowance Regulations 2008 (SI 2008/794) Sch.9 para.73 (Sums to be disregarded in the calculation of income other than earnings—Scottish short-term assistance)*

Provision for short-term assistance under s.36 of the Social Security (Scotland) Act 2018, thus falling within para.73, has been made by reg.42 of and Sch. to the Disability Assistance for Children and Young People (Scotland) Regulations 2021 (SSI 2021/174), with effect from July 26, 2021, and by reg.62 of and Sch. to the Disability Assistance for Working Age People (Scotland) Regulations 2022 (SSI 2022/54), with effect from March 21, 2022. 6.156

p.1556, *amendment to the Employment and Support Allowance Regulations 2008 (SI 2008/794) Sch.9 para.11(1)(a) (Capital to be disregarded)*

6.157 With effect from July 26, 2021, art.16(3) of the Social Security (Scotland) Act 2018 (Disability Assistance, Young Carer Grants, Short-term Assistance and Winter Heating Assistance) (Consequential Provision and Modifications) Order 2021 (SI 2021/886) substituted "72, 73 or 74" for "72 or 73". See the entry for p.1549 for the new para.74 of Sch.8.

p.1556, *amendment to the Employment and Support Allowance Regulations 2008 (SI 2008/794) Sch.9 para.11A (Capital to be disregarded—widowed parent's allowance)*

6.158 With effect from February 9, 2023, para.11(a) of the Schedule to the Bereavement Benefits (Remedial) Order 2023 (SI 2023/134) inserted the following after para.11:

> "**11A.** Any payment of a widowed parent's allowance made pursuant to section 39A of the Contributions and Benefits Act (widowed parent's allowance)—
> (a) to the survivor of a cohabiting partnership (within the meaning in section 39A(7) of the Contributions and Benefits Act) who is entitled to a widowed parent's allowance for a period before the Bereavement Benefits (Remedial) Order 2023 comes into force, and
> (b) in respect of any period of time during the period ending with the day before the survivor makes the claim for a widowed parent's allowance,
>
> but only for a period of 52 weeks from the date of receipt of the payment."

The legislation on widowed parent's allowance (WPA), abolished on April 5, 2017, and bereavement support payment (BSP) in operation for deaths after April 5, 2017, was declared incompatible with the ECHR by discriminating against children whose parents were cohabiting but not married to each other or in a civil partnership (see *Re McLaughlin's Application for Judicial Review* [2018] UKSC 48; [2018] 1 W.L.R. 4250 and *R. (Jackson) v Secretary of State for Work and Pensions* [2020] EWHC 183 (Admin); [2020] 1 W.L.R. 1441 in Vol.I of this series). The Remedial Order allows retrospective claims to be made for those benefits from August 30, 2018 onwards and accordingly for arrears of benefit to be paid if the conditions of entitlement are met. The new para.11A, and the amended para.60 on BSP, deal with the consequences of such payments on old style ESA entitlement, by providing for them to be disregarded as capital for 52 weeks from receipt. See the entry for p.682 on income support for the effect of the payment of arrears of WPA being in its nature a payment of income to be taken into account (subject to a £10 per week disregard under para.17(i) of Sch.8 to the ESA Regulations 2008) against entitlement in past periods (allowing revision and the creation of an overpayment) and the misleading state of para.7.15 of the Explanatory Memorandum to the Order.

pp.1558–1559, *amendments to the Employment and Support Allowance Regulations 2008 (SI 2008/794) Sch.9 para.27 (Capital to be disregarded)*

6.159 With effect from January 1, 2022, reg.7(8)(a) of the Social Security (Income and Capital Disregards) (Amendment) Regulations 2021 (SI

2021/1405) amended sub-para.(1A) by inserting ", child abuse payment, Windrush payment" after "Grenfell Tower payment" and amended sub-paras (2) to (6) by inserting ", a child abuse payment or a Windrush payment" after "Grenfell Tower payment" in each place where those words occur. All of those payments are defined in reg.2(1).

See the entry for pp.684–685 (Income Support Regulations Sch.10 (Capital to be disregarded) para.22) for some technical problems with the addition only with effect from January 1, 2022 of the disregards of payments from approved schemes providing compensation in respect of historic institutional child abuse in the UK and from the Windrush Compensation Scheme. All the schemes so far in existence provide payments in the nature of capital. That entry also contains information about the nature of the schemes involved, including the child abuse compensation schemes so far approved.

With effect from July 9, 2023, reg.3(8) of the Social Security (Income and Capital Disregards) (Amendment) Regulations 2023 (SI 2023/640) amended para.27(1A) by adding the following after "Windrush payment":

> ", Post Office compensation payment or vaccine damage payment."

Such payments are newly defined in reg.2(1), where there is now also an expanded definition of Grenfell Tower payments. With effect from the same date, the words substituted in sub-paras (2) to (6) have been further amended by substituting ", a Windrush payment, a Post Office compensation payment or a vaccine damage payment" for "or a Windrush payment". See the entry for pp.684–685 on income support in this Supplement.

With effect from August 30, 2023, reg.2(1)(f) of the Social Security (Infected Blood Capital Disregard) (Amendment) Regulations 2023 (SI 2023/894) amended para.27 by inserting the following after sub-para.(5):

> "(5A) Any payment out of the estate of a person, which derives from a payment to meet the recommendation of the Infected Blood Inquiry in its interim report published on 29th July 2022 made under or by the Scottish Infected Blood Support Scheme or an approved blood scheme to the estate of the person, where the payment is made to the person's son, daughter, step-son or step-daughter."

See the entry for pp.684–685 on income support for the background.

With effect from October 27, 2023, reg.8(3)(c) of the Social Security (Habitual Residence and Past Presence, and Capital Disregards) (Amendment) Regulations 2023 (SI 2023/1144) amended para.27(1) and (7) by inserting ", the Victims of Overseas Terrorism Compensation Scheme" after "the National Emergencies Trust" in both places. That scheme is newly defined in reg.2(1). See the entry for pp.684–685 on income support for the background.

With effect from October 10, 2024 reg.2(1)(a) of the Social Security (Infected Blood Capital Disregard) (Amendment) Regulations 2024 (SI 2024/964) amended para.27 by inserting the following after sub-para.(5A):

> "(5B) Any payment out of the estate of a person, which derives from a payment made under or by the Scottish Infected Blood Support Scheme or an approved blood scheme to the estate of the person as a result of that person having been infected from contaminated blood products."

See the entry for p.472 of Vol.II in Pt II of this Supplement for discussion of the terms of sub-para.(5B).

p.1559, *amendment to the Employment and Support Allowance Regulations 2008 (SI 2008/794) Sch.9 para.31 (Capital to be disregarded—payments in kind)*

6.160 With effect from January 1, 2022, reg.7(8)(b) of the Social Security (Income and Capital Disregards) (Amendment) Regulations 2021 (SI 2021/1405) amended para.31 by inserting ", a child abuse payment or a Windrush payment" after "Grenfell Tower payment". All of those payments are defined in reg.2(1). See also the entry for pp.684–685.

p.1563, *amendment to the Employment and Support Allowance Regulations 2008 (SI 2008/794) Sch.9 para.60 (Capital to be disregarded—bereavement support payment)*

6.161 With effect from February 9, 2023, para.11(b) of the Schedule to the Bereavement Benefits (Remedial) Order 2023 (SI 2023/134) amended para.60 by making the existing text sub-para.(1) and inserting the following:

> "(2) Where bereavement support payment under section 30 of the Pensions Act 2014 is paid to the survivor of a cohabiting partnership (within the meaning in section 30(6B) of the Pensions Act 2014) in respect of a death occurring before the day the Bereavement Benefits (Remedial) Order 2023 comes into force, any amount of that payment which is—
> (a) in respect of the rate set out in regulation 3(1) of the Bereavement Support Payment Regulations 2017, and
> (b) paid as a lump sum for more than one monthly recurrence of the day of the month on which their cohabiting partner died,
> but only for a period of 52 weeks from the date of receipt of the payment."

See the entry for p.682 on income support for the general background. The operation of this amendment is much more straightforward than that of the new para.111A on widowed parent's allowance. Although a payment of arrears of bereavement support payment (BSP) is in its nature a payment of income and attributable to the past period in respect of which it is due, the payment could not affect any entitlement to old style ESA in that past period because it would be disregarded entirely as income (Sch.8, para.68). The amount of the arrears would thus immediately metamorphose into capital, which would then be disregarded under para.60(2) subject to the 52 week limit.

pp.1565–1566, *annotation to the Employment and Support Allowance Regulations 2008 (SI 2008/794) Sch.9 (Capital to be disregarded)*

6.162 With effect from June 28, 2022 "Cost of living payments" under the Social Security (Additional Payments) Act 2022, both those to recipients of specified means-tested benefits and "disability" payments are not to be taken into account for any old style ESA purposes by virtue of s.8(b) of the Act. The same effect was achieved with effect from March 23, 2023 in relation to payments under the Social Security (Additional Payments) Act 2023 (s.8(b) of that Act). See Pt I of Vol.II for the text of both Acts.

p.1579, *amendment to the Employment and Support Allowance (Work-Related Activity) Regulations 2011 (SI 2011/1349) reg.2 (Interpretation)*

With effect from November 19, 2023, arts1(2) and 21(2) of the Carer's Assistance (Carer Support Payment) (Scotland) Regulations 2023 (Consequential Amendments) Order 2023 (SI 2023/1218) amended para. (1) by inserting ", "carer support payment"" after "carer's allowance". 6.163

p.1579, *amendment to the Employment and Support Allowance (Work-Related Activity) Regulations 2011 (SI 2011/1349) reg.3 (Requirement to undertake work-related activity)*

With effect from November 19, 2023, arts1(2) and 21(3) of the Carer's Assistance (Carer Support Payment) (Scotland) Regulations 2023 (Consequential Amendments) Order 2023 (SI 2023/1218) amended para. (2) by deleting the word "and" at the end of para,(2)(c) and inserting the new sub-paragraph "(ca) is not entitled to carer support payment; and". 6.164

Part V

Universal Credit Commencement Orders

p.1613, *amendment of the Welfare Reform Act 2012 (Commencement No.9 and Transitional and Transitory Provisions and Commencement No.8 and Savings and Transitional Provisions (Amendment)) Order 2013 (SI 2013/983) art.5A (Transitional provision where Secretary of State determines that claims for universal credit may not be made: effect on claims for employment and support allowance and jobseeker's allowance)*

With effect from March 30, 2022, art.5 and Sch.1 para.1(2) of the Welfare Reform Act 2012 (Commencement No. 34 and Commencement No. 9, 21, 23, 31 and 32 and Transitional and Transitory Provisions (Amendment)) Order 2022 (SI 2022/302) omitted the phrase "or article 4(11) of the Welfare Reform Act 2012 (Commencement No. 32 and Savings and Transitional Provisions) Order 2019 (no claims for universal credit by frontier workers)" in art.5A(1). But note also the next entry. 6.165

p.1613, *revocation of the Welfare Reform Act 2012 (Commencement No.9 and Transitional and Transitory Provisions and Commencement No.8 and Savings and Transitional Provisions (Amendment)) Order 2013 (SI 2013/983) art.5A (Transitional provision where Secretary of State determines that claims for universal credit may not be made: effect on claims for employment and support allowance and jobseeker's allowance)*

With effect from July 25, 2022, reg.11 of, and Sch. para.2(2) to, the Universal Credit (Transitional Provisions) Amendment Regulations 2022 (SI 2022/752) revoked art.5A. 6.166

p.1615, *amendments to the Welfare Reform Act 2012 (Commencement No. 9 and Transitional and Transitory Provisions and Commencement No. 8 and Savings and Transitional Provisions (Amendment)) Order 2013 (SI 2013/983) art.6 (Transitional provision: where the abolition of income-related employment and support allowance and income-based jobseeker's allowance is treated as not applying)*

6.167 With effect from March 30, 2022, art.5 and Sch.1 para.1(3) of the Welfare Reform Act 2012 (Commencement No. 34 and Commencement No. 9, 21, 23, 31 and 32 and Transitional and Transitory Provisions (Amendment)) Order 2022 (SI 2022/302) omitted the phrase "or article 4(11) of the Welfare Reform Act 2012 (Commencement No. 32 and Savings and Transitional Provisions) Order 2019 (no claims for universal credit by frontier workers)" in art.6(1)(e)(ii).

With effect from July 25, 2022, reg.11 of, and Sch. para.2(3) to, the Universal Credit (Transitional Provisions) Amendment Regulations 2022 (SI 2022/752) omitted para.(1)(e)(ii) in art.6 and the "or" preceding it.

pp.1663–1664, *annotation to the Welfare Reform Act 2012 (Commencement No.20 and Transitional and Transitory Provisions and Commencement No.9 and Transitional and Transitory Provisions (Amendment)) Order 2014 (SI 2014/3094)*

6.168 Article 6 of SI 2014/3094 (Transitory provision: claims for housing benefit, income support or a tax credit) was revoked with effect from July 25, 2022, by reg.11 of, and Sch. para.5 to, the Universal Credit (Transitional Provisions) Amendment Regulations 2022 (SI 2022/752).

pp.1670–1672, *amendment of the Welfare Reform Act 2012 (Commencement No.21 and Transitional and Transitory Provisions) Order 2015 (SI 2015/33) art.6 (Transitional provision: claims for housing benefit, income support or a tax credit)*

6.169 With effect from March 30, 2022, art.5 and Sch.1 para.2 of the Welfare Reform Act 2012 (Commencement No. 34 and Commencement No. 9, 21, 23, 31 and 32 and Transitional and Transitory Provisions (Amendment)) Order 2022 (SI 2022/302) omitted the phrase "or by virtue of article 4(11) of the Welfare Reform Act 2012 (Commencement No. 32 and Savings and Transitional Provisions) Order 2019" in art.6(11). But note also the next entry.

pp.1670–1672, *revocation of the Welfare Reform Act 2012 (Commencement No.21 and Transitional and Transitory Provisions) Order 2015 (SI 2015/33) art.6 (Transitional provision: claims for housing benefit, income support or a tax credit)*

6.170 With effect from July 25, 2022, reg.11 of, and Sch. para.3 to, the Universal Credit (Transitional Provisions) Amendment Regulations 2022 (SI 2022/752) revoked art.6.

p.1674, *annotation to the Welfare Reform Act 2012 (Commencement No.23 and Transitional and Transitory Provisions) Order 2015 (SI 2015/634) (General Note)*

6.171 Delete the letter "a" after "These" in line 3 of the General Note at para.5.116.

p.1681, *amendment of the Welfare Reform Act 2012 (Commencement No.23 and Transitional and Transitory Provisions) Order 2015 (SI 2015/634) art.7 (Transitional provision: claims for housing benefit, income support or a tax credit)*

With effect from March 30, 2022, art.5 and Sch.1 para.3 of the Welfare Reform Act 2012 (Commencement No. 34 and Commencement No. 9, 21, 23, 31 and 32 and Transitional and Transitory Provisions (Amendment)) Order 2022 (SI 2022/302) omitted the phrase "or by virtue of article 4(11) of the Welfare Reform Act 2012 (Commencement No. 32 and Savings and Transitional Provisions) Order 2019" in art.7(2). But note also the next entry. 6.172

pp.1681–1683, *revocation of the Welfare Reform Act 2012 (Commencement No.23 and Transitional and Transitory Provisions) Order 2015 (SI 2015/634) art.7 (Transitional provision: claims for housing benefit, income support or a tax credit)*

With effect from July 25, 2022, reg.11 of, and Sch. para.6 to, the Universal Credit (Transitional Provisions) Amendment Regulations 2022 (SI 2022/752) revoked art.7. 6.173

p.1732, *amendment to the Welfare Reform Act 2012 (Commencement No. 31 and Savings and Transitional Provisions and Commencement No. 21 and 23 and Transitional and Transitory Provisions (Amendment)) Order 2019 (SI 2019/37) art.2 (Interpretation)*

With effect from July 25, 2022, reg.11 of, and Sch. para.4(2) to, the Universal Credit (Transitional Provisions) Amendment Regulations 2022 (SI 2022/752) omitted "and article 8(2)(b)" in art.2(3). 6.174

p.1733, *amendment to the Welfare Reform Act 2012 (Commencement No. 31 and Savings and Transitional Provisions and Commencement No. 21 and 23 and Transitional and Transitory Provisions (Amendment)) Order 2019 (SI 2019/37) art.4 (Savings)*

With effect from June 8, 2024, art.2(2) of the Welfare Reform Act 2012 (Commencement No. 31 and Savings and Transitional Provisions) (Amendment) Order 2024 (SI 2024/604) amended art.4 by inserting after para.(2) the following new sub-paragraphs: 6.175

"(3) Nothing in regulation 6A (restriction on claims for housing benefit, income support or a tax credit) of the Transitional Regulations prevents a claim for housing benefit by a member of a mixed-age couple referred to in paragraph (1) where—

(a) they have been issued with a migration notice;

(b) they make the claim for housing benefit within three months beginning with—

  (i) in the case of a person who became entitled to universal credit by claiming before the final deadline, the day after their award of universal credit terminates; or

  (ii) in the case of a person who did not claim universal credit, or claimed before the final deadline but was not entitled, the day after their award of housing benefit terminates; and

(c) they meet the conditions for entitlement to housing benefit on that day.

(4) Where a person mentioned in sub-paragraph (b)(i) of paragraph (3) claims—

(a) housing benefit; or

(b) state pension credit (whether or not they also claim housing benefit), within three months beginning with the day mentioned in that sub-paragraph, any days on which they were entitled to universal credit are to be disregarded for the purposes of paragraph (2).

(5) In this article "Transitional Regulations" means the Universal Credit (Transitional Provisions) Regulations 2014 and "final deadline" and "migration notice" have the same meaning as in those Regulations."

p.1734, *amendment to the Welfare Reform Act 2012 (Commencement No. 31 and Savings and Transitional Provisions and Commencement No. 21 and 23 and Transitional and Transitory Provisions (Amendment)) Order 2019 (SI 2019/37) art. 6 (Transitional provision: termination of awards of housing benefit)*

6.176 With effect from July 25, 2022, reg.11 of, and Sch. para.4(3) to, the Universal Credit (Transitional Provisions) Amendment Regulations 2022 (SI 2022/752) substituted "in regulation 2 of the Universal Credit (Transitional Provisions) Regulations 2014" for "respectively in sub-paragraphs (h) and (l) of article 7(11) of the No.23 Order" in art.6(4).

p.1734, *amendment to the Welfare Reform Act 2012 (Commencement No. 31 and Savings and Transitional Provisions and Commencement No. 21 and 23 and Transitional and Transitory Provisions (Amendment)) Order 2019 (SI 2019/37) art. 7 (Transitional provision: application to housing benefit of the rules in universal credit for treatment of couples and polygamous marriages)*

6.177 With effect from July 25, 2022, reg.11 of, and Sch. para.4(4) to, the Universal Credit (Transitional Provisions) Amendment Regulations 2022 (SI 2022/752) substituted "regulation 6A of the Universal Credit (Transitional Provisions) Regulations 2014" for "article 6 of the No. 21 Order or article 7 of the No. 23 Order" in art.7(1)(a)(i).

p.1735, *amendment of the Welfare Reform Act 2012 (Commencement No. 31 and Savings and Transitional Provisions and Commencement No. 21 and 23 and Transitional and Transitory Provisions (Amendment)) Order 2019 (SI 2019/37) art. 8 (Transitional provision: where restrictions on claims for universal credit are in place)*

6.178 With effect from March 30, 2022, art.5 and Sch.1 para.4 of the Welfare Reform Act 2012 (Commencement No. 34 and Commencement No. 9, 21, 23, 31 and 32 and Transitional and Transitory Provisions (Amendment)) Order 2022 (SI 2022/302) inserted "or" at the end of art.8(1)(a) and omitted both art.8(1)(c) and the "or" preceding it. But note also the next entry.

pp.1735–1736, *revocation of the Welfare Reform Act 2012 (Commencement No. 31 and Savings and Transitional Provisions and Commencement No. 21 and 23 and Transitional and Transitory Provisions (Amendment)) Order 2019 (SI*

2019/37) art.8 (Transitional provision: where restrictions on claims for universal credit are in place)

With effect from July 25, 2022, reg.11 of, and Sch. para.4(5) to, the Universal Credit (Transitional Provisions) Amendment Regulations 2022 (SI 2022/752) revoked art.8. 6.179

p.1737, *amendment to the Welfare Reform Act 2012 (Commencement No. 32 and Savings and Transitional Provisions) Order 2019 (SI 2019/167) art.1 (Citation and interpretation)*

With effect from June 8, 2024, reg.3(2) of the Social Security (State Pension Age Claimants: Closure of Tax Credits) (Amendment) Regulations 2024 (SI 2024/611) inserted at the appropriate places in art.1 the following new definitions: 6.180

> "“migration notice” means a notice under regulation 44 (migration notice) of the Universal Credit (Transitional Provisions) Regulations 2014 or a notice under regulation 45 (migration notice) of the Universal Credit (Transitional Provisions) Regulations (Northern Ireland) 2016;"
> "“notified person” means a person to whom a notice has been issued under article 3A (tax credit closure notice);"
> "“state pension credit” means state pension credit under the State Pension Credit Act 2002 or the State Pension Credit Act (Northern Ireland) 2002;".

p.1738, *amendment of the Welfare Reform Act 2012 (Commencement No. 32 and Savings and Transitional Provisions) Order 2019 (SI 2019/167) art.1 (Citation and interpretation)*

With effect from March 30, 2022, art.4(3) of the Welfare Reform Act 2012 (Commencement No. 34 and Commencement No. 9, 21, 23, 31 and 32 and Transitional and Transitory Provisions (Amendment)) Order 2022 (SI 2022/302) omitted art.1(3). 6.181

p.1738, *amendment to the Welfare Reform Act 2012 (Commencement No. 32 and Savings and Transitional Provisions) Order 2019 (SI 2019/167) art.3 (Savings)*

With effect from June 8, 2024, reg.3(3) of the Social Security (State Pension Age Claimants: Closure of Tax Credits) (Amendment) Regulations 2024 (SI 2024/611) inserted "Subject to articles 3A (tax credit closure notice) and 3B (saving to cease following issue of tax credit closure notice)," at the beginning of art.3(1). 6.182

p.1741, *amendment to the Welfare Reform Act 2012 (Commencement No. 32 and Savings and Transitional Provisions) Order 2019 (SI 2019/167) by insertion of new arts 3A and 3B*

With effect from June 8, 2024, reg.3(4) of the Social Security (State Pension Age Claimants: Closure of Tax Credits) (Amendment) Regulations 2024 (SI 2024/611) inserted after art.3 the following new arts 3A and 3B: 6.183

"Tax credit closure notice

3A.—(1) The Secretary of State (or, in Northern Ireland, the Department) may, at any time, issue a notice ("a tax credit closure notice") to—

(a) a person who is entitled to an award of child tax credit, but not an award of working tax credit, and is—

(i) a single person who has reached the qualifying age;

(ii) a member of a couple both members of which have reached that age; or

(iii) a member of a protected mixed-age couple; or

(b) a person who is entitled to both an award of a tax credit and an award of state pension credit,

informing the person that their tax credit award is to end by a specified day ("the deadline day").

(2) The tax credit closure notice may contain such other information as the Secretary of State or the Department considers appropriate.

(3) The deadline day must not, subject to paragraph (4), be within the period of three months beginning with the day on which the tax credit closure notice is issued.

(4) The deadline day may be within such shorter period as the Secretary of State or the Department considers appropriate where—

(a) the person is entitled to an award of state pension credit when the tax credit closure notice is issued; or

(b) the tax credit closure notice is issued after cancellation of a previous tax credit closure notice or after cancellation of a migration notice issued to that person.

(5) If the tax credit award is to joint claimants the Secretary of State or the Department must issue a tax credit closure notice to each claimant.

(6) The Secretary of State or the Department may determine that the deadline day should be changed to a later day either—

(a) on the Secretary of State's or the Department's own initiative; or

(b) if the notified person requests such a change before the deadline day,

if there is a good reason to do so.

(7) Where the Secretary of State or the Department changes the deadline day in accordance with paragraph (6) they must inform the notified person or persons of the new deadline day.

(8) The Secretary of State or the Department may cancel a tax credit closure notice issued to any person—

(a) if it has been issued in error;

(b) in any other circumstances where the Secretary State or the Department considers it necessary to do so in the interests of the person, or any class of person, or to safeguard the efficient administration of state pension credit.

(9) In a case referred to in paragraph (8)(a) the Secretary of State or the Department may, instead of cancelling the tax credit closure notice, treat that notice as if it were a migration notice issued to that person and as if the deadline day in the tax credit closure notice were the deadline day in a migration notice.

(10) In this article—

"the Department" means the Department for Communities in Northern Ireland;

"protected mixed-age couple" means a mixed-age couple to whom article 4 (savings) of the Welfare Reform Act 2012 (Commencement No. 31 and Savings and Transitional Provisions and Commencement No. 21 and 23 and Transitional and Transitory Provisions (Amendment)) Order 2019 or article 4 (savings) of the Welfare Reform (Northern Ireland) Order 2015 (Commencement No. 13 and Savings and Transitional Provisions and Commencement No. 8 and Transitional and Transitory Provisions (Amendment)) Order 2019 applies,

and the reference in paragraph (1) to a person who is entitled to a tax credit includes a person who is treated as being so entitled by virtue of regulation 11(1) (ongoing awards of tax credits) of the Universal Credit (Transitional Provisions) Regulations 2014 or regulation 9(1) (ongoing awards of tax credits) of the Universal Credit (Transitional Provisions) Regulations (Northern Ireland) 2016.

Saving to cease following issue of tax credit closure notice

3B.—(1) Paragraph (1) of article 3 (savings) shall cease to apply to a notified person in relation to any of the cases mentioned in that article on—

(a) where the person makes a claim for state pension credit on or before the deadline day, the day on which the claim is made (or if, in the case of joint tax credit claimants there is more than one such claim, the day on which the first claim is made); or

(b) in any other case, the deadline day.

(2) Where article 3 ceases to apply in relation to an award of a tax credit in accordance with this article during a tax year, the amount of the tax credit to which the person is entitled for that tax year is to be calculated in accordance with the Tax Credits Act 2002 and regulations made under that Act as modified by Schedule 1 (modification of tax credits legislation (finalisation of tax credits)) to the Universal Credit (Transitional Provisions) Regulations 2014 or Schedule 1 (modification of tax credits legislation (finalisation of tax credits)) to the Universal Credit (Transitional Provisions) Regulations (Northern Ireland) 2016 in the same way as if—

(a) the claim for state pension credit had been a claim for universal credit; or

(b) the deadline day in the tax credit closure notice had been the deadline day in a migration notice."

p.1742, *amendment of the Welfare Reform Act 2012 (Commencement No. 32 and Savings and Transitional Provisions) Order 2019 (SI 2019/167) art.4 (Appointed day—coming into force of universal credit provisions and abolition of income-related employment and support allowance and income-based jobseeker's allowance: persons resident outside Great Britain)*

With effect from March 30, 2022, art.4(4) of the Welfare Reform Act 2012 (Commencement No. 34 and Commencement No. 9, 21, 23, 31 and 32 and Transitional and Transitory Provisions (Amendment)) Order 2022 (SI 2022/302) omitted art.4(11). 6.184

p.1745, *insertion of new Commencement Order at para.5.188 onwards.*

The Welfare Reform Act 2012 (Commencement No. 34 and Commencement No. 9, 21, 23, 31 and 32 and Transitional and Transitory Provisions (Amendment)) Order 2022

SI 2022/302 (C.12)

6.185 *The Secretary of State makes the following Order in exercise of the powers conferred by section 150(3) and (4)(a), (b)(i) and (c) of the Welfare Reform Act 2012:*

ARRANGEMENT OF ARTICLES

Citation

5.188 **1.** This Order may be cited as the Welfare Reform Act 2012 (Commencement No. 34 and Commencement No. 9, 21, 23, 31 and 32 and Transitional and Transitory Provisions (Amendment)) Order 2022.

Interpretation

5.189 **2.** In this Order—

"the No. 9 Order" means the Welfare Reform Act 2012 (Commencement No. 9 and Transitional and Transitory Provisions and Commencement No. 8 and Savings and Transitional Provisions (Amendment)) Order 2013;

"the No. 32 Order" means the Welfare Reform Act 2012 (Commencement No. 32 and Savings and Transitional Provisions) Order 2019.

Full commencement of universal credit

5.190 **3.** 30th March 2022 ("the appointed day") is the appointed day for the coming into force of the provisions of the Welfare Reform Act 2012 listed in Schedule 2 (universal credit provisions coming into force in relation to certain claims and awards) to the No. 9 Order, in so far as they are not already in force.

Removal of restriction preventing frontier workers from claiming universal credit

4.—(1) The amendments of the No. 32 Order set out in paragraphs (3) and (4) have effect from the appointed day. **5.191**

(2) The No. 32 Order is amended as follows.

(3) In article 1 (citation and interpretation), omit paragraph (3).

(4) In article 4 (appointed day—coming into force of universal credit provisions and abolition of income-related employment and support allowance and income-based jobseeker's allowance: persons resident outside Great Britain), omit paragraph (11).

Consequential amendments

5. The consequential amendments set out in the Schedule have effect from the appointed day. **5.192**

Article 5

SCHEDULE

CONSEQUENTIAL AMENDMENTS

1.—(1) The No. 9 Order is amended as follows. **5.193**

(2) In article 5A (transitional provision where Secretary of State determines that claims for universal credit may not be made: effect on claims for employment and support allowance and jobseeker's allowance), in paragraph (1) omit "or article 4(11) of the Welfare Reform Act 2012 (Commencement No. 32 and Savings and Transitional Provisions) Order 2019 (no claims for universal credit by frontier workers)".

(3) In article 6 (transitional provision: where the abolition of income-related employment and support allowance and income-based jobseeker's allowance is treated as not applying), in paragraph (1)(e)(ii) omit "or article 4(11) of the Welfare Reform Act 2012 (Commencement No. 32 and Savings and Transitional Provisions) Order 2019 (no claims for universal credit by frontier workers)".

2.—(1) The Welfare Reform Act 2012 (Commencement No. 21 and Transitional and Transitory Provisions) Order 2015 is amended as follows.

(2) In article 6 (transitional provision: claims for housing benefit, income support or a tax credit), in paragraph (11) omit "or by virtue of article 4(11) of the Welfare Reform Act 2012 (Commencement No. 32 and Savings and Transitional Provisions) Order 2019".

3.—(1) The Welfare Reform Act 2012 (Commencement No. 23 and Transitional and Transitory Provisions) Order 2015 is amended as follows.

(2) In article 7 (transitional provision: claims for housing benefit, income support or a tax credit), in paragraph (2) omit "or by virtue of article 4(11) of the Welfare Reform Act 2012 (Commencement No. 32 and Savings and Transitional Provisions) Order 2019".

4.—(1) The Welfare Reform Act 2012 (Commencement No. 31 and Savings and Transitional Provisions and Commencement No. 21 and 23 and Transitional and Transitory Provisions (Amendment)) Order 2019 is amended as follows.

(2) In article 8 (transitional provision: where restrictions on claims for universal credit are in place)—

(a) at the end of paragraph (1)(a) insert "or"; and

(b) omit subparagraph (1)(c) and the "or" preceding it.

Part VI

Transitional, Savings and Modifications Provisions

Part VII

Immigration Status and the Right to Reside

p.1793, *annotation to the Immigration (European Economic Area) Regulations 2016 (SI 2016/1052) (General Note—EEA nationals and their family members with pre-settled status)*

6.186 In *R. (Fratila) v SSWP* [2021] UKSC 53; [2022] P.T.S.R. 448 the Supreme Court allowed the appeal by the Secretary of State against a decision of the Court of Appeal which had found the domestic right to reside test unlawfully discriminatory contrary to art.18 of the TFEU for treating EU nationals with pre-settled status differently to UK nationals. The judgment of the Court of Appeal had become unsustainable following the decision of the CJEU, in *CG v Department for Communities* (C-709/20) [2021] 1 W.L.R. 5919, that such a provision is not contrary to art.18 of the TFEU, or Directive 2004/38.

However, what the Supreme Court elected not to address (since it was a new point, which would have required new evidence) was the implications for the domestic Regulations of what had also been said in *CG* about the Charter of Fundamental Rights of the European Union (the Charter). The Court of Justice had stated:

> "[93] . . . [Where] a Union citizen resides legally, on the basis of national law, in the territory of a Member State other than that of which he or she is a national, the national authorities empowered to grant social assistance are required to check that a refusal to grant such benefits based on that legislation does not expose that citizen, and the children for which he or she is responsible, to an actual and current risk of violation of their fundamental rights, as enshrined in Articles 1, 7 and 24 of the Charter. Where that citizen does not have any resources to provide for his or her own needs and those of his or her children and is isolated, those authorities must ensure that, in the event of a refusal to grant social assistance, that citizen may nevertheless live with his or her children in dignified conditions. In the context of that examination, those authorities may take into account all means of assistance provided for by national law, from which the citizen concerned and her children are actually entitled to benefit."

Important questions arising from *CG* are:

- whether the Charter has any ongoing application, since the end of the transition period in December 2020, for EU nationals resident in the UK on the basis of pre-settled status; and
- what if any substantive or procedural requirements are imposed on the Secretary of State by the obligation to 'check' that Charter rights will not be breached.

In *SSWP v AT (UC)* [2022] UKUT 330 (AAC) (December 12, 2022), a three-judge panel addressed those questions. It dismissed the Secretary of State's appeal against a decision that a destitute parent who was also a victim of domestic violence was entitled to UC. Though her only right of residence was on the basis of her pre-settled status, the refusal of UC would breach her Charter rights. The panel decided that by virtue of the Withdrawal Agreement, the Charter does indeed continue to apply following the end of the transition period where a person is residing in the UK with pre-settled status. It also decided that *CG* does indeed impose a requirement on the Secretary of State (and by extension the FTT) to check in individual cases that there is no breach of Charter rights. It gives guidance on how that check should be conducted. The Secretary of State made a second appeal to the Court of Appeal; the Court of Appeal unanimously dismissed it: [2023] EWCA Civ 1307 (November 8, 2023). On February 7, 2024, the Supreme Court refused the Secretary of State permission to appeal any further.

Several further questions about the operation of the domestic regulations still await definitive judicial determination.

First, is the domestic right to reside test unlawful in its application to people with PSS (or at least subject to disapplication in individual cases) on the basis that:

- there is a right to equal treatment under Art.23 Withdrawal Agreement for all those with pre-settled status, given the way that the UK implemented Art.18 WA? The argument runs that grants of pre-settled status constitute 'residence on the basis of this agreement' within the meaning of Art.23, which triggers an equal treatment right and distinguishes the position from pre-WA cases given that claimants such as *Fratila* and *CG* were not residing 'on the basis of' Directive 2004/38/EC, and as such had no equal treatment right. In a homelessness eligibility context, this argument has been accepted at county court level in one case, *Hynek v Islington* K40CL206 (HHJ Saunders, 24 May 2024), and rejected (obiter) in another, *C v Oldham* [2024] EWCC 1 (22 May 2024). It has been rejected by the High Court in *Fertre v Vale of White Horse District Council* [2024] EWHC 1754 (KB) (8 July 2024). No application for permission to appeal was made in either County Court case; in *Fertre*, the Court of Appeal has given permission to appeal, and a hearing is listed for 14–16 May 2025.
- it discriminates unlawfully against EEA nationals in comparison with third country nationals, contrary to Art.14 ECHR and s.3 HRA 1998? In *GA v Secretary of State for Work and Pensions* [2024] UKUT 380 (AAC) (25 November 2024), a claimant with PSS argued that she was is in a comparable position to a foreign national who could have made use of the Destitution Domestic Violence Concession due to having leave under Appendix FM of the Immigration Rules, and would in those circumstances have been able to gain access to means tested benefit; that she was refused benefit as a person with PSS; and that the differential treatment was unjustified. The Secretary of State conceded that the differential treatment was unlawful, the UT accepted that concession, and the appeal was allowed. But that concession turned on the particular factual matrix. In other types of case, whether there is art.14 discrimination against people with PSS may be much more contentious.

- it is ultra vires the enabling primary legislation? In *GA v Secretary of State for Work and Pensions* [2024] UKUT 380 (AAC) (25 November 2024), the Upper Tribunal records that it had refused permission to appeal on the ground that the FTT misdirected itself in law by failing to hold that regulation 9(3)(c)(i) of the Universal Credit Regulations 2013 is ultra vires section 4(5)(a) of the Welfare Reform Act 2012. The UT held that "there is no realistic prospect of success in arguing that the ratio of *Sarwar and Getachew* [*R v Secretary of State for Social Security ex p Sarwar and Getachew* [1997] CMLR 648 (CA)], by which the Upper Tribunal is bound, is not equally applicable to reg 9(3)(c)(i)."

Those arguments were raised in *AT* at the Upper Tribunal stage, but never required determination, because of *AT*'s success on her 'dignity' point.

Second, what kind of residence is necessary to be within the scope of Art.10 WA? Neither the decided *AT* 'dignity' basis for disapplying the domestic right to reside test in individual cases, nor the potential 'equal treatment' argument for setting the domestic right to reside test aside altogether, could apply where a person is outside the scope of the Citizens Rights part of the WA. Relatedly, is a grant of EUSS leave conclusive evidence that a person is in the scope of the WA, or does there exist a category of persons granted PSS or SS who have domestic law rights only? Art.10(1)(a) applies to 'Union citizens who exercised their right to reside in the United Kingdom in accordance with Union law before the end of the transition period and continue to reside there thereafter'. It might be suggested that the requirement to 'continue to reside there thereafter' requires residence in accordance with EU law (ie exercising a positive EU law right of residence) at least until, and perhaps even beyond, the end of the transition period. See *Secretary of State for the Home Department v Abdullah* [2024] UKUT 66 (IAC), e.g. [68]. However, the contrary – and, it is suggested, better – argument is that once there has been a pre-transition period of residence, continuous factual residence thereafter is sufficient. The 'continuous residence in accordance with EU law' position would be textually strained, and hard to reconcile with analysis of analogous wording in *Secretary of State for Work and Pensions v Gubeladze* [2019] UKSC 31, [2019] AC 885, [76]–[92]. It would also generate great uncertainty: it would mean that there was indeed a class of persons with PSS or SS who have domestic law rights only, but nobody would know who they were until a dispute arose about their rights, potentially years or even decades later.

Third, can people with leave under the EUSS who are neither EU citizens nor their family members (i.e. EFTA state members) rely on the AT principle of protection against a breach of the right to dignity?

p.1798, *annotation to the Immigration (European Economic Area) Regulations 2016 (SI 2016/1052) (General Note—Overview)*

6.187 In *FN v SSWP (UC)* [2022] UKUT 77 (AAC), Judge Ward records an example of the evidential problems which can arise for claimants seeking to demonstrate a right of residence under these Regulations:

> "[4] . . . On the (erroneous) basis that it was necessary to demonstrate that the husband was a 'qualified person', the claimant, by her social worker,

had informed the DWP that she and her daughter had fled the family home due to domestic violence and that the claimant had obtained a non-molestation order against her husband. His name, date of birth, national insurance number and details of his then current and previous employers were provided to the DWP, who were asked to contact them, as although the social worker had had some contact with the husband, he had been uncooperative in providing the information necessary.

[5] On mandatory reconsideration, the DWP upheld the original decision saying that the Data Protection Act prevented them from providing the information relating to the husband that had been requested.

[6] On appeal, the DWP indicated they could provide information if in response to a tribunal or court order. The claimant's representatives emailed the FtT on 6 February 2020 explaining this and asking for an order to be made. The email did not on its face identify that the claimant and her husband were estranged due to domestic violence and that may have contributed to why the District Tribunal Judge (DTJ) refused the application, saying, put shortly, that the husband should get them and send them to the DWP and that the FtT would only become involved if the parties had exhausted their own efforts. This prompted a follow-up email on 16 March 2020 explaining the background of domestic abuse and providing a copy of the non-molestation order. The DTJ remained adamant, indicating that the order did not prevent the claimant from contacting her husband through solicitors and until there was evidence that an attempt had been made to do so and had been unsuccessful the decision remained unaltered. Subsequently, on 26 May 2020 a registrar did make an order for the evidence to be supplied by DWP but it was not, despite the representative sending a follow-up email. The case was then listed as a paper hearing, without further notification to the claimant or her representative, and decided [adversely to the claimant]."

As the facts of *FN* indicate, problems are particularly likely where a right of residence may derive from a family member from whom the claimant is estranged. A Tribunal's failure to exercise the FTT's inquisitorial duty to seek evidence of a right of residence, including by establishing details about a relative's identity and possible rights of residence, may constitute an error of law. See, e.g. *AS v SSWP (UC)* [2018] UKUT 260 (AAC); *ZB v SSWP* CIS/468/2017 unreported April 25, 2019 ([21]: "an award of benefit is not a prize rewarding only the most adept"), and *PM v SSWP (IS)* [2014] UKUT 474 (AAC). It is clear from those decisions that the Tribunal can direct the Secretary of State to provide information she holds about an estranged family member. Further, while the Secretary of State appears to consider that due to her data protection obligations she can provide information about such a third party only if ordered to do so by a court or tribunal, there is room for doubt about whether that view is in fact correct, as noted in *ZB* at [19].

pp.1826–1829, *annotation to the Immigration (European Economic Area) Regulations 2016 (SI 2016/1052) reg.4 ("Worker", "self-employed person", "self-sufficient person" and "student")*

Self-employed persons

In *SSWP v VB (UC)* [2024] UKUT 212 (AAC) Judge Ward finds (at [47]) that a claimant who was not actually trading but was preparing to do 6.188

so "had taken steps appropriate to the business she was later to launch (and which was genuine and effective) to prepare for doing so. She had moved beyond the stage of a mere idea or intention"; that brought her into the scope of Art.49 TFEU and meant she had a right of residence as a self-employed person. The fact that she had only taken such steps a short while before the date of the DWP's decision under appeal was immaterial (at [47]).

Self-sufficient persons

In *VI v Commissioners for HMRC* (C–247/20 O) (September 30, 2021) at [56]–[64], AG Hogan's opinion described a "fundamental question" in that case as "probably" being whether free access to the NHS satisfies the requirement to have CSI, and lamented that the UK Government had not made any submissions about that issue. However, the AG did not express an opinion on the answer, and advised the Court not to do so either.

Surprisingly, the court's judgment ([2022] EUECJ C-247/20 [2022] 1 W.L.R. 2902) did give an answer, and the answer was that free access to the NHS does satisfy the CSI requirement:

> "[68] In the present case, it is apparent from the documents before the Court that VI and her son were affiliated during the period in question, namely from 1 May 2006 to 20 August 2006, to the United Kingdom's public sickness insurance system offered free of charge by the National Health Service.
>
> [69] In that regard, it must be recalled that, although the host Member State may, subject to compliance with the principle of proportionality, make affiliation to its public sickness insurance system of an economically inactive Union citizen, residing in its territory on the basis of Article 7(1)(b) of Directive 2004/38, subject to conditions intended to ensure that that citizen does not become an unreasonable burden on the public finances of that Member State, such as the conclusion or maintaining, by that citizen, of comprehensive private sickness insurance enabling the reimbursement to that Member State of the health expenses it has incurred for that citizen's benefit, or the payment, by that citizen, of a contribution to that Member State's public sickness insurance system (judgment of 15 July 2021, *A (Public health care)* (C–535/19) EU:C:2021:595 at [59]), the fact remains that, once a Union citizen is affiliated to such a public sickness insurance system in the host Member State, he or she has comprehensive sickness insurance within the meaning of Article 7(1)(b).
>
> [70] Furthermore, in a situation, such as that in the main proceedings, in which the economically inactive Union citizen at issue is a child, one of whose parents, a third-country national, has worked and was subject to tax in the host State during the period at issue, it would be disproportionate to deny that child and the parent who is his or her primary carer a right of residence, under Article 7(1)(b) of Directive 2004/38, on the sole ground that, during that period, they were affiliated free of charge to the public sickness insurance system of that State. It cannot be considered that that affiliation free of charge constitutes, in such circumstances, an unreasonable burden on the public finances of that State."

That decision is obviously inconsistent with a long line of domestic authority, cited in the main volume commentary: for example *Ahmad v*

Secretary of State for the Home Department [2014] EWCA Civ 988; *FK (Kenya) v Secretary of State for the Home Department* [2010] EWCA Civ 1302; *W (China) and X (China) v Secretary of State for the Home Department* [2006] EWCA Civ 1494 and *VP v SSWP (JSA)* [2014] UKUT 32 (AAC) and *SSWP v GS (PC) (European Union law: free movement)* [2016] UKUT 394 (AAC); [2017] AACR 7.

VI falls within the scope of art.89 of the Withdrawal Agreement (as a CJEU reference made before the end of the Transition Period). As such, it so far appears to be uncontentious that *VI* is directly binding, in relation to periods before December 31, 2020, and that the old domestic authorities should no longer be followed. See *WH v Powys County Council and SSWP* [2022] UKUT 203 (AAC), para.3.

In *SSWP v WV (UC)* [2023] UKUT 112 (AAC) the Upper Tribunal shows one way in which *VI* may have practical application for a person reliant on benefit income. A Belgian national was a carer for his disabled wife who received income-related ESA. The amount of social assistance decreased due to the claimant's presence in the household: the loss of some premiums, and the inclusion of carer's allowance (which is social security not social assistance), more than offset the increase to couple rates. UTJ Ward decided the claimant had a right to reside at that time as a self-sufficient person. Until *VI*, the claimant's argument would have foundered on the comprehensive sickness insurance requirement, but *VI* meant that the claimant met it. When the couple then claimed universal credit, the relatively modest additional cost which awarding that benefit to the couple rather than just awarding it to his UK national spouse as a single person (and only for the 23 months until the claimant qualified for settled status), along with the cost of similar such claims which would also now fall to be allowed, was not an "unreasonable burden" on the UK social assistance system. Consequently, the claimant did not lose his right to reside as a self-sufficient person, and was therefore entitled to a joint award of universal credit.

In *Secretary of State for Work and Pensions v Versnick* [2024] EWCA Civ 1454 the Court of Appeal dismissed the Secretary of State's appeal against the UT's decision in *WV*. The Court also refused permission to appeal to the Supreme Court. The Secretary of State did not renew the application for permission to appeal directly to the Supreme Court so the decision is now final.

p.1831, *annotation to the Immigration (European Economic Area) Regulations 2016 (SI 2016/1052) reg.6 ("Qualified person")*

In the General Note to this regulation, under the section *"Retaining worker status—"Duly recorded" and "registered as a jobseeker"*, there is discussion (at pp.1844–1845) of whether, in order to satisfy the requirement of registration, the claim for JSA (or IS) must be made immediately after the cessation of employment. This issue is considered in *SSWP v PC (UC)* [2024] UKUT 186 (AAC) where Judge Ward holds: (i) not all delay will cause loss of worker status, (ii) being able to point to having lived off one's own resources for a period may help justify delay, (iii) the weaker the evidence of jobseeking before registration with the authorities, the harder it will be to justify delay. On the facts of PC's own case, Judge Ward finds the three-month delay meant that worker status had not been retained. **6.189**

p.1889–1891, *modification to the Immigration (European Economic Area) Regulations 2016 reg.16 (SI 2016/1052) (Derivative right to reside)*

6.190 As explained in the main text, the 2016 Regulations continue to apply as saved and modified by the Immigration and Social Security Co-ordination (EU Withdrawal) Act 2020 (Consequential, Saving, Transitional and Transitory Provisions) (EU Exit) Regulations 2020 (SI 2020/1309).

With effect from February 2, 2023, by amending the 2020 Regulations, reg.5 of the Immigration (Restrictions on Employment etc.) (Amendment) (EU Exit) Regulations 2023 (SI 2023/12) makes additional modifications to the saved reg.16 of the 2016 Regulations:

- in paragraph (3)(b), after "a worker" insert "or a self-employed person";
- in paragraph (7), after sub-paragraph (c), insert— "(d) "self-employed person" does not include a person treated as a self-employed person under regulation 6(4);"

p.1890, *erratum—Immigration (European Economic Area) Regulations 2016 (SI 2016/1052), reg.16 (Derivative right to reside)*

6.191 There is an error in the first of the two parallel versions of reg.16(12) (i.e. the version stated as now applying to those with pre-settled status). The words "unless that decision" should be deleted from that version.

pp.1891–1892, *annotation to the Immigration (European Economic Area) Regulations 2016 (SI 2016/1052) reg.16 (Derivative right to reside)*

Primary carers of self-sufficient children

6.192 The main volume General Note discusses a pending reference to the CJEU in *Bajratari v Secretary of State for the Home Department* [2017] NICA 74. The Court's judgment (C-93/18) was delivered on October 2, 2019 ([2020] 1 W.L.R. 2327). It agreed with AG Szpunar and held (at [53]), that a Union citizen minor can meet the requirement to have sufficient resources not to become an unreasonable burden on the social assistance system of the host Member State during his period of residence, "despite his resources being derived from income obtained from the unlawful employment of his parent, a third-country national without a residence card and work permit".

pp.1892–1893, *annotation to the Immigration (European Economic Area) Regulations 2016 (SI 2016/1052) reg.16 (Derivative right to reside)*

Primary carer of children of migrant workers in education

6.193 The main volume General Note asserts: "Where primary carers are also jobseekers (in the EU sense of that term), they cannot be denied social assistance on the basis of the derogation in art.24(2) of the Citizenship Directive". There is now domestic authority for that proposition: *Sandwell MBC v KK and SSWP (HB)* [2022] UKUT 123 (AAC).

p.1893, *annotation to the Immigration (European Economic Area) Regulations 2016 reg.16 (SI 2016/1052) (Derivative right to reside)*

Primary carers of previously self-sufficient children with a right of permanent residence

Regulation 16(2) and reg.16(5) address the position of carers of *Chen* children and of *Zambrano* children respectively (*Zhu and Chen v Home Secretary* (C-200/02); *Zambrano v Office national de l'emploi (ONEm)* (C-34/09)). It might be thought that both groups are in essentially the same position, insofar as the carer's right of residence does not generate a right to reside triggering social security entitlement. However, the difference is that the *Chen* child may eventually acquire a right of permanent residence under Directive 2004/38 art.16. The situation of primary carers of *previously* self-sufficient children who *now* have a right of permanent residence is not recognised in domestic law. But in *FE v HMRC (CHB)* [2022] UKUT 4 (AAC) the Upper Tribunal decides that it is necessary to treat that category differently, and recognise their right of access to social assistance. 6.194

PART VII

FORTHCOMING CHANGES AND UP-RATING OF BENEFITS

FORTHCOMING CHANGES

Abolition of tax credits

There will be no new awards of tax credits with effect from April 6, 2025. 7.001

Migration from other legacy benefits to universal credit

The Minster for Social Security and Disability, Sir Stephen Timms, confirmed on November 12, 2024 that the DWP's intention was to send the final migration notices in early December 2025 and fully move all claimants to universal credit, closing all legacy benefits, by the end of March 2026 (*Completing the Implementation of Universal Credit*, HCWS205). For a detailed analysis see HC Library research briefing, *Managed migration: Completing Universal Credit rollout* (December 19, 2024). 7.002

Changes to disability benefits

The new Government's White Paper, *Get Britain Working* (CP 1191, November 26, 2024) stated that the current benefits system "focuses on assessing capacity to work instead of on helping people to adjust and adapt to their health condition" (para.90) and declared a broadly expressed ambition for a system that "moves away from binary categories of fit for work, or not fit for work, meaning people do not need to demonstrate they are too sick to work to access financial support" (para.91). A DWP written statement stated that "we will bring forward in the spring a Green Paper setting out proposals on reforming the health and disability benefits system. This will ensure that disabled people and those with health conditions have the same rights and opportunities as everybody else, including the right to work; that they are treated with dignity and respect; and that the system responds to the complex and fluctuating nature of the health conditions that so many people are living with today. We will work closely with disabled people and representative organisations as we develop our proposals." (Written Statement to House of Commons by SSWP, November 28, 2024, HCWS252). 7.003

Miscellaneous amendments including changes in relation to managed migration and the ending of tax credits

The Social Security (Miscellaneous Amendments) Regulations 2025 (SI 3/2025), mostly in force from January 27, 2025, make changes to various regulations relating to universal credit, pension credit, housing benefit and tax credits. The amendments also give effect to the Upper Tribunal decisions in *PR v SSWP* [2023] UKUT 290 (AAC) (relating to the discriminatory application of LCWRA waiting period on migration) and (with effect from June 1, 2025) *SSWP v JA* [2024] UKUT 52 (AAC) 7.004

(finding that transitional protection arrangements discriminated against people moving out of specified accommodation).

Payments from the Ministry of Defence's Lesbian, Gay, Bi-sexual and Transgender (LGBT) Financial Recognition Scheme

7.005 The Social Security (Income and Capital Disregards) (Amendment) Regulations 2025 (SI 44/2025), coming into force from February 28, 2025, amend various sets of regulations relating to means-tested benefits so as to disregard payments from the Ministry of Defence's Lesbian, Gay, Bi-sexual and Transgender (LGBT) Financial Recognition Scheme as income or capital.

Neonatal Care (Leave and Pay)

7.006 Section 1 (partially) and para.49 of the Sch. to the Neonatal Care (Leave and Pay) Act 2023 were brought into force on August 21, 2023 by the Neonatal Care (Leave and Pay) Act 2023 (Commencement No. 1) Regulations 2023 (SI 904/2023). Those provisions enabled HMRC to begin preparatory work for the making of payments of neonatal care pay for absences from work of employed parents (or others with a personal relationship) with a child who either is receiving or has received neonatal care. The Neonatal Care (Leave and Pay) Act 2023 (Commencement No. 2) Regulations 2025 (SI 41/2025) bring into force on January 17, 2025 regulation-making powers under section 2 of the Act and remaining provisions of the Schedule to the 2023 Act that create a statutory entitlement to neonatal care leave and neonatal care pay and make consequential amendments.

Scottish adult disability living allowance

7.007 The Disability Assistance (Scottish Adult Disability Living Allowance) Regulations 2025 (SSI 3/2025), in force from March 21, 2025, make provision for Scottish Adult Disability Living Allowance, a type of disability assistance awarded by the Scottish Ministers under s.31 of the Social Security (Scotland) Act 2018. It will not be open to new applications as all awards will result from case transfer from DLA as part of the devolution of disability benefits to the Scottish Government. In effect, therefore, Scottish Adult DLA replaces DLA paid by the DWP for those remaining adults in Scotland on the GB benefit.

Social Security (Amendment) (Scotland) Act 2025

7.008 The Social Security (Amendment) (Scotland) Act 2025 received Royal Assent on January 23, 2025. The measures covered by the 2025 Act include changes to the rules about making and challenging decisions about social security assistance in Scotland, including in relation to the right to request a late re-determination or appeal in exceptional circumstances, and the right to withdraw a request for a redetermination.

NEW BENEFIT RATES FROM APRIL 2025

NEW BENEFIT RATES FROM APRIL 2025

(Benefits covered in Volume I)

	April 2024 £ pw	**April 2025** £ pw
Disability benefits		
Attendance allowance		
higher rate	108.55	110.40
lower rate	72.65	73.90
Disability living allowance		
Care Component		
highest rate	108.55	110.40
middle rate	72.65	73.90
lowest rate	28.70	29.20
Mobility Component		
higher rate	75.75	77.05
lower rate	28.70	29.20
Carer's allowance	81.90	83.30
Maternity allowance		
Standard rate	184.03	187.18
Bereavement benefits and retirement pensions		
Widowed parent's allowance or widowed mother's allowance	148.40	150.90
Widow's pension		
standard rate	148.40	150.90
Retirement pension		
Category A or Category B (higher)	169.50	176.45
Category B (lower), Category C or Category D	101.55	105.70
New state pension	221.20	230.25
Dependency increase for child		
The only, elder or eldest child for whom child benefit is being paid	8.00	8.00
Any other child	11.35	11.35

	April 2024 £ pw	April 2025 £ pw
Industrial injuries benefits		
Disablement benefit		
100%	221.50	225.30
90%	199.35	202.77
80%	177.20	180.24
70%	155.05	157.71
60%	132.90	135.18
50%	110.75	112.65
40%	88.60	90.12
30%	66.45	67.59
20%	44.30	45.06
Unemployability supplement		
Basic rate	137.00	139.35
Increase for adult dependant	81.90	83.30
Increase for child dependant	11.35	11.35
Increase for early incapacity-higher rate	28.40	28.90
Increase for early incapacity-middle rate	18.20	18.50
Increase for early incapacity-lower rate	9.10	9.25
constant attendance allowance		
exceptional rate	177.40	180.40
intermediate rate	133.05	135.30
normal maximum rate	88.70	90.20
part-time rate	44.35	45.10
exceptionally severe disablement allowance	88.70	90.20
reduced earnings allowance-maximum rate	88.60	90.12
retirement allowance-maximum rate	22.15	22.53
Death benefit		
Widow's pension (higher rate) or widower's pension	169.50	176.45
Widow's pension (lower rate)	50.85	52.94
"New-style" jobseeker's allowance		
Personal allowances		
aged under 25	71.70	72.90
aged 25 or over	90.50	92.05
"New-style" employment and support allowance		
Personal allowances		
assessment phase-*aged under 25*	71.70	72.90
aged 25 and over	90.50	92.05
main phase	90.50	92.05
work-related activity component	35.95	36.55
support component	47.70	48.50

NEW BENEFIT RATES FROM APRIL 2025

(Benefits covered in Volume II)

Universal credit	**April 2024**	**April 2025**
	£ pm	£ pm
Standard allowances		
Single claimant-*aged under 25*	311.68	316.98
aged 25 or over	393.45	400.14
Joint claimants-*both aged under 25*	489.23	497.55
one or both aged 25 or over	617.60	628.10
Child element-*first child (if born before April 6, 2017)*	333.33	339.00
each other child	287.92	292.81
Disabled child addition-*lower rate*	156.11	158.76
higher rate	487.58	495.87
Limited capability for work element	156.11	158.76
Limited capability for work and work-related activity element	416.19	423.27
Carer element	198.31	201.68
Childcare element-*maximum for one child*	1014.63	1031.88
-maximum for two or more children	1739.37	1768.94
Non-dependants' housing cost contributions	91.47	93.02
Work allowances		
Higher work allowance (no housing element)		
one or more children	673.00	684.00
limited capability for work	673.00	684.00
Lower work allowance		
one or more children	404.00	411.00
limited capability for work	404.00	411.00
Pension credit	£ pw	£ pw
Standard minimum guarantee		
Single person	218.15	227.10
Couple	332.95	346.60
Additional amount for child or qualifying young person		
first child (if both before April 6, 2017)	76.79	78.10
each other child	66.29	67.42
Additional amount for severe disability		
single person	81.50	82.90
couple (one qualifies)	81.50	82.90
couple (both qualify)	163.00	165.80
Additional amount for carers	45.60	46.40
Additional amount for additional spouse in a polygamous marriage	114.80	119.50
Savings credit threshold		
single person	189.80	198.27
couple	301.22	314.34
Maximum savings credit		
single person	17.01	17.30
couple	19.04	19.36

NEW BENEFIT RATES FROM APRIL 2025

(Benefits covered in Volume IV)

HMRC-administered payments	**2023–24** £ pw	**2024–25** £ pw
Benefits in respect of children		
Child benefit		
only, elder or eldest child	25.60	26.05
each subsequent child	16.95	17.25
Guardian's allowance	21.75	22.10
Employer-paid benefits		
Standard rates		
Statutory sick pay	116.75	118.75
Statutory maternity pay	184.03	187.18
Statutory paternity pay	184.03	187.18
Statutory shared parental pay	184.03	187.18
Statutory parental bereavement pay	184.03	187.18
Statutory adoption pay	184.03	187.18
Income threshold	123.00	125.00
Scottish social security assistance	£ pw	£ pw
Adult disability payment		
Daily living component		
Enhanced rate	108.55	110.40
Standard rate	72.65	73.90
Mobility component		
Enhanced rate	75.75	77.05
Standard rate	28.70	29.20
Child disability payment		
Care component		
Highest rate	108.55	110.40
Middle rate	72.65	73.90
Lowest rate	28.70	29.20
Mobility component		
Higher rate	75.75	77.05
Lower rate	28.70	29.20
Scottish child payment	26.70	27.15
	£	£
Best start grants		
Pregnancy and baby grant		
First child	754.65	767.50
Subsequent child and additional payment for twins etc	377.35	383.75
Early learning payment	314.45	319.80
School age payment	314.45	319.80

HMRC-administered payments	**2023–24** £ pw	**2024–25** £ pw
Funeral expense assistance		
Standard rate	1,257.75	1,279.15
Rate where the deceased has left in place a pre-paid funeral plan	153.50	156.10
Maximum rate for removal of an implanted Medical device by a person other than a registered medical practitioner	25.35	25.80
Young carer grant	383.75	390.25
Child winter heating assistance	251.50	255.80
Winter heating payment	58.75	59.75
Carer's allowance supplement (bi-annual)	288.60	288.60

NEW BENEFIT RATES FROM APRIL 2025

(Benefits covered in Volume V)

	April 2024 £ pw	April 2025 £ pw
Contribution-based jobseeker's allowance		
Personal rates-*aged under 25*	71.70	72.90
aged 25 or over	90.50	92.05
Contribution-based employment and support allowance		
Personal rates-assessment phase-*aged under 25*	71.70	72.90
aged 25 or over	90.50	92.05
main phase	90.50	92.05
Components		
work-related activity	35.95	36.55
support	47.70	48.50
Income support and income-based jobseeker's allowance		
Personal allowances		
Single person-aged under 25	71.70	72.90
aged 25 or over	90.50	92.05
lone parent-aged under 18	71.70	72.90
aged 18 or over	90.50	92.05
couple-both aged under 18	71.70	72.90
both aged under 18, with a child	108.30	110.15
one aged under 18, one aged under 25	71.70	72.90
one aged under 18, one aged 25 or over	90.50	92.05
both aged 18 or over	142.25	144.65
dependent child	83.24	84.66
Premiums		
Family-ordinary	19.15	19.48
lone parent	19.15	19.48
Pensioner-single person (JSA only)	127.65	135.05
couple	190.70	201.95
Disability-single person	42.50	43.20
couple	60.60	61.65
Enhanced disability-single person	20.85	21.20
couple	29.75	30.25
disabled child	32.20	32.75
Severe disability-single person	81.50	82.90
couple (one qualifies)	81.50	82.90
couple (both qualify)	163.00	165.80
Disabled child	80.01	81.37
Carer	45.60	46.40

	April 2024 £ pw	April 2025 £ pw
Income-related employment and support allowance		
Personal allowances		
Single person-aged under 25	71.70	72.90
aged 25 or over	90.50	92.05
lone parent-aged under 18	71.70	72.90
aged 18 or over	90.50	92.05
couple-both aged under 18	71.70	72.90
both aged under 18, with a child	108.30	110.15
both aged under 18 (main phase)	71.70	72.90
one aged under 18, one aged 18 or over	142.25	144.65
both aged 18 or over	142.25	144.65
Components		
work-related activity	35.95	36.55
support	47.70	48.50
Premiums		
Pensioner-single person with no component	127.65	135.05
couple with no component	190.70	201.95
Enhanced disability-single person	20.85	21.20
couple	29.75	30.25
Severe disability-single person	81.50	82.90
couple (one qualifies)	81.50	82.90
couple (both qualify)	163.00	165.80
Carer	45.60	46.40

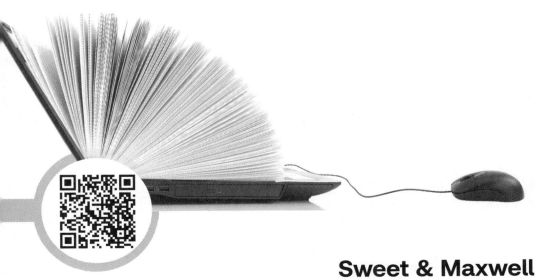